# THE YOUTH WORKER'S ENCYCLOPEDIA OF BIBLE-TEACHING IDEAS:

## New Testament

*Group*

Loveland, Colorado

**The Youth Worker's Encyclopedia of Bible-Teaching Ideas: New Testament**
Copyright © 1994 Group Publishing, Inc.

**Credits**
Compiled by Mike Nappa and Michael Warden
Edited by Mike Nappa, Michael Warden, Stephen Parolini, Rick Lawrence, and Amy Nappa
Cover designed by Liz Howe
Interior designed by Lisa Smith
Illustrations by Amy Bryant and Joel Armstrong
Copyedited by Stephanie G'Schwind
Typesetting by Joyce Douglas, Rosalie Lawrence, and Randy Kady

**Library of Congress Cataloging-in-Publication Data**

The youth worker's encyclopedia of Bible teaching ideas.

    Includes indexes.
    Contents: [1] Old Testament — [2] New Testament.
    1. Bible—Indexes. 2. Church work with teenagers.
I. Group Publishing.
BS432.Y685    1994    268'.433    94-12166
ISBN 1-55945-184-X : (O.T.)
ISBN 1-55945-183-1 : (N.T.)

10  9  8  7              03  02  01  00  99  98

Printed in the United States of America.

# CONTENTS

INTRODUCTION ...............................................................5

   Matthew ...................................................................7

   Mark .......................................................................61

   Luke.........................................................................89

   John .......................................................................125

   Acts ........................................................................165

   Romans...................................................................189

   1 Corinthians .........................................................211

   2 Corinthians .........................................................231

   Galatians.................................................................245

   Ephesians................................................................255

   Philippians .............................................................269

   Colossians ..............................................................279

   1 Thessalonians......................................................289

   2 Thessalonians......................................................297

   1 Timothy...............................................................303

   2 Timothy...............................................................313

   Titus.......................................................................319

   Philemon ................................................................323

   Hebrews..................................................................327

   James......................................................................341

   1 Peter ...................................................................355

   2 Peter ...................................................................363

   1 John ....................................................................369

   2 John ....................................................................377

   3 John ....................................................................381

   Jude........................................................................385

   Revelation ..............................................................391

SCRIPTURE INDEX.............................................................404

THEME INDEX ..................................................................407

TEACHING-STYLE INDEX ...................................................412

# CONTRIBUTORS

Many thanks to the following people, who loaned us their creative expertise to help bring together this volume of ideas:

Ann Cannon
Berry Richardson
Beth Snowden
Bill Zieche
Bob Easton
Bob Latchaw
Carol Davis Younger
Christine Yount
Chuck Hilgeman
Cindy Hansen
Cindy Whitman
David Adams
David Cassady
David Crim
Dean Feldmeyer
Dean Nadasdy
Denise Turner
Dennis Castle
Donald Hinchey
Doug Newhouse
Gary Wilde
Greg Tolle
James Gimbel
Jeanne Leland
Jennifer Root Wilger
Jim Pritchett
Jody Wakefield Brolsma
Karen Dockrey
Kathi B. Finnell
Katie Abercrombie
Keith Drury
Keith Luck
Kelli Dunham
Kim West

Kimberly Porter
Kirk Morledge
Larry J. Michael
Laurie Eynon
Lianne Bauserman
Linda Johnson
Linda Joyce Heaner
Linda Snyder
Lynn Potter
Mark Gilroy
Mark Killingsworth
Mark Reed
Martha Rodriguez
Michael Capps
Michael Warden
Mike Gillespie
Mike Nappa
Nancy Going
Pam Montgomery
Paul Woods
Rex Stepp
Rich Melheim
Rick Lawrence
Rick McKinney
Sam Simpson
Scott Linscott
Sheri Simpson
Stephen Parolini
Steven McCullough
Therese Caouette
Tom Miller
Walter John Boris
Wes Olds
Wesley Taylor

# INTRODUCTION

Once upon a time, a little publishing company in Colorado had a dream.

"What if," the people there said, "instead of simply *teaching* kids about the New Testament, we had a way to help them *learn* about it—a way to help them experience and apply the truths found in Scripture?"

So they went right to work. They contacted the most inventive minds in youth ministry and asked them to create innovative, New Testament-based learning experiences for teenagers. Then they compiled those ideas into this volume, ***The Youth Worker's Encyclopedia of Bible-Teaching Ideas: New Testament.***

Suddenly, it wasn't just a dream anymore. It was reality. And it was ready to be shared with youth workers around the world—with youth workers like you.

In the following pages, you'll find hundreds of active, guided experiences that take scriptural truths from the New Testament and bring them to life for kids. Your teenagers will gain a deeper understanding of the Bible through a variety of experiential activities such as:

- learning games,
- skits,
- affirmation activities,
- creative readings,
- retreats and overnighters,
- creative prayers,
- adventures,
- devotions,
- music ideas,
- object lessons,
- projects,
- and parties!

With such a wide variety of carefully planned, scripturally focused activities, your kids will never think of the Bible as "boring" again. Instead, they'll discover how to embrace New Testament truths for themselves and then apply those truths effectively to their lives.

***The Youth Worker's Encyclopedia of Bible-Teaching Ideas: New Testament*** is an essential tool for any youth worker interested in helping kids explore and understand the Bible. You can use it with your group in several ways—for Sunday school, midweek meetings, Bible study groups, camp and retreat meetings, or any other time you gather your youth group together. Try it today! You—and your teenagers—will be glad you did.

# MATTHEW

*"We saw his star in the east and have come
to worship him."*

*Matthew 2:2b*

# MATTHEW
# 1:1-17

---

## THEME:
Family histories

## SUMMARY:

In this PROJECT, teenagers research how their ancestors influenced them and how Jesus' ancestors influenced him.

---

PREPARATION: You'll need Bibles for all participants.

Plan a project in which kids research their own family trees. Send a blank family-record form (these can be found in the front of many Bibles, or you can create your own form) to each family in your youth group, along with a letter to parents requesting their help in this activity. Encourage kids to trace their family history back as far as they can, then to pick one special person in their family they admire. Have kids ask parents or other relatives for stories or other information about this family member. Encourage kids who were adopted or don't know much about their extended family to focus on a parent or sibling.

When kids have prepared their family trees, hold a meeting to discuss the results of kids' research. At your meeting, have kids form pairs and tell their partners about their special family members. Then have them discuss the following questions:

■ **What do you admire most in your special family member?**

■ **Do you see any of your spe-** cial family member's qualities in yourself?

After kids have had time to discuss the questions, call the group back together.

Say: **We can learn interesting things about ourselves by studying our family histories. Even though Jesus is God's Son, the writers of two books in the Bible, Matthew and Luke, thought it was important to record the history of Jesus' earthly family.**

Read Matthew 1:1-17 together, having kids take turns reading the verses aloud. Keep the tone light as everyone tries to pronounce the more unusual names.

Say: **These are the people God picked to be in Jesus' family. Let's learn more about some of them.**

Assign each pair one of the following passages. (If your group has more than twenty people, form groups of three or four. If you have five or fewer people in your group, assign each pair two or more passages.)

- Abraham — Genesis 15:4-6
- Ruth — Ruth 1:16-18
- Boaz — Ruth 2:1-13
- King David — 2 Samuel 7:18-29
- King Solomon — 1 Kings 3:4-14
- King Hezekiah — 2 Kings 18:5-7
- King Josiah — 2 Kings 23:1-3
- Zerubbabel — Ezra 3:8-13
- Joseph — Matthew 1:18-25
- Mary — Luke 1:26-38

Have pairs name one quality they admire in the person they read about and decide if any of that person's qualities are reflected in Jesus. Ask pairs to share what they've discovered with the entire group.

Close in prayer, thanking God for families and for sending Jesus to bring us into God's family.

VARIATION: Instead of having kids trace their physical family trees, have them create spiritual family trees. For example, a teenager might identify the person who first brought him or her to church or other important leaders or friends (spiritual "aunts," "uncles," "cousins," and so on).

# MATTHEW
# 1:18-23

THEME:
The promised savior

SUMMARY:
Use apples and this CREATIVE READING to help young people focus on the promise of Jesus' birth.

PREPARATION: You'll need a photocopy of the "Creative Reading for Matthew 1:18-23" handout (p. 11), an apple for each person, a bowl, lighted candles, and a Bible.

Say: **Let's experience a creative reading to help us focus on the promise of Jesus' birth as described in Matthew 1:18-23.**

Ask five people to volunteer to read the parts from the creative reading and give each volunteer one section from the handout. Sit in a circle with lighted candles and place a bowl of apples in the center. Then dim the lights and begin the reading.

# MATTHEW
# 2:1-12

THEME:
Jesus' birth and life

SUMMARY:
This ADVENTURE leads teenagers on a hunt around the church grounds as they retrace events in Jesus' life.

PREPARATION: Before class, prepare 12 newsprint stars. The stars can be as elaborate as you have time to make them. If possible, darken the church. You'll also need Bibles and flashlights.

On each star, write the reference to a Scripture passage from Jesus' life.

For example, you might use Matthew 1:18-25 (Jesus' birth); Matthew 2:1-12 (visit by the Magi); Luke 2:41-52 (the boy Jesus at the temple); John 2:1-11 (the wedding at Cana); Matthew 4:18-22 (Jesus calls his first disciples); John 3:1-21 (Jesus and Nicodemus); Matthew 8:23-27 (Jesus calms a storm); Matthew 14:13-21 (feeding of the 5,000); Matthew 21:1-11 (Jesus' triumphal entry); Matthew 27:11-56 (Jesus' crucifixion); Matthew 28:1-10 (Jesus' resurrection); and Acts 1:6-11 (Jesus' ascends to heaven). Number the stars in chronological order of Jesus' life and post them in

# CREATIVE READING FOR MATTHEW 1:18-23

**Directions:** Photocopy and cut apart this handout for use during the creative reading for Matthew 1:18-23.

------------------------------------------------------------

■ Reader 1: **Christians in the early church performed dramas to teach people the stories of the Bible. These became known as "miracle" and "mystery" plays.**

**The "paradise play" portrayed the Creation, the sin of Adam and Eve, and their expulsion from the garden of Eden. Since this play often concluded with the promise of the coming savior, it was performed around Christmas. A tree decorated with apples was used to symbolize the garden of Eden. Christians began to erect this "paradise tree" in their homes on December 24, the feast day of Adam and Eve.**

------------------------------------------------------------

■ Reader 2: **You're invited to take an apple, a symbol for the first sin of human beings. Look at it and think of sins or things in your life that you wish to turn away from.** (Pass the bowl of apples around the circle.)

------------------------------------------------------------

■ Reader 3: (Read aloud Matthew 1:18-23.)

------------------------------------------------------------

■ Reader 4: **The promise of Jesus' birth, spoken through the angel Gabriel, reminds us that we aren't trapped by sin—we have a savior, Jesus. One of the names for Jesus is "Immanuel," which means "God with us." God is with us and loves us. He will help us turn away from the negative and guide us in the best directions for our lives. Let's use this opportunity to be quiet and listen for God's direction.** (Bow your head.)

------------------------------------------------------------

■ Reader 5: (Allow a few minutes of silence before speaking.) **Let's pray. Dear God, this night we thank you for the birth of your Son, Immanuel. We celebrate your presence with us. We know that your love will give us the power we need to turn away from the things in our lives that hurt us. And you can turn us toward all that is good and helpful for our growth. In Jesus' name, amen** various locations around the church. A passage about Jesus' birth could be posted in the nursery, his childhood in a Sunday school room, his temptation on a balcony, or his healing miracles near a first-aid kit. Be creative and adapt the stories you choose to the settings your church has available. Put the last star outside the door of a closet or other small, dark room. Inside the closet, set up a simple nativity scene and hang a newsprint cross over the manger. On the cross, write "John 3:16."

At your meeting, have a group member read Matthew 2:1-12 aloud. Ask:

■ **Why do you think Jesus' birth was important to men from so far away?**

■ **Why is Jesus' birth important to you?**

Say: **The wise men may not have known the events that would occur in Jesus' life on earth, but they knew Jesus was going to be an important figure in history. Like the wise men, let's follow the stars to find out more about Jesus' birth and life.**

Form groups of two or three. Make sure each group has a Bible.

Say: **There are 12 stars around the church with various Scripture references on them. Stay with your group members and search for the stars in any order. At each star read the passage given and tell one reason this event was important in Jesus' life and why that event is important to us today. When you've found all the stars, meet at star #12.**

Have groups search the church. If the church is dark, have kids use flashlights to search for the stars. It's OK if several groups are at the same star at the same time, but encourage kids to work within their smaller groups instead of forming one large group.

When kids have gathered around the last star, open the door to reveal the nativity scene. Have kids recite or read John 3:16 together, then ask:

■ **Why are we wise if we, too, look for Jesus?**

■ **What have you found in your search for Jesus?**

Close by singing the first verse and chorus of "O Come, All Ye Faithful" together.

# MATTHEW 2:1-18

THEME:
Pride

SUMMARY:
Use this LEARNING GAME to examine the effects of pride.

PREPARATION: Gather masking tape, a wastebasket, scrap paper, and a Bible. Use masking tape to mark off a 10-foot circle on the floor. Place the wastebasket in the center.

Form two teams and declare one team the defending world champions. Privately tell teams the following instructions:

Say to the world champions: **You're defending your title, so you want to win even if it means breaking the rules.**

Say to the other team: **You want to win—but always play by the rules.**

Have teams stand around opposite sides of the masking tape circle. Give kids each 10 pieces of scrap paper to wad up and use as basketballs. Say: **Here are the rules: You must shoot from outside the circle. You may not re-shoot a ball someone else missed with, but you can re-shoot your own ball. Keep track of your own scoring.**

After one minute, have teams total their scores. Announce a winner. Then ask: **What happened in our game? How did it feel being a defending world champion? Why did some people resort to cheating?**

Have several volunteers read aloud Matthew 2:1-18. Ask: **How were Herod's actions like our defending champions' actions? How did pride fit into Herod's actions? How can pride hurt us? others?**

Say: **Pride doesn't always kill people, but it can kill relationships. It can also damage our relationship with God. But if we humble ourselves before him, he'll forgive us.**

# MATTHEW
# 3:1-12

**THEME:**
John the Baptist

**SUMMARY:**
This PARTY celebrates the life and message of John the Baptist.

PREPARATION: Plan this party near a river, lake, beach, or pool. Before the party, gather the following items: old clothes, fake fur, tissue paper, gummy worms (or candy insects), loaves of unsliced bread, and a bowl of honey. You'll also need a Bible.

Open the party by reading Matthew 3:1-12.

Say: **Today we'll have fun as we learn more about this interesting man and his message.**

Begin by having kids use the old clothes, fake fur, and tissue paper to create John the Baptist costumes. Have kids refer to Matthew 3:4 for hints about how John might have looked. When all costumes are ready, have a fashion show. Then ask:

∎ **What can we learn about John the Baptist from the clothes he wore?**

∎ **If he were alive today, what do you think he might look like?**

∎ **Would John the Baptist have any friends? If so, what would they be like?**

Next have kids work alone or in groups to present John the Baptist impersonations. Encourage kids to use any props available in your location to dramatize John's sermon from Matthew 3:7-12. For example, as one person preaches the message, members of his or her group could hold up rocks, pretend to chop down trees, and so on. When each group or person has performed, have kids tell what they think John's message means.

Serve a snack of gummy worms (or candy insects) and chunks of bread with a bowl of honey for dipping.

Ask a volunteer to read Matthew 3:1-3. Then have kids form pairs and discuss these questions together:

■ **What would you like to change about your heart and life?**

■ **What does it mean to you that "the kingdom of heaven is near"?**

■ **What can you do to be like John the Baptist and "prepare the way for the Lord"?**

Have everyone stand in the water (or around the edge of a pool) and hold hands. Take turns completing the following sentence: "One way I'd like to be more like John the Baptist is … " Then close with prayer, asking God for help in being outspoken Christians, even if it means being different from popular society.

VARIATION: If it's appropriate, you might close this party by having a baptismal service. Work with your senior pastor and announce it ahead of time so those wishing to participate may discuss with you or another church leader the significance of baptism prior to the party.

# MATTHEW 4:1-11

THEME:
Temptation

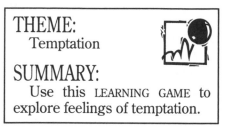

SUMMARY:
Use this LEARNING GAME to explore feelings of temptation.

PREPARATION: Gather straws, a paper cup, and a pitcher of water. You'll also need Bibles.

Form groups of four to six with one adult leader in each group. Give groups each an animal name —wolves, dogs, bears, lambs, or birds. Read aloud Matthew 4:1-11. Then have everyone form a large circle and stand next to people from different groups. Next give each person a straw. Place a small paper cup of water in the center of the circle. Tell the group to circle clockwise.

Say: **When I call out an animal name, everyone in that group must run to the center of the circle, sip from the cup with their straws and squirt the water at each other. Everyone must stay in the youth room. Remember to be careful not to slip on the wet floor.**

Begin calling out the names. Increase the pace gradually. Call two or three animal names at a time. Sooner or later, someone will use the cup instead of the straw to get the others really wet. When this happens, simply say not to do that again. Refill the cup from a pitcher of water. When the cup of

water has been thrown a few times, stop the game. Wrap up the experience by asking kids to discuss these questions:
■ **Were you tempted to throw the cup? Why or why not?**
■ **How did it feel to be tempted?**
■ **How is that feeling like the way Jesus might have felt when he was tempted?**
■ **How did Jesus deal with his temptation?**
■ **How can you deal with temptation in your own life?**

# MATTHEW
# 4:17-22

## THEME:

Telling others about Jesus

## SUMMARY:
Fishing lures are examined in this OBJECT LESSON about fishing for people.

PREPARATION: Ask the owner or manager of a fishing-supply store to prepare a brief tour of his or her store for your group. Have this person select common fly-fishing flies and explain how each fly is used. For example, a fly may be used to catch fish of a specific size, fish in murky water, fish that are close to the surface, or fish that prefer a certain type of insect.

Arrange transportation for your group to this location. You'll need Bibles, a variety of fishing lures, pens, 3×5 cards, and tape.

Take your group to the store and have the owner lead the tour. Ask him or her to point out and describe important equipment used in fly-fishing, such as rods, flies, tackle boxes, waders, and vests. After the tour, thank the owner and move the group to the parking lot or return to your meeting place.

Form groups of no more than four. Each group will need a Bible. Have kids read Matthew 4:17-22, then ask:
■ **How is telling others about Jesus similar to fishing?**
■ **Fishing flies are created to be attractive to fish. How can you make the good news about Jesus attractive to your friends?**
Give each person a fishing lure (or have kids make simple ones with feathers and string or wire). Then have each person choose a key phrase from the passage, write it on a 3×5 card, and hook or tape the lure to the card. Encourage group members to use these lures as reminders to tell others about Jesus.

# MATTHEW
# 5:1-12

## THEME:
Values

## SUMMARY:
In this DEVOTION, teenagers compare the values of celebrities to the values of Jesus.

PREPARATION: Gather newsprint, markers, and Bibles. If your youth group has a formal leadership structure, you might want to do this activity near the time you'll be selecting leaders.

EXPERIENCE

Form groups of no more than four. Assign each group a different celebrity from current society, such as the president or other politician, a popular movie star, a musician, or a sports figure. Try to pick people popular with kids in your group.

Say: **From what you know of your assigned celebrity, list this person's top 10 values. These are the 10 things this person believes are most important. For example, an athlete may value health, or a politician may value freedom of speech.**

Have groups each list their celebrity's values on a sheet of newsprint. If you have time, provide newspapers and current magazines that contain articles about the personalities you've selected. This will give kids more information as they create their lists.

After groups have finished their lists, tell them that their celebrities have requested leadership positions in the youth group. Groups are each to use the values they've listed to represent their celebrity in a campaign-style debate. Remind kids that they can't change the qualities on their lists; then give them several minutes to discuss campaign strategies.

After groups have discussed their strategies, start the debate. Have groups each post their values list near where they're sitting. You will act as the moderator and give each group a chance to respond to questions such as:

■ **What's the first thing your celebrity will do as youth group president?**

■ **What activities would the youth group do if this person were in charge?**

■ **Tell us why your celebrity is qualified for this position.**

Be sure to point out answers that are inconsistent with each group's posted values.

RESPONSE

Ask a volunteer to read Matthew 5:1-12 (if possible, from the New International Version of the Bible). As the volunteer reads the passage, write the following values on a new sheet of newsprint: "poor in spirit," "mourning," "meek," "hungry and thirsty for righteousness," "merciful," "pure in heart," "peacemaker," "persecuted for righteousness." Ask:

■ **Are any of these values named on your group's list?**

■ **How do the values of the celebrities we discussed com-**

pare to the values of Jesus?

■ **How do your own values compare to those of Jesus?**

CLOSING

Have kids take turns sharing one value named in Matthew 5:1-12 that they'd like others to see in their own lives. Then close with a short prayer asking God to help group members live out the values found in Matthew 5:1-12.

# MATTHEW 5:3-12

THEME:
The Beatitudes

SUMMARY:
Use this ADVENTURE to help kids explore the Beatitudes.

PREPARATION: You'll need Bibles and a cardboard tray.

Gather on a hillside and read aloud Matthew 5:3-12. Then assign each person one beatitude (verse) from Matthew 5:3-12. Say: **Find something on this hill that represents the verse you've been assigned. Then bring it back here if you can. Don't damage anything. Be prepared to talk about why the object you picked represents your verse.**

Allow kids to search the hillside for objects. When everyone is ready, have kids each read their assigned verse, then explain how the object they chose represents

that verse. Collect all the objects on a cardboard tray, then have kids create a collage of "Beatitude" symbols they can display in the youth group meeting room as a reminder of Jesus' teachings from the Sermon on the Mount.

# MATTHEW 5:4

THEME:
God's comfort

SUMMARY:
Kids will have a "pity PARTY."

PREPARATION: With an air of melodrama, have a meeting where kids come dressed for a pity party. Encourage kids to wear black clothing, hats, dark sunglasses, or anything else they think makes them look sad. You'll need recent newspapers and a Bible.

When everyone arrives, form a circle and have kids take turns making up the most exaggerated, soap opera-ish, sad stories they can. For example, someone might say, "On the way to youth group, I was eating an ice-cream cone, when a band of terrorist guerrillas surrounded me, called me names, and stole my ice-cream cone. Then, I stubbed my toe and fell down, and an ant bit me on the nose. Finally, I found out that I'm allergic to eating! Oh, woe is me!"

After each story, have the kids in the room "cry" if they think the story is sad. When everyone has had a turn, vote on the top three stories by a "cry-o-meter" (a volunteer who places an elbow on an open palm, then raises his or her forearm to indicate the strength of the "tears" for each story). The story that draws the loudest wails wins.

Afterward, read Matthew 5:4 and have kids discuss the following questions:

■ **How would you feel if your story had really happened to you?**

■ **Our sad stories were all exaggerated and funny. What are some real-life sad stories that people must deal with that aren't funny?**

■ **How do you comfort people who've experienced true sadness or tragedy? How does God comfort them?**

Distribute recent, local newspapers and have kids work in pairs to find real-life sad stories. Have pairs share their stories, then vote on which story kids would most like to help with. Contact the newspaper to find out what your group can do to provide help and comfort for those involved.

# MATTHEW
## 5:9-12, 21-22, 38-48

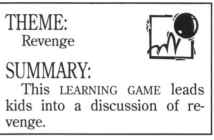

**THEME:**
Revenge

**SUMMARY:**
This LEARNING GAME leads kids into a discussion of revenge.

PREPARATION: Gather Bibles, a sheet of newsprint, tape, a marker, two pieces of 6-foot-long rope or clothesline, two pairs of scissors, a ruler, and two prizes. Make one rope 6 inches shorter than the other.

Write the following on newsprint: shorter by less than a foot = 100 points; longer by any measurement = 50 points; shorter by more than a foot = 0 points; getting even = end of contest, everybody wins. Tape the newsprint to the wall.

Form two teams. Give each team a length of rope and a pair of scissors. Tell teams they're going to compete for the prize by trying to outsmart the opposing team. There will be five rounds of play. In each round, team members will have one minute to decide how much of their ropes to cut off. Then teams will each cut their ropes. The ropes will then be compared to each other, and teams will be awarded points as indicated on the newsprint.

Refer to the scoring chart on the newsprint. Say: **As you can see, the goal of this contest is to get even—that is, to make your** ropes the same length. Having a longer piece than the other team gives you 50 points, but having a piece less than a foot shorter gives you 100 points. Be careful! Cutting your rope too short results in no points. If at any time the two ropes measure exactly the same in any round, the contest is over and everybody wins. If the ropes are never even, the team with the most points wins a prize.

Remind teams not to let each other know how much they intend to cut off. Then begin playing. After five rounds of comparing the two ropes' lengths or when ropes are even, declare the winners. Ask:

■ **How did you feel as you tried to outsmart the other team's members?**

■ **What happened to the rope as you tried to outsmart the others?**

■ **How is what happened to the rope like or unlike what happens to us when we try to outsmart others?**

■ **Have you ever tried to get even with someone? What happened?**

■ **Does getting even usually end the competition with everybody feeling like a winner? Why or why not?**

Have different volunteers read aloud Matthew 5:9-12, 21-22, 38-48. Then wrap up the activity by asking:

■ **What do these passages say about getting back at someone who hurts you?**

■ **Is there anything surprising about Jesus' view of enemies? Explain.**

■ **What changes do you need** to make to better reflect Jesus' attitude about revenge this week?

# MATTHEW 5:13

> **THEME:**
> Being "salty" Christians
>
>
>
> **SUMMARY:**
> In this PROJECT, kids will makes pretzels and compare salt to Christianity.

PREPARATION: Buy frozen bread dough, thaw it before your meeting, and gather the necessary utensils for baking. You'll also need a Bible.

Have kids work in pairs to twist the thawed frozen bread dough into a variety of pretzel shapes—hearts, sticks, balls, and so on. Follow the baking instructions on the frozen bread dough, but before baking, salt half of the pretzels.

When the pretzels are done, have a taste test and let the group determine whether the salted or unsalted pretzels are best. Have kids explain their choices.

Read Matthew 5:13-16, then ask:

■ **As we've tasted, salt can be used to add flavor. It can also be used as a preservative and for medicinal purposes. Keeping this in mind, what do you think it means to be the "salt of** the earth"?

■ Jesus called his followers both "salty" and "a light." What does being salty have to do with being a light for other people?

■ What do you think the world would be like without Christians acting as salt and light?

■ How can you be salt in your school or neighborhood?

Give each person a pretzel to take home to share with a friend. Encourage them to tell their friends about the importance of salt and the importance of knowing Jesus.

# MATTHEW
## 5:14-16

THEME:
Shining God's light

SUMMARY:
Boost your group members' self-esteem with this "shining" OBJECT LESSON/AFFIRMATION.

PREPARATION: Gather a Bible, paper bags, scissors, pens, quarters, and a flashlight.

Have kids form groups of no more than three with people they know and trust. Have the oldest person in each trio read aloud Matthew 5:14-16 for his or her group. Ask groups to discuss these questions:

■ Why do you think Jesus described his followers as "light"?

■ In what ways have you seen Christians be "light to the world"?

Challenge group members to think of several ways they've seen their partners shine God's light. For example, kids might think about a partner's helpfulness, encouraging attitude, or boldness in sharing about Jesus. Tell kids not to share their thoughts yet.

Next, give kids each a small paper bag with scissors, a pen, and a quarter inside. Have each person use the quarter as a pattern to cut at least six circles out of the bag. Have kids write each partner's name on three circles. On the other side of each circle, have kids write their thoughts about how God's light shines through that person.

Darken the room and give each group a flashlight. (If the number of flashlights is limited, have groups join together for the next part of this activity.) One at a time, have kids place their bags over a lighted flashlight. As the light shines through the holes of a person's bag, have his or her partners take turns telling how they see God's light shine through that person.

When everyone has had a turn, have kids give their paper-bag circles to the group members whose names are on them as a reminder to continually shine God's light.

# MATTHEW
## 5:27-28

**THEME:**
Lust

**SUMMARY:**
Use this SKIT to help kids see that lusting for someone is just as wrong as premarital sex.

## JUST LOOKING...?

SCENE: Two girls are sitting on a bench at a local shopping mall, watching people walk by.

PROPS: Chairs arranged to look like a bench. You'll also need Bibles for the discussion after the skit.

CHARACTERS:
**Stephanie** (a student who's not easily embarrassed)
**Lynette** (Stephanie's friend)

### SCRIPT
*(Stephanie and Lynette are sitting facing the audience. Occasionally, both turn their heads in unison as if watching someone walk by.)*
**Stephanie:** *(Watching someone walk by)* Six.
**Lynette:** Nine. Definitely a nine.
**Stephanie:** *(Turns to Lynette.)* How could you give *that* a nine?
**Lynette:** He's cute. And besides... I happen to know he has a great car.
**Stephanie:** A Camaro?
**Lynette:** A Camaro? Camaros haven't been cool for 10 years. He drives a Miata—a convertible, y'know?
**Stephanie:** Oh, I guess a cool car

can add a few points. *(Watching someone else walk by)* Seven.
**Lynette:** *(Nodding in agreement)* Seven.
**Stephanie:** *(Wide-eyed, with a big smile)* Look what's coming...a definite 10!
**Lynette:** A 10 plus!
**Stephanie:** What I wouldn't do to see the back seat of *his* car.
**Lynette:** *(Surprised, she turns to Stephanie.)* Stephanie! I don't believe you just said that!
**Stephanie:** What? What's wrong with what I said? I just happen to be a connoisseur of auto upholstery.
**Lynette:** *(Sarcastically)* Right. You don't know *anything* about cars.
**Stephanie:** *(With a knowing smile)* Yeah, *(continues watching as the person walks by)* but I know a good bucket seat when I see one.
**Lynette:** Stephanie! You shouldn't talk that way.
**Stephanie:** What's wrong with having a little fun? It's not like I really *did* anything wrong.
**Lynette:** No, but if you keep talking about sex, you're going to get yourself into trouble.
**Stephanie:** *(Indignantly)* Wait one minute, Little Miss Goody-Two-Shoes. What did *your* "10" mean? You liked his socks?
**Lynette:** No, I was grading his... *(pauses, then finds the right word)* his personality.
**Stephanie:** *(Surprised)* You know him?
**Lynette:** *(Pausing)* Um...no. But he *looks* like a nice guy.
**Stephanie:** *(Sarcastically)* Yeah... he *looks* great.
*(Both pause uncomfortably for a*

*moment, then watch silently as a few more people walk by. After a few moments both stand at the same time.)*

**Stephanie:** *(Awkwardly)* Maybe we should find a new place to sit.

**Lynette:** Yeah. It's getting a little hot over here.

*(Both get up and leave together.)*

If you use this skit as a discussion starter, here are possible questions:

■ **Why do people talk about sex so often?**

■ **How might the message of Matthew 5:27-28 apply to teenagers like Stephanie and Lynette?**

# MATTHEW 5:38-42

**THEME:**
Violence

**SUMMARY:**
Use this LEARNING GAME to examine the issue of violence.

PREPARATION: Gather marshmallows and a Bible.

Form two teams and have them move to opposite sides of the room. Designate one team as the cartoon team and the other team as the real-people team. Give each team a supply of marshmallows. Say: **Your goal is to get your opponents "out" by hitting them with marshmallows. You must stay on your side of the room. When you're out, you must stop tossing marshmallows and lie still on the floor. People on the real-people team are out when they're hit once by a marshmallow, but people on the cartoon team aren't out until they're hit five times each.**

Play the game until one team is completely out. Ask: **Was this a fair fight? Why or why not? How would you feel if the marshmallows had been bullets, knives, or fists? Is there really a winner when fighting or violence occurs? Why or why not?**

Have everyone stand on one side of the room. Then stand by yourself on the other side of the room. Say: **We're going to play the marshmallow game again, but this time you'll be one team, and I'll be the other team by myself. It'll take 10 marshmallows to get me out, but only one to get any of you out.**

On "go," simply stand in place without throwing any marshmallows. When you've been hit 10 times, fall to the ground and pause for a minute.

After you get back on your feet, read aloud Matthew 5:38-42. Ask:

■ **How did you feel when I didn't fight back?**

■ **What does this passage have to say about returning violence for violence? Do you agree? Why or why not?**

■ **Is it always wrong to fight back? Why or why not?**

■ **What can we learn from this game and this Scripture passage to help us respond to violence this week?**

# MATTHEW 6:19-21

**THEME:**
Possessions

**SUMMARY:**
In this AFFIRMATION, teenagers will affirm the treasures they see in others' lives.

PREPARATION: Check with several locksmiths in your area to see if they have old keys that could be donated to your group. Otherwise, purchase enough new keys for all group members.

Also, cut heart shapes about the size of an adult's hand out of red poster board. Make enough for each group member to have one. You'll also need a Bible, pens, and string for this activity.

Create a youth group museum with kids' most prized possessions. Invite kids to bring in one or more items they treasure and set them up in a display area. (If an item cannot be displayed because of size or value, have the person bring a picture of the treasure.) Near their display, have kids post one- or two-paragraph explanations of the items and why they're important. Then let kids tour the museum.

After the tour, ask:
■ **How would you feel if your prized possessions were stolen?**
■ **How would you feel if they were broken or destroyed by vandals?**
■ **Are any of these possessions replaceable? Why or why not?**
Read Matthew 6:19-21 aloud. Ask:
■ **What does Jesus mean by saying, "Your heart will be where your treasure is"?**
■ **What do the treasures in our "museum" reveal about our hearts?**
■ **How can we store up treasures in heaven? What keeps us from doing that?**
Give each person a poster-board heart, a pen, a key, and about 5 inches of string. Have kids use the pen to poke a hole along the outer edge of the heart. Then have them each thread string through the hole and tie a key to the heart. Last, have kids write their own name in small letters on the heart.
Say: **These are the keys to your hearts. Let's take time now to write on each other's hearts. Write one or two words that tell what good things, such as kindness, purity, and so on, you see locked away as treasures in that person's heart.**
Encourage kids to keep their keys and hearts as a reminder of the value of what's locked there.

VARIATION: Offer kids a challenge—for the next week you'll keep their possessions locked in your office. If they accept the challenge, they should spend time in prayer or read their Bibles each time they miss their possessions. Next time you meet, talk about what it was like to live without those items. Return kids' possessions, and challenge them to continue to pray each time they see the possessions and remember the experience.

# MATTHEW
# 6:25-34

## THEME:
Worry

## SUMMARY:
In this SKIT, a guy agonizes over missing a question on a test, thinking it will keep him out of Harvard.

## THE END OF THE WORLD?

SCENE: Two students are sitting next to each other in class. They're holding calculus tests that have just been graded.

PROPS: Two 10-page sections of continuous computer paper (folded up at the beginning of the skit). These are the students' calculus tests. You'll also need Bibles for the discussion after the skit.

CHARACTERS:
**Jared**
**Simeon**

### SCRIPT
*(Jared and Simeon are looking over the papers they've just been handed in calculus class.)*

**Jared:** Oh, no! My life is over. *(He melodramatically drops his head into his hands.)*

**Simeon:** What… what's the matter? Are you sick?

**Jared:** *(Raising his head to talk)* I'm going to be in a few minutes.

**Simeon:** Bad grade, huh?

**Jared:** Bad? It's the *worst!* My future's ruined.

**Simeon:** It can't be that bad. You *always* do well on calc tests.

**Jared:** *(Matter-of-factly)* I know. *(Looking at his paper again)* But this time I really blew it. Now I'll never make it to Harvard. *(He drops his head melodramatically again.)*

**Simeon:** C'mon, Jared. Don't be so down on yourself. One bad test isn't going to affect your grade that much.

**Jared:** *(Raising his head and speaking, oblivious to Simeon's comforting words)* Finished. That's what I am. Finished. I'm washed up. It's over. I'm dead meat. This is the end of the line. I'm a has-been. A nobody. A man without a future.

**Simeon:** *(Interrupting)* Hold on a minute, Jared. You worry too much. *(Suddenly concerned)* You didn't *flunk* the test, did you?

**Jared:** Flunk? Are you kidding? This is worse than flunking. *(Looking at his test again)* What am I going to do with my life now?

**Simeon:** All right, I give up. Tell me why you're so worried. How many questions did you miss? *(Jared begins to skim his test as if counting. The computer paper slowly spills over the front of his *desk. Near the bottom of the paper, Jared pauses, then points dramatically to the last page.)*

**Jared:** *That* one!

**Simeon:** *(Pausing, then with a confused look)* That *one?*

**Jared:** *(Repeating his pointing)* That *one!* What am I going to do? *(Suddenly interested in Simeon's test)* How many did you miss?

**Simeon:** *(Horrified)* Two. *(He pauses, looks at Jared.)*

**Jared and Simeon:** *(Simultaneously)* Our lives are ruined! *(They freeze in position.)*

Permission to photocopy this skit from *Youth Worker's Encyclopedia: NT* granted for local church use. Copyright © Group Publishing, Inc., Box 481, Loveland, CO 80539.

If you use this skit as a discussion starter, here are possible questions:

■ **Why do people worry so much about the little things that go wrong in life?**

■ **How does the message of Matthew 6:25-34 influence the way we deal with anxiety?**

# MATTHEW
# 6:28-34

**THEME:**
Worry

**SUMMARY:**
Teenagers will search for and photograph various flowers on this ADVENTURE.

**PREPARATION:** Borrow several instant-print cameras from church members and purchase film for each camera. Load each camera with one pack of film. You'll also need ballpoint pens and a Bible.

Prepare and photocopy a list of common flowers, such as dandelions, daisies, poppies, violets, pansies, marigolds, and various colors of roses. Include plants kids could find outdoors in common areas as well as indoor plants, such as African violets, that they might have to knock on doors and ask permission to photograph. Be sure to pick plants that are native to your area.

On a spring or summer day, form teams and send kids on a photo scavenger hunt. Give each team an instant-print camera and the list of flowers and other plants to photograph. Specify a return time and tell kids to photograph as many plants as they can using the time and film available to them.

When groups return, have kids share their photos and tell about their botanical adventures. Have groups examine each other's photos and vote on several favorites. Choose the best flower, the most colorful picture, the best photography, and so on. Post the favorite photos on a wall or bulletin board where everyone will be able to see them.

Distribute the remaining photos so that each person has one. Also distribute ballpoint pens at this time. Have kids look at their photos as you read Matthew 6:28-34.

Have kids form pairs.

Say: **Think of one thing you**

often worry about. **Tell your partner about this worry.**

Allow several minutes for sharing.

Say: **With your partner discuss what God wants you to do with your worry. Then exchange photos and write a note of encouragement at the bottom of your partner's photo. Keep this photo as a reminder that God cares about you.**

# MATTHEW
# 7:13-14

THEME:
The narrow way

SUMMARY:
This pizza PARTY includes a LEARNING GAME as kids hunt for the food.

PREPARATION: Hide pizza and soft drinks for your group somewhere on the church grounds. You'll also need Bibles.

Post directions to the pizza and soft drinks on self-stick notes around the church. Be sure to post notes in inconspicuous places, such as under cribs in the nursery, inside the refrigerator in the kitchen, or on the office photocopy machine, as well as in obvious places, such as on doors and on the pulpit. Don't give kids a direct route! Most of your notes should direct kids to another note, such as "Sorry. Try looking in the third-grade

room." Several notes might even say something like "No pizza here. Sorry."

Invite kids to the church for a pizza party. Gather in your classroom for an opening prayer, then say: **The pizza's around here somewhere, but it's up to you to find it!**

Have everyone hook elbows (or hold hands) and search for the pizza in one large group. Don't give any answers to kids' questions.

After the food has been found and eaten, have a volunteer read Matthew 7:13-14. Ask:

■ **How did you feel when you discovered it was up to you to find the pizza?**

■ **How is following the clues to find the pizza like following the narrow road?**

■ **What are the rewards of following the narrow road?**

Dismiss by thanking God for the rewards of following the narrow road and for the pizza.

# MATTHEW
# 7:13-14

THEME:
Walking the narrow road

SUMMARY:
In this LEARNING GAME, kids experience walking the "narrow road."

PREPARATION: Ask kids to bring

to the activity large suitcases filled with books or other heavy items. You'll also need a stopwatch and Bibles. Have kids set up a complicated obstacle course using objects available in your meeting room. Some areas in the course should be difficult to cross while carrying a piece of heavy luggage.

Form teams of no more than five. Show teams the obstacle course. Explain that each team will compete for the best time. Say: **I'll add up the individual times of each team member to determine the total time for each team. The team with the lowest time wins a prize.**

Have the first person on each team run the course. Record the time for each participant. Then hand the weighted suitcases to kids on one or two teams. Say: **For the next rounds, some kids will be required to carry a heavy suitcase through the course. If the suitcase is put down at any time, a 10-second penalty will be assessed.**

Although kids will complain about the unfair competition, continue until all teams have finished the race. Award a prize to the winning team. Form a circle and ask:

■ **If you had to carry luggage, how did you feel?**

■ **If you didn't have any luggage, how did you feel watching those who did?**

Next, have teams each read Matthew 7:13-14, then discuss these questions to wrap up the activity:

■ **What does this passage mean?**

■ **How is the narrow road like our obstacle course?**

■ **What kind of "baggage" makes it difficult for us to move down the narrow road?**

■ **What can we do this week to help us travel down the narrow road?**

# MATTHEW
## 7:24-29

THEME:
Building on a strong foundation

SUMMARY:
Use this beach ADVENTURE to explore what gives kids a solid foundation.

PREPARATION: You'll need buckets and Bibles.

Go to a nearby beach (or create your own beach if you're land-locked). Form two teams. Team 1 should build the strongest sand castle possible. Team 2 should build a castle out of rocks and shells. Set a time limit, then have teams each try to destroy the opposing team's castle using buckets of water.

Read aloud Matthew 7:24-29. Draw a line in the sand. Ask kids to think of things in their lives that have helped build strong foundations in them. Have them write those things in the sand on one side of the line. Then ask kids to write things that could weaken their foundations on the other side of the line.

Ask kids to think about the breadth, depth, and power of the ocean. Then encourage discussion by asking:

■ **How is Jesus like a rock in our lives that enables us to stand firm, even when something as powerful as the ocean comes against us?**

# MATTHEW
# 8:18-20

THEME:
Home

SUMMARY:
This DEVOTION helps teenagers understand that they, like Jesus, don't eternally belong on earth.

PREPARATION: Post signs on the doors of all the classrooms in the church. Each sign should say something like "No kids allowed," "Teenagers prohibited," "Under 21 not admitted," "Big kids, scram!" or "Adults only." On one door, post a sign that says, "Can't you see there's no place for you here? Why don't you just leave!" You'll also need a Bible.

EXPERIENCE
Meet youth group members in the parking lot.

Say: **We'll need to find a different room for our meeting.**

Lead kids from door to door.

When you come to the last door, say: **Well, I guess we'll just have to meet outside.**

RESPONSE
Find a place to sit; then have a volunteer read Matthew 8:18-20. Ask:

■ **How did you feel as we went from room to room?**

■ **How is this like how Jesus must have felt having no permanent home?**

■ **Why do you think Jesus responded to the potential follower in this way?**

■ **Where is the home Jesus wants us to have?**

CLOSING
Lead the group back to the room where you regularly meet.

Say: **This is our room. It's the home for our group. But our real home is with Jesus. Just as Jesus couldn't call earth his home, we should remember that this isn't our eternal home, either. Our eternal home will be either with Jesus or without him. It's our choice.**

Close in prayer, thanking God for sending Jesus to spend a short time on earth so that we could someday spend eternity with him in heaven.

# MATTHEW
## 9:9-13

---

### THEME:

Jesus came for sinners.

### SUMMARY:
Use this SKIT to help kids understand that Christians must reach out in love to non-Christians.

---

## EATING WITH SINNERS

SCENE: Three students are sitting together in the school cafeteria. An empty chair sits 10 feet from the three students.

PROPS: Four chairs. You'll also need Bibles for the discussion after the skit.

CHARACTERS:
**Jay**
**Tamara**
**Steve**
**Bill**

### SCRIPT

*(Jay, Tamara, and Steve are eating lunch together. Bill enters and sits in the lone chair across from them.)*

**Jay:** *(Looking Bill's direction)* Now isn't that a sorry sight.

**Tamara:** *(Looking around the room)* What...where?

**Jay:** Over there. Bill. He always seems to eat by himself.

**Steve:** Yeah, but there's a good reason. You know that awful stench in the guys' locker room?

**Jay:** *(Simultaneously with Tamara)* Yeah?

**Tamara:** *(Simultaneously with Jay)* No.

**Steve:** *(Nodding and pointing to Bill)* Bill.

**Tamara:** That's not very nice.

**Jay:** Maybe not, but it's not too far from the truth. I had to share a locker with Bill last year.

**Tamara:** Bill just doesn't get a break. I heard he was suspended for a whole week because he was smoking in class a couple months ago.

**Steve:** That's nothing. *I* heard he was arrested for stealing cigarettes from a gas station last month. His parents must've paid off the judge or something.

**Jay:** *I* heard his parents kicked him out. He's living at some uncle's house or something.

**Tamara:** It must be terrible to live that way.
*(After a long pause, Steve, Jay, and Tamara look at Bill for a moment, then get up to leave.)*

**Steve:** So...you guys coming to youth group tonight?

**Jay:** Wouldn't miss it. I like these game nights.

**Tamara:** Yeah. I can bring my non-Christian friends, and they don't get turned off by some *boring* sermon. What's the theme of tonight's meeting?

**Steve:** Reaching out to non-Christians or something like that.

**Tamara:** Sounds like fun.
*(They exit.)*

If you use this skit as a discussion starter, here are possible questions:

■ **How do you act toward the "Bills" you know at school? What would Jesus do if he were in your shoes?**

■ **How can we live the message of Matthew 9:9-13 at school?**

# MATTHEW
# 10:39

---

## THEME:
Commitment

## SUMMARY:
This DEVOTION helps kids understand how to find true life.

---

PREPARATION: You'll need newspapers, tape, markers, Bibles, and white crepe paper.

EXPERIENCE

Gather everyone in a circle and give each person five newspaper pages, tape, and a marker. Say: **Think of the five things in life you value most, outside of your relationship with God. Write each of those five things on a separate newspaper page. Then, using the tape, make your five pages into a newspaper "outfit" and put it on. Be sure your writing is visible to others.**

After kids have donned their garments, have them model their outfits and explain what they wrote. Then say: **Let's pretend** those paper garments represent who you are—your personality, your values, and your attitudes. What does Jesus have to say about your life?

Give kids each a Bible and have them turn to Matthew 10:39. Have kids take turns reading the verse out loud. Each time the verse is read, silently go around the room and rip off one part of each person's "garment." Don't explain what you're doing. After the last person reads the verse, rip off the remainder of kids' paper garments.

RESPONSE

Ask:

■ **How did you feel when I ripped off your garment?**

■ **How was this experience like death?**

■ **How does the verse you heard relate to the idea of giving up your life for God?**

■ **Why is it hard to put God's command to give up your life into practice?**

CLOSING

Give each person three or four feet of white crepe paper. Read aloud Colossians 3:9-10. As you read, have kids drape the crepe paper around each other's shoulders. Then say: **This crepe paper represents all that Christ is— love, power, wisdom, and joy. You couldn't wear this new garment as long as you wore the old garment. In the same way, we have to die to our own way of life in order for Christ's life to be real in us. We must lose our lives to find true life.**

# MATTHEW 11:28-30

## THEME:

Giving Jesus our burdens

## SUMMARY:
Teenagers carry burdens of rocks on this ADVENTURE hike.

PREPARATION: Before class, collect enough rocks for each person in your youth group to have one. Rocks should be small enough to be carried while walking but heavy enough so kids will get tired of carrying them. Map out a one-mile hike that will end up in a park or field. You may need to transport kids and their rocks to a starting point if there are no parks near your church. Be sure to bring a Bible.

W hen everyone has arrived, distribute the rocks and announce that you'll be going on a hike. Tell kids to bring their rocks because they'll need them at the end of the hike. Don't let kids abandon or exchange their rocks during the hike.

When you reach your destination, have kids stand, holding their rocks. Read Matthew 11:28-30.

Say: **Think of one burden you'd like to give to Jesus. Perhaps it's anger at a failed relationship. Or frustration with a parent. Let's form a pile of burdens with these rocks. As you set your rock on the pile, say the burden you'd like to lay down with it.**

When kids have all laid down their burdens, ask them to discuss how they felt carrying the rocks and what their reactions were when they gave them up. Then ask kids to compare this experience to how it feels to let Jesus carry our personal burdens.

After discussion, sing a song about giving God your burdens, such as "Down by the Riverside," and pray together before returning to your starting point—free of your burdens!

**Note:** Unless it's OK for you to leave a pile of rocks in your park, you'll probably want to designate an adult volunteer to collect the rocks after the activity.

# MATTHEW 13:1-23

## THEME:

The parable of the seeds

## SUMMARY:
In this PROJECT, teenagers will create a presentation for a group of younger children.

PREPARATION: Gather Bibles, magazines, markers, blank transparencies, and an overhead projector.

H ave kids create a "picture show" to tell the parable of the seeds to a group of younger children. Form two groups and give each group markers, several magazines, and a stack of blank transparencies. Assign one group the story (Matthew 13:1-9) and the other group the explanation (Matthew 13:18-23). Have groups read their passages, then brainstorm ideas for possible illustrations. Magazine pictures can be traced on the transparencies if your group is short on artists.

Have some group members work on the illustrations while others work on writing a script that presents the story and explanation in language young children can understand. Encourage kids to be creative by adding sound effects, songs, or other fun elements to the presentation.

After kids have finished their scripts and transparencies, practice the presentation several times. Arrange to present it to a children's Sunday school class the following week. After your presentation, talk about the "seeds" you've just sown with the younger kids.

# MATTHEW
# 14:22-33

## THEME:
Doubt

## SUMMARY:
This CREATIVE READING helps kids understand God's power over their doubts and fears.

PREPARATION: On a sheet of newsprint, write, "Lord, we're afraid of (blank). Help us to trust you." On a second sheet of newsprint, write, "Have courage. It is I. Do not be afraid." Post both sheets in the front of the room. You'll also need a Bible.

Form groups of no more than four. Have kids read Matthew 14:22-33 in their groups.

Say: **Peter had a hard time trusting Jesus because he was afraid. In your group, brainstorm a list of situations where you might be afraid. Be realistic. For example, it's not likely you'll be thrown into a pit of vipers, but you could be teased because you refuse to drink at a party.**

Give kids several minutes to brainstorm, then invite groups to share their situations.

Say: **Now choose one or more situations from your list that each person in your group can relate to.**

Write groups' choices on the newsprint that says, "Lord, we're afraid of (blank). Help us to trust you."

Next, lead the group in a responsive reading as follows:

Read the opening statement, then have groups take turns saying, "Lord, we're afraid of *(blank)*. Help us to trust you." Have kids fill in the blank with one of the situations written on the newsprint.

After a group reads a situation, have the rest of the kids respond by reading Jesus' quote from Matthew 14:27, written on the second newsprint.

Continue the reading until each group has had a chance to read at least one situation.

# MATTHEW
# 14:22-33

## THEME:

Overcoming doubt and fear

## SUMMARY:
This SKIT portrays a diver at a swimming meet who questions his ability to dive.

## WALKING ON WATER

SCENE: A teenager is preparing for a difficult dive at a school swim meet.

PROPS: A long, wide board. You'll also need Bibles for the discussion after the skit.

CHARACTERS:
**Trevor**
**Offstage Voice**

SCRIPT

*(Trevor is standing on the end of a long, wide board, talking to himself as he looks at the "pool" in front of him.)*

**Trevor:** I don't know about this, God. *(Looks around as if surveying the crowd.)* If there weren't such a big crowd here, I'd climb down this ladder right away. *(Pauses.)* Maybe I should do that anyway. Yeah, that's it. I'll go back down. Coach will understand. He's probably seen it hap-pen hundreds of times. *(Turns as if to climb back down, then stops.)* No, I've got to do this. *(Confidently prepares to jump.)* Here I go—Trevor Stephens, diving maniac... *(He stops in midmotion.)* What am I doing? That's a long way down. People have died falling out of chairs, and I climb 10 meters to jump into a pool that feels like concrete if you hit it wrong. What am I, crazy? *(He starts to turn around as if to climb back down again, then pauses.)* OK, OK... you're right, Lord. You *have* kept me safe every other time. Why should this be different? It's not like I have to walk on water or anything. *(He turns again as if preparing to dive, starts his diving motion, but is interrupted by Offstage Voice.)*

**Offstage Voice:** The next diver is our current leader and last year's state champion: Trevor Stephens from West High. *(Trevor is startled out of his self-talk and looks around the room.)*

**Trevor:** *(Smiles, waves to the imaginary crowd and walks confidently toward one end of the room. He's mumbling to himself as he walks.)* I hope they remembered to fill the pool... *(Freezes in midstep.)*

If you use this skit as a discussion starter, here are possible questions:

■ **In what area of your life do you face the most fears and** doubts?

■ How does Peter deal with his fears and doubts in Matthew 14:22-33?

■ What's God's plan for overcoming doubt?

# MATTHEW 15:1-20

> **THEME:**
> Hypocrisy
>
> **SUMMARY:**
> Teenagers will compare chocolates with a disappointing filling to Pharisees in this OBJECT LESSON.

PREPARATION: Purchase chocolate-flavored, quick-hardening ice-cream topping and cotton balls. Before class, dip the cotton balls in the topping, place them on waxed paper, and refrigerate until hard. Dip again to improve the appearance of the "candies."

Arrange the chocolates on a plate or tray—the fancier, the better. You may even want to put a doily under the chocolates or wrap the plate with colored cellophane. You'll also need a Bible.

Take the plate of chocolates to class and set it in a prominent place. When everyone has arrived, pick up the plate.

Say: **These are hand-dipped chocolates. They're an extra-special treat I like to share with friends. Because they're so spe-** cial, **they must be savored and eaten in a special way. I'll explain how to eat them after everyone has been served.**

Pass around the plate of chocolates and let everybody take one. Don't insist on everyone taking a chocolate, especially if some kids are suspicious. Simply shrug and move on to the next person.

Say: **First you must barely taste the chocolate with the tip of your tongue. The first bite must be a small nibble because these chocolates are so rich. Once you get used to the richness, you can gradually take bigger bites.**

As kids discover the cotton inside the chocolate coating, have them discuss the following questions:

■ **What were you thinking when you first saw the plate of chocolates?**

■ **What were you thinking when I explained how to eat the chocolates?**

■ **What was it like to discover cotton under the chocolate coating?**

Read Matthew 15:1-20, then ask:

■ **How are the Pharisees like the chocolate-covered cotton balls?**

■ **When do you find yourself acting like the Pharisees by trying to look good on the outside?**

■ **What can you do to be sure that both your words and actions honor God?**

VARIATION: Instead of chocolate-covered cotton balls you might consider creating chocolate-covered Brussels sprouts.

# MATTHEW
# 16:24-26

> ## THEME:
>
> The cost of following Jesus
>
> ## SUMMARY:
> In this DEVOTION, kids will miss out on a treat by clinging to a smaller one.

PREPARATION: Bring chocolate kisses and candy bars in a paper sack. You'll also need Bibles.

EXPERIENCE

Show kids the kisses but don't let them see the candy bars yet. Give kids each a chocolate kiss. Then ask: **Who would like to give away the chocolate kiss I've just given you?**

After kids volunteer to give up their candy, tell them they can give the candy to anyone. Once all those who want to give their candy away have done so, bring out the candy bars and give candy bars to the people who gave up their kisses. If no one gave candy away, bring out the candy bars and show them what they missed.

RESPONSE

Form groups of four and have groups each read aloud Matthew 16:24-26. Have group members discuss these questions:

■ **How did it feel to give up your kiss? to not give it up?**

■ **How is what Jesus is saying like or unlike what just happened with the candy?**

■ **What is Jesus asking us to do in this passage?**

■ **If we aren't supposed to seek to save our lives, what should we seek?**

CLOSING

Give everyone another chocolate kiss. Tell group members to give that kiss away this week as a symbol of their commitment to give their all in service to Jesus.

# MATTHEW
# 17:1-13

> ## THEME:
>
> Jesus changes our lives.
>
> ## SUMMARY:
> This OBJECT LESSON compares the changes in a glowing object to the changes Jesus makes in our lives.

PREPARATION: Before class, go to a toy store and buy an object that glows in the dark. You should be able to find objects such as balls, rings, bracelets, or even gooey substances from which to choose. Pick an object that doesn't look like it would glow in the dark. Remember to "charge up" the object by holding it under a bright light before your meeting. Be sure to bring a Bible.

In a well-lit room hold up the object and ask kids to observe as many characteristics of the object as possible. After a minute, have kids share the characteristics they observed. Compliment them on their keen observations, then say: **Let's look at one special characteristic of this object.**

Turn off the lights and hold up the object so kids can see it glow. Ask:

■ **How could you tell whether or not this object would glow in the dark?**

Keeping the lights off, hold the object so its glow falls on a Bible and ask a volunteer to read the story of Jesus' transfiguration from Matthew 17:1-13. Ask:

■ **What was different about Jesus when his appearance changed?**

■ **How did this change in Jesus affect his friends' perception of him?**

■ **How has your relationship with Jesus changed your life? Have others been able to see this change?**

Say: **If we've truly been transformed by Jesus' power, we should be glowing all the time in our dark world.**

With the lights still off, pass the glowing object around the room. As kids hold the object, have them tell one way they plan to "glow" around others in the coming week. For example kids might say, "This week I'll be a glowing light to my brother by doing one of his chores each day" or "I'll glow for Jesus this week by sending a note of encouragement to one of my friends."

# MATTHEW 18:1-5

**THEME:**
Being like a child

**SUMMARY:**
On this OVERNIGHTER, teenagers remember fun aspects of childhood.

PREPARATION: Lead kids back to childhood for a night. Plan a lock-in or overnight retreat around childhood themes. Instruct kids to bring their favorite childhood toy (or an object similar to this toy if they no longer have it around). You'll need to gather a Bible, games, and food as suggested below.

Use these ideas to carry out the theme:

■ Have kids carry around their favorite toys during the entire event. Between activities call on different kids to tell about the toys they've brought. Be sure each person has the opportunity to share.

■ Serve childhood snack favorites, such as presweetened cereals, peanut butter and jelly sandwiches, hot dogs, or SpaghettiOs during your event.

■ Play standard schoolyard games such as Kickball, Red Rover, and Dodge Ball.

■ Sing children's songs such as "Jesus Loves Me," "Deep and Wide," and other songs with motions.

■ Have kids share a favorite childhood memory.

■ Read Matthew 18:1-5 and discuss what Jesus meant in this passage. Have kids determine what childlike qualities are important to their relationships with God.

# MATTHEW 18:15-17

THEME:
Confrontation

SUMMARY:
In this LEARNING GAME, kids will push and catch each other.

PREPARATION: You'll need Bibles.

Form pairs and have partners stand about 2 feet apart, facing each other with palms out. Tell kids to plant their feet about a foot apart and try to knock their partners off balance using nothing but their palms against their partners' palms. Allow pairs several tries. Then ask:

■ **How did it make you feel to knock your partner off balance?**

■ **How did it feel to get knocked off balance?**

■ **How is this experience like confronting a person about a problem?**

Next, form groups of three and have kids take turns falling backward into each other's arms. Have the fallers close their eyes and make their bodies stiff as they fall. Once everyone has fallen at least once, ask:

■ **How did you feel falling backward?**

■ **How did it feel to catch your partners?**

■ **Between this and the last activity, which is more like confronting a friend about a problem? Explain.**

Form groups of three and have groups each read Matthew 18:15-17. In their groups, have kids discuss these questions:

■ **What do these passages say about confrontation?**

■ **What kinds of issues would lead you to confront a friend?**

■ **How do you know when you should confront someone?**

■ **How would these passages influence the way you presently relate to your friends?**

Say: **Confronting people can be a lot like catching them. When we see friends going in a direction that's bad for them, confronting them can be the most loving thing we can do.**

# MATTHEW 18:19-20

THEME:
Prayer

SUMMARY:
Teenagers will directly apply the passage as they pray this CREATIVE PRAYER together.

PREPARATION: Gather Bibles, pencils, and slips of paper.

Form pairs and have kids discuss requests they'd like other

group members to pray about. If you have an uneven number of kids in your class, either assign one trio or participate in this activity yourself. Remind kids to include prayers for themselves and others, as well as praises for prayers God has answered.

Distribute slips of paper and have pairs write down their top three requests. Then have kids place their requests on the floor all around the room.

Have pairs read Matthew 18:19-20 together.

Say: **Jesus promises that he's here with us when we pray together. To show we believe that, we're going to pray for each other's requests now. Pick up a request from the floor and pray with your partner about it. Move from request to request until you've prayed for each one.**

Close with a prayer similar to this one: **Dear God, thank you for hearing our prayers. We trust you to answer them, just like you promised. In Jesus' name, amen.**

With kids' permission, post the prayer requests on a poster or bulletin board in your room. Each week have kids check the list and mark off requests God has answered.

# MATTHEW
# 18:21-35

**THEME**
Forgiveness

**SUMMARY:**
Teenagers will play LEARNING GAMES demonstrating forgiveness.

PREPARATION: You'll need a Bible, a watermelon and a knife to cut it, and two or more Sorry! board games.

Begin this event by reading Matthew 18:21-35 and explaining that forgiveness is important, even when playing games.

Play familiar games but vary the rules slightly to emphasize the forgiveness theme. If your group is large, have kids form groups and have several games going on at once. The following game ideas will get you started:

■ **Watermelon-seed spitting contest:** Read Psalm 103:12, then see how far kids can get from their "sins."

■ **Sorry! game:** Read Romans 3:23-25 before beginning the game. When someone says "sorry," say, "I forgive you" and move the player's piece back to its original position. (Have two or more game boards available for play.)

■ **"Hug" Freeze Tag:** "Unfreeze" tagged people by hugging them. Read Ephesians 4:32 when the game is over.

Close your event by reading Matthew 18:21-35 again.

# MATTHEW
# 19:16-30

## THEME:
Money

## SUMMARY:
This DEVOTION uses board games to help kids evaluate the importance of money.

PREPARATION: Bring in several money-related board games, such as Monopoly or Life. Set up the games around the room, including items such as paper and pencils needed for scorekeeping. You'll also need prizes for the winners and Bibles.

EXPERIENCE

Explain that you'll be playing board games together. If your group is small enough, have kids play as individuals. For larger groups, have kids form pairs or teams of three to play.

Before kids start playing, announce the allotted playing time and the prizes you'll award to the winners. However, don't say what qualifies as winning.

After the allotted time has passed, have kids count up their money, including the value of any property they've purchased. Award prizes to those with the least amount of money in each playing group.

RESPONSE
Ask:
■ **What was your goal as you played your game?**

■ **How did you feel when I awarded the prizes to the people with the least money?**

Give each playing group a Bible and have kids read the story of the rich, young man in Matthew 19:16-30. Have groups discuss the following questions:

■ **How do you think the rich man felt about himself and his possessions before he approached Jesus?**

■ **How do you think he felt afterward?**

■ **How is that like or unlike the way you felt when I awarded the prizes?**

CLOSING
Have kids form small groups with those at their playing tables.

Say: **Think of the things you own. What would be hard to give up if Jesus asked you to? Share your answers with your group.**

After everyone has shared, have kids tell one item they'll be willing to give to a charitable organization this next week. During your next meeting, ask kids if they followed through with their commitments.

# MATTHEW
# 20:25-28

## THEME:
Service

## SUMMARY:
This PROJECT gives kids the opportunity to serve people in the church and community.

PREPARATION: Hold a planning meeting with teenagers to prepare for the actual mowing event. You'll need a Bible.

Read Matthew 20:25-28 and discuss ways teenagers can serve others in their homes, communities, and at church. Then have kids plan a lawn-mowing day for members of the church or community who are unable to do this chore for themselves. Kids will need to work on the following:

■ Creating a list of lawns to be cared for. A notice could be put in the church bulletin or posted in a neighborhood senior center to find those in need of your services.

■ Finding people willing to loan lawn mowers and other equipment. Be sure these items are returned in the condition in which they were borrowed—and with full gas tanks.

■ Raising funds to buy gas for the mowers. Perhaps a special offering could be taken in your class for a couple of weeks before the event.

■ Arranging transportation to the various homes.

On the day of the event, let kids be in charge of the project. This is their opportunity to serve others. Encourage kids to keep a good attitude as they're showing Jesus' love to those they serve.

**Note:** Because safety could be a concern with this activity, you'll want to make sure all lawn mowers are in good working order and that all kids involved know how to handle a lawn mower safely. You might also want to have parents sign permission forms that release the church from responsibility in case of an accident.

Depending on the climate where you live, you may want to have a snow-shoveling or leaf-raking event as well.

# MATTHEW 21:1-11

---

THEME:
Jesus, our King

SUMMARY:
This CREATIVE READING dramatizes Jesus' entry into Jerusalem.

---

PREPARATION: You'll need to select six or more group members to perform in this dramatic responsive reading. The roles are as follows: Leader, Speaker A, Speaker B, Jesus, and two Bicycle Pushers. If you have fewer than six teenagers, have kids read for more than one role. For larger groups, have as many people as you like read the parts of Speaker A and Speaker B in unison.

Make a photocopy of the "Creative Reading for Matthew 21:1-11" handout (p. 41) for each person participating. Gather enough brooms, mops, or feather dusters for those who are Speakers. You'll also need a bicycle with paper donkey ears and a tail attached to it, and Bibles.

Have your group members read Matthew 21:1-11 together as

# CREATIVE READING FOR MATTHEW 21:1-11

**Leader:** The king is coming!

**Speaker A:** Hosanna!

**Speaker B:** Praise to the king!

**Leader:** Surely our king is a powerful king.

**Speaker A:** The king is strong and mighty.

**Speaker B:** The king shall rule forever.

**Leader:** What shall we do to welcome the king?

**Speaker B:** We'll polish the silver.

**Speaker A:** Bring out the fine china.

**Speakers A and B:** Prepare a great feast. Invite him for dinner.

**Leader:** Who shall we invite to the feast for the king?

**Speaker A:** Ambassadors, presidents, heads of state.

**Speaker B:** Important people—others can wait.

**Leader:** Where shall the king stay while he's here on his visit?

**Speaker B:** At the Ritz.

**Speaker A:** At the palace.

**Speakers A and B:** Someplace with glitz!

**Leader:** What mode of transport shall we offer the king?

**Speaker A:** A Mercedes!

**Speaker B:** A Cadillac!

**Speaker A:** A stretch limousine!

**Speaker B:** A Learjet!

**Speaker A:** How about the space shuttle?

**Speaker B:** *(Shaking head)* Nah, it's out being cleaned.

**Leader:** Let's ready the streets for the king's motorcade! When he comes, he'll be greeted by grand parades.

*(Speakers walk up and down the aisles or around the room dusting and sweeping. As they work, have them speculate about how the king will arrive. After about a minute of sweeping, continue the reading.)*

**Speaker A:** What was that?

**Speaker B:** Did you hear that?

**Speaker A:** I bet that's his plane! It's a siren—it must be the king's motorcade!

*(Moment of silence as Leader and Speakers listen, holding their hands to their ears.)*

**Speaker B:** What's that squeak?

**Speaker A:** What's that clatter?

**Speakers A and B:** What's the matter?

*(Enter Jesus, dressed in ordinary clothes, sitting on an old bicycle which is being wheeled up the aisle by two silent Bicycle Pushers. After he nears the front, continue the dialogue.)*

**Leader:** Who are you? *(Pointing to the bicycle)* What's that thing? You can't be the king!

**Jesus:** This was to bring about what the prophet had said: "Tell the people of Jerusalem, 'Your king is coming to you. He is gentle and riding on a donkey, on the colt of a donkey.' "

*(Dim lights.)*

they prepare to present this reading. Discuss how the setting during Jesus' time might have been similar to or different from that created during this reading.

# MATTHEW 22:34-40

**THEME:**
Loving God

**SUMMARY:**
This LEARNING GAME helps kids understand the importance of serving God with all they have.

PREPARATION: You'll need a Bible.

Have kids remove their shoes and place them in a pile in the center of the room. Mix up the shoes.

Say: **I'm offering you a chance to complete the world's easiest game. All you have to do is put on your shoes. The only rule is that you must keep one hand behind your back at all times.**

Let kids begin hunting for and putting on their shoes. After all the kids have at least retrieved their shoes, ask:

■ **What was it like putting on your shoes with just one hand?**

Read Matthew 22:34-40. Then ask:

■ **How is putting on your shoes with one hand like trying**

to follow God with only part of yourself?

■ **What are ways we can love God with our hearts? our souls? our minds?**

Form pairs and have partners each share one way they can serve God with their whole heart, soul, and mind this week.

# MATTHEW 24

**THEME:**
The end times

**SUMMARY:**
In this OBJECT LESSON, teenagers will participate in a cereal taste test to explore Jesus' words about the end times.

PREPARATION: Gather Bibles, newsprint, markers, tape, blindfolds, cereal, and three bowls.

Using Matthew 24 as a guide, have kids make newsprint "signs of the times." For example, signs may say, "Wars and Stories of War" or "Earthquakes." Have kids tape these signs to the walls.

Place three bowls on a table. Say: **I'm going to fill each bowl with a different food, and I want you each to take a turn choosing which bowl to eat from. The catch is that you'll all be blindfolded.**

Blindfold all the kids and have them line up single file. Then secretly take the blindfolds off the first two kids. Give them each a note. One note should say to eat (or pretend to eat) and then give a negative response, such as whining about the taste, spitting out the cereal, or moaning. The other note should say to eat (or pretend to eat) and then give a positive response, such as praising the taste or asking for more. Tell these two kids to really ham it up.

Fill each bowl with a different cereal. While the kids are reading their notes, say: **We're going to use the first two people in line as guinea pigs. Let's see how well they choose.**

Have these kids each act out their response one at a time. Then tell the rest of the blindfolded kids they can change their order in line if they want to. Some kids will rush to the end. After they've reorganized themselves, have them remove their blindfolds. Ask:

■ **How did you feel as you heard the first two responses?**

■ **How did the first two responses affect where you wanted to be in line?**

Finish the activity by referring to the signs on the wall and asking:

■ **How are your feelings about waiting to experience this food similar to or different from your feelings about the end times?**

■ **How do you think Jesus wants us to view the end times?**

■ **What can you do this week to help you view the end times in that way?**

# MATTHEW 24:36-44

THEME:
Jesus' return

SUMMARY:
During this OVERNIGHTER, teenagers will be surprised by unexpected, fun events.

PREPARATION: Plan an all-night party for your group with the theme "Expect the Best!" Make arrangements to go to a variety of fun places, such as a skating rink, bowling alley, drive-in movie, community pool, and so on. (Some places offer group discounts or discounts for using their facilities late at night or very early in the morning.) Recruit adult drivers as needed and plan the evening so kids will go right from one event to the next. Schedule breakfast as your closing event. Be sure to have a Bible.

As you publicize this event, don't tell kids where you'll be going. Provide a list of items kids will need to bring without telling them why they'll need the items. For example, they'll need socks for skating and bowling, swimsuits and towels for swimming, and so on. To keep kids guessing, add a few unnecessary items, such as a needle and thread, a shoelace, or a roll of masking tape. List all items on a flier and tell kids to expect the best for the evening.

When kids arrive, ask them what they're expecting for the evening and assure them you've got the best activities planned. Then begin your trek from event to event.

Before stopping at your final destination (breakfast), gather the kids for a time of discussion. Ask:

■ **What were you expecting for this evening?**

■ **What gave you clues as to what we'd be doing?**

■ **How did you prepare for this event?**

■ **What would've happened if you hadn't prepared as suggested on the flier?**

Read Matthew 24:36-44 aloud and ask:

■ **What do you think it will be like when Jesus comes to take those who are ready to heaven?**

■ **What would it be like to miss Jesus' return?**

■ **Just as you had to prepare for this event, we have to prepare for Jesus' return. How should we prepare for Jesus to come?**

■ **Are you ready for Jesus to come? Explain.**

Lead the group to breakfast. Over the meal, talk about what heaven might be like and how each person can prepare to go there.

# MATTHEW 25:14-30

**THEME:**
Using God's resources

**SUMMARY:**
Use this PROJECT to help kids understand stewardship.

PREPARATION: You'll need Bibles.

After studying Matthew 25:14-30 with your kids, work with your youth group to try an experiment in stewardship.

In addition to the regular offering, take a youth group offering each week for a month. At the end of four weeks, add up the total amount of the additional offering for the month. Then divide that total by the number of kids who regularly attend your group. That'll give you a rough dollar figure per person.

On a predetermined Sunday, instead of collecting the additional offering, pass around plates full of dollar bills with the invitation for kids to take up to the amount of your dollar figure per person. Tell all those who take money that they've just become "servants" like the ones in the parable.

Tell kids that they must spend the next two weeks multiplying the money however they can. Tell participants to return in two weeks the money they took and whatever profit they've made.

Encourage kids to be creative in

the ways they multiply the money. Some might pool their money to buy ingredients for cookies, then hold a bake sale. Someone else might use the money to buy gas for his or her car, then sell "chauffeur rides" to school. (If you feel it's necessary, tell kids that gambling to multiply their money isn't acceptable.)

On the appointed Sunday, have kids turn in their money and report how they multiplied it. Discuss with kids how they can "multiply" on a regular basis the time, talents, and resources that God has given them. Use the multiplied money for future youth events.

**Note:** If for some reason the total amount of money isn't multiplied, use that as a teachable moment for kids. Discuss why the money wasn't multiplied and how that reflects the way we use our resources for God.

# MATTHEW
# 25:14-30

**THEME:**
Gifts and talents

**SUMMARY:**
In this AFFIRMATION, teenagers affirm the talents of others by writing the talents on bits of "gold"—painted rocks.

PREPARATION: Collect a bucket of rocks. (Gather more if you have a large group.) Find rocks that are smooth and are at least the size of golf balls. Spread these on newspaper and lightly coat them with gold spray paint. When the paint has dried, return the rocks to the bucket. Place the bucket of rocks in the front of your meeting room.

Gather Bibles and enough paper lunch sacks and markers for each person to have one of each.

Give each person a paper lunch sack and a marker. Have kids write their names on the sacks and set them along a wall in the room.

Show kids the bucket of gold rocks and say: **Here we have a bucket of gold. This gold is already valuable, but we're going to add to its value by writing words on the rocks.**

Have each person take a rock from the bucket, then form a circle.

Say: **On this piece of gold, I want you to write a couple of words describing a talent you've observed in the person to your left. This could be a talent such as singing or playing a musical instrument, or it could be a talent such as having a great laugh or encouraging those who feel down. After you've written on this bit of gold, find the bag with the name of the person you wrote about and put the gold in the bag. Then take a new piece of gold and begin writing about the talents of another person in the group. You can write on as many gold rocks as you like. Let's see how full we can fill each other's bags of talents.**

Allow time for kids to write on as many rocks as possible, then give kids the opportunity to read what others said about them. Afterward, gather kids together and have a volunteer read Matthew 25:14-30. Ask:

■ **Why are the talents God's given you more valuable than gold?**

■ **How have you seen people in our church use their gifts and talents for God?**

■ **What makes it hard to use your gifts and talents for God? What can you do about that?**

■ **What will you do this week with the talents God's given you?**

Have kids keep their bags of gold as reminders of the talents God's given them.

# MATTHEW
# 25:31-46

THEME:
Mercy

SUMMARY:
After learning about specific needs of people in the community, teenagers use this CREATIVE PRAYER/MUSIC IDEA to pray for those in need and those helping them.

PREPARATION: Ask a local charitable organization if they'd be willing to share some of their mail to help motivate your youth group to reach out to the needy in your community or congregation. Photocopy several thank-you letters from peo-

ple the organization has helped and several letters requesting the organization's help. (Ask the charitable organization if they'd like you to black out the names of the people who sent the letters before you distribute them to your youth group.) Return the original letters to the organization.

You'll also need Bibles, the songs suggested in the activity, and the equipment for playing them.

As kids arrive, randomly distribute the letters. Without any explanation, have kids read the letters aloud to the group.

Then play "Hollow Eyes" from *Petrified (The Very Best of Petra)* by the contemporary Christian music group Petra, "The Sheep And The Goats" from Keith Green's *The Ministry Years, 1980–1982, Volume 2,* or another song that's relevant to the passage. If the song you choose has a video and you have access to video equipment, have kids watch the video for an even stronger impact.

After the song, have kids form groups of no more than four. Have groups read Matthew 25:31-46 together. Ask:

■ **What kind of person is a sheep? Who is someone you know who is like this?**

■ **What kind of person is a goat?**

Say: **We're going to have a time of prayer now. I'll name a subject for prayer and give several minutes for you to pray together in your groups. Then I'll name another subject for prayer.**

Use this list as a guide for leading the groups in prayer:

■ Pray for those whose letters we just read.

■ Thank God for organizations that help those in need.

■ Pray for someone you know personally who is in need.

■ Ask God to show you a way to help a person in need this week.

VARIATION: Ask the organization for a list of ways teenagers could help them. Read this list after the meeting and provide information for those interested in helping.

# MATTHEW
# 25:31-46

## THEME:
Hard-to-love people

## SUMMARY:
Use this DEVOTION to explore how Jesus wants us to treat hard-to-love people.

PREPARATION: Gather shirts, hangers, markers, tape, and paper. You'll also need a Bible.

EXPERIENCE
Form groups of five or fewer. Give groups each an old shirt on a hanger, a marker, tape, and several sheets of paper. Have groups hang their shirts near where they're sitting. Say: **Sometimes we treat people badly because of the way they're dressed. But there are also lots of other things that make us treat people differently.**

In their groups, have kids write in big letters on each sheet of paper words that describe the most unattractive type of person they can think of (one word per sheet of paper). For example, kids might write "dirty," "cruel," "rude," and so on. Then have groups each make a "head" for their person by drawing a face on one sheet of paper and taping it to the shirt collar. Have them tape their paper words all over their shirt "people."

RESPONSE
Have groups discuss these questions:

■ **What would you say if you met that person in the school hallway?**

■ **How do you feel when you call someone one of the words written on the papers?**

■ **Why do people treat others that way?**

■ **Think about putting that shirt on yourself—how would you feel if people described you using the words you wrote?**

While kids are discussing the questions, silently go to each group's shirt and tape to it a sheet of paper with "Jesus" written on it. Then ask:

■ **Now how would the way you treat this person change? Why the change?**

CLOSING
Read aloud Matthew 25:31-46. Ask:

■ **How would Jesus want us to treat these people?**

■ **What can we do this week to act more Christlike toward people around us who are unattractive in some way?**

# MATTHEW 26:17-30

THEME:
The Passover

SUMMARY:
In this PROJECT, kids will research, plan, and participate in a Passover meal.

PREPARATION: Before presenting your group with this project, gather Bibles and information on resources kids can use.

Check with a local synagogue or "Jews for Jesus" to see if they can offer help or advice on preparing for this meal. Also check out books from your church library or local library on the history of the Passover meal, its symbolism, and how it is served.

Announce that everyone will be working together to plan and participate in a Passover celebration. Inform kids of the resources you've found and how they can be used. Then form the following groups to plan various aspects of the celebration:

■ **Meal research and preparation**—Have this group work with you or another leader to select, purchase, and prepare traditional Passover foods such as lamb, bitter herbs, and unleavened bread. Kids will need to find out how the foods should be prepared and be able to explain the significance of various foods to the entire group when the food is served.

■ **Scripture reading and presentation**—Have this group study and present Exodus 12:1-14; 15:1-21; Matthew 26:17-19, 26-30; and Hebrews 9:1-7, 11-15, 23-28. Encourage kids to include dramatic and responsive readings in their presentation. They could also type out portions of the Scriptures and set them under the plates for a reading by all at the Passover table.

■ **Song selection and leading**—Have this group choose worship songs. Scripture songs—especially those taken from Psalms—would be most appropriate, as well as other songs that express thanks and praise to God for his action in our lives. Kids will need to be ready to lead others in song or perform songs themselves if they like.

Encourage kids to be creative and plan the service so it will be meaningful for all. Have an adult or student leader from each group report the group's progress to you. These people can also work with you to plan a written program for the evening. This will help each group know when they're to share.

After the event, give kids the opportunity to share what they learned from this dinner.

# MATTHEW 26:17-46

## THEME:
The night of Christ's arrest

## SUMMARY:
This ADVENTURE will help your group get a deeper sense of the night of Christ's arrest by acting out the events of Matthew 26.

PREPARATION: Before the event, spend time studying in detail the Last Supper; Christ's heartfelt betrayal prayer at Gethsemane; and his arrest, trial, crucifixion, and resurrection. You'll need Bibles.

Shortly before Easter, have the group re-enact the Last Supper. Try to re-create the scene as accurately as possible, having a youth leader or respected teenager play the role of Christ. This portrayal will be most effective if principal actors memorize the scene and interact naturally.

As a memorable finale for the evening, have the group walk to a nearby secluded area. Assemble the group members and read the account of Jesus in Gethsemane (Matthew 26:36-46). Sing worship songs and then, as a surprise to the group, have soldiers and Judas (all portrayed by adults in the church) arrive to take Jesus away.

Return to church and let the group members discuss what happened and how they felt about it.

# MATTHEW 26:47–28:15

## THEME:
Easter

## SUMMARY:
Use this Easter SKIT to take a behind-the-scenes look at the people who crucified Jesus.

## IT'LL TURN UP

SCENE: Pilate sits on the throne, center stage. Advisers stand on both sides. The Three Women are on the right side of the stage.

PROPS: You'll need costumes that are appropriate for the characters, such as swords and shields for the Soldiers, a crown for King Herod, and so on. You'll also need Bibles for the discussion after the skit.

CHARACTERS:
**Soldier 1**
**Soldier 2**
**Mrs. Pilate**
**Pilate**
**Three Women**
**King Herod**
**Adviser 1**
**Adviser 2**
**Adviser 3**
**Maid**

### SCRIPT
*(Actors are frozen in place as lights come up. Scene opens as Soldier 1 runs down the center aisle toward Soldier 2 at left. Lights come up and Soldiers. Start the action while other actors remain frozen.)*
**Soldier 1:** Omigosh! Claudius!

The body's gone! The captain will have our heads!

**Soldier 2:** Don't worry, Flavius. It'll turn up. It'll turn up.

*(Soldiers freeze in place. Mrs. Pilate, her Maid, and a group of Three Women unfreeze and stand nodding in agreement.)*

**Mrs. Pilate:** I told him to leave this man alone.

**Maid:** She told him.

**Mrs. Pilate:** I told him to have nothing to do with this execution.

**Maid:** I heard it myself. With my own ears I heard it.

**Mrs. Pilate:** "Have nothing to do with him," I said. "This is a righteous man," I said. "Let Herod do his own dirty work," I said. But would he listen to me?

**Maid:** Would he listen to her? No. Not at all. Not one minute. He wouldn't listen to her one stinkin' minute.

**Mrs. Pilate:** Now we'll have a ghost after us.

**Maid:** A ghost. A dead, dead ghost. A ghost. *(Making a ghostly sound)* Ooo...

**Mrs. Pilate:** He said he's washed his hands of the whole thing, but my husband has this man's blood on his head.

**Maid:** His head. The blood is on his head. On his head? *(Looking at Mrs. Pilate quizzically)* On his head. Well, we'd better wash it off then, don't you think?

*(All freeze, then Pilate, Herod, and Advisers unfreeze. Herod is pacing. Advisers stand on both sides of Pilate.)*

**Herod:** They've stolen the body. That's the only logical explanation. They've stolen the body.

**Pilate:** You fool, Herod. Nobody stole anything. The guards were there the whole time.

**Herod:** They must have fallen asleep.

**Pilate:** Roman soldiers do not fall asleep.

**Adviser 1:** These men know the penalty for sleeping on duty is death.

**Adviser 2:** Even those who didn't fall asleep are put to death if one of them dozes off. The squad leader kills them one by one and then falls on his own sword.

**Pilate:** They didn't fall asleep.

**Herod:** If they didn't fall asleep, then what happened? Where's the body? They'll be telling people that he's alive.

**Adviser 1:** So what? It's only rumors.

**Adviser 2:** Rumors aren't flesh and blood.

**Adviser 3:** Rumors can't hold a sword.

**Pilate:** He's dead. And no dead man can give us any trouble.

**Herod:** If they stole his body and say he's alive, the whole movement might gain popular support.

**Pilate:** Relax, would you? These people are like a bunch of dumb sheep. You strike down the shepherd, and the sheep scatter.

**Adviser 1:** He's right. They've all run away. If any of them dare start any "resurrection" rumors, we'll just pressure them to stop. They'll crack soon enough.

**Adviser 3:** Crack.

**Herod:** And what if they don't?

**Adviser 2:** Listen, all we need is just one from Jesus' inner circle to admit it's all a lie, and it's over!

**Herod:** But what if they still stick to their story?

**Adviser 2:** We know how to get them to talk.

**Adviser 3:** We've had lots of practice.

**Pilate:** No one sacrifices his life for a lie.

**Herod:** I don't know. I have a bad feeling.

**Pilate:** Think about it. Who could possibly be a threat to us? His men from Galilee? Uneducated fishermen, most of them! They can't even read!

**Herod:** But they can talk. What about the man Simon, the one they call Peter, the "rock"?

**Pilate:** Peter?! Ha! I'm told he was hiding in the shadows through the trial.

**Adviser 1:** Too afraid to even show his face.

**Pilate:** No, Peter's no danger. A little pressure on him and he'll deny the whole thing to save his skin.

**Herod:** There's Matthew...

**Pilate:** The tax collector?

**Adviser 2:** No one in all Israel will listen to a tax collector, Herod. Surely you know that.

**Adviser 3:** No one.

**Pilate:** Who else?

**Herod:** Mark or John might...

**Pilate:** Mark who? John who?

**Herod:** Mark's a young one. And John, well, he's a dreamer, I suppose.

**Adviser 1:** No one will take them seriously.

**Adviser 3:** Not a soul.

**Pilate:** All right, who else?

**Adviser 1:** There's Luke.

**Adviser 2:** He's educated.

**Adviser 3:** Smart.

**Adviser 1:** He's a doctor, with some credibility.

**Adviser 2:** And James, the man they call Jesus' brother.

**Adviser 1:** And the Pharisee Nicodemus and Joseph of Arimethea, who gave him the tomb.

**Pilate:** So what are you afraid of, Herod? Do you seriously think such a small, varied group of men will come together to raise up a new world religion?

*(All except Herod laugh. Soldiers walk up to guard either side of the throne.)*

**Soldier 1:** New world religion! Ho, ho, ho! That's a good one!

**Pilate:** Think about it—this carpenter's son from a nowhere town is really the Son of God. Sure, everyone will believe it.

**Adviser 3:** We crucified God! Ha!

**Pilate:** Well, they'll probably claim he planned it that way—stripped and nailed to a cross. *(All laugh but Herod.)* And then they'll claim he's somehow immortal... risen from the dead!

*(Three Women join the growing crowd, laughing.)*

**Adviser 3 and Women:** From the dead!

**Pilate:** Yes, I see hundreds—no—thousands of people worshiping the dead king Jesus and praying to him.

*(Maid and Mrs. Pilate walk in, laughing.)*

**Maid:** Why not millions?

**Pilate:** Yes, millions wearing crosses as an ornament around their necks—all in tribute to Jesus!

**Adviser 3:** Tribute!

**Pilate:** It's just a matter of time before the whole world starts celebrating his birthday every year! *(Laughter grows—even Herod joins in.)*

**Herod:** His birthday?

**Pilate:** Why, yes, of course. They'll even rewrite the Roman calendar—they'll number it from the year he was born!

**Herod:** Rewrite the calendar. Ha! Stop. I can't take it anymore! *(All laugh uncontrollably.)*

**Herod:** OK, OK. I guess you're right. Nobody will believe this. It's too far-fetched to even consider. I guess...I guess I was just a bit paranoid. *(He takes a deep breath.)* Wearing crosses as ornaments. That's good!

**Pilate:** I give this whole mess two or three weeks. Then the fishermen will be back to their boats, the tax collector back at his tables—if we let him keep his job.

**Herod:** Are you sure it'll be over that soon?

**Pilate:** As sure as Jesus is dead and never coming back.

**Herod:** And the body?

**Pilate:** *(He pauses, gets up from his throne, walks to center stage, and peers into space.)* It'll turn up, Herod. It'll turn up.

# MATTHEW 27:32–28:7

## THEME:
Good from bad

## SUMMARY:
In this OBJECT LESSON, kids will break open a coconut and eat its fruit.

PREPARATION: Gather coconuts, markers, and Bibles.

Form groups of no more than four and give each group a coconut and a marker. Have kids each think of a bad time in their lives that worked for the best in the end. For example, kids might think of a time they failed a homework assignment, but doing so made them study harder to do well on a test.

On their coconut, have each group's members write a word, phrase, or symbol that represents their situation. For example, a person could draw a truck to symbolize leaving good friends when his family moved to a different state. Have kids each tell their group about their situation.

Once everyone has shared, tell groups to take their coconuts outside and do whatever it takes to break them open. Supervise groups to make sure they don't endanger themselves or the church property. And be sure they don't totally destroy their coconuts.

When groups have accomplished their task, have them gather their coconut pieces and go back to the meeting room. Invite group members to feast on the sweet-tasting coconut meat. Ask:

■ **How did you feel as you destroyed your group's coconut?**

■ **How is breaking open the coconut and finding something good inside like having good things come out of a bad situation?**

Assign each group one of these passages: Matthew 27:32-50 or Matthew 28:1-7. Have each group come up with a one-sentence summary of its assigned passage. Then ask groups to discuss these questions to wrap up:

■ **How is Jesus' death like breaking open the coconut?**

■ **How is Jesus' resurrection like tasting the good food inside the coconut?**

■ **What does Christ's death mean to you personally?**

■ **What difference has it made in your life?**

# MATTHEW
## 27:62–28:15

## THEME:
Jesus' resurrection

## SUMMARY:
This SKIT helps teenagers visualize the Resurrection from a guard's point of view.

# A GUARD'S-EYE VIEW

SCENE: Jesus' tomb

PROPS: You'll need to construct a large stone out of cardboard. This can be leaned against the back of your stage area with the Angel hiding behind it. Additional costumes and props will add to the skit but aren't required. Have actors pantomime any actions done without props. You'll also need Bibles for the discussion after the skit.

CHARACTERS:
**Felix** (a Roman guard)
**Anthony** (a Roman guard)
**Angel**
**Chief Priest**

SCRIPT

**Anthony:** *(To audience)* It all started that night Felix and I got called up from the reserves to patrol the streets during Passover. I'll never forget what happened that night.
*(Enter Felix. Anthony begins speaking with Felix instead of audience.)*

**Felix:** *(Scowling)* When I volunteered for the Roman Army National Guard, I didn't expect to get called up to duty!

**Anthony:** You know how unruly these Jews get during their holiday times. Besides, it's only for a few days. It could be worse—we could be posted at their temple. Those animal sacrifices make my stomach turn.

**Felix:** I guess we'd better finish sealing this stone. I don't know who would want to steal a dead body anyway.

**Anthony:** It beats me. But those are our orders, and unless we want to join that guy in the cave, we'd better get to work.

*(Anthony and Felix begin pounding the cardboard stone to ensure it's tightly wedged into the tomb. They could place chairs in front of it, pretend to glue it, and so on.)*

**Felix:** *(Proudly)* That ought to hold 'er, wouldn't you say?

**Anthony:** If it doesn't, I'm sure those chains will make enough noise to get our attention.

*(Felix and Anthony get settled in. They lean up against the sides of the stone and begin watch. After a minute, they begin shaking, as if feeling the first rumblings of an earthquake. Suddenly the earthquake strikes, knocking them both off their feet. Angel, from behind the rock, pushes the rock aside and stands up.)*

**Felix:** Huh? Hey! What the— *(Bumps his head against the stone.)*

**Anthony:** Oof! Ow! *(Sees the angel and gasps.)* Hey, Felix!

*(Felix ignores him—he's rubbing the bump on his head.)*

**Anthony:** *(Louder)* Hey, Felix! You better look at this!

**Felix:** What! What is it?

*(As Felix turns to look, he faints, and Anthony covers his eyes and huddles as if hiding.)*

**Angel:** *(Speaking to the audience and not looking at Felix or Anthony)* Don't be afraid. I know that you are looking for Jesus, who has been crucified. He is not here. He has risen from the dead as he said he would. Come and see the place where his body was. And go quickly and tell his followers, "Jesus has risen from the dead. He is going into Galilee ahead of you, and you will see him there."

*(Anthony faints next to Felix. Dim lights and have the Angel leave the stage, taking the rock along. Bring lights back on.)*

**Felix:** *(Nudging Anthony)* Anthony! Wake up! Where's the stone? I thought you said we'd hear the chains! Now look at the mess we're in!

**Anthony:** *(Still a little groggy)* No, no. I heard voices, but no one was there...

**Felix:** You're crazy. Come on. We've got to go report this now, before someone else does.

*(Felix drags Anthony up by the hand. Anthony looks back with a puzzled expression on his face. They walk to other side of stage, where Felix knocks on a door.)*

**Chief Priest:** *(Moving toward the door)* Who is it?

**Felix:** It's Felix and Anthony, sir. We've run into a bit of trouble.

**Chief Priest:** *(Opening the door)* Trouble, you say?

**Felix:** Well, yes, sir. You tell him, Anthony.

**Anthony:** Well, sir, the man in the tomb is gone.

**Chief Priest:** What do you mean he's gone? Didn't I tell you to seal that tomb?

**Felix:** Oh, yes, sir. And we sealed it good. Didn't miss a spot.

**Chief Priest:** Do you know who tampered with the seal?

**Anthony:** Well, that's just it, sir. The seal just sort of opened by itself.

**Chief Priest:** *(Very skeptically)* Opened by itself? What have you been drinking, soldier? Listen here. You go back to that tomb and keep guarding it as if nothing has happened. If anyone asks you, the man's followers came during the night and stole the body while you were asleep. And here's a little something for your trouble. *(He counts out money into Felix's hand, then moves to Anthony, who refuses.)*

**Anthony:** I can't take that, sir. I know it sounds strange, and you probably don't believe me, but I really did hear something. Maybe the man did rise from the dead.

**Chief Priest:** *(Forcing the money into Anthony's hand)* Nonsense. You heard nothing. You saw nothing. Now get back to work before I notify the governor of your little hallucination. *(He slams the door and moves offstage.)*

*(Anthony runs away. Felix shrugs his shoulders and moves in other direction offstage. Anthony stands facing audience.)*

**Anthony:** I just know he's alive. Hmm, I wonder how far it is to Galilee.

*(Anthony exits, lights fade.)*

After the skit, form groups of no more than three to discuss the following questions. As they're discussing the questions, have kids refer to Matthew 27:62–28:15 for more details about Jesus' resurrection.

■ **Who do you identify with more—Felix or Anthony? Why?**

■ **How do you think you'd have responded if you'd been present at Jesus' resurrection?**

■ **What would've been scary for you?**

■ **What would've been exciting?**

■ **The skit ends with Anthony thinking about risking his job and possibly his life to meet the risen Jesus. What risks do you have to take by having a relationship with Jesus?**

■ **How has knowing Jesus changed your life?**

# MATTHEW
## 28:1-7

**THEME:**
Easter

**SUMMARY:**
Use this SKIT around Easter time to help kids get a fresh perspective on the Resurrection.

## CEMETERY ANGEL

SCENE: A cemetery

PROPS: You'll need a shovel and Bibles for the discussion after the skit.

CHARACTERS:
**Howard** (an older man who's a cemetery groundskeeper)
**Derek** (teenager visiting a grave)
**Tyrone** (teenager visiting a grave)
**Christine** (teenager visiting a grave)

SCRIPT

*(Lights up on Howard, who stands with a shovel, stage right.)*

**Howard:** *(To audience)* Howdy. They told me you'd be comin'. I was waitin' here for ya. See, if you don't meet folks here at the gate, they're likely to turn right around and head home. Cemeteries have a way of turnin' people around.

*(Walking with the shovel to center stage)* They said you'd like to learn a little somethin' about... well... dyin'. Can't say I'm an expert on the subject, since I myself have never died firsthand. *(He chuckles.)* But I've worked here 24 years, and that puts me closer to the subject than most will ever get. We live in a white house over there by the big oak. Livin' with dyin' is the way it's been for us. *(Silence.)*

*(Looking out at audience)* Suppose you're wonderin' about the shovel. The answer's no; I haven't just dug a grave. *(Setting shovel down)* I was just sprucin' up Marlys *(pronounced "Marlis")* Potter's grave over there *(pointing to stage right)*. Went to school with Marlys. Always liked her a lot. *(Silence.)*

Oh, by the way, the name's Howard. Howard Wallace. *(Walking to stage right)* I know why you're here today. It happens every year. Come Easter, all of a sudden, people start talkin' about dyin' and risin' and livin' forever. You understand, though, that in my line of work, it's Easter almost every day.

*(Derek, Tyrone, and Christine enter stage left and stand facing the audience as if around a grave. Howard continues talking to the audience.)*

**Howard:** I learn as much about livin' around here as I do about dyin'. I watch 'em come and go—all the families and the friends, I mean. *(Notices the threesome.)* Like those three. They've been comin' quite regular since February. 'Bout three times a week. You'd like 'em. It's the girl's brother who died. Car accident, they said. Sixteen years old. The boys there were in the car with him. They're havin' a hard time with it. I've talked with them before. Say, you just follow along, will ya? But keep quiet. *(He walks over to the three; stands center stage.)*

**Howard:** So... back again, huh?

**Derek:** Right.

**Christine:** You're not closing yet, are you?

**Howard:** Nope.

**Christine:** That's right. Forgot. Howard, it looks good.

**Derek:** It's important to us. We appreciate it.

**Tyrone:** We come because he was our friend.

**Howard:** It's a good thing you're doin'.

**Christine:** I'm sure you see a lot of people like us.

**Howard:** You'd be surprised. Most come at first, then less and less. They mean well—all of 'em do. But the livin' begins to take over again, and the dyin'... well, the dyin' is left here where it belongs.

**Derek:** What do people do when they come?

**Howard:** They pray. They stand. Most cry. Some will try to break the barrier and talk.

**Derek:** The barrier?

**Howard:** The wall between those who live and those who've died. Some'll try to talk and tell themselves they're being heard.

**Derek:** They're wasting their time, aren't they?

**Howard:** Maybe. But the heart will always hunt for hope when death takes a loved one.

**Tyrone:** You sound like a preacher.

**Howard:** It rubs off, you know. I've been to a lot of funerals.

**Christine:** I've only been to one— Kevin's. The preacher talked about it being Kevin's time. How could he know it was Kevin's time? Kevin was 16!

**Howard:** Sometimes even preachers say more than the Good Book itself allows.

**Christine:** What do you mean?

**Howard:** Just that sometimes we say more than we have a right to say.

**Tyrone:** So what do you say?

**Howard:** What do I say about what?

**Tyrone:** What do you say about Kevin dying?

**Howard:** I say it hurts. I say it must hurt a lot.

**Tyrone:** You got that right. I say it stinks. I say it's unfair. It should never have happened. *(Silence.)* Kevin's time? What a joke! People are living to be 100 all over the country. It's no more Kevin's time than it's my time.

**Derek:** Howard, what do you say when people wonder about the fairness?

**Howard:** I'm afraid I wonder right along with 'em. Listen, you don't dig a grave for a baby who dies in the night with no explanation and not wonder about the fairness of it. I've got myself a son over there *(pointing back stage)*. Buried him when he wasn't much older than Kevin here. I put him near where he used to sled in the winter *(pointing)* way up the hill there, just this side of the tall fir. I buried him myself.

**Tyrone:** How could you do that?

**Howard:** Bury him, ya mean? *(Tyrone nods.)* Years ago, folks used to do it all the time—lay their kin to rest. The buryin' for me wasn't so bad. I do it for a livin'. His dyin', though, that was different. I still walk up there and see him slidin' down that hill and rollin' off the sled near the bottom. Sometimes I'll try to break the barrier myself, but it ain't no use. He's gone. There'll be no more talkin' this side of heaven.

**Tyrone:** I guess you know how we feel.

**Howard:** Ya don't work in a cemetery for 24 years and not learn about the way folks handle dyin'. Ya see it on their faces. 'Til the boy died, though, I probably never really knew. The Bible calls it a sting, I think.

**Christine:** A sting. That's not bad. It stings all right.

**Howard:** What happens next is the sting turns into an ache. At least that's the way it's been for me.

**Derek:** So when does it all go away? When do the sting and the ache and the whole thing just stop?

**Howard:** I'm not sure it ever has—for me, with the boy dyin', I mean. It comes back, even after all these years. Don't know why it is, but when the snow hits that hill up there, the tears come like the two were somehow hooked up.

**Christine:** I'd give anything to have Kevin back.

**Howard:** Bet you'd tell him some things you never got to say.

**Christine:** I would.

**Derek:** So would I.

**Howard:** Strange how we don't say what we need to say to the people closest to us. And that's true with almost everybody. Maybe if everyone who comes here with somethin' left to say had said it when they had the chance, the world would be a kinder place.

**Derek:** Maybe so.

**Howard:** Say, will ya excuse me for just a minute?

**Tyrone:** Go ahead. We'll be here awhile.

**Howard:** *(Moving to stage right as the three huddle closer, speaking to the audience)* See how folks come here searchin'? They all come lookin,' hopin' that somehow the sting and the ache will go away. As I recall, people came to a cemetery on the first Easter, too. They knew about the sting. But they never really experienced the ache 'cause the one in the grave wasn't there anymore. *(Silence.)*
I'll tell you a little secret. Remember how, on the first Easter, the people who came to the cemetery were first greeted by the angel—the one who told them what had happened? The angel is my hero. I like to think of myself as givin' people the news that there's livin' to be done after dyin'. *(Silence.)*
You have to go easy, though, and wait until people are ready. That's usually when they say somethin' like "I'd like to believe I'll see him again" or "I have this feelin' part of her is still alive." *(Looking over at the threesome)* So, if ya don't mind, I'll be joinin' my three friends over there... doin' the work of the cemetery angel. You're welcome to stay for a while, if you like. *(Walking to stage left)* You have a happy Easter. *(He joins the other three.)* Say, we'll be closin' the gates fairly soon. You kids may want to be headin' home.

**Christine:** OK. *(Silence.)* Something pulls us here, Howard. What is it? Why do we keep coming back?

**Howard:** I ain't a psychologist, but *(turning)* I know it's the same thing that has me lookin' up that hill. It's love... or hope. It's real, though. I know that.

**Derek:** If only we could see him again.

**Howard:** *(Smiles at the audience. To Derek)* Do you want to believe that—that you'll see him again?

**Christine:** I think we all do.

**Howard:** Then let me tell you about what keeps me goin' when the first snow flies and I'm walkin' that hillside up there. *(Putting arms around two characters' shoulders)* Don't worry about the gate. We'll just leave it open awhile.

*(Characters exit.)*

# MATTHEW 28:18-20

## THEME:
Following Jesus

## SUMMARY:
In this DEVOTION, kids will do mirror-image movements to demonstrate discipleship.

PREPARATION: You'll need a Bible.

### EXPERIENCE
Form pairs and have partners sit facing each other. Tell one person in each pair to mirror the other's actions. After a minute, reverse roles. Instruct pairs to each make up a short skit in which they do mirror-image movements. For example, partners could wave with one hand, wave with the other hand, shrug their shoulders, then fall backward.

### RESPONSE
Have volunteers share their skits. Ask:
■ **How did you feel being a mirror?**
■ **How did you feel being a model?**
■ **In what ways does a Christian disciple mirror Jesus?**
■ **How would you define a Christian disciple?**

### CLOSING
Read aloud Matthew 28:18-20. Ask:
■ **What does Jesus say about discipleship?**
Say: **Being Jesus' disciple is kind of like the activity we just did. Just as we mirrored others' actions by watching them, we become a disciple of Jesus by watching and following what we see him doing.**

# MARK

*"This is a voice of one who calls out in the desert: 'Prepare the way for the Lord. Make the road straight for him.'"*

*Mark 1:3*

# MARK
# 1:9-11

## THEME:
The Trinity

## SUMMARY:
In this OBJECT LESSON, kids will compare Neapolitan ice cream to the Trinity.

PREPARATION: Buy enough Neapolitan ice cream for everyone in your group. Gather a Bible, bowls, and spoons.

Have a volunteer read aloud Mark 1:9-11. Ask:

■ **In what different ways is God revealed here?**

■ **Why do you think God is called a "Trinity"?**

■ **What did each person of the Trinity do in this passage?**

■ **What is the role of each person in the Trinity?**

Serve everyone a bowl of Neapolitan ice cream, making sure each person gets a little of all three flavors. While eating, ask:

■ **What's your favorite flavor?**

■ **How is this Neapolitan ice cream like or unlike the Trinity?**

Say: **This Neapolitan ice cream is one thing in one package, yet there are three distinct flavors within the one package. God is one being with three distinct "flavors"—the Father, the Son, and the Holy Spirit.**

# MARK
# 1:9-13

## THEME:
Temptation

## SUMMARY:
This ADVENTURE leads kids into a local "wilderness" to learn more about temptation.

PREPARATION: Arrange transportation for your group to a local "wilderness." This could be a shopping mall, a downtown area, an inner city neighborhood, or a high school.

You'll also need Bibles, pencils, and paper.

Form groups of no more than four and have each group read Mark 1:9-13 together.

Say: **What? No holding hands? No singing songs? No potluck dinner? No, the Bible tells us that immediately after being baptized, Jesus was sent into the wilderness.**

Ask:

■ **From this passage, what three things do we know about Jesus' time in the wilderness?**

Say: **We're going to venture into a modern wilderness and see if we can find examples of these same experiences.**

Provide each group with pencils and a sheet of paper.

Say: **Form three columns on your paper. Label these "Temptation," "Wild Animals," and "Caring Angel." As you trek through the wilderness, record** your observations of these three items. For example, an advertisement could be a "temptation." A potentially dangerous place or situation might be a "wild animal," and an "angel" might be as simple as accessibility for handicapped people.

Transport your group to "the wilderness," tell kids where and when to meet, and then send the groups out on their adventure.

When they return, invite groups to give their best example of each of the three things they were asked to observe and record. Ask:

■ **How did you see things differently from how you have before?**

■ **How have things changed since biblical times?**

■ **How have they stayed the same?**

■ **Where is the wilderness today? What would God have us do about it?**

End with this prayer: **Lord, give us courage to stand firm as Jesus did when we're in the wilderness of tempting situations. Amen.**

# MARK
## 2:1-12

### THEME:
Friendship

### SUMMARY:
This DEVOTION helps kids learn how important the faith of friends can be.

PREPARATION: You'll need a strip of soft cloth to tie the hands of each person in your group. You'll also need a Bible and equipment to play either volleyball or basketball.

EXPERIENCE

As kids enter the room, ask them each to put their hands out in front of them. Bind each person's wrists together with a strip of cloth. Make the bindings strong enough to be secure without being uncomfortable.

When everyone has arrived and been bound, play a game of volleyball or basketball together. Be sure everyone stays bound during the game.

RESPONSE

After the game, gather everyone together with hands still bound and ask:

■ **How did you feel trying to play with your hands bound?**

■ **When do you feel as if something is "tying you up" in real life?**

Read Mark 2:1-12 for the group. Then ask:

■ **How is our being bound like the man's paralysis described in Mark 2:1-12?**

■ **How does sin make you feel bound or paralyzed?**

■ **What can you learn about the paralyzed man's friends from their actions described in Mark 2:1-12?**

■ **What was so important about the faith of these four friends?**

■ **How can friends be a healing presence in our lives today?**

■ **How can you use your be-**

lief in Jesus to help others find healing?

CLOSING

Go to the nearest person and say: **I am your friend, and I have faith that Jesus can free you.**

Then untie that person's hands. Invite him or her to join you in freeing the next person, and so on, throughout the room until all are free.

Return to your game of volleyball or basketball now that everyone can play freely.

# MARK
## 2:13-17

---

### THEME:

Accepting others

### SUMMARY:
In this ADVENTURE, kids will search for items mentioned or implied in Mark 2:13-17.

---

PREPARATION: You'll need to gather Bibles to prepare the following Scripture scavenger hunt. Using Mark 2:13-17 as a guide, list any related item that's mentioned or implied in the passage. For instance, potential items might include water from the lake (verse 13), dusty footprints from the crowd (verse 13), a tax receipt from the tax collector's booth (verse 14), hamburger wrappers from the dinner with the tax collectors and sinners (verse 15),

certificates of achievement for the Pharisees who were lawyers (verse 16), and a doctor's bill for sick sinners (verse 17).

Form teams of five or fewer and give each team a list of all the items in the passage. On "go," send teams out for one hour to scavenge the neighborhood or town for items from the list. At the end of the time limit, have teams each return and read aloud the passage while illustrating it with the items.

After the hunt, have groups combine their items to create a "museum" display that describes the passage. Have kids label each item with a description of its significance to the passage.

Then use the following questions to spark discussion about kids' experience and Mark 12:13-17. Ask:

■ **What's your impression of Jesus after reading Mark 12:13-17 and going on your Scripture scavenger hunt? Explain.**

■ **How did going on this scavenger hunt help you learn more about who Levi was?**

■ **How can learning about who people are help you be more accepting of them?**

■ **Why do you think Jesus showed his acceptance of Levi in such a public way, when he knew others wouldn't like it?**

■ **Why do you think Mark included this story in his gospel?**

■ **What changes would we need to make this week to imitate the attitude of acceptance that Jesus expressed in Mark 12:13-17?**

# MARK
## 2:15-17

---

### THEME:

Including or excluding others

### SUMMARY:
Kids will experience being either included or excluded in this DEVOTION.

---

PREPARATION: You'll need several sheets of paper in two colors, such as yellow and green. Cut the paper into enough small slips for each person in the group to have one. On the yellow slips write, "Hold this paper. Don't let anyone else see it. Do nothing special." These are the "out" crowd.

On the green slips write, "Congratulations! You're part of a special, select group. Find other people with green slips of paper and congratulate them on their good fortune. Don't speak to anyone who doesn't have a green slip of paper." These are the "in" crowd.

You'll also need Bibles and cookies for everyone.

### EXPERIENCE
As kids come in, distribute the slips of paper randomly and allow kids to mill about the room for several minutes.

Invite the group to be seated but specify that those with green slips of paper should sit in the front, while the rest of the group should stand in the back. Also hand out cookies to those with green slips.

Have a volunteer from the green crowd read Mark 2:15-17.

### RESPONSE
Collect all slips of paper, create an equitable seating arrangement, and ask:

■ **Who were the insiders and what was so special about them?**

■ **Who were the outsiders and what was wrong with them?**

■ **How did it feel to be an outsider? an insider?**

■ **In biblical times, there was a clear division between the insiders and outsiders. How are insiders and outsiders divided today?**

■ **How did the scribes and Pharisees feel about including others?**

■ **How did Jesus feel about it?**

■ **Why did Jesus associate with "undesirable" people?**

■ **What can we do to follow Jesus' example? What should we not do?**

### CLOSING
Have each person who was in the "in" crowd take a cookie and give it to someone who was in the "out" crowd. Then have everyone join hands and sing "They Will Know We Are Christians by Our Love" or another song of unity.

# MARK
## 3:31-35

### THEME:
God's family

### SUMMARY:
This picnic PARTY involving children from your church will help teenagers broaden their understanding of the "faith family."

PREPARATION: Help teenagers plan a picnic involving younger children from your church. For example, have your group make arrangements for the third- and fourth-grade classes to join them for an afternoon at a local park. Let your teenagers know they'll be assigned a younger "brother" or "sister" for the event.

Have kids prepare food for the event, as well as games that will be fun for younger children. Be sure to include games that involve pairs, such as a three-legged race, an egg toss, and various relays. Make games such as volleyball more fun for the younger kids by lowering the volleyball net, playing with a beach ball to give them a better chance, and changing the rules so a little sister or brother has to hit the ball before it can be returned.

You'll also need a Bible.

W hen everyone has gathered to leave for the picnic, have a volunteer read Mark 3:31-35 aloud.

Say: **Jesus reminds us that those who do the will of God are his brothers and sisters. Let's treat each other as special brothers and sisters today.**

Assign a big brother or sister to each child and explain that these pairs are to remain together for the picnic, joining together in games, eating, and other activities. As much as possible, assign same-sex pairs. Also, make these assignments yourself instead of letting kids pair up themselves. This will bypass the problem of anyone playing favorites or a younger child feeling unwanted if they're not quickly picked.

When the picnic is over, invite youth group members to reflect on the event and how it felt to function as a family in the church. End the day by reading Mark 9:35-37 and thanking God for the little brothers and sisters he has given us in our faith family.

# MARK
## 4:1-9, 13-20

### THEME:
Spiritual growth

### SUMMARY:
This OBJECT LESSON uses plants to help kids compare different growth conditions in nature to growth conditions of the heart.

PREPARATION: Gather paper cups, potting soil, gravel, flower seeds, and ryegrass seed. You'll also need a Bible.

Form four groups. Have those in group A put soil into their cups and set flower seeds **on top of** the soil. Tell them to sprinkle water over the soil every day. Before kids leave, remove the seeds from the top of the soil (it's OK if kids see you do this).

Have those in group B put soil into their cups and liberally sprinkle the ryegrass seed over it. Then give each person two flower seeds to take home. Tell these kids to sprinkle water over the soil every day and, after four days, to plant their flower seeds in the soil and continue watering. When the grass sprouts, they should water ever other or every third day.

Have those in group C fill their cups with gravel, then sprinkle with flower seeds. Instruct them to sprinkle water over the gravel every other day.

Have those in group D fill their cups with soil and plant flower seeds. Instruct them to water their plants every day or every other day to keep the soil moist.

Tell kids to bring their plants back in two weeks. After two weeks, gather everyone together with their plants (or cups of dirt or gravel). Read Mark 4:1-9 and ask:

■ **Which part of the story does your plant resemble?**

■ **How is the way your plant grew (or didn't grow) like the way people respond to hearing about God?**

■ **How is hearing about God like a seed?**

■ **What kind of person is represented by each kind of soil?**

■ **Which growth condition best represents your heart?**

End the session by reading Mark 4:13-20.

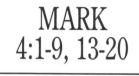

# MARK
## 4:1-9, 13-20

**THEME:**
Seeds and soil

**SUMMARY:**
In this DEVOTION, kids will compare themselves to types of soil.

PREPARATION: Gather Bibles, paper cups, plastic spoons, paper, and pencils. Make one photocopy of the "What Kind of Soil Is This?" handout (p. 70) and cut it apart as indicated.

EXPERIENCE

Give each group member a cup and a plastic spoon. Give kids five minutes to go outside and fill their cups with dirt that describes themselves in some way. For example, someone might choose rocky soil because he sees himself as "rough and tumble." Someone else might choose mud because she thinks she's "rich and creamy."

When everyone is ready, have kids each explain their choice. Then ask a volunteer to read aloud Mark 4:1-9. Ask other volunteers to explain what point Jesus is trying to get across by telling this parable. Then read aloud the explanation of the parable in Mark 4:13-20.

RESPONSE

Form four groups and give them each a sheet of paper, a pencil, and one section from the "What Kind of Soil is This?" handout. Give the groups five minutes to answer the questions and follow the directions on their sections.

CLOSING

When groups are finished, have them each explain their drawings. Then ask:

■ **What kind of soil do you identify with right now in your life?**

■ **What kind of soil do you want to be like? Explain.**

Have kids form a circle around group 4's drawing as you pray this prayer to close: **Lord, help us grow in faith today, this week, this year, and for the rest of our lives. In Jesus' name, amen.**

Encourage kids to take home their dirt-filled cups as a reminder of what they learned during this devotion.

# MARK
## 6:1-6

THEME:
Jesus' rejection

SUMMARY:
This CREATIVE READING focuses on the way Jesus was treated by those who thought they knew him best.

PREPARATION: Make six photo-copies of the "Creative Reading for Mark 6:1-6" handout (p. 71). Have six volunteers practice reading the script until they are comfortable with their lines. During the reading, have "Jesus" stand in front of the audience with the Narrator off to the side. Have the Voices scattered throughout the group. They may speak while sitting, but they should speak loudly enough for everyone to hear. You'll also need a Bible.

# MARK
## 6:7-13

THEME:
Expressing Jesus to others

SUMMARY:
As in the passage, teenagers form pairs and go on an ADVENTURE to let others know about Jesus.

PREPARATION: Arrange transportation for your group to a shopping mall, airport, or a local kids' hangout. This activity can also be done in your church's neighborhood.

You'll need a Bible and snacks for the group.

Have kids pair up. Then say: **We're going on a special assignment today. With your partner, do something that just by your actions will show Jesus**

*(continued on p. 72)*

# WHAT KIND OF SOIL IS THIS?

**Directions:** Photocopy and cut apart this handout for use during the devotion for Mark 4:1-9, 13-20.

---

■ **Group 1: The Road (Mark 4:4)**—What kind of soil is this? Draw a picture of the kind of person this soil represents. What would he or she look like? What might he or she do? Describe his or her lifestyle.

---

■ **Group 2: The Rocky Ground (Mark 4:5-6)**—What kind of soil is this? Draw a picture of a person who is like this kind of soil. What would he or she look like? What might he or she do? Describe his or her lifestyle.

---

■ **Group 3: The Weeds (Mark 4:7)**—What kind of soil is this? Draw a picture of a person this kind of soil represents. Do you ever feel "choked" by activities in your life? Do the activities overwhelm your faith? What are some things that are choking your life right now? Explain.

---

■ **Group 4: The Good Ground (Mark 4:8)**—What kind of soil is this? Draw a picture of a person this kind of soil represents. Describe his or her lifestyle. How can you tell this person from people who are more like the other types of soil mentioned in the passage?

# CREATIVE READING FOR MARK 6:1-6

**READERS:**
**Narrator**
**Jesus**
**Four Voices**

**Narrator:** Jesus left there and went to his hometown, and his followers went with him. On the Sabbath day he taught in the synagogue.

**Jesus:** A man had two sons. The younger son said to his father, "Give me my share of the property." So the father did.

**Voice #1:** Why that's Jesus, isn't it? Mary's boy?

**Jesus:** Then the younger son gathered up all that was his and traveled far away to another country. There he wasted his money on foolish living.

**Voice #2:** I knew his father, Joseph. Built my dining room table. Did a nice job on it, too. Good carpenter, that Joseph.

**Jesus:** After he had spent everything, a time came when there was no food anywhere in the country, and the son was poor and hungry. So he got a job with one of the citizens there who sent the son into the fields to feed pigs. The son was so hungry that he wanted to eat the pods the pigs were eating, but no one gave him anything.

**Voice #3:** I wonder why he didn't become a carpenter like his father.

**Jesus:** When he realized what he was doing, he thought, "All of my father's servants have plenty of food. But I am here, almost dying with hunger. I will leave and return to my father and say to him, 'Father, I have sinned against God and have done wrong to you. I am no longer worthy to be called your son, but let me be like one of your servants.' " So the son left and went to his father.

**Voice #2:** He didn't seem like anything special when he was a kid. Who does he think he is with all this preaching?

**Voice #4:** Kind of odd, isn't it? I mean, we've known him all of his life, practically raised him, and now he comes back here and has the nerve to tell us how to live our lives.

**Jesus:** While the son was still a long way off, his father saw him and felt sorry for his son. So the father ran to him and hugged and kissed him. The son said, "Father, I have sinned against God and have done wrong to you. I am no longer worthy to be called your son."

**Voice #3:** I wonder if this is one of those autobiographical stories? You suppose he came back home to live with his parents? Guess he couldn't make it as a preacher.

**Voice #1:** Hardly recognized him after all these years. Taller than his father.

**Voice #2:** And a good speaking voice, too. Too bad he didn't make it on his own.

**Jesus:** But the father said to his servants, "Hurry! Bring the best clothes and put them on him. Also, put a ring on his finger and sandals on his feet. And get our fat calf and kill it so we can have a feast and celebrate. My son was dead, but now he is alive again! He was lost, but now he is found!" So they began to celebrate.

**Voice #4:** Such a disappointment to his parents. He would have made a good carpenter.

**Voice #3:** Probably broke his mother's heart.

**Voice #2:** Some gall he has, preaching to us. What kind of story is this anyway?

**Narrator:** So the people were upset with Jesus. Jesus said to them…

**Jesus:** A prophet is honored everywhere except in his hometown and with his own people and in his own home.

**Narrator:** So Jesus was not able to work any miracles there except to heal a few sick people by putting his hands on them. He was amazed at how many people had no faith.

*(NOTE: The story of the prodigal son that's referred to in this reading is from Luke 15.)*

*(continued from p. 69)*
to others. **Discuss with your partner what you'll do as we prepare to leave on this adventure. For example, you might offer to carry groceries for elderly shoppers, clean trash out of a parking lot, or bring a guitar and lead a street-corner song fest.**

Take kids to the selected site or have them leave to walk around the neighborhood. Be sure they know when and where to meet again.

When everyone has gathered again, serve snacks and have each pair tell about their experiences.

Read Mark 6:7-13 and ask:

■ **Why did Jesus send his disciples out in teams?**

■ **Did having a partner make the experience easier for you than if you'd had to do it alone? Explain.**

■ **Why did Jesus instruct his disciples to travel light?**

■ **What kind of impression do you think your appearance had on those you encountered?**

■ **Did you experience people rejecting you or not listening to you? Explain.**

■ **What does it mean to "shake its dust off your feet"?**

■ **What problems occur if we carry the "dust of rejection" with us?**

End with a prayer of thanksgiving for the opportunity to spread God's love to the world.

# MARK 6:30-44

**THEME:**
God's provision

**SUMMARY:**
In this SKIT, three teenagers at a football game decide to share with everyone what little food they have.

## MORE THAN ENOUGH?

SCENE: Three high school friends are sitting in the stands at a school football game.

PROPS: Part of a hot dog bun and three chairs. You'll also need Bibles for the discussion after the skit.

CHARACTERS:
**Jesse**
**Lori**
**Julie**

SCRIPT
*(Jesse, Lori, and Julie are sitting in chairs representing bleachers at a football game. A small section of a hot dog bun is sitting offstage, out of view.)*

**Jesse:** I'm getting hungry. How about you two?

**Lori:** Hmm...yeah.

**Julie:** Me too.
*(All three suddenly stand up and cheer loudly as their team scores a touchdown. Then they sit down again.)*

**Lori:** I'll get the food. What do you guys want?

**Jesse:** *(Handing money to Lori)* I'll take two burgers, a hot dog, three slices of pizza, two nachos, and a Diet Coke.

**Lori:** A *Diet* Coke?

**Jesse:** Hey, I'm trying to watch my weight, OK?

**Lori:** How about you, Julie?

**Julie:** *(Staring incredulously at Jesse)* Just get me a small bag of chips.

**Lori:** OK. I'll be back soon. *(Lori exits the stage and picks up the piece of the hot dog bun.)*

**Julie:** Can you really eat all that food?

**Jesse:** Sure. I've got an active metabolism. At least that's what my doctor says.

*(Jesse and Julie stand up and begin to cheer, then sit down dejectedly as their quarterback throws an interception. Lori enters with the piece of a hot dog bun.)*

**Jesse and Julie:** What's that?

**Lori:** You're not going to believe this. This was all they had at the concession stand. *(She holds up the bun.)* I'm lucky I got *this.* The people behind me got nothing. *(She hands Jesse his money back.)*

*(All three stare at the bun.)*

**Jesse:** *(Dejectedly)* You eat it, Lori. You're the one who had to wait in line for it.

**Lori:** No, you can have it. I was hoping for a slice of pizza. Besides, when I saw the looks on the faces of the people in line when they found out I got the only food left, I kinda lost my appetite.

*(Pause.)*

**Julie:** Wait a minute. Maybe we could share it...

**Jesse:** Yeah, I'll take a third, Lori can have a third, and...

**Julie:** No, I mean like Jesus in the feeding of the 5,000.

**Lori:** The other people in line did look pretty hungry...

**Jesse:** It's just crazy enough that it might work!

*(Lori tears off a bite from the bun, then passes it to Julie, who does the same and then passes it to Jesse. Jesse shrugs and eats the whole rest of the bun.)*

**Lori:** Oh great. Way to go, Jesse. Now there's not enough for anyone else to have any.

**Julie:** *(Annoyed)* Yeah, we were trying to feed the 5,000 just like Jesus did.

**Jesse:** *(Swallowing)* I know. But we forgot one thing. We're not Jesus.

**Julie:** *(Slight pause, then, with awe)* I guess you're right. Wow. Imagine—just imagine feeding more than 5,000 people with only five loaves of bread and two fish. *(Shaking her head in amazement)* Jesus is pretty awesome, huh?

*(Lori and Jesse nod in agreement, then all freeze.)*

If you use this skit as a discussion starter, here are possible questions:

■ **How was this skit like or unlike the story of Jesus feeding the 5,000 in Mark 6:30-44?**

■ **What do you think it might've been like to be present when Jesus fed the 5,000?**

■ **How does God provide for us in everyday circumstances?**

# MARK
## 6:32-34

THEME:
Helping others

SUMMARY:
In this LEARNING GAME, teenagers blow Ping-Pong balls through a windy area to learn about helping others who are going astray.

PREPARATION: Mark a line across the center of a wood or tile floor with masking tape. You'll need about 20 Ping-Pong balls. Mark half of the balls with a red marker so they're easily distinguished from the others. Place all the marked balls against the wall on one side of the room and all the unmarked ones against the opposite wall. Place one or two oscillating fans at each end of the masking tape line so they'll blow into the playing area. You'll also need a Bible.

Form two teams and have each team line up against one of the walls where the Ping-Pong balls are.

Say: **The object of this game is for each team to blow its Ping-Pong balls across the floor and over the line. No hands may be used, but everyone may blow at the same time. The winning team is the one that finishes blowing all its Ping-Pong balls across the line first.**

Turn on the fans and let the game begin.

When the game is over, congratulate the winning team and read Mark 6:32-34. Ask:

■ **How were these Ping-Pong balls like sheep without a shepherd?**

■ **Have you ever seen or been part of a group of people who acted like sheep without a shepherd? Explain.**

■ **How did you feel trying to blow the balls in one direction with all the interference?**

■ **How do your feelings compare to those Jesus had when he saw the people acting this way?**

■ **When you see people wandering through life without direction, how do you react?**

■ **How did Jesus react when he met such a group?**

■ **What can you do to help others who are being blown around like Ping-Pong balls?**

# MARK
## 6:32-44

THEME:
Gifts and talents

SUMMARY:
This PROJECT helps kids see, as did the disciples, that God has given them sufficient resources for serving those in need.

PREPARATION: Invite a representative from your church's missions committee to come and briefly share a need of a person in your church or of a group your church supports. This should be an immediate need, such as a person whose children need warm coats and gloves for the winter, or an organization providing relief for those involved in a recent natural disaster.

Other than inviting this representative and gathering a Bible, don't do any further preparation. The point of this project is to demonstrate to your kids that the resources they bring to a situation are often adequate.

When the invited speaker is finished, thank him or her, then turn to your group.

Say: **Let's do something to help right now! We can raise some money for this cause! But first, let's go to the Bible for guidance.**

Read Mark 6:32-44. Ask:

∎ **What problem did the disciples have?**

∎ **Outside of the miracle, what did Jesus do?**

Say: **Jesus conquered the situation by doing three things: First, he took inventory of the resources available. Second, he got organized by dividing the people into groups. Third, he asked for God's blessing on the resources he had. We can follow Jesus' example.**

Help your group follow Jesus' example. First, inventory your resources by brainstorming to the question: **What can we do, in the next couple of hours, to raise money to help those in need?** For example, group members might say, "Sell hugs after church," "Wash car windows," "Serve coffee," "Beg," "Entertain

for handouts," or "Run off some coupons and sell them for a car wash to be held at a later date."

After brainstorming, have the group select an idea and move into the second step: organization. Have kids list tasks that need to be done for the fund-raiser to be successful and then form teams to accomplish those tasks.

When the plan is fully in place, move on to the third step: prayer. Give kids the opportunity to ask God's blessing on the group's efforts. Then move ahead with your plan and expect God to use your group in meeting this need!

# MARK 6:45-51

**THEME:**
Jesus calms life's storms.

**SUMMARY:**
This CREATIVE READING involves kids in acting out Mark 6:45-51.

PREPARATION: You'll need enough photocopies of the "Creative Reading for Mark 6:45-51" handout (p. 77) for each reader to have one. Go through the script with the readers several times so everyone is comfortable with what they're to do. During the performance of the reading, have only the Narrator and "Jesus" use their scripts. Everyone else should be able to remember their actions.

Arrange about six chairs in several short rows. This will be a boat for the Disciples. You will need a water-filled squirt gun for each person representing the Storm. You'll also need a Bible.

After the reading, lead your group (including the readers) in a discussion of Mark 6:45-51. Focus on the "storms of life" that harass them and how Jesus can control these storms.

# MARK
# 7:1-13

## THEME:
Tradition

## SUMMARY:
This RETREAT helps students examine tradition and its place in the church.

PREPARATION: Make arrangements for a two-day retreat. You'll need to gather items according to the activities you choose for the event and a Bible.

During the first day of the retreat, do only traditional retreat activities—things you have done on other retreats. Play volleyball, eat pizza or hot dogs, play games you've recently played, and sing songs most popular with your group.

To open the second day of the retreat, read Mark 7:1-13, then announce that you are going to break the old traditions. Here are some possible ways to break tradi-

tion on your retreat:

■ Serve uncommon foods, such as duck, sushi, matzo, or prune danish.

■ Eat dinner food at breakfast and breakfast food for lunch. Or eat meals at unusual hours.

■ Sing the words to one song using the melody of another song.

■ Get everyone up earlier or later than in the past.

■ Introduce new games. Or mix several games together, such as playing volleyball with a football or inventing new rules for Capture the Flag.

■ Do nothing the old way!

End the retreat with a discussion of traditions in your church. Ask:

■ **What traditions can you identify?**

■ **Why do we hold on to traditions?**

■ **Why are traditions sometimes valuable?**

■ **When do traditions stop being helpful?**

■ **What are some traditions that our group wants to hang on to and why?**

■ **What traditions does our group want to re-evaluate?**

**Note:** The film *Fiddler on the Roof* provides an excellent resource in examining the role of tradition in a culture or society. If you don't want to use the whole film, play the opening song where the main character explains his understanding of tradition.

# CREATIVE READING FOR MARK 6:45-51

**READERS:**
**Narrator**
**Jesus**
**Disciples**
(up to 12 people)
**Storm**
(three or four people armed with squirt guns)

**Narrator:** Jesus told his followers to get into the boat and go ahead of him to Bethsaida across the lake.

*(Jesus points, and Disciples get into the boat and reluctantly begin rowing.)*

**Narrator:** He stayed there to send the people home. After sending them away...

*(Jesus waves toward audience.)*

**Narrator:** he went into the hills to pray.

*(Jesus kneels and prays.)*

**Narrator:** That night, the boat was in the middle of the lake, and Jesus was alone on the land. He saw his followers struggling hard to row the boat...

*(Jesus shades eyes and looks toward Disciples as they pretend to struggle with rowing the boat.)*

**Narrator:** because the wind was blowing against them.

*(Storm moves toward Disciples and harasses them, blowing them back and squirting them with squirt guns.)*

**Narrator:** Between three and six o'clock in the morning...

*(All cast members stop and pantomime looking at watches.)*

**Narrator:** Jesus came to them, walking on the water...

*(Jesus casually strolls out.)*

**Narrator:** and he wanted to walk past the boat.

*(Jesus starts to walk past Disciples.)*

**Narrator:** But when they saw him walking on the water, they thought he was a ghost and cried out.

*(Disciples cry out and cower in the boat, hugging each other in fear.)*

**Narrator:** But quickly Jesus spoke to them and said...

**Jesus:** Have courage! It is I. Do not be afraid.

**Narrator:** Then he got into the boat with them...

*(Jesus gets into boat, and Disciples are very happy to see him, hugging him and pretending to be talking about the storm.)*

**Narrator:** and the wind became calm.

*(Storm freezes, then quietly walks offstage.)*

**Narrator:** The followers were greatly amazed.

# MARK
# 7:14-23

## THEME:
Sin

## SUMMARY:
Teenagers will eat a "dirty" dessert and see the difference between what we put into our bodies and what comes out of our minds and hearts in this DEVOTION.

PREPARATION: Crush chocolate sandwich cookies to the consistency of crumbs. Then make chocolate pudding and pour it into a clean bucket. Cover the pudding with a thick layer of the cookie crumbs. Gather a clean trowel, spoons and bowls, paper napkins, a dictionary, a Bible, and a trash can.

EXPERIENCE
Say: **I've brought along a snack for us today. A bucket of dirt!**

Show kids the bucket of "dirt" and see if anyone wants a shovelful to eat. Then tell them the dirt is actually a chocolatey dessert. Pass out spoons, bowls, and napkins and give kids a chance to shovel out a bowlful.

RESPONSE
While everyone is eating, ask:
■ **What did you think when I told you I'd brought dirt for our snack?**
■ **Would eating actual dirt make you dirty inside?**
■ **Is there anything that you**

**wouldn't eat? Explain.**
Read Mark 7:14-23. Invite kids to go through the words in verses 21-22 and define the terms. Depending on the version of Bible your group uses, a dictionary may be helpful. Ask:
■ **If food doesn't make us sinful, what things do?**
■ **Why is what comes out of our minds and hearts more important than what goes into our mouths?**
■ **How can we keep our minds and hearts clean?**

CLOSING
Have kids form a circle around the trash can. As they take turns tossing their dirty napkins into the trash, have kids tell one thing they'll do in the coming week to keep clean inside.

# MARK
# 8:27-30

## THEME:
Describing Jesus

## SUMMARY:
This LEARNING GAME focuses on descriptions of objects and leads into a discussion of ways we describe Jesus.

PREPARATION: Gather a variety of objects, such as a soup can, a rock, a baseball, a sock, a candy bar, a spoon, a stick of gum, a ring, and so on. Place all items in a box. You'll also need a Bible.

Form teams of three to six. Select one person from each team to be a guesser. Send the guessers out of the room and show the remaining kids an object from the box. Return the object to the box and place it out of view. Then have the guessers return to the room.

Have teams take turns saying one word to the guessers as a clue about what the object is. Even though all the guessers will hear the clue, teams will want their own guesser to guess the correct object. Teams are not allowed to name the object or use a brand name. They may only describe objects, using only single-word adjectives on each turn.

When the object has been guessed, the team whose guesser guessed correctly gets a point. Then select a new guesser from each team and repeat the activity. Continue until you've used all the objects in your box, then name the team with the most points the winners. Ask:

■ **How can one object be described with so many words?**

■ **Suppose there were a picture of Jesus in the box. What words would you use to describe him?**

Have a volunteer read Mark 8:27-30. Wrap up the activity by asking:

■ **How did the people of Jesus' day describe him? Why?**

■ **What was significant about Peter's description of Jesus?**

■ **How can we describe Jesus to those who don't know him?**

■ **How are our lives descriptions of Jesus Christ?**

■ **Would people be able to recognize Jesus Christ through the descriptions we give of him in the way we talk and live? Why or why not?**

# MARK
# 9:1-8

THEME:
Prayer

SUMMARY:
This CREATIVE PRAYER helps kids see how easy it is to pray with comfortable rituals instead of listening to God.

PREPARATION: Select a volunteer to assist you in this prayer. This person will need a handful of coins and a plate. You'll also need Bibles. Rehearse the prayer with your assistant before the meeting.

Have kids follow along as you read Mark 9:1-8 aloud.

Say: **Peter witnessed a holy and miraculous event. He was overwhelmed and didn't know what to do, so he fell back on the familiar. It was a common practice then to build small altars or shrines on the sites of sacred events. Peter was focusing on tradition without focusing on Jesus.**

Ask kids to close their eyes for prayer.

Say: **Lord, often we don't**

spend enough time or energy focusing on you. **Sometimes it's easier to sing instead.** (Assistant sings first line of a worship song.) **Or we like to talk.** (Assistant says, "Praise the Lord! Amen!") **Sometimes we give money.** (Assistant drops coins in a plate.) **It's easier to pray old prayers that we've memorized.** (Assistant recites first lines of the Lord's Prayer in singsong voice.) **But you desire that we listen, really listen to you. OK, Lord. We're going to listen now. We're going to listen quietly for one brief minute.** (Have 60 seconds of silence.) **Amen.**

After the prayer, discuss what makes listening to God difficult. Have kids commit to spending two minutes in listening prayer each day this week.

# MARK
## 9:33-37

THEME
Being the greatest

SUMMARY:
This CREATIVE READING humorously portrays Mark 9:33-37.

PREPARATION: Select kids to do the reading and have them rehearse before your meeting. Each person will need a photocopy of the "Creative Reading for Mark 9:33-37" handout (p. 81). You'll also need a Bible.

# MARK
## 10:17-27

THEME:
Possessions

SUMMARY:
Kids carry a variety of large items through an obstacle course in this LEARNING GAME.

PREPARATION: Arrange a couple chairs or other pieces of furniture to form a simple obstacle course in the room. Gather the items below. Write the following boldface words on slips of paper and pin or tape them to the following items:

**Security**—A large stuffed animal

**Money**—A big purse or handbag

**Cars**—A handful of loose keys

**Knowledge**—Three big books

**Food**—Four cans of food items

**Wardrobe**—A duffel bag full of old clothes

You'll also need a Bible and a stopwatch or watch with a second hand.

Say: **These items I've gathered represent various forms of wealth. You've probably heard the saying "You can't take it with you," but I'm going to let you try! As you run through the obstacle course, you'll have to carry all these items with you. This may mean making two trips!**

Have kids line up to be timed going through the obstacle course.

# CREATIVE READING FOR MARK 9:33-37

**READERS:**
Narrator
Jesus
Peter
James
John
Thomas

**Narrator:** Now Jesus and his disciples were on the road to Capernaum, and he heard them bickering and arguing with each other.

**Peter, James, John, and Thomas:** Oh yeah? Yeah! Oh yeah? Yeah! Says who? Says me! Oh yeah?

**Narrator:** When they got to the house where they were going, Jesus asked...

**Jesus:** What were you discussing on the way?

**Narrator:** But they were too embarrassed to tell him.

**Thomas:** Oh, nothing. It wasn't important. Just a little theological debate is all. No big deal.

**Narrator:** But Jesus knew better. *(Jesus gives the disciples a knowing, doubtful look.)*

**Narrator:** Finally, they came clean.

**Peter:** Well, see, Jesus, we were just talking about...Well, it's just that... Uh, see, we were all kind of wondering...uh... *(rushing)* Which one of us is the greatest.

*(Jesus looks at the other disciples)*

**James:** It was John's idea.

**John:** You wanted to know, too.

**James:** Did not.

**John:** Did so.

**James:** Did not.

**John:** You wish.

**Peter:** We all wanted to know.

**Thomas:** Not me. It was you guys!

**Jesus:** *(Raising hands to silence them)* Whoever wants to be the most important must be last of all and servant of all.

**Peter:** *(After a pause)* That's kind of vague, Lord. If it's not asking too much, uh, could you be a little more specific?

**Jesus:** *(Leaning closer, speaking slower)* Whoever wants to be the most important must be last of all and servant of all.

**Peter:** *(Slowly dawning)* Oh...OK. So if I want to be great, I have to be humble, right?

*(Jesus smiles.)*

**John:** No problem! I can be humbler than any of these guys!

**James:** Not me. You can't be humbler than me! I'm the humblest guy here! I'm humbler than any of you.

**Peter:** Can I get you a glass of water, Jesus?

**John:** No, let me.

**James:** I got it. Get back—I said I got it!

**John:** I had it first.

**James:** Did not.

**John:** Did so!

**Thomas:** No, me! Let me get it! Another sandwich, Peter?

**James:** Shine your shoes, John?

**John:** Let me carry that for you, Thomas.

**Narrator:** They still didn't get it. So Jesus took a child who was in the house and placed the child on his lap and said...

**Jesus:** Whoever accepts a child like this in my name accepts me. And whoever accepts me accepts the One who sent me.

**Peter, James, John, and Thomas:** I got it! No you don't—I got it! Do not. Do so. Do not! I'm humbler than you, so let me have it. No! I'm the humblest.

**Narrator:** But it took a long time for the lesson to sink in.

Begin timing kids before they begin loading their arms with the objects so that "packing" time is included in the final time. Putting objects into pockets or into another object (such as putting the loose keys into the purse or the suitcase) isn't allowed. Record each person's time and congratulate the person who made it through the course with everything in the shortest amount of time. Ask:

■ **Consider what each item represents. Which would you be most willing to give up in life? Explain.**

■ **Which would you be least willing to give up? Explain.**

Read aloud Mark 10:17-27 and lead kids in a discussion about what Jesus requires his followers to sacrifice.

# MARK
# 10:17-31

THEME:
Riches

SUMMARY:
In this SKIT, a guy becomes so obsessed with buying things that he forgets to live life.

## THE ONE WITH THE MOST TOYS

SCENE: Two friends are walking together along the road. One, Steve, stops frequently to pick up aluminum cans and places them in a paper bag he's carrying.

PROPS: Paper bag, aluminum cans, and a plastic container. You'll also need a Bible for the discussion after the skit.

CHARACTERS:
**Steve**
**Ray**

### SCRIPT
*(Steve and Ray are walking along a road. Every once in awhile, Steve stops and picks up an aluminum can, then places it into his paper bag. This happens a few times before Ray says anything. Ray simply looks on as Steve picks up the cans until he finally can't keep quiet any longer.)*

**Ray:** What's with the aluminum cans, Steve?

**Steve:** I pick 'em up.

**Ray:** I know that, Steve. Why do you pick them up?

**Steve:** *(Matter-of-factly)* I need 'em for my car.

**Ray:** Oh. *(He stares at Steve.)* I didn't know you had a car!

**Steve:** Exactly.

**Ray:** *(Puzzled, shaking his head)* I don't get it, Steve. Last week you were collecting glass bottles...

**Steve:** *(Interrupting)* For my stereo.

**Ray:** Right, for your stereo. Two weeks ago, you were collecting newspapers for your...for your...

**Steve:** For my computer.

**Ray:** Right. *(Pauses.)* But, Steve...

**Steve:** *(Still focusing on picking up cans)* Yeah?

**Ray:** You don't have a car, a stereo, or a computer.

**Steve:** *(Turning to look at Ray)* And I'm never going to get them without a lot of money, am I?

*(He turns back, looking for more cans.)*

**Ray:** So you collect aluminum cans, glass bottles, and newspapers for the money?

**Steve:** Yep. And I work two part-time jobs—for my snowmobile. I mow seven lawns a week in the summer—for my video games. And I invest all the money I make in high-yield savings accounts—for my basketball shoes.

**Ray:** When do you have any time for fun?

**Steve:** Who has time? The rest of my time I have to study so I can get into the best business school in the country... *(pause)* for my house. *(He looks around, then picks up a plastic bottle and studies it before tossing it back onto the ground.)*

**Ray:** Y'know, they pay 2 cents a pound for plastic like that down at the recycling center.

**Steve:** *(Retrieving the plastic container)* Aha... *(He puts it into his paper bag.)* For my cruise around the world. *(Characters freeze.)*

If you use this skit as a discussion starter, here are possible questions:

■ **How is Steve's attitude like the attitude of the wealthy man in the story told by Jesus in Matthew 10:17-31?**

■ **According to this passage, what is the most important thing in life?**

# MARK 12:41-44

**THEME:**
Value

**SUMMARY:**
In this AFFIRMATION, kids will affirm and encourage others to use what they have for God.

PREPARATION: Gather enough pennies for half of your students to have one. You'll also need Bibles.

Have group members form pairs and give each pair a penny. Instruct pairs to read Mark 12:41-44 together. Ask:

■ **What's the value of a penny?**

■ **Why were the widow's pennies so valuable in Jesus' eyes?**

■ **What made the large amounts of money given by the rich less valuable?**

Have pairs discuss the questions then share their answers with the entire group.

Say: **When something is all you have, it suddenly becomes bigger, more valuable, and more important. If all you have in life is one penny, giving it away can be difficult. That's what God desires of us—not dollars or pennies, but all we have.**

Have each person holding a penny complete this sentence for his or her partner: "I see that you have *(name a positive quality)*. Use this valuable quality for God." For example, someone might say, "I see that you have patience. Use this valuable quality for God." Someone else might say, "I see that you have the ability to make others laugh. Use this valuable quality for God." Then have those who spoke give their pennies to their partners. Have all those with pennies find new partners to affirm. Continue until everyone has been affirmed several times.

Close in prayer, thanking God for the value of each youth group member and asking that each one will give what he or she has to God.

# MARK
## 14:32-40

THEME:
Focusing on God

SUMMARY:
In this PROJECT, teenagers will compare keeping focused on a worship service to Jesus' disciples keeping focused in the garden of Gethsemane.

PREPARATION: Have kids bring sack lunches for a picnic after the worship service. Also, make enough photocopies of the "Worship Service Project" handout (p. 85) for each person to have one. Gather pencils and a Bible.

Distribute the handouts and pencils to youth group members as they prepare to enter your church's worship service. Plan to meet for lunch after the service.

At lunch, have kids share what they wrote on their handouts and discuss how easy or difficult the questions were to answer. Then have a volunteer read Mark 14:32-40 aloud.

Say: **An hour can be a long time. Even Peter, James, and John had a hard time staying focused for an hour while Jesus prayed. Jesus had asked them to stay awake and pray with him, but they were just too tired and distracted.**

Ask:

■ **Do you ever feel unfocused, distracted, or even tired on Sunday morning during the worship service? Explain.**

■ **How was your situation in the worship service like or unlike that of the disciples in the garden?**

■ **Would you have been able to stay awake in their situation? What might you have done to follow Jesus' request?**

■ **How can we, as regular participants in the worship service, keep focused on the message?**

# MARK
## 15:15-32

THEME:
Jesus' suffering

SUMMARY:
In this DEVOTION, teenagers will examine Jesus' suffering.

# WORSHIP SERVICE PROJECT

■ What hymns were sung?

■ How did they connect with the rest of the worship service?

■ What verses were used in the sermon?

■ What were the main points of the sermon?

■ What was the focus of the prayers?

■ How did various parts of the sermon relate to real life?

■ What part of the service was the most meaningful to you and why?

■ Was there an area that you thought needed more explanation? Explain.

■ How can this service of worship change your life?

PREPARATION: Before the activity, create a simple human figure, 6 to 12 inches high, out of modeling clay. Set out the figure, straight pins, pencils, pushpins, and rubber bands on a table. You'll also need Bibles.

**Caution**: Some teenagers may have a strong reaction when they picture the brutality that Jesus suffered as it's acted out on the clay figure. Be prepared to help kids work through their feelings without compromising the truth of Jesus' suffering.

EXPERIENCE

Have kids gather around the table. Say: **When we think of suffering in the Bible, we most often think of the suffering Jesus went through for us.**

Assign kids each a different verse from Mark 15:15-32. It's OK if kids have more than one verse or the same verse. Say: **This clay figure represents Jesus. We're going to use this clay figure to help us understand what Jesus went through at the time of his arrest and crucifixion. Please maintain a quiet, serious, and thoughtful attitude while we do this.**

Encourage kids to take this seriously and imagine that the clay figure really is Jesus as the activity proceeds.

Read through the passage twice. Have kids listen the first time. The second time through, use the supplies to demonstrate on the clay figure the kinds of punishment Jesus endured. For example, you might use the rubber bands to illustrate Jesus' whipping, the pushpins to illustrate Jesus' crown of thorns, and a pencil to illustrate Jesus' beating. Use two pencils for Jesus' cross and straight pins or pushpins for the nails through Jesus' hands and feet.

RESPONSE

Afterward ask:

■ **How did you feel as you saw what the clay Jesus went through?**

■ **How might you have felt if you'd been the one to make the clay Jesus suffer?**

■ **How is this like or unlike what the real Jesus endured?**

■ **Why do you think Jesus had to go through so much suffering?**

CLOSING

Tear off bits of clay and pass one piece to each person in the group. Encourage kids to prayerfully take the clay and place it in a prominent place in their homes to remind them of the suffering Jesus endured for them.

# MARK
# 15:21

THEME:
Serving Jesus

SUMMARY:
This CREATIVE READING shows Simon of Cyrene serving Jesus and helps kids see ways they, too, serve Jesus.

PREPARATION: Make enough photocopies of the "Pick Up That Cross, Simon of Cyrene!" handout (p. 88) for each reader to have one. Select someone to read the lines of Simon and have three or more kids read the lines of the People. You'll also need a Bible.

# MARK
# 16:1-8

## THEME:
Jesus' death

## SUMMARY:
In this PROJECT, kids plant a garden to understand death and new life.

PREPARATION: Gather a Bible and gardening hand tools such as hoes, spades, claws, and a hose. You may also need potting soil and plant fertilizer. Make necessary arrangements with the church gardener or groundskeeper to have your class plant flowers for Easter.

Tell kids you'll be decorating an area of the church grounds for Easter. Announce a date within the week before Easter for everyone to meet at the church for flower planting. Invite group members to bring potted daffodils to transplant.

On the designated day, work together to transplant the daffodils in a garden area. Encourage kids to make this area as beautiful as they can.

When the garden is planted, have kids gather around it as you read Mark 16:1-8. Then explain to the class that daffodils are perennial flowers, meaning they will bloom again each year at about the same time. But they must die before they can bloom again. Each spring they are resurrected to new life.

Close with a prayer similar to this: **Lord, the daffodil reminds us of your promise that after death, resurrection is possible in Jesus Christ. Help us to hold tightly to that promise for the rest of our lives. In Jesus' name, amen.**

# PICK UP THAT CROSS, SIMON OF CYRENE!
### (A Creative Reading for Mark 15:21)

**READERS:**
**Simon**
**The People**

**Simon:** I didn't ask for this, Lord. I didn't come seeking it.

**People:** Yet you choose your servants. You call them out of the crowd.

**Simon:** I was minding my own business. Not bothering anyone.

**People:** Walking home from work. Thinking about my job, my family, my problems, politics, committees. I'm a busy person. No time for nonsense.

**Simon:** There was a huge traffic jam in the city. People everywhere.

**People:** Avoid crowds. Be comfortable. Go your own way. Keep life simple.

**Simon:** But what was I going to do? Going around the city would add another two hours to my journey.

**People:** Go to McDonald's. Grab a sandwich. Wait it out. Take it easy. Stay out of it. Don't get involved.

**Simon:** So there I was, and this cop grabs me out of the crowd.

**People:** I have plenty of my own crosses to bear, thank you. I don't need any more. Besides, I'm too busy. I have to get home. I have a meeting to go to. Work to do.

**Simon:** Please find someone else.

**People:** Not me. Anyone but me.

**Simon:** I'm just too busy right now.

**People:** Maybe another time.

**Simon:** But he wouldn't listen. He wouldn't take no for an answer.

**People:** He insisted.

**Simon:** Suddenly, I looked at Jesus, and I got the feeling it was what he wanted me to do, too—to take up his cross and follow him. So I picked up the cross. And I turned to face my world...

**People:** Hunger, injustice, racism, poverty, disease, hate...

**Simon:** And I put the cross on my shoulder and started following in Jesus' footsteps through the mocking crowd.

**People:** War, crime, violence, abuse, drugs...

**Simon:** And I've been carrying that cross ever since.

**People:** The cross of Christ. On my shoulders.

**Simon:** Once you pick it up, it's hard to put down. But I would not trade it for anything.

**People:** Amen.

# LUKE

*"Today your Savior was born in the town of David. He is Christ, the Lord."*

*Luke 2:11*

# LUKE
# 1:26–2:20

## THEME:
Jesus' birth

## SUMMARY:
In this CREATIVE READING, kids will act out responses to the Christmas story.

PREPARATION: You'll need a Bible.

Say: **The Christmas story has a special message if you've ever felt like a nobody. Jesus didn't come like the king he was. To most of the people, he was just another baby—a nobody. Let's respond to the story of Jesus' birth through this reading.**

Form six groups and assign each one a different response to words you'll read from the "First Noel" story that starts on this page.

■ **Mary**—Point to yourself, tilt your head to the side, and say, "Who, me?"

■ **Joseph**—Shrug your shoulders and say, "What now?"

■ **Manger**—Form a cradle with your arms and say, "What a bed!"

■ **Shepherds**—Hold your nose and say "P-U!"

■ **Jesus**—Cross your arms over your chest and say, "I love you."

■ **Angel**—Flap your arms like wings and yell "Hallelujah!"

Have groups practice their responses. Encourage kids to be wild and crazy as you read the story. Pause for responses every time you see a word in boldface.

## THE FIRST NOEL

This is the story of the birth of **Jesus. Jesus'** mother, **Mary,** was pledged to be married to **Joseph,** but before they came together, **Mary** was found to be pregnant through the Holy Spirit. **Joseph** was a good man. **Joseph** did not want to disgrace **Mary.** He was going to leave **Mary** quietly.

But an **angel** appeared to **Joseph** in a dream and said, "**Joseph,** do not be afraid to take **Mary** home as your wife because what is conceived in her is from the Holy Spirit. **Mary** will give birth to a son, and you are to give him the name **Jesus** because he will save his people from their sins." When **Joseph** woke up, he did what the **angel** said and took **Mary** home as his wife.

And in those days, there was a census to be taken, and people were to go to their hometowns to be registered. So **Joseph** and **Mary,** who was pregnant with **Jesus,** traveled to Bethlehem to be registered. While they were there, the time came for **Jesus** to be born, and **Mary** gave birth to **Jesus. Mary** wrapped **Jesus** in cloths and placed **Jesus** in a **manger** because there was no room in the inn.

And there were **shepherds** watching their flocks in the fields nearby. An **angel** appeared to the **shepherds,** and the **shepherds** were terrified. But the **angel** said to the **shepherds,** "Do not be afraid. I
*(continued)*

bring you good news of great joy. Today your Savior, **Jesus,** has been born in the city of David. You will find **Jesus** wrapped in cloths and lying in a **manger.**"

When the **angel** left, the **shepherds** went to find the baby **Jesus** in the **manger.** When the **shepherds** found **Mary** and **Joseph** and **Jesus,** who was lying in the **manger,** the **shepherds** spread the word to all. And all who heard it were amazed at what the **shepherds** said to them about the baby in the **manger.**

# LUKE
## 2:7

### THEME:
No room at the inn

### SUMMARY:
This LEARNING GAME works great around Christmastime.

PREPARATION: You'll need a Bible.

Say: **We all love the closeness that Christmas brings. Families are together, and we seek to include others in our festivities. But we also remember that the Christmas story begins with an exclusion.**

Ask a volunteer to read aloud Luke 2:7. Have kids form a circle, locking arms. The circle will represent the inn. Choose a guy and a girl to represent Joseph and Mary and have them stand outside the circle. Tell them their task is to find "room at the inn." They can try to talk their way back into the circle by begging or reasoning with "innkeepers," or they can try to force their way into the circle. The innkeepers' task is to keep the circle tight, excluding Mary and Joseph by saying, "There's no room in the inn!"

After a few minutes, have kids sit down. Wrap up the game by asking:

■ **How did Mary and Joseph feel?**

■ **How did the innkeepers feel?**

■ **How do we keep God from breaking into our lives during this Christmas season?**

■ **How might we exclude others?**

# LUKE
## 2:21-40

### THEME:
Parents

### SUMMARY:
This PARTY lets kids express their appreciation for their parents.

PREPARATION: Have kids work with you to plan a party expressing appreciation to their parents. Kids can work in one or more of the following areas:

■ **Food**—Have this committee prepare snacks and beverages for the party.

■ **Invitations**—Those on this committee can design and send invitations to the parents of each youth group member.

**Note:** Let kids with stepparents determine if they'll invite one or both sets of parents. Those raised primarily by another family member (such as a grandparent), by foster parents, or by another person should invite these people.

■ **Decorations**—This committee will decorate the room on the day of the party. One idea is to make a collage on the bulletin board with pictures of kids and their parents. Funny captions can be added if kids like. This group could also provide or make corsages for parents.

■ **Entertainment**—Have this committee write and perform a song celebrating parents. Or have them collect thank-you letters from kids to their parents to be read aloud or delivered during the party. This group could also plan a few icebreaker activities with which to begin the party.

You'll need a Bible at the party.

During the party, have everyone form groups of three or four. Include at least one teenager and one adult in each group. Parents and kids from one family should not be in the same group. Allow a minute for everyone to introduce themselves.

Read Luke 2:21-40 aloud. Ask:

■ **How did Mary and Joseph fulfill their responsibilities as parents of Jesus?**

■ **What are the responsibilities of parents today?**

■ **What does each parent see as his or her most important responsibility?**

Close this time with a short prayer thanking God for the parents. If you like, continue the party with games and singing.

# LUKE
# 4:1-13

**THEME:**
Temptation

**SUMMARY:**
In this OBJECT LESSON, kids will compare their feelings of temptation to Jesus' temptation.

PREPARATION: Make arrangements to have a variety of tempting snacks such as brownies, pizza, a bowl of M&M's, and so on. Place these on a table in the front of your meeting room. Have an adult volunteer ready to interrupt your meeting at the appropriate time. You'll also need a Bible.

As kids enter the room, explain that the snacks are for later. Begin leading the group in a crowdbreaker game. Just as the group starts the game, have your volunteer come to the room and call you out for a moment. Step away from the room, closing the door behind you, for several minutes.

When you return, quietly note

whether any snacks are missing. Have the group finish the game, then call everyone together.

Have a volunteer read Luke 4:1-13. Compare the temptation kids felt while you were out of the room to the temptations Jesus endured. If some kids did sneak food, give them the opportunity to share how they felt doing this. Discuss how Jesus withstood temptation. Have kids share ways they avoid or stand up to temptations each day. Then eat!

# LUKE 4:31-35

THEME:
Knowing Jesus

SUMMARY:
In this PROJECT, teenagers will create posters describing Jesus through his many names.

PREPARATION: Collect a variety of art supplies, such as stamp pads, stencils, sponges, paint, calligraphy markers, and so on. Set these out on one or more tables. Provide a large piece of poster board for every four kids in your group. You'll also need Bibles.

Form groups of no more than four. Have each group read Luke 4:31-35 together and discuss the following questions:

■ **How did the evil spirit know who Jesus was?**

■ **How do we know who**

Jesus is?

■ **This verse describes Jesus as God's Holy One. What are some other names for Jesus or God?**

Ask each group to use the art supplies to create a poster expressing names for Jesus. If kids need more ideas for names, they can look in Isaiah 9:6 or scan Psalms.

Have groups share their posters and discuss how Jesus' many names help us know who he is. Hang the posters in a prominent place as a reminder of what group members learned during this project.

# LUKE 6:17-49

THEME:
The Sermon on the Mount

SUMMARY:
This CREATIVE READING takes place during a hike.

PREPARATION: Plan a day hike to a local mountain, forest, or park. Have kids bring light snacks and water for the hike. Take along a Bible, too.

Say: **Jesus' most famous sermon took place outside. Today we'll hear portions of what he said as we enjoy the outdoors, too.**

Begin hiking together and encourage kids to appreciate the beauty of God's creation.

Stop five times during the hike for rest and refreshment. Have a different person read one of the following sections at each stop: Luke 6:17-26; 6:27-36; 6:37-42; 6:43-45; and 6:46-49. After each reading, have kids find a partner to discuss what this passage means during the next section of the hike. Kids should find new partners after each reading.

# LUKE
# 6:27-31

## THEME:
Loving your enemies

## SUMMARY:
Kids race to fill buckets of water only to find they'll need a second water source to win in this LEARNING GAME.

PREPARATION: Prepare a relay race. You'll need two buckets and one cup for each team. Set up the relay course with buckets a little more than half-full of water on one end of the room. Place empty buckets on the other end. You'll also need doughnuts (or another prize) for everyone and a Bible.

**H**ave kids form two teams. Say: **The goal of this relay is to be the first team to have its bucket filled to overflowing. Fill your empty bucket by taking turns running from one end of the room to the other with full cups of water. The first team with an overflowing bucket gets doughnuts** (or another prize).

Begin the relay. If kids complain they don't have enough water to fill the bucket to overflowing, just shrug. Don't allow kids to leave the room to find a new water source. The point of this relay is that no team can win without the help of the other team. When the teams figure out they must join together, everyone wins.

After the relay, serve the doughnuts and sit down as a group. Ask a volunteer to read Luke 6:27-31. Ask:

▪ **How does this passage relate to our game?**

▪ **How did you discover you needed the "enemy" team's help to win?**

▪ **Have you ever needed the help of someone you didn't like to succeed in real life? Explain.**

▪ **Why should we love our enemies?**

▪ **How can praying for someone you don't like change your attitude?**

VARIATION: Give each team a puzzle to complete, but switch a few pieces so kids must cooperate with the other team to finish.

# LUKE
# 6:43-45

## THEME:

Producing good fruit

## SUMMARY:

In this OBJECT LESSON, teenagers find fruits to represent qualities of other group members.

PREPARATION: Ask each person to bring a dollar to spend. Arrange transportation for your group to a local grocery store or farmers market. You'll also need a sharp knife and a Bible.

Have kids form groups of no more than four.

Say: **We're going shopping for fruit. As you look at the fruit available, select one fruit to represent each member of your group. For example, if someone is especially honest, you might buy cherries to represent the story of George Washington's admitting he'd chopped down the cherry tree. Or if a group member looks tough on the outside but is soft-hearted, you might buy a banana. Pool the money in your group to buy as much as you can with your money.**

Go to a local farmers market or grocery store. Remind the group to be considerate of other shoppers.

Return to your meeting room and form a circle. Ask each group to tell a little bit about the fruit they bought and how each piece represents a group member.

Ask a volunteer to read Luke 6:43-45. Then ask:

■ **How do we identify different kinds of trees?**

■ **How do we know what kind of person someone is?**

■ **How does being a Christian affect the fruit we produce?**

Wash and cut the fruit so that everyone has a chance to taste all of the different kinds.

# LUKE
# 6:46-49

## THEME:

Building on a strong foundation

## SUMMARY:

Teenagers visit a building site to compare a building's foundation to various foundations in life in this OBJECT LESSON.

PREPARATION: Make arrangements with a building contractor to visit a building site. Ask him or her to give you a tour describing how a house or other building is built. Also arrange transportation to the visited sites, informing kids beforehand of any safety concerns at the sites (such as the need for hard hats). Bring along a Bible.

During the tour, encourage kids to ask questions. Have the contractor explain the importance of a well-made foundation and what happens to a building if the foundation is inadequate. Perhaps you can also visit a building with a foundation that is failing in some way.

After your group tours the sites, find a place to sit for a brief discussion. Ask:

■ **What did you find most interesting at the building site?**

■ **If a builder wanted to cut costs, would the foundation be a good place to scrimp? Why or why not?**

Have a volunteer read Luke 6:46-49. Then ask:

■ **How does the foundation of a building compare to the foundation Jesus describes?**

■ **How do we build our lives upon this foundation?**

■ **What foundations are people tempted to build their lives upon?**

Ask group members to spend a few moments reflecting on the foundation on which they're building their lives.

Close with a prayer asking for God's help in hearing his words and putting them into practice.

# LUKE
# 6:46-49

## THEME:
Jesus, our rock

## SUMMARY:
This ADVENTURE takes kids rock climbing to help them understand the strong foundation Jesus offers.

PREPARATION: Plan a day of rock climbing or rappelling for your group. In the interest of safety, have an expert lead this adventure. Many camps and outdoor education facilities offer these programs. Or check with your local parks and recreation department for a referral.

Be sure to bring along a Bible.

Spend the day climbing and hanging from rocks with the kids. Be sure the person leading this adventure explains the importance of driving pitons and other equipment into solid rock.

When the group has climbed to its destination, or after you've returned from your trip, gather together for discussion.

Read Luke 6:46-49 and ask:

■ **What amount of faith would you have had in a rope anchored in a pile of sand?**

■ **What gave you faith in your ability to complete this climb?**

■ **How is Jesus like the rocks we climbed?**

■ **How is Jesus a rock in your life?**

■ **What sandy areas are you dangerously hanging from or**

standing on that need to be replaced with rock?

# LUKE
## 6:46-49

THEME:
Obeying Jesus

SUMMARY:
In this AFFIRMATION, kids will affirm one another by writing words of encouragement on a foundation of bricks.

PREPARATION: You'll need enough bricks for each person to have one. Gather several black markers and a Bible.

Read Luke 6:46-49 aloud. Say: **Jesus says we build a strong foundation by obeying him. According to Mark 12:28-31, the most important commandments to obey are to love God and to love others.**

Ask:

■ **How can we build up one another by obeying these commandments?**

■ **How can obeying these commandments build a strong foundation for our group?**

Give each person a brick and a marker. Have kids write their names on their bricks and then place them against the walls around the edges of the room to represent a foundation. (If your group is small, have kids place all bricks on the same wall.)

Say: **Let's strengthen our group by building one another up. Move to various bricks around the room and write words of encouragement on them. The words should reflect positive qualities you see in that person.**

Leave the bricks around the room to remind kids to continue building a strong foundation by building others up. After several weeks, allow kids to take their bricks home.

# LUKE
## 8:16-18

THEME:
Gifts and talents

SUMMARY:
In this LEARNING GAME, kids hide and search for flashlights to help them understand the value of using their talents instead of hiding them.

PREPARATION: Gather a Bible and two flashlights with bulbs of different colors. If you can't find a bulb other than white, cut a circle of colored transparency material and place it over the end of one flashlight to change the color of its light. This game must be played in a large, darkened room, such as the church sanctuary or outdoors at night.

Have kids form two teams. Give each team one of the flashlights. Say: **We're going to move into a darkened area. Your team will have five minutes to hide your flashlight from the other team. When I call out "Lights!" your team must turn on the flashlight in its hiding place, leave it, and begin searching for the other team's flashlight. The first team to find the other team's flashlight wins.**

Allow teams five minutes to hide their flashlights, then call "Lights" to signal teams that it's time to turn on their hidden lights. Congratulate the winning team and play again if you like.

When the game is over gather kids in the dark. Ask:

■ **Outside of playing this game, why would anyone turn on a light and then hide its beam?**

Have a volunteer read Luke 8:16-18, using a flashlight to read by.

Say: **Just as it's foolish to hide a light when you could be using its glow, it's foolish to hide our gifts and talents when we could be using them to serve Jesus. Let's share our hidden talents so others don't have to hunt and find them.**

Pass a flashlight around the group. As each person holds the light, have him or her share a gift, talent, or ability others may not know about. Encourage kids to find ways to use these talents to serve our God.

**Note:** If you have more than 15 in your group, you may want to gather extra flashlights and form additional teams.

# LUKE
# 8:22-25

## THEME:
Jesus calms life's storms.

## SUMMARY:
During this OVERNIGHTER camping trip, kids will focus on how storms of various kinds affect us and on Jesus' ability to control these storms.

PREPARATION: Plan an overnight camping trip using "Jesus calms life's storms" as the theme. Have kids form committees to plan meals, arrange for tents, find a location, plan activities, and so on. During the trip, give kids as much responsibility as possible. For example, let everyone take his or her turn with food preparation and cleanup.

Bring along a portable tape player (don't forget batteries!) and a tape of thunderstorms and heavy rain. ("Environments" by Warner Brothers or a series called "Solitudes" are carried by major music stores.) Be sure to bring a Bible.

Play the thunderstorm tape during your sharing time. Talk about how a storm would affect your camping trip. Ask:

■ **Can good come from a storm?**

■ **How would a storm make our group work together?**

■ **What's scary about a storm?**

Then read Luke 8:22-25. Have kids share "storms" they are facing or have faced, such as parents divorcing, failing a subject, losing a friend, and so on. Ask:

■ **How do these storms affect day-to-day life?**

■ **What good, if any, comes from these storms?**

Discuss ways Jesus is in control of these storms and how he can calm them.

VARIATION: If an actual storm hits on your trip, skip the cassette tape and hold your discussion during the real thing!

# LUKE
## 8:26-39

---

## THEME:
Fear

## SUMMARY:
This ADVENTURE helps kids face fear as they learn about people who were afraid of the power of Jesus.

---

PREPARATION: This is a spontaneous adventure in which kids will think of an idea and carry it out immediately. It's possible kids will select an adventure that involves traveling to another location, so you may want to have transportation available. You'll need several Bibles.

When the kids arrive, invite them to share about a time when they were overcome by fear. Then say: **Let's confront fear**

**right now. Think of an activity our group can do right now that will bring about these same feelings of fear you've just described.**

Help the kids brainstorm and choose an activity that would cause most of the participants to feel afraid. You could walk through a cemetery at night; stroll through a dark, wooded area; or even walk through the halls of your church building when it is empty, dark, and silent. Be sure kids don't choose an activity which poses true danger, such as walking over a rickety railroad truss or standing blindfolded on a freeway.

After completing your activity, gather in your meeting room. Form groups of no more than three. Have groups discuss the following questions. After kids have shared with their partners, allow each group to share with the larger group.

■ **Was this activity as scary as you thought it would be?**

■ **How did you feel about confronting your fear?**

Have kids read Luke 8:26-39 in their groups. Ask:

■ **Why did the people ask Jesus to go away?**

■ **Why do you think they were so afraid of him?**

■ **Do you ever feel afraid of Jesus? Explain.**

■ **In what ways is it sometimes scary to follow Jesus?**

Close with prayer, asking God to help us overcome our fears and follow him with joyful enthusiasm.

# LUKE
## 9:46-48

**THEME:**
Being like a child

**SUMMARY:**
Teenagers plan a variety of activities for younger children to express the love of Jesus in this PROJECT.

PREPARATION: Arrange with a local day-care center or children's home for your group to lead a morning or afternoon of activities for the children. Gather Bibles and supplies as needed for the activities you choose.

As you introduce this project to your group, read Luke 9:46-48. Discuss how people usually view children and how Jesus feels about children. Ask the group to think about why Jesus uses children in this example.

Say: **Let's make the time we have with these children special. We can really show them the love of Jesus.**

Then have kids form teams to plan a special morning or afternoon for the children. Encourage kids to use the theme of Jesus' love in whatever they plan. As kids plan, remind them to keep in mind the types of activities appropriate for the age-group you'll be visiting. For example, children younger than 4 can't do complicated crafts, while school-aged kids won't have much interest in singing nursery rhymes.

Here are suggestions for various teams and responsibilities:

■ **Singing**—This team may want to teach one or two new songs as well as lead kids in favorite songs. *Wee Sing* songbooks, available at toy stores and libraries, have words and music to most favorite children's songs. Have group members bring along guitars or other portable instruments to accompany the singing.

■ **Stories**—Visit your local or church library for entertaining storybooks. Have teenagers on this team practice reading the stories and adding funny voices or dramatics to further amuse the children.

■ **Games**—Younger children love playing London Bridge, while older ones can play Dodge Ball or other simple games. Or teach the children a new game. Remind teenagers to help children enjoy the games and not to become too competitive.

■ **Crafts**—This team can gather necessary supplies and lead children in using their creative skills.

**Note:** If you choose an organization that receives federal funds, you'll need to choose a nonreligious theme. Consider themes related to the season, animals, or people who are helpers. However, continue to emphasize that each child is special and important. Let teenagers know that even if they can't talk about Jesus, their actions will still express his love.

# LUKE
## 9:57-62

THEME:
Following Jesus

SUMMARY:

In this LEARNING GAME, kids compare the cost of material things to the cost of following Jesus.

PREPARATION: Gather department store catalogs and advertisements and cut out pictures of items your group members want most. These could be televisions, clothing, jewelry, games, and so on. On a separate piece of paper, note the cost of each item you've selected. Post the pictures around the walls of the room.

Collect paper and pencils for everyone and a Bible. You'll also need a bag of small candies, such as chocolate kisses.

Give each person a sheet of paper and a pencil. Have kids walk around the room and write down what they think each item costs. When everyone has priced the items, reveal the actual prices. After revealing each price, award the person who guessed closest to the actual price (without going over) a piece of candy. Then ask:

■ **Did these items sell for what you expected?**

■ **What might be hidden costs involved in purchasing these items?**

Read Luke 9:57-62. Ask:

■ **Why do you think Jesus responded in this way?**

Say: **Many people think the man's father wasn't dead yet. The man was probably waiting for his father to die. Maybe he even wanted to wait in order to receive his inheritance.**

■ **What was this man unwilling to "pay" to follow Jesus?**

■ **What kinds of costs are associated with following Jesus? Are you willing to live with these costs?**

■ **In some countries, being a Christian can mean punishment or being cut off from one's family. Would you be willing to pay this cost? Explain.**

# LUKE
## 10:30-37

THEME:
The good
Samaritan

SUMMARY:

In this DEVOTION, teenagers will act out the story of the good Samaritan without knowing it.

PREPARATION: Gather construction paper, markers, several pairs of scissors, and a Bible.

EXPERIENCE

As kids enter the room, whisper one of the following directions to each one:

■ **For the next few minutes, act tough and mean.**

■ **For the next few minutes, ignore anyone who complains.**

■ **For the next few minutes, complain about an injury or lie on the floor as if you're in pain.**

To only one person, whisper: **For the next few minutes, show concern for those who complain or act injured.**

RESPONSE

After a few minutes, have kids stop. Read aloud Luke 10:30-37. Ask:

■ **Who did you portray in the story?**

■ **How did your attitude at the start of class compare to the attitudes of the people described in the parable?**

■ **How are people today like the priest and the Levite?**

■ **Why was the good Samaritan willing to help the injured man?**

■ **What did the Samaritan receive for his trouble?**

CLOSING

Form pairs and give each pair a sheet of construction paper, scissors, and a marker. Have pairs each design a business card for the good Samaritan based on how he handled himself. Then have pairs each tell about their good Samaritan business card. Ask:

■ **Would you be able to write your name on the business card? Why or why not?**

■ **As a friend, how are you like or unlike the good Samaritan?**

# LUKE
# 10:30-37

**THEME:**
The good Samaritan

**SUMMARY:**
In this CREATIVE READING, kids will do "still life" scenes of the good Samaritan story.

PREPARATION: Choose youth group members to portray the characters. Gather the corresponding costumes and accessories. You'll also need a Bible.

CHARACTERS:
**Narrator**
**Man** traveling from Jerusalem to Jericho—backpack, cane
**Two robbers**—two bandannas
**Priest**—Bible
**Levite**—briefcase
**Innkeeper**—apron, towel
**Samaritan**—two coins

Instruct actors that the parable will be presented through "still life" acting. Group members will portray scenes of the parable by freezing in their posed positions for three to five seconds while that portion of the Scripture is read. Then an offstage leader will snap his or her fingers, and the characters will quickly take their places for the next scene.

Here are several ideas for still life scenes for this parable:

■ **Luke 10:30**—The man lies on the floor as two robbers appear to beat him.

■ **Luke 10:31**—The man on the floor reaches out as the priest holds a Bible and looks at him.

■ **Luke 10:32**—The man continues to reach out as the Levite looks at him.

■ **Luke 10:33-34**—The Samaritan pretends to tend to the man's wounds and prepares to take him to the innkeeper.

■ **Luke 10:35**—The Samaritan takes out two coins and gives them to the innkeeper.

■ **Luke 10:36-37**—All characters stand in a line in front of the audience.

When everyone is ready, have kids assume their opening positions, then begin reading Luke 10:30-37 for the group.

have Jesus' light shining through our eyes.

Say: **Look at your partner's eyes and draw them on your paper. Next to your drawing, write at least one way you see the light of Jesus shining through your partner.**

When everyone is ready, have partners share with each other what they drew and wrote.

Form groups of four by having pairs join with another pair. Ask kids to introduce their partners to the other pairs by telling about their eyes.

Close by singing several songs about light, such as "I Am the Light of the World," "Pass It On," or "Walking in the Light."

# LUKE
## 11:33-36

THEME:
The lamp of the body

SUMMARY:
Teenagers affirm their partners in this AFFIRMATION by drawing each other's eyes and sharing how Jesus' light shines through a person's eyes.

PREPARATION: Gather paper, colored markers or crayons, and several Bibles.

Have kids form pairs. Distribute paper and markers or crayons to each person.

Have pairs read Luke 11:33-36 together. Discuss what it means to

# LUKE
## 11:37-41

THEME:
Being beautiful inside

SUMMARY:
In this OBJECT LESSON, kids compare the wrappings and contents of gifts to the actions and hearts of the Pharisees.

PREPARATION: Gather and wrap enough presents for each person in your group to have one. Choose a variety of small but desirable items (such as candy bars, a cool bookmark, or a fast food gift certificate) as well as disgusting things (like mud or a piece of rotten fruit). Wrap some gifts beautifully and others in a tacky or sloppy manner. Put a few (but not all) of the disgusting things in the beautiful packages and vice versa. You'll also need a Bible.

One at a time, let kids choose their packages, tell the group why they chose that package, and open it. Ask each person to show the group what he or she received. Continue until each person has opened a gift.

Read Luke 11:37-41. Ask:

■ **How are the Pharisees like the packages that looked good on the outside but were disgusting on the inside?**

■ **What do people today do to look good to others?**

■ **How is it possible to be ugly inside but beautiful outside?**

■ **What can you do to be more beautiful on the inside?**

# LUKE
## 12:13-21

THEME:
Greed

SUMMARY:
This CREATIVE READING examines different attitudes toward material possessions.

PREPARATION: Have four kids volunteer for this creative reading. Provide a photocopy of the "Creative Reading For Luke 12:13-21" handout (pp. 106–107) for each one and let kids read through the

script before reading for the entire group. You'll also need a Bible.

After the reading, ask a volunteer to read Luke 12:13-21. Discuss the importance of material wealth compared to treasures stored in heaven. Ask:

■ **Why do we want more stuff?**

■ **How we can be content with what we have?**

# LUKE
## 12:13-21

THEME:
Materialism

SUMMARY:
In this DEVOTION, teenagers will select items they'd like to have and discuss what their choices reflect.

PREPARATION: Gather paper, pencils, old catalogs, glue, scissors, and a Bible.

EXPERIENCE
Give kids each a sheet of paper and a pencil. Ask them each to list six things they wish they could have—tell them not to worry about the cost or how difficult it might be to get the items.

Next, distribute catalogs, glue, and scissors. Have kids look through the catalogs and select several items they would like to have. Tell kids to cut out the items and glue them on the paper to form a collage.

*(continued on p. 108)*

# CREATIVE READING FOR LUKE 12:13-21

**Reader 1:** I have it all, but I don't really care.

**Reader 2:** I have it all and want more!

**Reader 3:** I don't have enough and want more, MORE, **MORE!**

**Reader 4:** "Stuff" just isn't important to me.

**Readers 1, 2, and 3:** Well it is to us!

**Reader 2:** I want those new tennis shoes! If only I could have them now, I would be so happy. I wonder if my parents would float me another loan. Wow! What cool shoes!

**Reader 1:** *(Yawning)* Yes...well...I do enjoy mine.

**Reader 2:** I mean, really, I only have two pairs of tennis shoes. Can you believe it? Just two! I mean, how am I supposed to compete without the newest shoes? What's $100, anyway? These shoes are a deal, I'm telling you—a bargain!

**Reader 3:** $100? For shoes? I can't believe it. My family had our water cut off because we couldn't pay for it, and I know it cost less than $100. And you want shoes that cost a $100 so you can run faster and jump higher? It's your fault that people like me don't have anything. You greedy people don't leave anything for the rest of us.

**Reader 2:** Hey, I'm not hurting you. I just want those shoes. And a pool for the back yard. Hey, maybe my parents can qualify for another loan.

**Reader 1:** Well, yes, the pool is nice...as long as you have a pool service to take care of it. Otherwise, your parents will make you do it.

**Reader 2:** Yuck!

*(Continued)*

# CREATIVE READING FOR LUKE 12:13-21 *(continued)*

**Reader 3:** A pool. Now I really can't believe it. You want a pool, and I can barely scrape up lunch money. My parents worry themselves sick over paying the bills!

**Reader 1:** Bills. Yes, well, you can hire an accountant to take care of those, too.

**Reader 4:** This stuff you have and want. It isn't important.

**Readers 1, 2, and 3:** What?

**Reader 4:** It's not important.

**Reader 2:** Of course it's important. How can anyone know who you are or how important you are if you don't have the right stuff?

**Reader 4:** Stuff isn't important—not to God, anyway. He measures us by who we are and not what we have.

**Reader 2:** But what about all this great stuff?

**Reader 4:** God wants us to be happy with what we have. Stuff is nice, but it doesn't mean anything. It doesn't bring us joy.

**Reader 3:** But what if you don't have *anything?* They have all the stuff!

**Reader 4:** You have God, your friends, your family, and your life. Use those things to build up your treasure in heaven, where it really matters.

**Reader 1:** Hmm. I wonder what I'll do with all this stuff while I work on building up treasure in heaven.

**Reader 2:** I'll take it! Uh...well, maybe you should give it to someone who really needs it.

# LUKE
# 12:35-40

*(continued from p. 105)*

RESPONSE

Read aloud Luke 12:13-21. Ask:

■ **How would you define greed?**

■ **How do you think Jesus would define it?**

■ **What do you think Jesus means in verse 21?**

Form groups of no more than three. Have group members look at their collages as they discuss these questions:

■ **What did you select?**

■ **How expensive were the items?**

■ **How many did you select?**

■ **Would you want to be known by what you selected? Why or why not?**

■ **Do the selections reflect your true identity as a Christian?**

■ **What does this statement mean to you: "Life is not measured by how much one owns"?**

CLOSING

Gather kids in a circle and say: **To close, let's sing a song to remind us of the importance of not letting our possessions distract us from our relationship with God.**

Lead the group in singing a song such as "Seek Ye First" or "More Precious Than Silver." (Both of these songs are available in *The Group Songbook,* published by Group.)

---

## THEME:

Jesus' return

## SUMMARY:

Use this DEVOTION to help kids understand preparing for Christ's return.

PREPARATION: Before the activity, prepare slips of paper with various commands such as "Stand in the corner" or "Sit on your hands." Prepare one command for each group member. You'll need snacks and a Bible.

EXPERIENCE

After everyone has arrived, distribute the commands and have kids follow the instructions written on their slips of paper. While kids are following their commands, tell them you have to leave for a moment but that you'll be right back. Tell kids it's important for them to keep doing their commands until you return.

RESPONSE

Leave the room for at least five minutes. When you return, shout: **I'm back as I promised!**

Some kids will be surprised and scamper to do their commands. Read aloud Luke 12:35-40. Ask:

■ **How did you feel when I came back into the room?**

■ **Were you doing what you were commanded? Why or why not?**

■ **How is this activity like**

waiting for Christ's return?

■ **What should we do while we wait for Christ's return?**

CLOSING

Say: **Only God knows when Jesus will come to take us home. We simply need to remember to be faithful to do the things God asks us to do in the Bible so that we'll be prepared at any time for Jesus' return.**

Before ending the activity, give a snack reward to everyone who faithfully followed your commands while you were away.

# LUKE
## 13:18-30

**THEME:**
The kingdom of God

**SUMMARY:**
In this SKIT, two girls talk about the kingdom of God after church, but one of them fixates on heaven.

## LATER...

SCENE: Two friends are talking with each other after church.

PROPS: You'll need a Bible for the discussion after the skit.

CHARACTERS:
**Cindy**
**Tyra**

SCRIPT
*(Cindy and Tyra are standing, talking after church.)*

**Cindy:** *(Excitedly)* Didn't that sermon really get to you?

**Tyra:** It *did* get me thinking. Pastor's ideas about the kingdom of God were...interesting.

**Cindy:** What do *you* think heaven will be like?

**Tyra:** Hmm... I guess I haven't thought about it much.

**Cindy:** Well, I think it's going to be like a big party. *(She begins to dance around.)* Everyone's gonna be singing and dancing. And the food—I think it's gonna be the best!

**Tyra:** What did you think about the idea that we're a part of God's kingdom today, too?

**Cindy:** Did he say that? Oh, I don't know. I just can't wait until heaven. *(Thoughtfully)* I wonder if we'll be able to fly in heaven?

**Tyra:** I think you missed the point of the sermon.

**Cindy:** *(Distracted)* Wouldn't it be great to fly wherever you wanted to go? Heaven is going to be incredible. *(Turning to Tyra)* Um...what were you saying?

**Tyra:** I was saying that I think you missed the point of the sermon.

**Cindy:** *(Adamantly)* I did *not* miss the point of the sermon. It was about the kingdom of God—it was about heaven.

**Tyra:** Yeah, but Pastor's point was that the kingdom of God begins now—here on earth. He said that by serving others, reading the Bible, sharing our faith with friends, and generally living out God's will, we're experiencing a taste of God's kingdom. Heaven is just a bonus...

**Cindy:** I don't want a *taste* of God's kingdom—I want the whole thing. *(Lost in her own thoughts)* I wonder if we'll be able to date in heaven...

**Tyra:** *(She looks around, then interrupts.)* Cindy, my mom's waiting for me. See you tonight at youth group?

**Cindy:** Oh, I can't make it tonight. I've got too much other stuff to do. Besides, I'm not thrilled about going to some dirty, old homeless shelter. You can be sure they won't have homeless shelters in heaven...

**Tyra:** But, Cindy, you're still missing the...

**Cindy:** *(Interrupting)* Oh, there's my dad. Gotta go now. Later. *(She exits.)*

**Tyra:** *(She pauses. Then, to herself)* Yeah, later.

If you use this skit as a discussion starter, here are possible questions:

■ **Is heaven the goal of living the Christian life or just a bonus? Explain.**

■ **Based on Jesus' description of the kingdom of God in Luke 13:18-30, what is it? In what way does it exist today?**

■ **What does it mean to be in the kingdom of God?**

# LUKE
# 14:15-24

## THEME:
Excuses

## SUMMARY:
Use this PROJECT to help kids explore excuses people give for not following Jesus.

PREPARATION: You'll need a contest prize (such as a fast-food gift certificate or a contemporary Christian CD) and Bibles.

At the end of one of your youth meetings, invite kids to participate in the "World's Greatest Excuse for Not Having Finished Homework" contest. Show kids your contest prize, then explain the following rules for the contest:

1. The object is for contestants to interview friends, family, co-workers, church members, and anyone else outside the youth group to find the most creative, *actual* excuse someone gave for not turning in homework on time. For example, an excuse might be "My dog ate my homework" or "I had to donate my homework to a scientific experiment at the university."

2. A contestant may not enter an excuse that he or she has used—excuses must be someone else's.

3. Contestants may enter up to 10 excuses.

4. All excuses are due by the beginning of the next youth meeting.

At the beginning of the next

youth meeting, collect the excuses. While the meeting is underway, have a team of two or three volunteer judges preview the excuses in another room. Have judges select the 20 or 30 most creative entries to present to the group.

About midway through the meeting, read the excuses to the youth group and have them applaud for their favorite excuses. Award the title of "World's Greatest Excuse for Not Having Finished Homework" to the excuse that earns the loudest applause. Give the prize to the contestant who entered that excuse in the contest.

Afterward say: **The excuses we make about not turning in homework are often humorous, but Jesus once told a story about people who made excuses not to follow God. Let's read that story now.**

Form groups of no more than three. Have the person wearing the most blue in each group read Luke 14:15-24 aloud for his or her group. Then wrap up the project (and the meeting) by having trios discuss these questions:

■ **How do the excuses in our contest compare to the excuses people gave in Luke 14:15-24?**

■ **What point do you think Jesus wanted to make by telling this story?**

■ **Why do you suppose people make excuses for not responding to God's invitation?**

■ **What can you do this week to help you avoid making excuses to God?**

# LUKE
## 15:1-10

**THEME:**
Reaching out to non-Christians

**SUMMARY:**
When kids hunt for a "lost" friend, they find a surprise PARTY.

PREPARATION: Find a hiding place in your church where you can have a party. This might be a small room, a large closet, or even the church balcony. Before the meeting, hide party food and other supplies in this place. Hide a Bible there, too. At the beginning of the meeting, ask one group member to "disappear" and hide in the prearranged place.

As you begin your meeting, say: **Well, it looks like everyone is here, so let's get started.** (Name of hidden person) **is going to open our time with prayer. Wait a minute. Where's** (hidden person)**?**

Let everyone wonder and discuss it for a moment.

Then say: **I know** (hidden person) **is here somewhere. Let's look for** (him or her).

Ask everyone to spread out around the church and look for the hidden person.

As kids begin to find the hidden group member, have that person encourage them to hide with him or her. When everyone has found the lost friend, pull out the party supplies and have a celebration.

While everyone enjoys the goodies, pull out your Bible and have the formerly lost person read Luke 15:1-10 aloud. Ask:

■ **How did you feel when you found our lost youth group member?**

■ **How does it feel to lose something and then find it?**

■ **How does Jesus feel when a "lost" person chooses to follow him?**

Close the party by having each person pray for someone they'd like Jesus to find and bring into his family.

# LUKE
# 15:11-32

## THEME:
The prodigal son

## SUMMARY:
In this CREATIVE READING, kids will pantomime the story of the son who left home.

PREPARATION: Gather Bibles and write each of the following Scripture references on separate slips of paper: Luke 15:11-13; Luke 15:14-19; Luke 15:20-24; and Luke 15:25-32.

Form four groups. Give each group a Bible and a slip of paper with a reference on it. Tell groups to each read their passage and create a pantomime (no words allowed) to portray their verses to the others.

After five minutes, say: **On with the show!**

Have groups present their pantomimes in order. As one group pantomimes its passage, the others groups are the "script writers"—they call out the lines the pantomiming kids would say if they could talk. For example, a group could pantomime verses 20-24 by having members act as the son; the father; and the servants, who dress the son in a robe, ring, and sandals. The script writers then could think of lines such as "Son, I love you so much, I want to give you some presents," "Dad, I don't deserve all this," and "We servants agree. Why don't you give these gifts to your older son? Or better yet, we could use them for our families."

After all passages have been pantomimed and scripted, read the story from the Bible. Ask:

■ **What were some of the missed opportunities in this passage?**

■ **What was the "second chance" described in the passage?**

■ **How did you feel acting out your passage?**

■ **In real life, when have you felt most like the father? the younger son? the older son? the servants?**

# LUKE
## 15:11-32

### THEME:

The prodigal son

### SUMMARY:
Use this "teenspeak" SKIT of the classic parable to help kids understand God's love and forgiveness.

## THE TOTALLY TUBULAR TALE OF BIFF, THE PRODIGAL SON

SCENE: Farmer Bob's farm.

PROPS: Provide a simple stage with a podium off to the side (for the Narrator) and two chairs (for the taxi cab). You'll also need a bag of coins, a jacket, a Time magazine, a paper cup, a camera, and a Bible for the discussion after the skit.

CHARACTERS:
**Narrator**
**Farmer Bob** (a hick with Shakespearean tendencies)
**Penelope** (his daughter)
**Biff** (his son)
**Cabby**
**Jacket Seller**—with a jacket
**Rich Man**
**Rich Woman**
**Chorus** (anyone in the cast who's not on stage)

### SCRIPT
*(Narrator stands behind the podium. Farmer Bob, Penelope, and Biff stand center stage with their backs to the audience.)*

**Narrator:** Welcome to "The Totally Tubular Tale of Biff, the Prodigal Son." Our story begins like this: In a small town somewhere between California and New Jersey, there lived a farmer who often said things like ...

**Farmer Bob:** *(Turning around)* Forsooth, forthwith, heretofore—I'm Farmer Bob.

**Narrator:** Farmer Bob had two kids. The older one was Penelope. She often said things like ...

**Penelope:** *(Turning around)* Dad, isn't there some more work for me to do on this swell farm? I love chores. Can I be a farmer when I grow up? Can I? Huh? Can I?

**Narrator:** And she meant it. The younger one was Biff. He often said things like ...

**Biff:** *(Turning around)* Hey, dudes! I want out of this cheesy place so I can *(laughs)* see the big city. I want to party it up on a surfing safari!

**Narrator:** And he meant it. So one day, Biff asked his dad ...

**Biff:** Yo, Pops. Could I have a little advance on my allowance?

**Farmer Bob:** Yup. How much do you want?

**Biff:** Oh, however much you were planning on giving me in your will. I don't see the point in waiting 'til you kick the can before I get out of this chicken roost. I'm not cut out to be a ditch-diggin', cow-kickin', chicken-cuttin', food-farmin', over-the-hill hillbilly like yourself.

**Farmer Bob:** *(Dramatically)* Hark! How thou breaketh my

heart! But, alas, if that is your wish, then you must "to be" what you chooseth "to be." Here's your share of the farm. *(He hands Biff a bag of coins.)*

**Biff:** Wow! How'd you fit half the farm in this little bag, Daddy-O?

**Farmer Bob:** I truly hateth to see this happen to you, Biff. I hate to see an innocent boy transformed into... *(dramatically)* the prodigal son.

*(Cabby enters and sits in the driver's chair.)*

**Chorus:** Honk! Honk!

**Biff:** That's my ride. Later days and better waves, dude! *(Biff enters the cab. Farmer Bob and Penelope exit.)*

**Cabby:** Where to, Mac?

**Biff:** The big city—and hurry!

*(Cabby and Biff pantomime a wild ride. Chorus provides sound effects.)*

**Narrator:** The first thing Biff wanted to do was buy some flashy clothes.

*(Jacket Seller enters holding a jacket. Biff gets out of cab.)*

**Jacket Seller:** Attention, sidewalk shopper! Need a jacket?

**Biff:** Excellent! Tailor, fit me with your finest threads!

**Jacket Seller:** *(Handing Biff the jacket)* It's $780.

**Biff:** *(Handing Jacket Seller a bill)* Here's a thou; keep the change. *(Biff returns to the cab. Jacket Seller exits.)*

**Biff:** Driver, take me to this town's best party place.

**Cabby:** But it's only two doors down.

**Biff:** Drive on, anyway, dude—and step on it! *(Biff and Cabby lurch backward, then forward quickly)*

Keep the motor running while I indulge myself.

*(Biff gets out of cab and looks around. Chorus enters and gathers around Biff. Biff speaks to Chorus.)*

**Biff:** Cigarettes! Drugs! Booze! Ladies! Life in the fast lane! Here, dudes, have some money. *(He freely hands out cash to Chorus.)*

**Chorus:** Hooray! All right! Biff is our friend!

**Narrator:** Time passed quickly. *(Cabby leaves car and paces while reading a Time magazine.)*

**Narrator:** And Biff's money eventually ran out.

**Chorus:** *(Exiting stage left)* Goodbye, Biff. It was fun while it lasted.

**Cabby:** Hey, Mac, you owe me 780 bucks!

*(Biff shows him his empty pockets and empty coin bag. Cabby points to Biff's jacket. Biff looks sadly at his prized possession, hugs it, kisses it, and gives it to the Cabby. Cabby exits.)*

**Narrator:** So, Biff was left penniless on the street.

*(A member of the Chorus throws a cup to Biff. Biff holds the cup, puts on his sunglasses, and starts to beg. Rich Man and Rich Woman enter stage left with a camera. Jacket Seller drifts on stage behind them.)*

**Rich Man:** Oh, look, mumsy, a poor man. Let's get our picture taken with him. *(To Jacket Seller)* Excuse me, good fellow, but would you mind taking our picture? *(He hands camera to Jacket Seller, who takes the picture, then sneaks the camera into* *his own pocket, and leaves.)*

**Rich Woman:** *(Exiting, unaware of the theft)* See, honey? I told you there'd be poor people here.

**Biff:** *(Taking off sunglasses)* I'm so bummed. Nothing is worse than this—not even the farm. Maybe Penelope and Pops would take me back as a hired hand. If they only knew what I've been through. Hey, that rhymes *(He laughs mournfully.)*

**Narrator:** So, Biff began the long walk back to the farm. *(Biff walks in a small circle to the side of the Narrator.)* Seconds became minutes, minutes became hours, hours became days, days turned into weeks, weeks plodded into months...

**Biff:** Hey, I'm gettin' dizzy over here!

**Narrator:** *(Sighs.)* Then he saw his father's farm in the distance! Then he saw his father! But his dad had already seen him and was running toward Biff.
*(Farmer Bob enters, running in slow motion toward Biff. Biff runs in slow motion toward Farmer Bob. They finally reach each other and embrace.)*

**Biff:** Yo, Daddy-O. I've been like the biggest cheesehound in four counties, you know? I'm big-time sorry, but I blew your bucks, and I've got nothin' to show for it. Would you, could you take me back on as one of your hired hands? I'd be strictly a minimum wager, you know, and you wouldn't even have to give me dental benefits, if you didn't want.

**Farmer Bob:** Hark! At last my son hath returned from squan-dering his fortune. Oh, ye apple of my eyeball, Biff. 'Tis good to see you! Servants, bring forth all my shiny things and put them on my son. Then go cook a really big meal. There shall be a hoedown tonight.

**Chorus:** Hooray! Everyone is happy.

**Narrator:** Except Penelope.

**Penelope:** *(Entering)* Father, it's not fair. Biff got so out of hand, and you reward him for it. You throw him a party. But I've been cleaning stables all this time, doing just what's expected of me, and you've never so much as baked me a cake!

**Farmer Bob:** You misjudge me, fair daughter. I have always loved you, just as I loved Biff. All that I have here I have shared with you. But my son was lost, and now he is found again. Should I not rejoice over his return?

**Penelope:** OK, you've got a point. But can I have a party, too? Maybe next weekend?

**Farmer Bob:** You may have your heart's desire, my child.
*(Farmer Bob and Penelope embrace, then Biff comes in and joins the hug.)*

**Narrator:** And that is "The Totally Tubular Tale of Biff, the Prodigal Son."
*(Everyone bows and leaves.)*

If you used this skit as a discussion starter, here are possible questions:

■ **Read the story of the prodigal son in Luke 15:11-32. How would you summarize the theme of this story in one sentence?**

■ **When have you felt like a "prodigal son"? What did you do about it?**

■ **In what ways are we all prodigal children to God?**

■ **What can we do about it?**

# LUKE
# 16:1-12

THEME:
Faithfulness

SUMMARY:
In this LEARNING GAME, kids will be tempted to be unfaithful in a task.

PREPARATION: Purchase a bag of miniature candy bars. Gather a Bible and an object to be touched (a book, an eraser, or almost anything).

Form two groups—a candy group and a guard group. Give the candy group a bag of miniature candy bars. Have the guard group stand and form a circle facing out. Place an object in the center of the circle. Have kids in the circle link elbows and guard the object. The guards should not let the candy group touch the object.

The candy group should try to lure the guards away with candy. Once a guard is lured away, the guard group cannot close a gap left by a missing guard. The candy-group members can then touch the guarded object. Once the guarded object is touched, the game is over.

After several minutes or when the object is touched, ask:

■ **How did you feel during this game?**

■ **How easy or difficult was it to do your job?**

■ **How easy or difficult was it to endure temptation?**

Read aloud Luke 16:1-12. Ask:

■ **What is a "little thing" that you're required to be faithful in?**

■ **What temptations do you face that might keep you from being faithful in that thing?**

■ **How do you endure those temptations?**

■ **What "big thing" might God be using this little thing to train you for?**

# LUKE
# 17:11-19

THEME:
Giving thanks

SUMMARY:
This Thanksgiving PARTY offers the opportunity for kids to express their appreciation toward others and God.

PREPARATION: Plan a Thanksgiving party. Include Thanksgiving-themed party favors, decorations, and food (such as pumpkin pie and sugar cookies cut into turkey shapes). Gather paper, pens, envelopes, and a Bible.

Include these activities at your party:

■ Sing traditional Thanksgiving songs as well as contemporary songs of thanks.

■ Have a time for kids to express thanks to anyone else in the group for any reason, large or small.

■ Let kids use the paper and envelopes to write thank-you notes to friends, family, teachers, coaches, or any other people they'd like. Encourage kids to deliver the notes within three days.

■ Read Luke 17:11-19 and discuss why giving thanks is important.

■ Take turns offering one-sentence prayers of thanks to God.

# LUKE 17:11-19

THEME:
Appreciating others

SUMMARY:
Teenagers write notes of thanks to each other in this AFFIRMATION.

PREPARATION: Buy printed thank-you cards or design your own. You'll need one for each member of your group. Also gather pens and a Bible.

Begin the meeting by reading Luke 17:11-19. Ask:

■ **Why do you think the nine didn't thank Jesus?**

■ **Why don't we always remember to say "thanks" to God or others?**

Say: **Today we're going to make time to say thank you. I have a thank-you note for each person in this room.**

Distribute the cards and pens. Have each person write his or her name on the outside of the card. Then have kids pass the cards around and write short sentences inside telling the person whose card they have why they appreciate him or her. Be sure to participate in the activity yourself and affirm each group member in this way.

# LUKE 18:9-14

THEME:
Bragging

SUMMARY:
In this SKIT, three friends complain about a bragger, not realizing they have the same problem.

## I'M THE BEST

SCENE: Three friends are sitting around a cafeteria table.

PROPS: Set up a table and three chairs. You'll also need a Bible for the discussion after the skit.

CHARACTERS:
**Matt**
**Juan**
**Ryan**

SCRIPT

**Matt:** Can you believe what Tom said?

**Juan:** He has such a big head.

**Ryan:** The thing is, he really *believes* he can do it.

**Juan:** There's no way.

**Matt:** Tom? Impossible.

**Ryan:** Well *he* certainly thinks he can do it.

**Juan:** *(Sarcastically)* Yeah, when trees fly. I'll bet he doesn't even make the first cut.

**Matt:** If that.

**Ryan:** What *is* it with these people who think they can do anything?

**Juan:** Well, you know. One lucky shot in a scrimmage, and suddenly Tom's "Mister Basketball."

**Matt:** "Mister Lucky" is more like it.

**Ryan:** Yeah, then he goes around telling everyone he's a shoo-in for making the team.

**Juan:** Everyone knows that *no one* is a shoo-in.
*(All three pause, then look at each other.)*

**Matt:** Except us, of course.

**Ryan:** You got that right.

**Juan:** Yeah, here we are—three-fifths of this year's starting line-up.

**Matt:** We're the best.

**Ryan:** No doubt.

**Juan:** Primo.
*(They pause, then continue talking as they get up from the table.)*

**Juan:** I can't believe that Tom...

**Matt:** I've never known anyone who brags as much as he does.

**Ryan:** Can't wait to see the look on his face when we make the team and "Dr. Braggo" doesn't...
*(They laugh and exit.)*

If you use this skit as a discussion starter, here are possible questions:

■ **What's the difference between self-confidence and bragging?**

■ **How does Jesus deal with pride and humility in Luke 18:9-14?**

■ **How can we avoid the trap of pride this week? the trap of false humility?**

# LUKE
## 19:1-10

**THEME:**
Truth

**SUMMARY:**
Create suspense and improve Bible knowledge in this LEARNING GAME by having kids role play different versions of the story of Zacchaeus and Jesus.

PREPARATION: You'll need newsprint, a marker, and Bibles.

Form one or more pairs and assign each pair the task of role playing Luke 19:1-10. However, ask each pair to alter the story in some way when they present it. Allows pairs to leave the room for a few minutes to prepare their role plays. Don't allow the rest of the group to read the passage beforehand.

When pairs are ready, have them each present their role-play. After each presentation, have the rest of the group work together to offer one guess about what's wrong with the story line. Keep track of kids' guesses on newsprint but don't tell them whether they're right or wrong until all the pairs have presented their role-plays.

After all the pairs have finished, have each pair tell how they changed the story.

Then have the whole group form pairs and read Luke 19:1-10 with their partners to verify what actually happened. Ask pairs to discuss these questions:

∎ **We know what was wrong with the Scripture presentations that the pairs role played, but what would you say was wrong with the way people perceived Zacchaeus?**

∎ **Why do you think Jesus refused to see Zacchaeus the way others did?**

∎ **In what ways are you like Zacchaeus? like the people who called Zacchaeus a sinner?**

∎ **What can we learn from the story of Zacchaeus to help us be more like Jesus this week?**

# LUKE
# 21:1-4

## THEME:
Giving

## SUMMARY:
In this DEVOTION, kids will hear about a man who gave his life for another and compare this to the kind of giving Jesus wants from them.

PREPARATION: You'll need a copy of *The Body: Being Light in Darkness,* by Charles Colson (Word Publishing, 1992). Check your local library or the libraries of your church or pastor. Or ask members of the congregation to lend you the book or buy it for your youth group.

Read chapter 23, "Who Are You?" and familiarize yourself with the story of Father Maximilian Kolbe. If time allows, plan to read the entire chapter to your group. Otherwise, summarize the first half of the chapter for your group members and begin reading aloud with the paragraph beginning, "By the end of July, 1941 ... " You'll also need a Bible.

EXPERIENCE

Form groups of no more than four and assign each group member one of the following roles:

∎ Maximilian Kolbe
∎ Prisoner #5659, who was allowed to live
∎ Brono Borgowiec, the prisoner who was attendant to the death cells
∎ A guard observing the events

(If you have groups of fewer than four, have one person play two roles. If you have groups of more than four, have two people play the same role.)

Have groups each form a circle. Tell kids to silently act out in their circles the actions described for their characters as you read the selected sections of the chapter for your group. Remind kids that the story you're going to read is true and ask them to keep a serious, thoughtful attitude as you read and they act.

Afterward, ask groups to discuss these questions:

■ **What's your reaction to this story? Explain.**

■ **Why do you think Maximilian Kolbe did what he did?**

Say: **Imagine you are your assigned character, actually living the events in this story. With your group, discuss the feelings you might have during this series of events.**

Allow several minutes for discussion, then have kids form four new groups—one group made up of everyone who played Maximilian Kolbe, one group made up of everyone who played Prisoner #5659, and so on. Have kids each share with their new group members what they discussed in their previous group. Ask:

■ **How are your feelings alike or different?**

RESPONSE

Have kids remain in their groups as you ask the following questions. Have kids answer the questions in their groups, then share one or two answers with the

larger group. Ask:

■ **How did having various perspectives of the same event cause different emotions?**

■ **What would it take for you to willingly do what Father Kolbe did?**

Have a volunteer from each group read Luke 21:1-4. Ask:

■ **How are this widow and Father Kolbe alike?**

■ **How can a small offering be of great worth?**

■ **What would it take for you to give sacrificially instead of out of your relative wealth?**

CLOSING

Ask each person to share one way he or she can give sacrificially in the next week. Be sure kids understand giving goes beyond money to include time, talent, and even friendship.

Close with a prayer asking God to give group members hearts that are generous and sharing.

# LUKE
## 21:5-38

THEME:
Signs of the end times

SUMMARY:
In this CREATIVE PRAYER, kids will pray for those hit by natural and human-caused disasters.

PREPARATION: You will need newsprint, a marker, tape, a Bible, paper, and pencils. Tape the newsprint to the wall in the front of the room.

Brainstorm with your group specific natural disasters that have occurred in the past year, such as earthquakes, tornadoes, hurricanes, floods, and so on. Also think of disasters caused by people, such as wars, bombings, drug abuse, and so on. List all of these things on the newsprint. Discuss what it must be like for the people involved in these crises.

Distribute pencils and sheets of paper. Ask each person to choose one of the situations on the newsprint and write a short prayer for the people affected by it.

After kids have written these prayers, read Luke 21:5-38 aloud. Ask:

■ **Do you think we are near the end of the age? Why or why not?**

■ **How will we know when the end of time is near?**

■ **What should Christians do while we wait?**

Have kids take turns reading their prayers to God. Close by asking God to help everyone in your group be ready for Christ's return.

# LUKE
# 22:39-46

**THEME:**
Prayer

**SUMMARY:**
Teenagers will create a slide show of pictures and share prayers during this CREATIVE PRAYER/PROJECT.

PREPARATION: You'll need a Bible, newsprint, a marker, one or more cameras, slide film, and a slide projector and screen for viewing the slides.

Read Luke 22:39-46 to your group. Ask:

■ **Have you ever prayed as diligently as Jesus did during this crisis in his life? Explain.**

■ **What people and situations are you aware of that need serious prayer?**

List kids' responses to the second question on the newsprint. Then have kids work together to create a slide show with pictures representing each of the areas on this list. Kids will need to list what they'll photograph to represent each item, then go together or in small groups to shoot each picture. Encourage kids to be creative in choosing what to photograph.

When the film has been developed, have kids decide which slides to use and how to arrange them. Have each person write a prayer about one or more of the represented topics.

Show the slides and have kids take turns reading the prayers they wrote while the images representing this topic are being viewed. The entire church may want to join in this time of prayer.

VARIATION: If kids are uncomfortable praying aloud, record the prayers before the showing and play the recording during the slide show.

# LUKE
# 24:13-35

THEME:
Celebration

SUMMARY:
This PARTY/MUSIC IDEA uses songs to focus on the various emotions felt by Jesus' friends after his death and resurrection.

PREPARATION: Prior to the party, ask several kids to help you select some of the group's favorite songs in two categories: sadness or struggle and praise or celebration. Make arrangements for someone to lead singing and for musicians to accompany the group.

D ecorate the room in a festive manner with bright streamers and balloons. Have a variety of refreshments for kids to enjoy. Also gather a Bible, small candles, and matches.

Begin the party with all the lights off and the room in darkness. As kids enter, give each one a lit candle. Ask everyone to be seated and to keep the mood serious at this time.

Begin singing the songs of sadness and struggle. Say: **Imagine how Jesus' followers must have felt after he was crucified. Suppose what the rumors about his body being gone must have made them think. They must have been confused, scared, worried, and maybe even a little hopeful—but hoping against hope. Imagine yourself in this story as I read it to you.**

Read Luke 24:13-35. Discuss the elation the disciples must have felt to discover their Lord was alive. Ask a few volunteers to tell the group about a time they experienced this feeling of joyous discovery and relief.

Say: **We can all share in the joy the disciples experienced at Emmaus. We were once burdened and loaded down by sin, but he has lifted that load from us. What a relief! What a joyful feeling! We are his children, and we share in his resurrection!**

Turn on the lights so everyone can see the brightly decorated room. Sing the praise songs together, holding hands, hugging, and celebrating. We truly have a reason to rejoice!

# LUKE
## 24:13-35

## THEME:
Friendship with God

## SUMMARY:
In this ADVENTURE, teenagers will discuss their friendship with God while they're taking a walk.

PREPARATION: You'll need Bibles.

Read aloud Luke 24:13-35. Then direct group members to form pairs and take a 20-minute walk. Ask partners to talk about their friendship with God in three parts:

■ past—what it's been;

■ future—what I want it to be; and

■ present—what it is now, and what they'll do to make it better. Play music or honk your car horn to signal the end of the walk.

When kids return, form groups of four and have kids share again what their present friendship with God is like. Then have groups pray together for God's grace to help them grow in their relationships with God.

# JOHN

*"God loved the world so much that he gave
his one and only Son so that whoever
believes in him may not be lost,
but have eternal life."*

*John 3:16*

# JOHN
## 1:1-5, 14

THEME:
Jesus, the Word

SUMMARY:
In this LEARNING GAME, kids send messages using themselves as the message to understand how Jesus is God's message to us.

PREPARATION: You'll need Bibles.

Have kids form teams of no more than four. Say: **You may have played the game Telephone before, where the object is to pass a message to others without confusing the message. This is a similar game. First, each team will need to think of the secret message they want to send.**

Give teams time to do this.

Say: **Now, instead of whispering this message, your team members must become the message. For example, if your message is "We're for world peace," you might sing a song about the world while hugging each other.**

Give teams time to determine how to become their messages. Then give each team one minute to send their message while the other teams try to guess what it is. Congratulate any teams that successfully send their messages. Ask:
- **How difficult was it to become the message?**

- **What's the difference between saying a message and actually being a message?**

Have kids read John 1:1-5, 14 in their groups.

Say: **"The Word" is Jesus. The Greek word for "word" is "logos." Logos can also be translated as "message." Read the passage again and substitute "message" for "Word."**

Ask:
- **How is Jesus Christ God's message?**
- **What is the message God sent in Jesus?**
- **Why is it important that Jesus not only spoke the message but was the message?**

Close by having each person share one part of God's message that is meaningful to him or her.

# JOHN
## 1:35-51

THEME:
Jesus, our power source

SUMMARY:
In this OBJECT LESSON, kids compare the power in batteries to the power of Jesus.

PREPARATION: Purchase or borrow four battery-operated toys like the ones in battery commercials on TV. These toys should be the type that move forward in some manner—not ones that remain stationary while making a noise, flashing lights, and so on. Purchase and install new batteries in two of the toys. Leave older batteries in the other toys but be sure the toys at least work. You'll also need Bibles.

Have kids form four teams. Give each team a toy as its "mascot" for a series of contests. Encourage kids to cheer for their mascots.

Use these contests or make up your own:

■ All toys race from a starting point to a finish line.

■ Determine which toy goes in the straightest direction.

■ Race with obstacles placed randomly in the path to see which toy gets the farthest.

When all the contests are completed, congratulate the team with the most successful mascot. Ask:

■ **What was the power source that "energized" your toys?**

■ **How did the amount of power left in your battery affect the success of your toy?**

Have kids read John 1:35-51 in their teams. As you ask the following questions, have kids first discuss their answers in their teams; then let teams take turns sharing their answers with the whole group. Ask:

■ **What was the power source that energized these men?**

■ **How was that power source like or unlike the one we used?**

■ **In what way is the power source described in the Bible available to us?**

■ **What kinds of things happen when a person is energized by this power source?**

■ **Describe a time when you have been energized by this**

**same power source.**

Close by challenging kids to remember their power source and become energized this week!

# JOHN
## 3:1-10

THEME:
New birth

SUMMARY:
In this LEARNING GAME, kids will shoot paper wads and examine what it means to be "born again."

PREPARATION: Gather scrap paper, a wastebasket, Bibles, and pencils.

Form teams of no more than three. Give teams each nine pieces of scrap paper and ask kids to wad each piece into a ball. Place a wastebasket in the center of the room. Have all teams gather in a circle around the wastebasket so that each team is standing about 10 feet away from it.

Say: **This activity is called the New-Birth Olympics. The object is for your team to throw as many paper wads as possible into the wastebasket. Each person on your team will have three chances to throw—there are nine separate "events" in these olympics. We'll take turns until we've completed all nine events.**

Have teams all shoot at the same

time for each event. Have teams each keep track of how many paper wads they shoot into the basket. Call out the following events:

■ **Close your eyes and shoot.**

■ **Look to your right as you shoot.**

■ **Use your left hand if you're right-handed, and vice versa.**

■ **Shoot over your left shoulder.**

■ **Shoot the paper wad from your mouth.**

■ **Shoot into an upside-down basket.**

■ **Hold hands with someone and shoot holding the paper wad together.**

■ **Throw the paper wad in the air and bat it toward the basket.**

■ **Shoot the paper wad with your foot.**

After the competition, congratulate the winners, then say: **The goal of these events was to shoot the wad into the basket. But that goal was difficult— sometimes impossible—to achieve because our assigned methods were ineffective. We need new ways of shooting paper wads if we're going to be effective.**

Give teams each a Bible, a sheet of paper, and a pencil. Ask teams to read John 3:1-10, then discuss and write responses to these questions:

■ **What is the kingdom of God?**

■ **How is entering the kingdom like getting a paper wad into the basket?**

■ **There are several ways to get a paper wad into the basket, but John 3:1-10 teaches that there's only one way to get into the kingdom of God. Why do**

you suppose that's so?

■ **What do you think Jesus meant when he told Nicodemus that he needed to be born again?**

■ **What must you do to be "born again"?**

Have volunteers from each team share their responses. Then have one or two kids stand at the line and toss a paper wad into the wastebasket. Say: **Discovering what it means to be born again in Christ is a lot like discovering the best way to toss the paper wad into the basket. But with God, there is only one possible way to see his kingdom—through a new birth in Christ.**

# JOHN 3:16

THEME:
God's gift of Jesus

SUMMARY:
In this AFFIRMATION, kids will give "gifts" to other kids.

PREPARATION: Gather construction paper, markers, pencils, and a Bible.

Have everyone sit together in a circle. Tell group members to think of what Christmas presents they'd like to give to each person in the group if the cost didn't matter. Encourage kids to choose personal gifts based on their friends' interests and needs. For example, someone might give a friend a scholarship to a particular college, a set of loving parents, or a giant chocolate bar. Tell kids the sky's the limit, but no unkind gifts are allowed.

Give each person a sheet of construction paper, a marker, and a pencil. Tell group members to decorate their papers to look like gift boxes and to put their names at the top. Have kids then pass their "boxes" to the right. Each time kids get a new box, have them read the name at the top, write in pencil (or marker, if there's enough room) the gift they'd like to give to that person, and sign their name next to their gift idea. Continue passing the boxes until everyone has his or her own paper back.

Allow time for kids to read their boxes silently, then let volunteers read aloud their gift lists. Ask the gift givers to tell why they chose particular gifts for others in the room.

Close by reading aloud John 3:16. Ask kids to share what they think God would say if he were asked why he chose to give the gift of his Son over all the other gifts he might have given.

# JOHN
# 3:16-18

THEME:
God's love

SUMMARY:
In this OBJECT LESSON, kids compare eternity to the amount of time it takes to eat candy.

PREPARATION: You'll need Tootsie Pop suckers for everyone, paper, a pencil, and a Bible.

Give each person a Tootsie Pop. Ask for and record everyone's predictions on how many licks it will take to get to the chocolate center. Then have everyone begin licking. Tell kids to keep track of their own number of licks. No biting allowed!

After a few minutes have kids pause. Ask:

■ **Do you think you'll ever get to the middle?**

■ **How much longer do you think it will take?**

Read John 3:16-18 aloud. Ask:

■ **Because God loves us, we can have eternal life. A minute ago, it seemed like eternity until we'd get to the middle of our suckers. But how does eternity compare with the time licking to the middle of a sucker?**

■ **What do you think eternity will be like for Christians? for non-Christians?**

■ **In what ways can we plan for our eternity?**

Continue licking as you talk about God's loving provision for us for eternal life—which lasts a long, l-o-n-g time! If you have any Tootsie Pops left over, award the rest to the person coming closest to his or her number-of-licks prediction.

# JOHN
# 4:1-26

## THEME:

Jesus knows and loves us.

## SUMMARY:
In this LEARNING GAME, kids see how much they know about their partners and realize that Jesus knows everything about them.

PREPARATION: You'll need prizes as suggested below, paper, pencils, and a Bible.

Form pairs and have partners sit back to back. Give each person a pencil and a sheet of paper.

Say: **This is a contest to see how well you know your partner. Some people may have the advantage of knowing their partners better than others, but do the best you can in answering the questions.**

Read the following questions. Without allowing kids to confer with their partners, have them write their answers on their paper.

▪ **What is your partner's full name?**

▪ **On what street does your partner live?**

▪ **Does your partner have a job? If so, what does he or she do?**

▪ **What is your partner's favorite radio station?**

▪ **When was the last time your partner petted a dog?**

▪ **What's your partner's ring size?**

▪ **What was the first name of your partner's first-grade teacher?**

Have kids talk over their answers with their partners and count how many answers were correct. If the correct answer to a question is unknown (such as ring size or the teacher's name) no credit is given. Find out which pairs knew the most about each other and award funny prizes to the winners. For example, containers of Secret deodorant because this pair has no secrets from each other, a package of Twinkies because they're so much alike, or a roll of breath mints because these two are so close all the time.

Say: **It's impossible for any of us to know everything about another person. There are some things we don't even know about ourselves! Let's read about a woman who found someone who did know all about her.**

Read John 4:1-26, then have your group discuss what Jesus knew about the Samaritan woman and compare this to what Jesus knows about us. Also discuss how that should affect the way we live.

Say: **Jesus loved this woman in spite of the wrong things she'd done and in spite of the prejudice against her. He knew her and he loved her. This is the same way he knows and loves each of us.**

# JOHN
# 4:4-26

THEME:
Accepting others

SUMMARY:
In this DEVOTION, some kids will try to join a circle of other kids.

PREPARATION: Before the activity, prepare two 3×5 cards. On each card, write a different set of these instructions:

**Card #1**—Choose a spot to break into the circle. Whisper, "God is great" in the ear of the person to the right of the spot you've chosen. Whisper, "God is good" in the ear of the person to the left of the spot you've chosen. Then yell "Cowabunga!" to break into the circle.

**Card #2**—Choose a spot to break into the circle. Whisper, "Let's thank God" in the ear of the person to the right of the spot you've chosen. Whisper, "for this food" in the ear of the person to the left of the spot you've chosen. Then yell "Cowabunga!" to break into the circle.

EXPERIENCE
After everyone has arrived, recruit two volunteers to form a "minicircle" by placing their hands on each other's shoulders. Secretly show them each the Card #1 instructions and instruct them to resist anyone who doesn't follow the instructions exactly.

Say to the whole group: **The only way you can participate in this activity is by joining the minicircle formed by our two volunteers. And the only way to join the circle is by following the instructions I will show you. Once you're in the circle, don't allow anyone else to join unless they follow the exact instructions you did.**

Have kids line up. One at a time, have them each approach the circle. Show each person one set of instructions, randomly alternating the cards after every few people. Have kids each follow the instructions you show them and try to join the circle.

RESPONSE
When kids have all tried to join the circle, stop the activity and have everyone sit down in a circle. Ask:

■ **How did it feel to be excluded from the circle?**

■ **What was your attitude toward those in the circle?**

■ **How did those of you who did join the circle feel?**

■ **What was your attitude toward those who didn't make it in?**

Read aloud John 4:4-26. Say: **The Samaritan woman probably felt a lot like those of you who couldn't break into the circle. Some Jews refused to associate with Samaritans, even though the Samaritans had no control over their ethnic background.**

Ask:

■ **Have you ever avoided someone just because he or she was different from you? Why or why not?**

■ **Why do you think Jesus treated the Samaritan woman differently than other Jews would have?**

■ **What do Jesus' actions tell us about his attitude toward people who were different from him?**

CLOSING

Say: **Let's take a moment to celebrate and thank God for creating each of us to be uniquely different individuals.**

To close, have kids take turns completing this prayer about the person on their right: "Lord, thanks for giving *(name)* the unique ability of *(blank)*." For example, kids might finish the prayer by saying, "making others feel special," "making me smile," or "helping people learn more about you."

# JOHN
# 6:1-13

THEME:
Feeding the 5,000

SUMMARY:
In this PROJECT kids follow Jesus' example by providing an item for 5,000 people.

PREPARATION: Before your meeting, research the needs of various charities in your area or organizations that your church supports. Find several charities that can use 5,000 of one item. For example, a food bank might need 5,000 cans of food; an organization for the homeless might need 5,000 washcloths, toothbrushes, or bars of soap; or a mission agency might need 5,000 bottles of vitamins. Also research the cost of the items. Compile a list of three or more needs to present to your youth group. Bring a Bible to your meeting, too.

Read John 6:1-13 to your group and have kids determine where they might have seen 5,000 people before; for example, at a sporting event, a huge rally, and so on.

Say: **Five thousand is a lot of people, but Jesus was able to care for their needs. There are still people in need today. Let's follow Jesus' example and meet a need of 5,000 people.**

Tell your group about the needs you've researched and let them decide which need to meet. Then have kids plan how to gather, store, and distribute the 5,000 items. They may need to plan a fund-raiser or another event to gather items or contributions. Let kids be in charge of this and let your role be that of a facilitator and guide.

When the 5,000 items have been gathered, put them on display so everyone can see the fruits of the youth group's labor. You may even want to have a party to celebrate the success of all the hard work kids have done. (Be sure the cost of the party doesn't come out of the money raised for the needy.)

Again read John 6:1-13.

Say: **Each item here repre-**

sents one person that was fed when Jesus distributed the five loaves and two fish among the people. When Jesus multiplied the food for the 5,000, he demonstrated his love for those people. It's great to see how hard you've worked to show your love for others as well.

Distribute the goods as kids have arranged.

# JOHN
# 7:25-32, 45-49

**THEME:**
Questions about our faith

**SUMMARY:**
This LEARNING GAME focuses on silly questions, then moves on to serious questions kids have about Jesus and their faith.

PREPARATION: Gather 3×5 cards, pencils, and Bibles.

Have kids form pairs and give each pair a 3×5 card and a pencil.

Say: **Discuss with your partner questions that are always burning in your mind. Questions like "Why do guys wear ties?" "Why does Jell-O gel?" or "What makes yawning contagious?" Choose a question and write it on your card.**

After kids have written their questions, collect the cards, mix them up, then randomly distribute them again. Have each pair write a creative answer to the question they receive. Then gather the cards again and read the questions and answers aloud for all to enjoy.

Turn kids' attention to a portion of Scripture by having pairs read John 7:25-32, 45-49 together. Discuss what kinds of questions the guards might have had during these events and how the guards' questions might be like questions teenagers have about Jesus.

Encourage discussion and affirm kids for being willing to talk about questions regarding their beliefs.

**Note:** Try to avoid answering questions with pat answers. Encourage kids to look to the Bible for answers. Also provide additional resources, such as Bible dictionaries or commentaries, for them to study if they desire.

# JOHN
# 8:1-11

**THEME:**
God's perspective

**SUMMARY:**
In this AFFIRMATION, kids affirm each other's value as seen by God and others.

PREPARATION: Bring a package of Nickelodeon Gak (made by Mattel and sold in most toy departments), a Bible, newsprint, and a marker. Tape the newsprint in front of the room.

Take the Gak out of its package and toss it to a group member. Have kids pass it around and take a small piece to hold and play with during the discussion. (If you have a large group, bring two or more packages of Gak.) Ask:

■ **What would a little kid think about receiving this as a gift?**

■ **What might that child's parent think when the child received this as a gift?**

■ **Why do people have different opinions or perspectives about the same thing?**

Read John 8:1-11 and ask:

■ **What was the human point of view in this case?**

■ **What was Jesus' perspective?**

■ **Why was it different?**

Write the word "gak" on the newsprint, cross it out, and then write "gac."

Say: **If we change the spelling of "gak," we could say the letters now stand for "guilty as charged." That would be our point of view regarding all the things we've done wrong. But from God's perspective, these letters could stand for "grace at the cross."**

Have kids each take their Gak and give it to another person while completing this sentence about that person: "From God's point of view and my point of view, you're *(end sentence with a positive quality about that person)*." For example, someone might say, "From God's point of view and my point of view, you're a caring person" or "you're a real encouragement to those around you."

The person who has just been affirmed then takes the lump of Gak and affirms another person, giving him or her the Gak. Continue until there's one large lump of Gak and everyone has been affirmed.

Close by challenging kids to choose to believe and trust God's perspective for their lives.

# JOHN
# 8:1-11

**THEME:**
Forgiveness

**SUMMARY:**
In this SKIT, three teenagers struggle to ask God's forgiveness for terrible mistakes.

## THE POWER TO FORGIVE

SCENE: Three teenagers stand facing the audience. They're each praying aloud to God. After each person speaks, he or she freezes in position while the next person speaks.

PROPS: You'll need Bibles for the discussion afterward.

CHARACTERS:
**Sarah**
**Lynnea**
**Tremaine**

SCRIPT
**Sarah:** Dear God, I've gotten myself into trouble before, but nothing like the trouble I'm in now. You see...I was with this guy last night and...and... *(sud-*

*denly frustrated)* do I <u>have</u> to tell you what I did? I really don't want to admit it—besides, you're God, and you already know, don't you? *(Freezes.)*

**Lynnea:** Father, I've done a terrible thing. I really didn't mean to, but I just got so caught up in the moment. I was out with friends yesterday, and we saw Tremaine at the mall. Now *you* know I like Tremaine, but my friends, well, they don't like him all that much... *(Freezes.)*

**Tremaine:** All right, God, I give up. I don't know where else to turn. I just did a stupid thing, and I feel awful. I didn't want to, but those people, they made fun of me and called me names. How else could I prove them wrong? *(Freezes.)*

**Sarah:** OK, OK. I'll admit my mistake, Lord. I slept with Tremaine. I know it's wrong, Lord, but I really *like* Tremaine. And he really likes me—at least he *did.* Now I don't know *what* he thinks of me. *(Pause.)* I shouldn't have come on so strong. I didn't think he'd actually want to go through with it—he's always been so polite and patient... *(Freezes.)*

**Lynnea:** So when my friends started teasing Tremaine and saying he was, you know, gay, I just joined in. I didn't want to, Lord, but these were my friends—I didn't want to look like some goody-two-shoes... *(Pause.)* You're right, as always, Lord. I shouldn't have let my friends influence what I know is right. But now what do I say to Tremaine? *(Freezes.)*

**Tremaine:** I guess it was wrong to let others' taunts bother me. But it hurt, Lord. And besides, Sarah and I really care for each other. I just didn't expect that she'd really want to sleep with me. I should've been strong and said no like I always told myself I would. Now what do I say to Sarah? *(Freezes.)*

**Sarah, Lynnea, and Tremaine:** *(In unison)* Dear God, how will you ever forgive me?
*(All three close their eyes and bow their heads. After a moment, they look up, smiling.)*

**Sarah, Lynnea and Tremaine:** *(In unison)* Thank you, God.
*(All three turn to each other and begin hugging each other while saying, "I'm Sorry" or "Please forgive me." Then they freeze in a hug.)*

If you use this skit as a discussion starter, here are possible questions:

■ **When have you felt like these characters?**

■ **Why is it difficult to ask God for forgiveness?**

■ **What does Jesus' forgiveness in John 8:1-11 tell us about the breadth and power of Jesus' forgiveness?**

# JOHN
## 8:12

### THEME:

Jesus, the light

### SUMMARY:
In this DEVOTION, kids compare the light of a candle to Jesus.

PREPARATION: Gather candles, matches, and a Bible. Bring popcorn for refreshments.

EXPERIENCE

Have your regular program in a totally dark room. Start with songs, a game, announcements, and refreshments (serve popcorn).

RESPONSE

When all this is done, light a small candle. After so long in the dark, the light should be a welcome relief. Ask kids to look around the room. Point out the mess made by the popcorn and the other activities. Ask:

■ **How did you like meeting in the dark? Explain.**

■ **Was it easy to work together? Why or why not?**

■ **Did we trust each other in the dark?**

■ **How is meeting in the dark like living without Jesus?**

Read aloud John 8:12. Ask:

■ **How is this candle like Jesus?**

■ **What's good about having God's light in our lives?**

■ **What's difficult about it?**

CLOSING

Pass out candles, then pass the light around. Ask:

■ **How does our presence in the world affect the lives of people around us?**

■ **Do you think people enjoy having a light near them? Why or why not?**

# JOHN
## 8:31-36

### THEME:

Truth and freedom

### SUMMARY:
Being bound while attempting various tasks helps kids understand being bound by sin in this LEARNING GAME.

PREPARATION: Gather strips of soft cloth to tie hands and ankles and to make blindfolds. (Strips torn from an old sheet will work nicely.) You'll need enough strips for each person to have one. Also bring a Bible. Before the game, clear the room of obstacles such as tables and chairs.

Distribute the cloth strips to kids and have them form three groups. Instruct one group to loosely tie each other's hands behind their backs (you'll have to help the last person). Have another group use the strips to loosely tie each person's ankles together. Have the remaining group use its strips as blindfolds.

Say: **I'm going to call out various actions. You're to do each one in the best way you can.**

**Shake hands.**

**Touch your toes.**

**Walk across the room.**

**Wave to a friend.**

**Take one giant step.**

**Sit cross-legged on the floor.**

**Hop on one foot.**

**Point to the west.**

**Wink at someone.**

Have kids remain as they are as you ask:

■ **What kinds of problems are you having? Explain.**

■ **What can be done to solve these problems?**

■ **This game has taken away some of your freedom. What kinds of things bind us and take away our freedom in real life?**

■ **How can we be free from these things?**

Read John 8:31-36, then walk around the room freeing kids from their bonds.

Form discussion groups of up to five and have kids talk about these questions:

■ **What kind of freedom does Jesus give?**

■ **What does it mean to be free?**

■ **What is truth?**

Before closing, allow time for discussion groups to share with the large group any insights they gain.

# JOHN
# 9:1-34

## THEME:

Being important

## SUMMARY:
This LEARNING GAME focuses on the difference between what makes someone important in the world's eyes and in God's eyes.

PREPARATION: You'll need a stack of 3×5 cards, pencils, and a Bible.

Give each person three 3×5 cards and a pencil.

Say: **Think of things that make a person important. Perhaps it's being a millionaire or driving a new sports car. Or it could be doing something big, such as finding a cure for cancer or winning the Super Bowl. On each of your cards, write one thing that would make you feel very important.**

When kids have completed their cards, have them form pairs.

Say: **With your partner, play Rock, Paper, Scissors. The person who wins may choose one of his or her partner's cards.**

If kids don't know how to play Rock, Paper, Scissors, explain that on the count of three, kids must show either a "rock" (fist), "scissors" (two fingers), or "paper" (a flat hand). Rock breaks scissors, scissors cut paper, and paper covers rock. If kids show the same thing, they should play again until one beats the other.

Have kids find new partners and play the game again. Each winner may choose one of the loser's cards. Play for up to five minutes, then see who has the most cards. Have this person read his or her cards aloud so everyone can hear how important he or she is. Ask:

■ **If all you had were the items listed on the cards you have left (if you have any left at all), how would that make you feel about yourself?**

Next, have the winning person read the first four verses of John 9:1-34 and pass the Bible to someone else to read the next four verses. Have kids continue reading and passing the Bible until the entire passage has been read. Ask:

■ **Based on the things we wrote on our cards, how would you say we define "being important"?**

■ **From John 9:1-34, how would you say Jesus defined "being important"?**

■ **How do our definitions of importance compare with Jesus' definition?**

■ **How important do you think the blind man felt after Jesus healed him?**

■ **In Jesus' time, what made a person important in the eyes of the religious leaders?**

■ **What was it about Jesus that made the leaders think he wasn't important?**

■ **What important things about Jesus did these men not understand?**

Close by having kids tell one way they can help another person feel important in the next week.

# JOHN
# 10:10

THEME:
Giving thanks

SUMMARY:
Using this CREATIVE PRAYER, kids will give thanks through the alphabet.

PREPARATION: Before the activity, cut out squares of paper and put one letter of the alphabet on each one. You'll need a Bible, too.

Distribute the letters of the alphabet evenly among your group members. Read aloud John 10:10. Then ask kids to think of things that make life full.

Tell kids they're going to offer a group prayer of thanksgiving to God. Go through the alphabet, having each person stand when his or her letter is called and tell one thing beginning with that letter for which they're thankful; for example, apple pie, baby brothers, cars, or a drama team at school.

Afterward, see who can remember all the things kids mentioned in the group prayer.

# JOHN
# 11:1-43

**THEME:**
Friendship

**SUMMARY:**
In this LEARNING GAME, kids will discover qualities Jesus brings to a friendship.

PREPARATION: On separate 3×5 cards, write 10 qualities of a friend, such as loyalty or being a good listener, and 10 things friends do together, such as goofing off or talking on the phone. Place each card in a separate envelope and hide the envelopes in the room. You'll need Bibles, pencils, and paper.

When kids arrive, form groups of no more than six. Say: **People are always looking for the perfect friend. In this room, I've hidden sealed envelopes that contain information about a perfect friend. You'll have three minutes to find the envelopes, but don't open them.**

When all the envelopes have been found, ask kids to open them one at a time and read aloud the enclosed cards. Ask kids to identify other qualities of a perfect friend and things to do with a friend. Ask:

■ **How is this hunt for envelopes like or unlike the hunt for friends? Explain.**

■ **Which of these qualities of a friend does Jesus bring to a friendship?**

■ **How do Jesus' qualities** compare with the qualities of friends you have now?

■ **How can you do with Jesus the things you'd do with a friend?**

Give each group a Bible, a pencil, and a sheet of paper. On their paper, have them make two columns—one labeled "Jesus" and the other labeled "Jesus' friends." Have groups each read aloud John 11:1-43. As groups read, have them list the friendship qualities of Jesus and his friends in the appropriate columns. Afterward, ask:

■ **How does Jesus show his friendship to us?**

■ **How do we show our friendship to Jesus?**

# JOHN
# 11:1-44

**THEME:**
Death

**SUMMARY:**
This ADVENTURE takes kids through a cemetery as they examine their feelings about death.

PREPARATION: Arrange for transportation for your group to a local cemetery. Bring a Bible along on the trip.

Take your youth group to a nearby cemetery. Have kids walk silently through the grounds by themselves or with a partner, reading grave markers. Remind kids to be respectful and subdued as they walk.

After 15 to 20 minutes, gather kids and have everyone sit together on the lawn. Have kids share anything they noticed during their walk, such as a large family buried together, touching words engraved into the stones, or the grave of a young child.

Next, have kids form pairs or trios and read John 11:1-44. Help kids debrief their experience by asking groups to discuss these questions:

■ **How do you think people feel when they come here to visit these graves?**

■ **How do you think Lazarus' sisters felt when Jesus came too late?**

■ **Jesus knew he could raise Lazarus. Why do you think he cried?**

■ **How do you feel about death?**

■ **How does (or would) being a Christian affect the way you feel about death?**

# JOHN
## 12:1-11

THEME:
Giving

SUMMARY:
Kids choose a gift to give and carry out their plan of action in this PROJECT.

PREPARATION: You'll need a Bible, newsprint, tape, and a marker. Tape the newsprint on the wall at the front of the room.

Read John 12:1-11 to your group. Say: **The perfume Mary poured over Jesus' feet cost about a year's wages. But Mary thought Jesus was worth this extravagance. Judas, on the other hand, was stingy toward Jesus. He was stealing money from Jesus and the disciples and thought about himself instead of Jesus when it came to extravagant gifts.**

Ask:

■ **In what ways do people today demonstrate stinginess toward Jesus?**

■ **In what ways are people extravagant toward Jesus?**

Say: **Sometimes, doing a simple act of service can be an extravagant gift. Let's find a way to give extravagantly to Jesus through a simple act of service to another person or group.**

Have kids brainstorm a variety of actions or gifts they could give. For example, they might treat several new mothers from the church to an afternoon at the movies. While the mothers are gone, some kids could entertain their children, while other kids could thoroughly clean these women's homes and prepare a nice meal for when the women and their families return. Or perhaps there's a church member who's been sick and homebound for a long period of time. Kids could write notes, bring flowers or meals, or even prepare a variety show to be performed in this person's home.

When kids have listed a variety

of options, have them vote on which one they'd like to do. When a decision has been made, guide kids in determining how to carry out the plan. Take action as soon as possible to keep kids enthusiastic.

# JOHN 12:12-19

THEME:
Heroes

SUMMARY:
In this AFFIRMATION, kids affirm others for heroic actions that demonstrate commitment to Jesus.

PREPARATION: Cut 8×11-inch sheets of construction paper into shields. These should be similar in shape to the shield on Superman's costume, which has a large S on it. Avoid using dark colors because writing won't show up on it. You'll need one shield for each person. Collect markers, pens, straight pins or safety pins, and a Bible.

When your meeting begins, ask:
■ **Who are your heroes?**
■ **How do you show your heroes your dedication to them?**
Have a volunteer read John 12:12-19 aloud. Ask:
■ **How were people showing Jesus they considered him a hero?**

■ **How do you show Jesus you consider him a hero?**
Say: **When we were young, many of us probably loved dressing up as our favorite superheroes. Today, let's take a moment to be children again and dress up as heroes to give us an opportunity to encourage others to be heroic in their actions toward each other.**
Give each person a paper shield and place the markers in a central location.
Say: **Write your name on one side of your shield. On the other side, draw your first initial very large, like the S on Superman's costume.**
Allow time for kids to do this, then say: **Now we're going to pass these shields around the room. When you receive someone else's shield, think about a heroic action you've seen this person take. Remember—we're thinking of "heroic" in terms of showing Jesus' love. Perhaps you've noticed a person in our group who always comes early to set up or stays late to straighten up our room. Or maybe when you were new here, another person welcomed you and sat with you during our meeting. Think of actions like these. Write a note on each person's shield, encouraging or thanking them for their actions.**
When kids have all been affirmed, have them pin their completed shields to their chests and wear them for the remainder of your meeting. Encourage kids to take their shields home as reminders to be heroes for Jesus.

# JOHN
## 12:20-26

**THEME:**
Jesus' death

**SUMMARY:**
In this OBJECT LESSON kids compare the various stages in the growth and usage of wheat to Jesus' life and death.

PREPARATION: Gather uncracked grains of wheat (most health-food stores carry this), a container of flour, a loaf of bread, a knife, butter or margarine, and a Bible. If you can find stalks of wheat at a farm or other location, bring these, too.

Talk about the various stages a kernel of wheat goes through before it becomes bread. The seed is planted, grows, then dies. When it grows again, many more seeds are produced. These seeds can either be planted again to grow more grain or gathered, threshed to separate out the chaff or unwanted parts, ground into flour, mixed with other ingredients, and baked to make bread. As you discuss the various stages, show kids the corresponding items.

Read John 12:20-26. Ask:

■ **What do you think Jesus meant by this?**

■ **How is what Jesus went through like or unlike the process a kernel of wheat goes through to produce bread?**

■ **How are we like grains of wheat?**

■ **How can we "plant" ourselves like wheat to grow more "seeds" for Jesus to harvest?**

Serve the bread with butter or margarine and encourage kids to reflect on Jesus' gift as they eat the bread. Give each person a kernel of wheat to serve as a reminder to plant themselves and create more seeds for Jesus to harvest.

# JOHN
## 13:1-17

**THEME:**
Service

**SUMMARY:**
This foot-theme PARTY is a fun way to remind kids that Jesus gave an example of love and service through washing his friends' feet.

PREPARATION: Plan a party with a foot theme. Create posters in the shape of large footprints to publicize the event. Gather food and other items as suggested in the activities below. You'll also need a Bible.

Welcome everyone to the party by having them remove their shoes and socks. Then proceed with the festivities! Here are suggested activities:

■ Have a footrace where all contestants run barefooted.

■ Have a foot shoelace-tying contest where kids tie their laces with their toes. Award the winner a blue ribbon to tie around his or her toe.

■ Contact a local dance school and invite ballerinas or tap dancers or cloggers to entertain with their fancy footwork. Perhaps an instructor could teach your kids a few steps in the dance.

■ Serve food with "foot" names, such as foot-long hot dogs and "Froot by the Foot." Have a sheet cake cut and frosted to look like a huge footprint.

■ Have volunteers stand behind a sheet with only their feet showing. See if others can guess the owner of each set of feet.

■ Let kids make casts of their feet in plaster of Paris.

■ To conclude the event, read and discuss John 13:1-17. Invite kids to wash each other's feet as a symbol of their desire to follow Jesus' example of service. Provide a couple of basins with warm, soapy water and several wash cloths and towels. Have kids take a cloth and wash the feet of one or more people.

As this can be embarrassing for some, don't force everyone to participate. Do, however, see that through your actions or those of student and adult leaders the feet of all kids participating are washed.

# JOHN
# 13:1-17

## THEME:
Service

## SUMMARY:
In this SKIT, two girls talk (as they clean up after a service project) about how hard it is to serve.

## YOUR SERVE

SCENE: Tanya and Gloria are cleaning up after helping their youth group paint the house of an elderly church member.

PROPS: You'll need a bucket of water, towels, and a Bible for the discussion after the skit. Also, both characters must wear shoes and socks for this skit.

CHARACTERS:
**Tanya**
**Gloria**

### SCRIPT
*(Tanya and Gloria enter, looking exhausted.)*
**Tanya:** I'm really beat...
**Gloria:** Yeah, that hot sun really takes a lot out of you.
**Tanya:** *(Plopping down into a chair)* This servant stuff really is tough.
**Gloria:** You're telling me. *(She helps Tanya remove her shoes.)* It's all work and no play.
**Tanya:** Too much dirt and sweat, if you ask me.
**Gloria:** *(Helping Tanya remove her socks)* I thought it would make

me feel good to help out.

**Tanya:** Me, too. I mean, I'm glad we're helping, but I just feel so tired and dirty.

**Gloria:** *(Gets a towel and begins to clean Tanya's feet using the water from the bucket.)* Yeah. I feel worse than after the youth group camping trip.

**Tanya:** *(Pointing to her feet)* And look at these feet! There's enough dirt here to plant a garden...
*(Pause.)*

**Gloria:** Do you think Mrs. Jordan appreciates our work?

**Tanya:** Who knows? She doesn't think all that clearly these days, y'know. And she doesn't hear too well, either.
*(Gloria finishes drying Tanya's feet, then the two switch positions. Tanya begins to help Gloria clean her feet.)*

**Gloria:** I'm not sure I want to come back tomorrow.

**Tanya:** I was thinking the same thing. I'm not cut out for this servant stuff. I really thought I'd feel good helping someone out. But it's not much fun if no one notices all the work we're doing...

**Gloria:** There's just no glory in serving.
*(Characters freeze.)*

Permission to photocopy this skit from *Youth Worker's Encyclopedia: NT* granted for local church use. Copyright © Group Publishing, Inc., Box 481, Loveland, CO 80539.

If you use this skit as a discussion starter, here are possible questions:

■ **Do you agree with Gloria's statement that there's no glory in serving? Why or why not?**

■ **How did the girls' actions demonstrate servanthood?**

■ **What does this skit say about having a servant's heart?**

■ **How can we apply the message of John 13:1-17 to this skit? to our lives?**

# JOHN
## 13:1-17

**THEME:**
Servanthood

**SUMMARY:**
Try this interesting twist on a foot-washing activity with this PROJECT.

PREPARATION: Ask kids to come to the activity with dirty or worn, old shoes. Gather different kinds and colors of shoe polish, rags, and brushes, as well as several pairs of brightly colored shoelaces. You'll also need a Bible.

Begin by reading aloud John 13:1-17. Tell kids that in Jesus' day, when guests entered a home after walking about on dusty paths, they would have their feet washed by the servants of that house. Jesus washed his disciples' feet to show them they should be servants to one another.

After discussing the meaning of servanthood, let the kids serve one another by "renewing" the shoes of a partner, either with a glowing shoeshine or with a new pair of colorful laces. Not only the shoes, but the whole group will feel renewed through serving one another.

# JOHN
## 13:31-35

**THEME:**
Love

**SUMMARY:**
In this PROJECT, kids create new things, just as Jesus gave a new commandment.

PREPARATION: Gather poster board, markers, a Bible, and newsprint. On the newsprint, write the questions given in the activity.

Form four groups and assign the following projects:

■ **Group 1** is to create a new breakfast cereal. Have them make up a slogan, design a package using poster board and markers, and produce (act out) a commercial for their new product.

■ **Group 2** will invent a new car design. Their finished product should include a picture, description, a slogan, and name for the car.

■ **Group 3** will create a new television show. They'll need to formulate a cast (using either people in the group or church, or famous actors), determine the general theme of the show, and prepare a brief clip of the show to perform.

■ **Group 4's** task is to create a new music group, complete with name, description, motto, and album cover. They should also include one verse of their latest hit.

Allow plenty of time for preparation. When everyone is ready, have groups each present their new item. Be sure to applaud loudly for each group.

Have groups remain intact and read John 13:31-35. Write the following questions on newsprint and post them in front of the room. Have kids discuss the questions in their groups.

■ **What was significantly new about what your group created?**

■ **What was new about Jesus' command?**

■ **What was significant about the timing of this command?**

■ **In what ways can you carry out the command in verse 34?**

■ **List four specific things your group will commit to doing this week to love others as Jesus loves you.**

# JOHN
## 14:1-4

**THEME:**
God's house

**SUMMARY:**
Touring model homes gets kids thinking about their eternal home in this ADVENTURE.

PREPARATION: Make arrangements for your group to tour several model homes in nearby areas of development. If your group is large, the construction company may appreciate your making an appointment for a tour. Bring a Bible with you.

As you tour the homes with your group, ask kids what they like about the homes and what changes they'd make if there were no financial restrictions. Let each person tell what his or her "dream home" would be like.

When the tour is over, gather everyone and read John 14:1-4. Ask:

■ **What do you picture when you hear the term "God's house"? Describe it.**

■ **How will God's house, as described in John 14:1-4, be better or different from the homes you toured? What do you hope your "room" will be like?**

■ **How does it make you feel to know that God is preparing a place just for you?**

Let kids know that while we don't know exactly what our rooms will be like, Christians are assured a special place in God's eternal home. Take time to thank God for getting these rooms ready.

# JOHN
## 14:6

**THEME:**
Jesus is the way to God.

**SUMMARY:**
Kids take photographs along various routes to the same location on this ADVENTURE about the one route to God.

PREPARATION: Plan a party at a local pizza restaurant or at someone's house. Before the event, determine three different routes to the location. Make these routes complicated, even taking kids in the wrong direction for a while. With your church as the starting point, write the directions you've decided upon. Photocopy as necessary, so that every group of four to five kids will have one of the three directions.

Borrow enough instant-print cameras so that each group will have one. Purchase and load film in the cameras. You'll also need a Bible and a prize for the winning group, such as gift certificates for ice-cream cones or hamburgers.

Arrange for several adults or responsible group members to be drivers for this event.

Have everyone meet at the church and form groups of four or five, depending upon how many cars and drivers you have. Give each team's driver a set of directions and a camera.

Say: **In order to ensure that**

you take the exact route to our final destination, you'll need to take pictures along the way to prove you were actually there. Every mile, stop the car at the nearest landmark, such as a restaurant or gas station, and take a picture of your group there. There's no prize for arriving first, but you must arrive within 30 minutes. Prizes will be awarded to the group with the most creative photographs of their trip.

Send kids on their way and go to the destination to wait.

When everyone arrives, have each group tell about their journey and show their pictures. Decide which team gets the prize for most creative photographs and make your awards.

While kids eat their pizza, see if anyone can think of other routes they could have taken to the destination. Talk about the variety of routes people can take in life. Ask if anyone can think of a place that can be reached in only one way. (Usually even remote places can be reached by walking and by helicopter.)

Close out your adventure by having kids form discussion groups of no more than four. Have groups read John 14:6 and answer these questions before they leave:

■ **If you took photographs of the routes people have taken to reach God, what would those pictures show?**

■ **How do a person's actions show he or she believes Jesus is the only possible route?**

■ **Why do you think Jesus claims to be the only way to God? What do you think about Jesus' claim? Explain.**

■ **How does what you believe about Jesus' claim in John 14:6 affect the way you live?**

VARIATION: If you're unable to find enough instant-print cameras, give each group a tape recorder instead. Have kids record the voices of people along their route, such as a gas station attendant, a convenience store clerk, and so on. Kids might also use video cameras, if they're available.

# JOHN
# 14:6

THEME:
Truth

SUMMARY:
In this DEVOTION, kids will examine the difficulty of being truthful about ourselves.

PREPARATION: You'll need a Bible.

EXPERIENCE
Form two equal lines facing each other. Read aloud John 14:6. Say: **Philosophers say truth is a statement or an idea, but Jesus says truth is a person. Jesus is the truth. There is nothing false or hidden in him. He is completely honest and truthful with us. It's hard for us to be completely honest and truthful with others because when we've**

been honest and truthful...

■ people have laughed at us.

■ people have betrayed us.

■ people have hurt us.

■ people have misunderstood us.

Say: **This is a safe place. We can trust each other not to laugh, not to betray, not to hurt, and not to misunderstand. We can see truth in our faces. Stand exactly across from someone in the other line. Every time I say "move," move so you're facing someone new. Try to always keep eye contact with the person across from you. Let's do this in silence, except for the things I say.**

Read aloud the following questions, leaving time for kids to think about them:

Say: **Think about...**

■ **How much do you know about this person? Move.**

■ **Does this person know the real you? Move.**

■ **What would you like to learn about this person? Move.**

■ **What's the most mysterious thing about this person? Move.**

■ **What could you do to get to know this person better? Move.**

■ **What keeps you from showing more of who you are to this person?**

RESPONSE

Have kids form a circle and hold hands. Ask:

■ **How did it feel to think about revealing your true self?**

■ **How did it feel to think about really knowing others?**

■ **How can we be more gen-**uine in our relationships?

Say: **Jesus has called us to be like him, and that includes being truthful about ourselves with one another. Just think of how free we would be to care about each other if we allowed ourselves to really be known for who we are! Jesus has set us free to celebrate ourselves—to share who we are with each other.**

CLOSING

Close with prayer, asking God to help young people be truthful with each other.

# JOHN
## 14:7-14

THEME:
Fathers

SUMMARY:
Dads join in this OVER-NIGHTER with activities based on a "fathers" theme.

PREPARATION: Plan an overnight activity with a father theme. Invite dads (or dad representatives, such as stepfathers, grandfathers, uncles, or male family friends) to join kids for the event. Gather supplies as needed for suggested activities and a Bible.

Begin by welcoming everyone to the event and having each group member introduce his or her father or father representative.

Then lead the group in a variety of "dad" activities such as:

■ Show slides (or pictures mounted on poster board and posted around the room) of famous fathers and have everyone guess their identities. These could include George Washington (the father of our country), the fathers of church staff members, television or movie dads, and so on.

■ Have a contest for dads to see how much they know about their kids. Ask questions about music, clothes, hobbies, food, sports, school, and so on. Reverse the game and have kids see how much they know about their dads.

■ Make root beer floats using Dad's root beer and ice cream.

■ Have father/teenager pairs compete in a timed obstacle course based on stereotypical-dad activities. For example, teenagers must push a lawn mower around the parking lot, then dads must hit a golf ball into a hole, teenagers have to hammer three nails into a plank, then dads and teenagers must toss a football back and forth four times, and so on. Award a prize to the pair with the quickest time.

■ Read or act out humorous sections from Bill Cosby's book, *Fatherhood* (Doubleday Publishing Company, 1986). **Note:** Be sure to preview any sections you'll use to make sure they're appropriate for your youth group.

■ Have kids work with their fathers to compile a list of characteristics for the perfect father. Discuss similarities and differences between earthly fathers and our heavenly Father, God. Have pairs read John 14:7-14 and talk about how each person is like or unlike their earthly father, and how they'd like to be more like their heavenly Father.

# JOHN
## 14:15-24

THEME:
Jesus is the way to God.

SUMMARY:
In this LEARNING GAME, kids try to reach a prize by stepping on bits of tape.

PREPARATION: Before your meeting, clear chairs, tables, and other obstacles from the center of the room. Place a chair against one wall where space has been cleared. Place 2- to 3-inch strips of masking tape randomly on the floor. Kids will be stepping from tape to tape from various points in the room heading toward the chair, so arrange tape strips so that some are close together while others require a bit of a jump for kids to reach for them. Don't place any tape within five feet of the chair.

Gift-wrap a Bible and place it on the chair. You may want to put the Bible in a box before wrapping so it won't be obvious what the package contains.

When kids arrive, say: **The person who can figure out how to reach the prize while always stepping on a piece of**

**tape wins the prize.**

Let kids attempt to reach the prize. Don't allow them to pick up and move pieces of tape. (If your group is large, have several kids at a time moving about the area.) After all have tried, acknowledge their efforts but declare no winner.

Go over to the area where there's no tape and add one long piece of tape reaching to the prize. Now have a volunteer step on the tape pieces to reach the prize. Have that person open the present and read John 14:15-24 to the group. Ask:

■ **How is God like the prize you were trying to reach in this game?**

■ **The only way to reach the prize was with a bridge. How is Jesus like a bridge to God?**

■ **How do people today try to reach God? Why do these ways fail?**

■ **How does Jesus tell us to show our love for him?**

Have each person tell one way he or she will be obedient to Jesus' teaching in the next week.

PREPARATION: Gather 3×5 cards, pencils, newsprint, a marker, tape, and a Bible. Write the following open-ended statements on the newsprint and tape this in front of the room:

■ I'm worried that...
■ I'm afraid of...
■ My heart hurts when...

Give each person three 3×5 cards and a pencil. Have kids work alone to complete the sentences written on the newsprint. When everyone has completed this, read John 14:26-27.

Say: **Jesus wants us to have peace in our hearts, so he has left the Holy Spirit as our comforter and helper. Let's ask for peace, comfort, and help from God, who cares about our concerns and feelings.**

Have kids form pairs and share what they've written on their cards. Have kids pray for the concerns of their partners. Then have kids complete this sentence with their partners: "I feel the Holy Spirit's care most strongly when ... " Have partners thank God for showing his love in this way.

# JOHN
# 14:26-27

THEME:
The Holy Spirit

SUMMARY:
Kids pray for the concerns of a partner in this CREATIVE PRAYER.

# JOHN
# 15:1-4

THEME:
Jesus, the vine

SUMMARY:
Kids compare trees to Jesus and their relationship with him in this OBJECT LESSON.

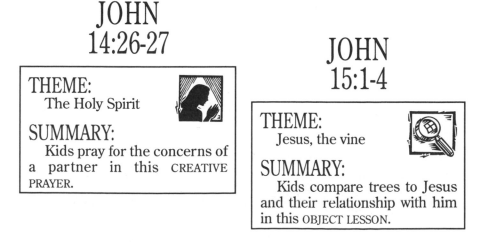

PREPARATION: Select a park, the church grounds, or another location where there are several large trees growing. Fruit trees would be ideal, but other trees will work as well. You'll need several Bibles, too.

Take your group to the selected tree location. Form groups of no more than five and have each group select a tree. Have kids lie under the trees, looking up at the branches. Have a volunteer in each group read John 15:1-4, then have kids answer questions about themselves and their trees in their groups.

Say: **Imagine this tree is a picture of Christ and his followers.** Ask:

■ **Which part of the tree would you label as Christ? Explain.**

■ **Which part would be his followers? Why?**

Have kids look for branches that are dead and need pruning. Ask:

■ **Why do branches die?**

■ **How might someone become spiritually dead, like a dead branch?**

Look for new growth. Ask:

■ **In what ways have you experienced new growth spiritually?**

Look for evidence that the tree is reproducing, such as seeds or fruit. Ask:

■ **What areas of your Christian life are producing fruit?**

Have each person choose a branch that is most like him or her spiritually and explain why they've chosen this branch. For example, someone might say, "This branch

is like me because it has lots of new growth, and I've been growing a lot in my faith recently."

Close by having groups each form a circle around their tree and pray that they'll grow in Christ, the true vine (or tree!).

# JOHN
# 15:5-11

THEME:
Jesus, the vine

SUMMARY:
Kids will act out motions in this CREATIVE READING.

PREPARATION: Prepare enough plant cuttings for each person to have one. You'll need a Bible, too.

Tell group members you're going to read and act out John 15:5-11 (from Today's English Version), and they're to repeat everything you say and do. Read aloud the passage and include the motions indicated in parentheses. Pause after each phrase-and-motion combination to allow time for it to be repeated. Say:

**I am the vine,** *(make a swaying motion)*

**and you** *(point to group)*

**are the branches.** *(Hold arms outstretched from shoulders.)*

**Whoever remains in me,** *(hug person next to you)*

**and I in him,** *(get person next to you to hug you)*

**will bear much fruit;** *(make a*

*lifting motion)*

**for you can do nothing** *(wave hands in front of you)*

**without me.** *(Cross arms, turn back on group.)*

**Whoever does not remain in me** *(turn and gently push away person you hugged)*

**is thrown out like a branch** *(make a throwing motion)*

**and dries up;** *(make a withering motion)*

**such branches are gathered up** *(make a gathering motion)*

**and thrown into the fire,** *(make a throwing motion)*

**where they are burned.** *(Jump away from the fire as if you were burned.)*

**If you remain in me** *(hug person next to you)*

**and my words remain in you,** *(get person next to you to hug you)*

**then you will ask anything you wish,** *(reach out hand, palm up)*

**and you shall have it.** *(Close hand, bring to chest.)*

**My Father's glory is shown** *(raise hands to heaven)*

**by your bearing much fruit;** *(hold arms out, lifting)*

**and in this way you become my disciples.** *(Put your arms around the people who are standing next to you.)*

**I love you** *(place your crossed hands on your chest)*

**just as the Father** *(point to heaven)*

**loves me;** *(point to self)*

**remain in my love.** *(Put arms around those people near you.)*

**If you obey my commands,** *(make emphasizing gesture on "obey")*

**you will remain in my love,** *(put arms around those near you)*

**just as I have obeyed** *(point to self)*

**my Father's commands** *(point to heaven)*

**and remain in his love.** *(Hug self.)*

**I have told you this so that my joy may be in you** *(take someone's hands and dance that person around)*

**and that your joy may be complete.** *(Jump around and cheer.)*

After the reading, give each person a plant cutting. Ask kids to think about what chance these cuttings have to survive without being connected to the plant or without having roots. Tell group members that we, too, need to be connected—to Christ. Ask kids to think of ways they're connected to Christ during the upcoming week.

# JOHN
## 15:10-11; 16:24

**THEME:**
Joy

**SUMMARY:**
In this PROJECT, kids produce a video to bring joy to others.

PREPARATION: Arrange for your group to visit a nursing home. You'll need a Bible, pencils, and paper. Afterward you'll need a video camera.

When your group meets together to visit the nursing home, read John 15:10-11; 16:24. Tell kids that this visit is the beginning of a project to bring joy to the residents of the nursing home.

Say: **During your visit, find out what various residents would like to see again. Since most aren't able to leave the home, they may miss seeing kids playing in a park, the ocean, their homes, and so on. Make the information you gather as specific as possible. Be sure to write it all down.**

Explain that after the visit, kids will work together to videotape as many of the requested scenes as possible. Don't have kids tell residents what they'll be doing in case kids are unable to locate some scenes.

After the visit, have kids compile their information and determine which scenes they can record. Encourage kids to be creative. For example, if a resident expressed the wish to see the ocean again, and you live in Arizona, try recording the shore of a lake. Then let kids begin recording. Also feel free to ask for help from friends or relatives in other parts of the country.

When the video is finished, arrange another visit to the home for a special showing. Leave the video as a gift of joy to those living there.

# JOHN
# 15:12-16

THEME:
Friends

SUMMARY:
Kids share songs about friendship, then tell others how they personify these songs in this MUSIC IDEA/AFFIRMATION.

PREPARATION: Before the meeting, ask kids to bring a favorite song about friendship to share with the group. Specify what kind of equipment will be available, such as a CD player or a cassette player, and have that equipment set up for the meeting. If you like, have kids print key phrases from the song they'll be bringing on an overhead transparency so everyone can listen for those words while the music plays.

Tape a sheet of newsprint to the front wall and have a marker there. Bring a Bible to the meeting, too.

Let kids take turns playing the songs they brought to share. Write the name of each song on the newsprint before it is played, then have the person who brought the song briefly tell what it has to do with friendship. If several people have brought the same song, have them all share before the song is played to avoid repeats.

After a song is played, encourage kids to share their comments about the song. Did it remind them of a special friend or time in their lives? What feelings did it bring out?

When all songs have been played, have a volunteer read John 15:12-16. Talk about the similarities between the friends described in the songs and the friends God calls us to be. Ask:

■ **What makes a good friend?**

After your discussion, have kids form groups of no more than five and sit in circles around the room.

Say: **Let's encourage each other in the area of friendship by using the songs we've heard. Take turns having each person in your group sit in the middle of your circle. When a person is sitting in the middle, everyone else can say a song title or a line from a song that reminds them of this person and explain why; for example, "Alondra, the Michael W. Smith song 'Friends' reminds me of you because you've been a faithful friend to me for a long time."**

**You can refer to the list of songs on the wall if you can't remember all the songs we heard.**

Remind kids to be positive in their comments to each other. Continue until each person has been affirmed by his or her group.

# JOHN 15:12-17

**THEME:**
Sacrificial love

**SUMMARY:**
Kids write stories for each other and younger children in this PROJECT.

PREPARATION: You'll need a copy of *The Way of the Wolf,* by Martin Bell (Ballantine Books, 1983) or another story that illustrates sacrificing something for a friend. You'll also need a Bible, lined paper, and pens.

Read the story "Barrington Bunny," from *The Way of the Wolf,* (or any other story that illustrates sacrificing something for a friend) to your group. Then have a volunteer read John 15:12-17. Discuss how the story illustrates the passage.

Distribute paper and pens, then say: **The story we read is only one example of expressing a biblical truth through a modern story. Even Jesus shared his message by telling stories to help others understand more clearly. Let's make a book of stories or poems to help young kids in our church understand Jesus better.**

Have kids use John 15:12-17 as the basis for their stories. If kids are unsure about their writing talents, have them think about how the passage could be explained through something that's happened to them or someone they know. This can then be made into a story.

When all stories are completed, compile them into a book and make photocopies for the children's Sunday school teachers. Be sure to keep a few copies in your meeting room so kids can read what others wrote.

**Note**: If any group members have access to a computer, see if they'd be interested in inputting the stories to make a nicer finished product. Kids with artistic talents may want to include illustrations for the readers as well. This project can be as detailed as teenagers want.

# JOHN
# 15:13

## THEME
Sacrifice

## SUMMARY:
Use this DEVOTION to help kids understand Jesus' sacrifice for us.

PREPARATION: You'll need newspaper and a Bible.

EXPERIENCE
Form groups of three or four. Tell kids to imagine that your youth group is on a cruise and the boat is sinking. Each small group has access to a lifeboat, but it won't hold everyone. One person in each group must choose to be left be- hind to save the rest of the passengers. Encourage kids to each convince their group why they should be left behind to save the others.

RESPONSE
After five minutes, tell kids that a rescue helicopter has flown in to save them all. Then ask:

■ **How did it feel to try to convince others that you should be the one left behind?**

■ **How do you think your attitude would change if you really were on a sinking ship?**

Read aloud John 15:13. Ask:

■ **How is Jesus like a person who stays behind on a sinking ship so that others can be saved?**

■ **Why do you think Jesus loved us enough to die for us?**

■ **Who are friends that you'd be willing to die for? Why would you be willing to die for them?**

■ **What are ways we can show Jesus' sacrificial love in all our friendships?**

CLOSING
Give everyone a sheet of newspaper and have them all make paper boats (see diagram) to take home as a reminder of Jesus' sacrificial love for them.

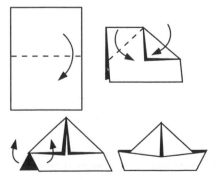

# JOHN
## 16:32-33

### THEME:

God's peace

### SUMMARY:
Kids focus on their need to be close to God in this DEVOTION.

PREPARATION: Plan to meet in a room that can be completely darkened. It may be necessary to cover windows with dark paper. You'll need a candle, matches, and a basket. For each person, you'll need a postcard, a pen, and a postage stamp.

### EXPERIENCE

Form a circle and have everyone hold hands. Turn out all the lights. Say: **Let go of one another's hands and walk to a place away from everyone else. Please remain silent.**

Pause for kids to move, then allow several moments of silence.

Say: **This may be how the disciples felt when, just before he was taken away, Jesus told them, "Listen to me; a time is coming when you will be scattered, each to his own home. That time is now here. You will leave me alone, but I am never really alone, because the Father is with me."**

**The pains and pressures in our lives can make us feel scattered and far away from God's love and his peace. Take time now to think of things that make you feel scattered and far away from God.**

Have a full minute of silence, then light the candle.

Say: **Quietly walk toward the light to form our circle again as we hear Jesus' words of peace from John 16:32-33: "I told you these things so that you can have peace in me. In this world you will have trouble, but be brave! I have defeated the world." Jesus offers us peace as we follow him.**

### RESPONSE

Have kids form pairs. Say: **Tell your partner what you were thinking and feeling when you stood alone in the dark.**

Have kids share with their partners an area in which they need to find God's peace in their own lives. Give each person a postcard, a stamp, and a pen and have kids write their partner's name and address on it. Then have kids each write a note to remind their partners of God's peace and strength to defeat problems. Kids shouldn't show their partners what they've written.

### CLOSING

Have the group form a circle again. Place a basket in the center of the circle. Say: **Let's take turns walking to the basket and dropping our postcards in it. As you take your turn, silently pray for your partner.**

When all postcards have been placed in the basket, close with prayer asking for God's peace and love in our lives. Mail the postcards this week!

# JOHN
## 17:20-23

**THEME:**
Unity

**SUMMARY:**
This CREATIVE READING for the entire group focuses on being one with God and other Christians.

PREPARATION: Make enough photocopies of the "Creative Reading for John 17:20-23" (p. 159) for each person to have one. Each person will need a pencil, too.

Distribute pencils and photocopies of the handout. Have kids read through and mark which passages they'll be reading, then begin!

**Note:** If a line from the reading goes unclaimed (for example, if no one has hair reaching past his or her shoulders), then go ahead and read that line for the group.

# JOHN
## 18:15-18, 25-27

**THEME:**
Peer pressure

**SUMMARY:**
This CREATIVE READING compares the pressure Peter felt to deny Christ to the pressures kids feel today.

PREPARATION: Photocopy the "Creative Reading for John 18:15-18, 25-27" handout (p. 160). Select volunteers to read the parts and give each reader a handout. Have them practice several times before the meeting.

**Note:** The role of Reader 1 is written for a girl, and Reader 3 for a guy. If you choose members of the opposite gender to read these roles, be sure to change the pronouns in their scripts.

After the reading, discuss how Peter's fear of letting others know he was Jesus' follower is like the fear of standing up to peer pressure. Encourage kids to stand up for their beliefs. Remind them that Jesus forgave Peter, and Jesus will forgive failures to stand for him today, too.

# JOHN
## 19:1–20:18

**THEME:**
Easter

**SUMMARY:**
During this RETREAT, kids take on the roles of those present at Jesus' death and resurrection.

PREPARATION: Plan a retreat with an Easter theme. (The retreat doesn't need to be over Easter weekend, but it would be a unique way of celebrating the holiday.) You'll need newsprint, a marker, name tags, and a Bible. Also gather supplies as suggested in the activities.

# CREATIVE READING FOR JOHN 17:20-23

**Everyone:** Jesus prayed, "I pray for these followers, but I am also praying for all those who will believe in me because of their teaching."

**Those wearing blue:** All those years ago, Jesus was praying for me and for you (point to others), and you, and you!

**Those with less than 50 cents in their pockets:** You mean Jesus was talking to God about me?

**Those wearing socks:** Not me. I'm not in the Bible.

**Those not wearing socks:** Yes, you are—because Jesus was praying for everyone who would believe in him in the future. That's now! If you believe, he was talking about you!

**Everyone:** Jesus continued, "Father, I pray that they can be one. As you are in me and I am in you, I pray that they can also be one in us. Then the world will believe that you sent me."

**Those who have jobs:** Being unified means we need to work together. This is a group effort.

**Those with hair reaching past their shoulders:** He says we need to be one, so others can believe. That's a lot of responsibility on our shoulders.

**Those wearing jeans:** Yeah, like we need to be loving and understanding of each other so that those watching us can know who we're following.

**Those shorter than 5½ feet:** They'll see Christ in our actions, not just in what we say.

**Everyone:** Jesus then said, "I have given these people the glory that you gave me so that they can be one, just as you and I are one."

**Those with one or more pierced ears:** I hear Jesus saying he's helping us to be one.

**Those in tennis shoes:** He helps us by his example here on earth. Jesus knows what it's like to walk in my shoes!

**Those who can drive a car:** He helps us through his words in the Bible. It's like a road map to life!

**Those who play an instrument:** He helps us by giving us guidance through the Holy Spirit. That's like a conductor showing everyone where they fit into the music.

**Everyone:** God wants us to be unified as one with him. He's given us the resources; now it's up to us to follow through!

# CREATIVE READING FOR JOHN 18:15-18, 25-27

READERS:
**Narrator**
**Girl**
**Peter**
**Reader 1**
**Reader 2**
**Reader 3**
**Servant**

**Narrator:** After Jesus was arrested, Simon Peter and another one of Jesus' followers went along after Jesus. This follower knew the high priest, so he went with Jesus into the high priest's courtyard. But Peter waited outside near the door. The follower who knew the high priest came back outside, spoke to the girl at the door, and brought Peter inside. The girl at the door spoke to Peter.

**Girl:** Aren't you also one of that man's followers?

**Peter:** No, I am not!

**Reader 1:** *(Pretending to talk on phone)* He's totally awesome—I mean, like, I can't believe he asked me out to the party of the year! Yeah, I know everyone will be drinking. Well... like, what's a drink or two? I have to impress this guy, and he won't think I'm cool if I just stand there without a drink! I mean, these are the kinds of things everyone expects, aren't they? Besides, everyone does it!

**Narrator:** It was cold, so the servants and guards had built a fire and were standing around it, warming themselves. Peter also was standing with them, warming himself. They spoke to him...

**Narrator, Girl, and Servant:** Aren't you one of that man's followers?

**Peter:** *(Louder than last time)* No, I am not.

**Reader 2:** It's not really cheating. I'm just helping him out. Everybody works together on these tests. Maybe that's not what the teacher had in mind, but this way we're all working together, helping each other. So how can that be bad?

**Narrator:** One of the servants of the high priest was there. This servant was a relative of the man whose ear Peter had cut off. The servant spoke...

**Servant:** Didn't I see you with him in the garden?

**Peter:** *(Very loudly)* No. I am not!

**Reader 3:** You're just *supposed* to—I mean, everyone is always trying to score on a date. That's what dating's for, isn't it? Besides the girls expect it. If I didn't try, they'd think something was wrong with me!

**Narrator:** At once a rooster crowed.

**All:** *(Crow once loudly.)*

---

Begin your retreat by reading John 19 aloud. As the name of each character in the chapter is read, list it on newsprint. Also include groupings of people such as the priests, soldiers, and crowds. Although the disciples aren't listed, add them to the list after the reading.

After the reading, explain that during this retreat the group will be remembering Jesus' death and resurrection by assuming the roles of various people involved in this scene. Assign or let kids pick from the listed roles. If your group is small, focus on the major roles. Larger groups can use every name on the list, with extras being part of the groupings.

Have kids make name tags with the name of the biblical person they represent and wear these during the retreat. Have kids think about how this person would act or respond in various situations and try to carry this out in their actions over the weekend.

During your Saturday meetings, focus on how various people and groups of people might have felt knowing that Jesus was dead. Let those representing each group share their thoughts first.

Ask questions such as:

■ **Were the disciples worried now that their leader and friend was gone?**

■ **Could they believe in what he'd taught?**

■ **How did the soldiers who had killed Jesus feel about their role? What about Pontius Pilate?**

■ **Were the Pharisees finally glad? Or did they have a few worries that Jesus might not be dead after all?**

On Sunday morning, have the person playing Mary Magdalene surprise everyone by waking them and exclaiming, "He is risen! I have seen the Lord!" Bring the group together and read John 20:1-18. Have a time of singing and celebration, focusing on Jesus' resurrection.

At breakfast, have each person tell what it felt like to be the character he or she portrayed. Also discuss how each person felt when Mary awakened them with the good news. Were the Pharisees angry? Were the soldiers afraid?

Close the weekend by having kids tell how Jesus' death and resurrection has changed their lives.

# JOHN 20:11-18

**THEME:**
Easter

**SUMMARY:**
Kids bring an Easter party to a group of special people in this PROJECT.

PREPARATION: Find a local nursing home, home for kids with special needs, or other similar organization that would like to have your group bring an Easter party to their facility. You'll need a Bible and supplies as indicated in the activities you choose.

Announce to your group the special opportunity they have to show Jesus' love by giving a party for an often forgotten group. Then have kids work together or in smaller groups to plan this fun event.

■ A decorations group can gather decorations to bring along, such as balloons, flowers, and filled Easter baskets. Make sure you can leave these at the site so the residents there can continue to celebrate.

■ One group can organize activities such as an Easter egg hunt using plastic eggs filled with candy and a Scripture verse. This group should work with the facility's activity director to plan the best party possible for the residents.

■ If the facility's activity director thinks the residents may enjoy singing, have a group gather hymnals or song books and guitars or other instruments.

■ Be sure to plan time for visiting with the residents. Many will be thrilled to have visitors!

Before the party begins, gather your group together and read John 20:11-18. Pray that today you'll see the angels at the tomb and Jesus in the garden and that the residents will see Jesus' love in your group.

After the party, take time to talk about where each person saw Jesus today. Close with a prayer of thanksgiving for a special Easter celebration.

# JOHN
# 20:24-29

## THEME:
Doubt

## SUMMARY:
In this OBJECT LESSON, a "telescope" will help kids understand doubt.

PREPARATION: Gather sheets of paper and a Bible.

Give kids each a sheet of paper and ask them to make a telescope by rolling the paper into a cylinder. They can adjust the "lens" to get a wide or narrow view. Then assign each person a simple task to do, such as rearranging a set of chairs, cleaning a chalkboard, or emptying the trash can. Tell kids they must do the task looking only through their telescopes (the other eye must be closed).

**Note:** For added fun, choose lots of tasks that require kids to move around the meeting room. They'll have quite a time avoiding each other.

Once kids have accomplished their tasks, ask:

■ **How did it feel to accomplish your task looking only through your telescope? Explain.**

■ **Did you feel cautious or doubtful of your surroundings? Why or why not?**

■ **Why do people tend to doubt something if they don't "see it with their own eyes"?**

Read aloud John 20:24-29. Ask

kids to describe Thomas; for example, "skeptical" or "weak in faith." Then ask:

■ **How did the telescope create doubt as you worked on your task?**

■ **How is that like real life?**

■ **How is that like Thomas' experience?**

■ **In what ways are you like or unlike Thomas?**

■ **How did Thomas' doubt change?**

Say: **Sometimes getting rid of doubt is just a matter of opening our eyes to see a bigger picture of God than we did before. When we understand how big he is and how much he loves us, we usually discover that our doubts just disappear.**

# JOHN 21:15-17

## THEME:
Feeding God's sheep

## SUMMARY:
In this AFFIRMATION, group members will encourage each other by identifying ways they care for "God's sheep."

PREPARATION: Prepare by thinking of each teenager in your group and remembering ways each one has cared for others in or outside of the group. Bring a Bible to the meeting.

Begin by having a volunteer read John 21:15-17. Discuss what Jesus means by "feed my sheep." Talk about Peter's failings and how Jesus still called him to be a leader. Have kids each share how they feel God has called them to "feed my sheep" and care for others.

After the discussion, have the group sit in a circle. Standing behind a group member, put your hands on his or her shoulders and complete this sentence: **I've seen** (person's name) **following God's call to feed his sheep by...** For example, you might say, "by openly telling others about her faith." Give the rest of the group members the opportunity to share as well. When one person has been affirmed, move to the next person in the circle and repeat the affirmation. Continue until all group members have been affirmed.

Close with prayer, thanking God that even when we fail he still calls us to be leaders and asking God to help us each follow his call.

# ACTS

*"But when the Holy Spirit comes to you, you will receive power. You will be my witnesses— in Jerusalem, in all of Judea, in Samaria, and in every part of the world."*

*Acts 1:8*

# ACTS
## 1:7-14

**THEME:**
Jesus' return

**SUMMARY:**
In this ADVENTURE, kids will imagine what it would be like if Jesus returned while they were watching the sky.

PREPARATION: You'll need Bibles.

Take your group to an open area where they'll be able to sit back and look up into the sky. If you meet at night, take your group to an observatory, if there's one nearby, or find an open area away from city lights where stars can be seen. Have kids gaze into the sky silently for a few minutes. Then ask:

■ **What do you think about when you gaze at the sky?**

■ **What makes the sky mysterious?**

■ **What mystery about the sky do you wish you understood?**

Give the kids several more minutes to think and gaze, then read aloud Acts 1:7-11. Ask:

■ **What do you think the disciples were feeling as they watched Jesus being taken up into the sky? Explain.**

■ **What promise is given in verse 11?**

■ **How is the way you feel about the mysteries of the sky like or unlike the way you feel about Jesus' return?**

Have a volunteer read aloud Acts 1:12-14. Ask:

■ **What do you think these people prayed about when they were together?**

■ **How is the way these people expected Jesus' soon return like the way we expect Jesus to return any day?**

■ **How does knowing that Jesus could return any day affect how you live your life?**

Close the time by having kids describe as they gaze into the sky what it might be like if Jesus were to return right now.

# ACTS
## 2:5-13

**THEME:**
The Holy Spirit

**SUMMARY:**
In this DEVOTION, kids listen to many different languages and learn the importance of telling others about Christ in their own language.

PREPARATION: You'll need Bibles, snacks hidden around your meeting room, several different foreign-language tapes (check your local library for these), and a cassette player for each tape. (If necessary, have kids bring cassette players from home to the meeting.) If you can't find foreign-language tapes, record five-minute segments of foreign-language cable TV channels.

On a separate cassette, record a five-minute message in English, greeting many of your kids personally and telling them how to find the hidden snacks.

EXPERIENCE

After kids arrive, loudly play all the tapes (including the English tape) at the same time but don't explain why. After about five minutes, gather the group together and ask how many of them paid attention to the tapes.

Play the tapes again, only this time tell kids to listen closely and follow the instructions they hear. After they've listened to the tapes (and found the hidden snacks), form trios for discussion. Ask:

■ **Even though there were several different languages playing at the same time, how were you able to pick out what was being said on the English tape?**

RESPONSE

Have a volunteer from each trio read aloud Acts 2:5-13. Then have trios discuss these questions one at a time, pausing every two minutes or so to report their answers to the large group before moving on to the next question:

■ **How is the way you were able to pick out your language from all those being played like the way the people heard the good news in their own languages?**

■ **Why was it important for people to hear in their own languages the great things God has done?**

■ **What does this say about how we should talk to those around us concerning Christ?**

CLOSING

Have kids communicate messages of encouragement to their trio partners. Tell kids to create messages that describe why their partners can confidently communicate God's love to others. For example, someone might say, "I know you can tell others about Christ because you're so easy to talk to" or "Because you're a caring person, others will listen to what you say about your faith."

# ACTS
## 3:1-10

THEME:
Jesus can heal us.

SUMMARY:

In this LEARNING GAME, kids participate in a race while disabled, then participate in a race without the limitations of the disability.

PREPARATION: You'll need strips of cloth or rope and Bibles.

"**D**isable" everyone by using cloth strips or soft rope to tie teenagers' right hands to their left feet. Then have kids run a race from one end of the building to the other. Congratulate the winner but don't let kids free themselves yet.

Form groups of no more than four. Have the person wearing the most buttons read Acts 3:1-10 for his or her group. Then have groups discuss these questions:

■ **How would your social life be different if you were tied like this permanently?**

■ **How would things be different for you economically?**

■ **How was it possible for the disabled man in Acts 3:1-10 to survive?**

■ **How would you feel if you were in his condition?**

Free kids from their "disability," then run the race again. Afterward, ask:

■ **What was it like to run the same race without having your hand tied to your foot?**

■ **How is that like or unlike the way the crippled man felt after he was healed?**

■ **How can God heal us today?**

# ACTS
## 3:17-26

THEME:
Following Jesus

SUMMARY:

In this ADVENTURE, kids will follow a leader as he or she walks in the wrong direction, then discuss how the Jews thought they were following God.

PREPARATION: For this activity, you'll want to have teenagers meet at a location that's about a 10-minute walk from an ice-cream parlor or a popular fast-food restaurant. Tell teenagers they'll need to bring their Bibles and enough money to purchase an ice-cream cone or a cold drink at a fast-food restaurant.

When everyone has arrived at your specified location, tell the group you're going to lead them on a walk to a surprise destination. Begin leading the kids in a direction away from your actual destination—the ice-cream parlor or fast-food restaurant. After about 10 minutes, turn around and retrace your steps before walking to your destination.

When kids arrive at the ice-cream parlor or fast-food restaurant, allow a few minutes for everyone to purchase a treat, then form groups of no more than three. Have the oldest person in each group read Acts 3:17-26. Then ask the following questions and have kids discuss them in their groups:

■ **How did you feel when you discovered we had been walking in the wrong direction for 10 minutes?**

■ **How is that like the way the Jews may have felt when they were told they'd been walking away from God when they thought they were serving him?**

■ **What struggles did the Jews have in deciding to turn around and walk in the opposite direction—to truly follow God?**

■ **If someone told you the direction you were headed in was wrong, how would you respond?**

After they've finished their snacks, lead the kids back to your meeting place. As they walk, ask teenagers to silently think about the direction their lives are heading in and evaluate if they need to go in the opposite direction in any area.

When you return to your meeting area, have volunteers tell how they need to change direction in their lives. Give kids a few minutes to pray silently and ask God to help them make those changes. Then have kids pray aloud for each other to have the courage to change.

# ACTS
# 4:1-21

## THEME:
Faith and actions

## SUMMARY:
In this DEVOTION, kids will participate in a courtroom simulation exploring the importance of acting on their faith.

PREPARATION: Set up the room to look like a courtroom. You'll need Bibles, newsprint, a marker, and a copy of *Foxe's Book of Martyrs* (check your local library or Christian bookstore to find the book).

EXPERIENCE
Ask four volunteers to portray two defendants and two prosecutors.

Say: **The defendants are on trial for being Christians. The prosecutors will take turns asking questions to prove the two defendants are Christians.**

Privately instruct one of the defendants to give honest answers and the other to give vague answers such as "I believe in God, so I'm OK"; "I'm just as good as other people, maybe even better than most"; "Jesus was a really good teacher, and he helped people a lot"; "The Bible has some good things to say"; or "I'm a Christian because I go to church."

Then have the prosecutors ask the following questions (and any others they think will help them prove the defendants are Christians):

■ **If someone were to ask you how to make it to heaven, what would you tell them?**
■ **How is your life different from those around you?**
■ **Who do you think Jesus is?**
■ **How might others see a difference in your life because of your belief in Christ?**
■ **What do you believe about the Bible?**

Have the rest of the kids be the jury. After the prosecutors ask their questions, have the jury decide whether or not to "convict" the defendants of being Christians.

RESPONSE
Form groups of no more than three and assign the following roles within each group: a reader who reads Acts 4:1-21, a reporter who reports his or her group's answers to the large group, and an encourager who urges everyone to participate in the discussion. Ask:

■ **How do you know that**

Peter and John were Christians?
■ **How did their actions match what they said?**

■ **If you were on trial for being a Christian, what evidence would prove your "guilt"?**

■ **How much would you be willing to suffer simply because of your faith?**

In their groups, have kids briefly tell one thing they can do in the next seven days to make their actions match their faith. Then have partners commit to doing those things during the week.

CLOSING

Read a few stories from *Foxe's Book of Martyrs* to the group. Ask:

■ **Just like in these stories, the only crime Peter and John committed was being Christians. Was their treatment worth it? Why or why not?**

Have kids close by praying for each other to be confident in their faith, even in the face of opposition.

# ACTS
# 4:32-35

## THEME:
Sharing

## SUMMARY:
In this PROJECT, kids will explore how they might help others with their own money, talent, and time.

PREPARATION: Make a list of at least five Christian charities, prefer-ably from your local area (check out charities your church supports, the Yellow Pages, and volunteer centers, or ask your local resource librarian for ideas). You'll also need Bibles.

When kids arrive, read aloud Acts 4:32-35. Then ask:
■ **What does this passage teach about Christians and their belongings?**

■ **How might our world be different if the church acted today as it did in this passage?**

■ **What kinds of resources are available in our youth group that could be used to help others?**

■ **How does it feel to consider giving away your money? Explain.**

Have kids vote on the two organizations they'd most like to help out. Then say: **Let's brainstorm ways we can help out these organizations. Then we can put into practice what the passage in Acts teaches us the church is all about.**

Form groups of no more than four and have groups come up with several ideas for raising funds or helping out each charity. Some suggestions are having a rummage sale (have kids each donate at least one item that's important to them), a bake sale, or a car wash; volunteering to serve meals and clean up; collecting dry goods; or sponsoring a clothing drive.

After each group has shared its ideas, have kids vote on one or two of their favorite projects. Then put volunteers in charge of each project and have kids plan out how to complete those projects within the next 30 days. Check on kids' progress as they prepare for the events, offering guidance and assistance when it's needed.

# ACTS
# 4:32-37; 9:23-27;
# 11:22-30

---

## THEME:

Encouraging each other

## SUMMARY:
In this LEARNING GAME, teenagers will build a human bridge to help each other cross an imaginary obstacle.

---

PREPARATION: Tape two 5-foot lengths of masking tape on the floor, approximately 10 feet apart. You'll also need Bibles.

Have kids stand behind one of the taped lines. Say: **The object of this activity is for you to build a human bridge to get everybody in our group across this 10-foot-wide "river." But no more than three people can touch the river. Once the bridge is built, we'll all have to cross the river without touching the ground.**

After everyone has crossed, ask:

■ **How did you feel as you built your bridge?**

■ **How did you encourage or support each other as the bridge was being built?**

■ **How are encouragers like bridges across tough times?**

■ **How does it feel to actually be a bridge for others?**

Have volunteers read aloud Acts 4:32-37; 9:23-27; and 11:22-30. After each passage, ask how it describes encouragement. Then ask:

■ **What does it mean when someone says, "A friend is someone who encourages you"?**

■ **How do your friends encourage you? How do you encourage them?**

■ **What does encouragement do for people?**

Say: **Even though he never really gets any credit for being a great leader in the Christian church, Barnabas stood by Paul when Paul needed him. Paul couldn't have been as effective if it hadn't been for Barnabas' encouraging him from the background. Think of someone you know who needs your encouragement right now.**

Close with prayer, asking God to help kids each encourage the person they thought of.

# ACTS
# 5:1-11

---

## THEME:

Consequences

## SUMMARY:
In this OBJECT LESSON, kids explore Bible characters' actions and discuss how our actions are followed by positive or negative consequences.

PREPARATION: You'll need a supply of dominoes and Bibles.

Form groups of no more than four and give each group a supply of dominoes. Have groups set up domino designs that'll cause all dominoes to fall when one domino is pushed.

After kids have created their domino designs, have someone in each group tap the first domino to make them all fall down.

Then have one person in each group read Acts 5:1-11. Have groups discuss these questions, pausing before each new question to report their answers to the group:

■ **What did Ananias and Sapphira do that was wrong?**

■ **Why were they judged so harshly?**

■ **How are the consequences of sin like the consequences of pushing a domino as we did in our activity?**

■ **What were the consequences of Ananias and Sapphira's sin?**

■ **What can we learn about our actions from this event?**

Say: **We all sin. And just as Ananias and Sapphira discovered, our actions have consequences.**

Before closing, have volunteers share positive or negative consequences they've experienced from things they've done. For example, a teenager might tell how studying helped him pass a tough exam, or someone else might tell how she lost a friend because she treated that friend unkindly.

Dismiss by having each group ask God to help them make good choices about their actions in the coming week.

# ACTS
## 6:8-15; 7:51–8:1

THEME:
Stephen's stoning

SUMMARY:
In this LEARNING GAME, teenagers will play a variation of Dodge Ball and compare it to Stephen's stoning.

PREPARATION: You'll need Bibles and scrap paper for paper wads.

Say: **Acts 6 and 7 tell us about Stephen, who was a leader of the early Christians. The Jewish leaders were jealous because he was very wise. They falsely accused him and arrested him. Eventually he was stoned to death.**

Form pairs and have one partner read Acts 6:8-15 and the other read Acts 7:51–8:1.

Say: **Let's play a game to help us experience in a safer way what it might've been like to be present at Stephen's stoning. The game is a variation of Dodge Ball, only we'll use paper wads instead of balls.**

Form two teams. Call one the "Stephens" and the other the "stone throwers." Have the stone throwers form a large circle and have the Stephens gather in the center. Give each stone thrower a wad of paper—representing a stone.

On "go," have the stone throwers throw their stones at the Stephens. Tell the Stephens to try to dodge the stones. Award the stone throwers 1 point for each stone that hits a Stephen. Then have stone throwers and Stephens switch roles for a new round. Play four to six rounds, with teams switching roles each round.

Afterward, have kids process their experience with these questions:

■ **What thoughts went through your head during this game?**

■ **When have you felt like you were a target of other people's laughter or opposition?**

■ **Have you ever hurt others by what you said to them? How is this like stone throwing?**

■ **Why do you think God allowed Stephen to face the stoning?**

■ **Why do you think God allows us to face others' laughter or opposition?**

■ **If Stephen were teaching this lesson, what do you think he'd want us to learn from his experience?**

# ACTS
# 7:51-60

**THEME:**
Taking a stand

**SUMMARY:**
In this SKIT, a guy is ridiculed for taking a stand against drugs and drinking.

## STICKS AND STONES

SCENE: Two friends are talking in a high school hallway between classes.

PROPS: You'll need Bibles for the discussion afterward.

CHARACTERS:
**Jared**
**Adam**
**Steve**

### SCRIPT
*(Jared and Adam stand talking at their lockers.)*

**Jared:** *(Angry)* I couldn't believe it! We invite the guy over to have a drink, maybe smoke some marijuana, and he starts coming unglued!

**Adam:** You're kidding!

**Jared:** It's the truth! You'd think he appointed himself police officer or something, telling us how the stuff is illegal, and then when that didn't work, saying it's bad for us.

**Adam:** What a jerk!

**Jared:** That's not all—he just kept preaching at us. He wouldn't shut...

*(Steve enters and tries to go to his locker.)*

**Steve:** Hi... *(The other two block his way.)* Excuse me.

**Adam:** *(Mockingly)* Oh, you're excused. Wouldn't want to get in the way.

**Jared:** *(Sarcastically)* Or do something "wrong."

**Adam:** *(Melodramatically)* Heavens, no! We might get in trouble.

**Jared:** It might be against the rules.

**Adam:** It might be bad for us! *(They let Steve by, then push him hard.)*

**Steve:** *(Angry)* Hey! I can't help it if you don't like to hear the truth! I just know that what you were planning was wrong, and you needed to hear it!

**Jared:** Jerk! What do we care what you think?

**Adam:** You're nothin'! And we're going to keep doing what we want—no matter what you say!

**Jared:** By the way, I hear your parents are separated. I s'pose neither one wants you living with 'em.

*(Steve turns away and looks at the floor.)*

**Adam:** Probably neither one cares whether he lives or dies!

*(Steve slumps to the floor. They laugh and turn to leave.)*

**Jared:** *(As they leave)* Keep out of our lives and get one of your own. *(They laugh.)*

**Steve:** *(Putting his head in his hands)* They don't know what they're saying.

If you use this skit as a discussion starter, here are possible questions:

■ **When is it hardest for you to stand up for God?**

■ **Read Acts 7:51-60. What would you have done if you'd been in Stephen's shoes?**

# ACTS 7:54–8:1

**THEME:**
Persecution

**SUMMARY:**
In this ADVENTURE/ CREATIVE PRAYER, kids will research other countries and pray for Christians in those countries.

PREPARATION: Make a list of 10 countries (include the United States). You'll need paper, pencils, and Bibles. Plan to meet at your local library.

**S**ay: **Sometimes it's not easy being a Christian. Depending on where you live, you could face everything from laughter to prison to death because of your faith in God. Let's do a little research to see what it might be like to be a Christian in several modern countries.**

Distribute paper and pencils to everyone, then assign each person (or group of teenagers) a country from your list. Tell kids to find and write down the following informa-

tion about their assigned countries:
- population,
- religions of the country (and how many people follow each),
- largest cities,
- type of government,
- main industries,
- language used the most, and
- special problems.

Encourage kids to check encyclopedias, almanacs, travel guides, and other library references to find the information they need. When kids have finished their research, go to a meeting place where you can talk (outside, if the weather is good).

Have kids take turns telling each other what they discovered about their assigned countries, then place their information papers in different places around the meeting area.

Read aloud Acts 7:54–8:1 Ask:

- **Why do people oppose the Christian faith?**

- **Do you think Stephen was stoned because of his message or because of the method he used to deliver it? Explain.**

- **What can we do this week to share the message of Jesus in a positive way in our country?**

Say: **Stephen believed so much that Jesus was the Christ that he was willing to die. Although telling about Jesus in most countries won't cost you your life, it may cause you problems in different ways, such as being shunned or ridiculed. Those who are willing to risk telling about Christ need our prayer support.**

Have kids form prayer groups of no more than three and station themselves in front of the information papers spread throughout the room. Have groups read the information about a country (so that they have a better feel for the people they're praying for), then pray for the Christians in that country. Encourage kids to ask God to give strength and encouragement to the missionaries and Christians in that country who may be persecuted because of their faith.

# ACTS
## 8:1-8

THEME:
Opposition to the faith

SUMMARY:
Through this LEARNING GAME, kids will explore how the persecution of the early church helped spread the news of Jesus to the world.

PREPARATION: You'll need several colors of sidewalk chalk, marbles, two basketballs, and Bibles.

In your church parking lot, use the sidewalk chalk to draw two large targets with at least four rings. Make the targets 10 to 20 feet in diameter and label each bull's eye "Jerusalem." Then label each circle outside of Jerusalem with a point value, increasing as they go farther out (10 points between Jerusalem and the first ring, 20 points between the first and the second rings, and so on).

Form two teams and have them each stand near a target. Give each team a basketball and 20 marbles to place on its bull's eye. Team members will take turns throwing the basketball on Jerusalem, scattering the marbles throughout the target. After each turn, points are added up based on where in the target the marbles have rolled. Then the marbles are gathered and returned to the center of the target for the next person to scatter.

Tell kids that the object is to have as many marbles as possible land outside of Jerusalem. Add up the points for each person on a team. Marbles landing outside the target count for 50 points each. After tallying the scores, declare the winning team.

Next, have kids each choose a partner from the opposing team to form pairs. Have one partner in each pair read aloud Acts 8:1-8 and the other summarize it in one sentence. Then ask:

■ **How was the persecution of the early church like this game?**

■ **In what way did the persecution help to spread the news of Jesus to remote areas of the earth?**

■ **How do you think the early Christians felt about their persecution? Explain.**

■ **What can we learn about how God works from this example of the early church?**

# ACTS
# 10:9-16, 34-36

## THEME:
Favoritism and cultural differences

## SUMMARY:
Kids will explore God's view on favoritism at this dinner PARTY and explore cultural differences as they eat foods from different countries.

PREPARATION: About a week before your party, assign kids to bring different foods from different parts of the world for an "international" dinner. Invite kids' parents to help out as necessary to ensure a variety of foods. For example, kids might bring spaghetti, crepes, tabouli salad, tacos, and so on. You'll need a Bible at the dinner.

As kids arrive, place all the different foods on a sheet in the middle of the room.

Before eating, have a volunteer read Acts 10:9-16.

Say: **Because of rules given in the Old Testament, the Jews of the early church felt it was sinful to eat certain foods that other cultures ate. When people from other cultures became Christians, they didn't necessarily feel the same way as the Jews.**

**As recorded in Acts, God gave insight to Peter into this matter through a vision. As you enjoy foods from different cultures, discuss with those around you**

things that some Christians today might call sin that are actually only cultural differences.

After eating, have volunteers share the results of their dinner discussions. Then ask:

■ **What do you think verse 15 means?**

■ **If it was OK for Peter to eat any kind of food, why were the Jews given dietary laws through Moses?**

■ **How do you think Peter felt about eating previously forbidden food?**

■ **How do you think people from other cultures respond to the dietary customs of our country?**

Ask a volunteer to read aloud Acts 10:34-36. Ask:

■ **What does this passage tell you about God's view of favoritism?**

■ **Since the United States was largely founded on Christian principles, do you think God is more pleased with our culture than with other countries' cultures? Explain.**

End your dinner party by praying for people in other cultures to come to know Christ and for Christians to be accepting of cultural differences without compromising God's standards.

# ACTS 13:46-52

## THEME:

Responses to evangelism

## SUMMARY:
In this DEVOTION, kids will create a dance and song to illustrate the Bible passage.

PREPARATION: You'll need Bibles.

EXPERIENCE

Form three groups. Have groups each read Acts 13:46-52 and create a song and dance called the "Shake off the Dust Shuffle," based on the message of the passage.

Let groups know that they can pick a current song and change the words to it, write a rap, or create an original tune. The lyrics must contain all of the following words:

■ "Paul,"
■ "Barnabas,"
■ "people of other nations,"
■ "Iconium,"
■ "the Holy Spirit," and
■ "Jews."

Give groups 10 minutes to complete their songs and dances, then have them give their performances in front of the whole group.

RESPONSE

Form a circle and ask:

■ **What feelings did you have during this activity? Explain.**

■ **How are those feelings like or unlike the way Paul and**

Barnabas might've felt in Acts 13:51?

■ What are some reasons people reject the news of Jesus?

■ When it comes to telling others about Jesus, how do you know when to "shake the dust from your feet"? How do you know when to keep trying?

Have kids describe times they felt they were wasting their time telling someone about their faith.

CLOSING

Have kids mime the act of shaking dust off their feet just before you lead them out of the room. As you're leaving the room, close in prayer, asking God to help you know when to shake the dust from your feet and move on.

# ACTS
## 15:1-2, 22-31

THEME:
Unity

SUMMARY:
Through this ADVENTURE, kids will explore other churches' beliefs and compare them to their own.

PREPARATION: You'll need Bibles.

Form three groups. Take each group of kids to a different church in your area for a Sunday night or midweek service. Ask teenagers to look for similarities and differences between your church and the one they visit. Encourage kids to interview the churches' pastors if possible and collect information about each church's doctrine.

At your next meeting, have kids share their experiences and tell about the differences and similarities they found. Ask:

■ What was it like to be in a different church setting?

■ What was the most difficult part of the experience? the easiest?

Form groups of no more than three and have group members number off from one to three.

Say: The churches in Antioch and Judea had a difference in opinion, which caused sharp debate. Yet both churches survived and reached an agreement on basic issues.

Discuss the next few questions in your groups. Then I'll call out a number from one to three. The person in your group whose number I call out will be responsible for sharing your group's answer.

Have the ones in each group read aloud Acts 15:1-2, 22-31. Then wrap up the adventure by asking the following questions, pausing after each to allow time for discussion. Call out a different number after each discussion time to select new people from each group to report answers. Ask:

■ Why are some Christians critical of other Christians' beliefs?

■ What are essential issues to agree on within Christianity? What are nonessential issues?

■ **Based on Acts 15:1-2, 22-31, how should we handle differences of opinion on essential issues? on nonessential issues?**

■ **How should we respond if we find we can't agree with someone about an important issue?**

# ACTS
# 16:16-35

---

## THEME:
God's control

## SUMMARY:
Kids will create SKITS about God interceding and saving someone in the midst of trouble.

---

PREPARATION: You'll need a Bible and photocopies of the "Skit Ingredients" handout (p. 181). You'll also want to copy onto a sheet of newsprint the skit guidelines listed below:

### SKIT GUIDELINES
In your skits...

■ someone must be stuck inside your assigned location through no fault of his or her own (tell how and why),

■ that person must be rescued supernaturally;

■ you must show how something good came from this experience;

■ the owners of each establishment must make a commitment to Christ; and

■ you must use every person in your group in at least one role.

Form groups of no more than five. Read aloud Acts 16:16-35. Then say: **Even when our actions are right, things can work out badly. But God is always in control and is able to make bad things work out for the ultimate good, as in the passage we just heard.**

Give each group one section from the "Skit Ingredients" handout. Following the skit guidelines, have groups each create a skit that somehow includes the ingredients on their handouts.

When everyone is ready, have each group present its skit. After the skits, have kids discuss how God can reach into any situation and make good things come from bad situations. Use questions such as these to spark discussion:

■ **In what ways did our skits mirror the situation described in Acts 16:16-35?**

■ **How would you have responded in Paul and Silas' situation?**

■ **When have you felt like God "saved the day" for you?**

■ **How do you respond when it seems like God hasn't saved the day?**

# SKIT INGREDIENTS

**Directions:** Photocopy and cut apart the sections below for kids to use to create their skits. You'll need one slip for every group of up to five.

### Skit #1 Ingredients:
**Place:** An ice-cream parlor.
**Things to include in the skit:** A blender, a wooden spoon, whipped cream, a paper cup, a banana, and a mouse.

### Skit #2 Ingredients:
**Place:** A gas station.
**Things to include in the skit:** A radio, a crescent wrench, an old tailpipe, a bathroom key, a spare tire, and a really lazy dog.

### Skit #3 Ingredients:
**Place:** A movie theater.
**Things to include in the skit:** Popcorn, candy, sticky floors, a broken seat, a tall hat, and a grouchy usher.

# ACTS
# 17:16-34

## THEME:
Putting God first

## SUMMARY:
In this OBJECT LESSON, kids will create clay sculptures, then reshape them to symbolize God's place in their lives.

PREPARATION: You'll need a supply of modeling clay and Bibles.

Form pairs. Give clay to each pair. Have partners make representations of things people worship today (cars, money, movie stars, sports, education, or themselves). After five minutes, ask several pairs to tell about what they made.

Then place the objects on a table. Ask:

■ **How would you feel if I asked you to worship these clay objects? Explain.**

Have one partner in each pair read Acts 17:16-34 and the other partner summarize the message of the verses. Ask pairs to discuss these questions:

■ **How are the things our clay objects represent like the gods discussed in this passage?**

■ **Why is it wrong to place other things above God?**

■ **Why is it easy for people to worship things they make with their own hands?**

■ **What changes could we make this week to follow the message of Acts 17:16-34?**

Have kids work together to re-form the clay objects into one large cross. Then have the group hold hands, stand around the cross, and pray silently to always seek God above all else.

Close by singing songs about the lordship of Christ, such as "Trust and Obey," "He Is Lord," "Jesus, Name Above All Names," and "Lord Be Glorified."

# ACTS
## 18:24-26

**THEME:**
Learning about our faith

**SUMMARY:**
In this PROJECT, teenagers will plan a series of studies to help fifth- and sixth-graders learn more about the basics of the Christian faith.

PREPARATION: You'll need newsprint, a marker, paper, pencils, and Bibles. You might also want to check with the fifth- and sixth-grade Sunday school teachers in your church to see if your teenagers can lead their classes for three weeks.

Open your planning time by having kids read Acts 18:24-26 and describe a time they felt like Apollos—when they spoke boldly about their faith but didn't really know what they were saying. Then form three groups (a group can be one person).

Have groups plan a three-week series for children to come and experience what Apollos experienced in Acts 18:24-26. Explain that this basic series will explain the way of God more adequately to upper-elementary students.

Write the topics below on newsprint and have each group choose one topic and create a lesson for fifth- and sixth-graders about that topic. Encourage groups to use the questions that follow each topic to spark discussion.

**Topic #1: What does it mean to be a Christian?**

■ Why should I become a Christian?

■ How do people become Christians?

**Topic #2: Who is God?**

■ Why does God want us to know him?

■ How do I grow closer to God?

**Topic #3: What is God's will?**

■ How can I discover God's will for my life?

■ How can I live out God's will in everyday life?

**Topic #4: What is the appropriate role of the arts and media in my life?**

■ What are biblical guidelines for what I choose to watch or listen to?

■ How much TV is too much?

**Topic #5: What is my role in the church?**

■ What can I do to make a difference in the church?

■ Why should I even go to church?

**Topic #6: How do I tell others about Christ?**

■ Why must I share my faith?

■ How can I tell others about Christ without offending them?

Make your curriculum library available to teenagers while they plan their lessons. Encourage them to study the way the curriculum producers have put together their lessons and to use those lessons as a guide. One valuable curriculum resource teenagers might want to use is *Group's Hands-On Bible Curriculum™, Grades 5 & 6,* available from Group Publishing.

When groups are ready, schedule dates for them to take their lessons into the fifth- and sixth-grade Sunday school classes in your church. After all groups have taught their lessons, hold a debriefing session where you help kids explore their reactions to the task of "explaining the way of God more adequately" to upper-elementary students.

# ACTS 19:11-20

**THEME:**
Ambition

**SUMMARY:**
In this AFFIRMATION, kids will be affirmed as they discuss who they wish they could be like and explore Acts 19:11-20, which tells about the Jews' ambition to be like Paul.

PREPARATION: You'll need Bibles, newsprint, a marker, paper slips, and a pencil. Before your meeting, write the words listed below on separate slips of paper and put them in a bowl. You'll need one slip for each person in your group. If you have more than 15 group members, you might want to add your own ideas on paper slips or make more than one slip with the same phrase on it.

■ Play football
■ Play basketball
■ Play baseball
■ Play tennis
■ Play golf
■ Play hockey
■ Act
■ Sing
■ Teach
■ Be funny
■ Get good grades
■ Write
■ Draw or paint
■ Speak
■ Dress

At your youth group meeting, write this sentence on newsprint: "I wish I could *(topic)* like *(person)*."

Have kids take turns drawing a slip of paper from the bowl. Then have them each complete the newsprint phrase, filling in the topic blank with their word or phrase and filling in the person blank by saying the name of a famous person they admire for being successful in that area. For example, someone might say, "I wish I could <u>play football</u> like <u>Troy Aikman</u>."

After everyone has had a turn, have a volunteer read aloud Acts 19:11-20. Then have group members stand while you ask the following questions. When one person shares an answer, kids who thought of the same answer and have nothing more to add can sit down. When everyone is seated, ask the next question and repeat the process. Ask:

■ **Even though they weren't Christians, why do you think the Jews tried to use the name of Jesus to cast out a demon?**

■ **Why did these Jews want to be like Paul?**

■ **Why do we wish for shortcuts to success?**

■ **What are the dangers of wishing we could be like someone else?**

■ **What good can come from desiring to be like someone else?**

Say: **The Jews in this passage wanted to have the same power and status they thought Paul had. They wanted the power but were looking for a shortcut to get that power.**

**Instead of looking for shortcuts, we can work toward our goals and affirm each other for what we already do well.**

Form a circle and have kids take turns completing the follow-

ing sentence for the person on their left: "I'm glad *(name of person on left)* is who *(he/she)* is because without *(him/her)* we wouldn't have *(blank)*."

Remind kids to keep their comments positive. For example, someone might say, "I'm glad John is who he is because without him, we wouldn't have as much fun in our meetings."

# ACTS
## 20:17-24

THEME:
Reactions to the gospel

SUMMARY:
In this DEVOTION, kids will tell about God's work in their lives, then receive an unpredictable "reward."

PREPARATION: You'll need strips of paper, a pencil or pen, cream pies (whipped topping scooped onto a paper plate), candy bars, soft drinks, doughnuts, plastic garbage bags, and towels for cleaning up. You'll also need Bibles.

Before your meeting, cut out 30 small strips of paper. On 10 of them write, "Pie in the face!" On the other 20, list different prizes such as "candy bar," "soft drink," or "doughnut." If you have other prizes available, list those, too.

## EXPERIENCE

Ask volunteers to tell the whole group about how God is working in their lives. Explain that each person who speaks will receive some type of reward—but don't specify what kind of reward it will be.

After a person speaks, have him or her draw a strip of paper, then give that person the appropriate reward. For example, if someone draws "Pie in the face!" cover that person with a plastic garbage bag, then give him or her a whipped cream pie in the face in front of the whole group.

Play until everyone has had a chance to speak. Afterward, give everyone who got a pie in the face a towel to clean themselves off and a real reward such as a candy bar, soft drink, or doughnut.

## RESPONSE

Form two circles, one within the other. Have the inner circle face outward and the outer circle face inward. Have teenagers pair up with the person in front of them and read Acts 20:17-24. Explain that Paul didn't know what was going to happen when he shared the gospel. Then have pairs discuss the following question:

■ **How is the way you didn't know what you'd get as a reward like Paul's experience in this passage?**

Have one person from each pair report answers to the large group. Then tell kids to rotate one space to the right in their circles and form new pairs to discuss the next question. After discussion, have pairs report answers to the large group. Repeat this process for each remaining question. Ask:

■ **How would it affect your attitude if you knew that everyone you talked to about your faith would be attentive and gracious?**

■ **How would it affect your attitude if you knew your audience would be hostile?**

■ **How is this game similar to the real-life risks or rewards of telling others about our faith in Jesus?**

■ **What can you do to make your audience more receptive to hearing about Jesus?**

## CLOSING

Close by having kids pray for their partners, either silently or aloud. Tell group members to ask God to prepare their partners for whatever responses they might get when telling others about their faith.

# ACTS
# 21:39–22:16

**THEME:**
Faith stories

**SUMMARY:**
Through this LEARNING GAME, kids creatively tell how they became Christians.

PREPARATION: In the middle of your meeting room, lay out as many of the following items as you can find to be used as props: a packet of seeds, a flower, a blank sheet of paper, several balloons, a fork, sandals or tennis shoes, a telephone, a newspaper, several pieces of wood, bubbles, a dust rag, finger paints and paper grocery bags, a brick, a pillow, a banana peel, a flashlight, a harmonica, an empty cup, and a bar of soap. You'll also need Bibles.

Read aloud the story of Paul's conversion to Christianity in Acts 21:39–22:16.

Say: **Paul's story of how he became a Christian is exciting, but it's no more unique than your story. Take a few minutes to think about how you became a Christian. Then think about ways you might use one or more of these props to explain to others the story of how you became a Christian.**

Form two teams. Have as many kids who are willing use as many props as they can to tell the whole group how they became Christians. Allow only the same number of kids from each team to share. Award teams 1,000 points for each prop used by its team members. Props may be used more than once but not in the same way that someone else previously used them. After each person has had a turn, tally the points and congratulate the winning team.

Next have kids choose a partner from the opposite team to form pairs. Wrap up the game by asking pairs to discuss these questions:

■ **Why do we sometimes get more excited about "extraordinary" conversion stories like Paul's than "ordinary" ones?**

■ **Are people better or worse**

**Christians based on how they were before they became Christians? Explain.**

■ **What are some creative ways to tell others about how you became a Christian?**

■ **Why is it important to use different methods in telling how we became Christians?**

# ACTS
# 24:5-16

THEME:
False accusations

SUMMARY:
In this DEVOTION, kids will explore how Paul was falsely accused and how he defended himself.

PREPARATION: You'll need paper, pencils, Bibles, and several Bible concordances.

EXPERIENCE
Form three groups. Give each group paper and a pencil for notes. Assign each group one of the following "slams" against Christianity:

■ Christianity is for people who are needy.

■ Churches are places where hypocrites go every week.

■ The Bible isn't true.

■ People can't be sure they're going to heaven.

■ Christianity is a bunch of outdated do's and don'ts.

■ How can God be love when so many bad things happen?

■ Christians always force their beliefs on others.

Give groups 10 minutes to come up with defenses against the accusations. Tell groups to support their defenses with Scripture as well as personal experience. Provide concordances for kids to use.

As each group presents its defense, have other groups challenge and try to discredit the defense.

RESPONSE

After the defenses have been given, have kids read Acts 24:5-16. Ask:

■ **How is the way you defended your faith against these accusations like or unlike the way Paul defended himself?**

■ **What is it like to hear people falsely accuse you?**

■ **What can we learn from Paul's defense techniques that will help us when we're falsely accused because of our faith?**

CLOSING

Form a circle. Have each group member take a turn telling the person on his or her right one true, positive "accusation" about that person's faith. For example, kids might say, "Your faith in Jesus shows in the way you're kind to others" or "Your faith in Jesus shows in your joyful attitude."

# ACTS 26:8

THEME:
God's power

SUMMARY:
Perform a CREATIVE READING about God's unlimited ability.

PREPARATION: You'll need Bibles, pencils, and paper.

Use this creative reading to bring home the awesomeness of God's power. Read each of the statements below, pausing where indicated for teenagers to recite in unison Acts 26:8. You might want to use this New Century version of that Scripture:

"Why do any of you people think it is impossible for God to raise people from the dead?" (Acts 26:8).

Say: **In Exodus 14:21-22, the Bible tells us how God split the sea so the Israelites could cross over on dry land. If God can part the sea...** (Pause and prompt kids to recite Acts 26:8.)

**In Exodus 17:6, God gave the Israelites water from a stone. If God can make water come from a rock...** (Pause and prompt kids to recite Acts 26:8.)

**In Numbers 21:4-9, God miraculously saved the Israelites from poisonous snakes. If God can heal his people from the bites of poisonous snakes...** (Pause and prompt kids to recite Acts 26:8.)

**In Joshua 10:6-14, God**

made the sun and moon stand still. If God can make the stars and planets halt in their celestial courses... (Pause and prompt kids to recite Acts 26:8.)

In 1 Kings 17:17-23, God, through Elijah, raised a child from the dead. If God can bring a boy back to life... (Pause and prompt kids to recite Acts 26:8.)

In Luke 17:11-19, Jesus healed lepers. If God can heal people with deadly diseases... (Pause and prompt kids to recite Acts 26:8.)

In John 2:1-10, Jesus transformed water into wine. If God has power over the elements...

(Pause and prompt kids to recite Acts 26:8.)

In John 2:18-22, Jesus promised to rise from the dead. If Jesus says he can defeat death... (Pause and prompt kids to recite Acts 26:8.)

After the reading, give each person a sheet of paper and a pencil. Have kids each write down a problem that's bothering them.

Then say: If God can raise the dead, surely God can help you with your problems.

Have kids pray silently for God to reach into their lives and help them deal with the problems they listed on their papers.

# ROMANS

*"When people sin, they earn what sin pays—death. But God gives us a free gift—life forever in Christ Jesus our Lord."*

*Romans 6:23*

# ROMANS 1:16-17

## THEME:

The power of good news

## SUMMARY:

In this DEVOTION, kids will see how good news can change a situation.

---

PREPARATION: You'll need Bibles.

EXPERIENCE

Form pairs. Say: **You've all probably heard jokes that start with "I have some good news and some bad news." Well today I'm going to read some bad news. You and your partner must then choose one situation from this list and create good news (either serious or silly) that would change your outlook on this situation into a positive one.**

**For example, the bad news might be that you overhear someone spreading untrue rumors about you. Then for good news, you might say that a good friend sets the record straight before the rumor spreads any further.**

Read aloud these bad-news situations, and have pairs take turns sharing their ideas for good news.

■ **You develop a severe case of acne just before a first date.**

■ **Your biology teacher schedules a comprehensive, closed-book final instead of an open-book quiz.**

■ **A preschooler you know learns how to use scissors by cutting up the only copy of your term paper for English.**

■ **You spill a tray of food on yourself in the cafeteria—just before class pictures are to be taken.**

■ **You overhear someone saying something about you that isn't true.**

■ **Your best friend finds out that his/her parents are getting a divorce.**

■ **You get turned down for the part-time job you really wanted.**

Give pairs 30 seconds to create good news for one of the bad situations. Then have volunteers tell the whole group the good news that changed their bad news.

RESPONSE

After kids give examples of good news, have pairs discuss these questions:

■ **What kind of power does good news have? What can it do?**

■ **How can good news turn a situation around?**

Say: **Good news can make a powerful difference to us when we really need it. Let's read about the good news of Jesus in Romans 1:16-17.**

Have one partner in each pair read Romans 1:16-17 and the other partner summarize the passage in one sentence. Then ask:

■ **How is the message of Jesus presented in the Bible like good news for bad times?**

■ **How has God's good news changed your life?**

CLOSING

Have kids tell their partners one

reason they're thankful for the good news written in Romans 1:16-17. Then have partners tell each other one way they want to be more open to the good news revealed in the Bible. Close by having partners pray for each other, focusing on what they've shared.

# ROMANS 2:1-3

## THEME:
Judging others

## SUMMARY:
In this SKIT, two girls enjoy judging others at the mall until they realize they're being watched as well.

## JUDGE NOT

SCENE: Two girls are leaning against a wall at a busy mall.

PROPS: You'll need Bibles for the discussion afterward.

CHARACTERS:
**Annie**
**Cynthia**

### SCRIPT
*(Annie and Cynthia are standing around, looking cool, and scoping out everyone around them.)*

**Cynthia:** What a great idea! You go, "Let's go to the mall." And I go, "Sure, let's do it." And here we are!

**Annie:** How do I look?

**Cynthia:** Great! You always look

great. How 'bout me?

**Annie:** Oh, stunning, of course. You always look... Ohmigosh! *(She looks across the mall at something.)* Cynthia, did you see that? That girl with the *(pantomiming big hair)* and the *(pantomiming a big derrière)*.

**Cynthia:** She's like a "before" picture if I ever saw one!

**Annie:** "Before" she's put out of her misery, maybe! *(She sees someone else.)* Look over there, isn't that Sid and Nancy? They must think the mall's celebrating Geek Week or something. Look how they're dressed!

**Cynthia:** *(Mockingly)* C'mon, Annie. Don't you know polyester and polka dots are in? It's the *Brady Bunch* look! People just have no taste!

**Annie:** I think I'm gonna gag. *(She covers her mouth and turns, then sees something.)* Cynthia—look over there. *(Quickly, as Cynthia starts to look)* But don't look like you're looking!

**Cynthia:** *(Taking pains to look while she tries not to look like she's looking)* What am I not looking at? All I don't see are some kids across the mall near the "Burger-on-a-Stick" stand.

**Annie:** *(Excited and upset)* Exactly! They're looking right at us!

**Cynthia:** Annie, you're, like, getting your shorts in a knot over this! People are starting to stare!

**Annie:** Don't you see? That's the point! They're looking at us and saying bad stuff about us. I just know it!

**Cynthia:** They are? *(Starting to get upset)* No way!!

**Annie:** Yes way—I can't stand this!

**Cynthia:** How dare they? *(Looking at them)* They're all like trying not to look like they're looking! How rude!

**Annie:** *(Unable to control herself, shouting across the mall)* YOU PEOPLE ARE SO LAME, YOU KNOW THAT? *(Cynthia, about to die of embarrassment, runs off.)* MY FRIEND AND I THINK YOU'RE ABOUT THE RUDEST, MOST INSENSI-TIVE... *(She looks to Cynthia for support, and, seeing she's gone, quickly looks around for her, then runs off.)*

If you use this skit as a discussion starter, here are possible questions:

■ **Why is it so easy for us to judge others?**

■ **Do you think Romans 2:1-3 bans us from making judgments about others? Why or why not?**

# ROMANS
## 3:21-28

**THEME:**
God's grace

**SUMMARY:**
Kids will play a LEARNING GAME they can't win and get the prize anyway.

PREPARATION: You'll need Bibles, paper, a marker, pencils, a whistle, and candy or other snacks for this game. Before kids arrive, write each of the following activities on a separate sign and place them at "activity stations" around your meeting room:

■ Run 2 laps around the room (10 points)

■ Do push-ups (1 point each)

■ Make up poems (10 points per four-line poem recited)

■ Sing songs (5 points for each song that you sing)

■ Hug someone (2 points per hug)

Place a scorekeeper (an adult or someone who's not playing the game) at each of the activity stations.

Form five teams (a team can be one to four people). If you have more than five teams, play in rounds, with an equal number of teams competing each round. Give each team a sheet of paper and a pencil to give to the scorekeeper at each station. Tell kids that you'll give a reward to each team that earns at least 500 points in five minutes. Explain that teams will have one minute at each station.

Have teams each begin at a different station. Begin the game, then blow a whistle or flash the lights every minute to let teams know when to rotate.

When the game is over, tally team scores and determine if anyone reached 500. Then have kids join with members of each of the other teams to form discussion groups of no more than five. Ask:

■ **How did it feel to work**

hard and still fall short of the points you needed to earn?

■ **How is this game like the way we fall short of doing all God wants us to do?**

Present everyone with a reward (candy or another snack). In each group, have the person who lives closest to the church read Romans 3:21-28 for his or her group. Then ask:

■ **How is the reward you just received like the reward God gives us?**

■ **How does it feel to know God's grace is free?**

■ **How should this knowledge affect the way we live?**

After discussion, have kids form a circle and take turns telling one important thing they've learned through this activity.

# ROMANS
## 3:23-24; 6:23

---

## THEME:
Rescued from sin

## SUMMARY:
In this DEVOTION, teenagers explore what it means to be rescued from the penalty of sin.

---

PREPARATION: You'll need Bibles.

EXPERIENCE

Form groups of no more than three. Say: **In your trios, describe a time that you were rescued from something. For example, maybe you were saved from**

drowning, or maybe your parents' advice saved you from making a bad mistake. **Have the oldest person in your group go first, then the second oldest, and so on. You have one minute to think about what you'll say, then each trio member will have one minute to share a "rescue experience."**

Give kids a minute of "think time," then have group members begin telling about their experiences. After four minutes, have kids pick one rescue story to share with the entire group.

RESPONSE

When each of the selected rescue stories has been told, say: **The Bible teaches that all Christians have been rescued by Jesus. Let's read about that now.**

Have the youngest person in each trio read Romans 3:23-24, and the oldest person read Romans 6:23. Ask trios:

■ **How is the way Jesus rescues us from sin like or unlike the way you were rescued in your stories?**

■ **Why do you think Romans 3:23 can say that everyone has sinned?**

■ **How does it make you feel to read in Romans 6:23 that the penalty for sin is death? Explain.**

■ **How can Jesus rescue us from the penalty of sin?**

After discussion, have trio members share with the class any insights they gained.

CLOSING

To close, sing a worship chorus

or hymn about how Jesus saves us from the penalty of sin. For example, you might sing "I've Been Redeemed" or "Amazing Grace" (both of these songs are found in *The Group Songbook,* available from Group Publishing).

After the meeting, you might also offer to talk to anyone who wants to know more about how to accept Jesus' payment for sin.

# ROMANS 4:4-6

## THEME:
God's grace

## SUMMARY:
In this SKIT, an overachieving student thinks her future is more dependent upon her standardized test results than God's grace.

## AND THE WINNER IS...

SCENE: Joan, an overachiever, is sitting at the kitchen table passing the time waiting for the mail to arrive. She's reading a book.

PROPS: You'll need a book, a stack of mail, an envelope with a piece of paper sealed inside, and a Bible for the discussion afterward.

CHARACTERS:
Joan
Sarah

### SCRIPT
**Joan:** *(Sits at table and reads a book for a few moments, then looks at her watch. Shouting offstage to Sarah)* Sarah! Did you see the mail carrier yet?

**Sarah:** *(Offstage)* Yeah—I put the mail on the counter. *(Joan goes to the counter and quickly finds a certain envelope. She sits down and looks hard at it without opening it. Sarah walks in.)* Anything good? *(No response.)* Yoo-hoo! Earth to Joan!

**Joan:** What?... Oh, I'm sorry, just thinking about my future.

**Sarah:** As what—an envelope inspector?

**Joan:** *(Chuckling)* No, these are my standardized test scores. *(She continues staring at the envelope.)*

**Sarah:** Do they test you for X-ray vision or what? Open it!

**Joan:** I'm afraid to.

**Sarah:** What?

**Joan:** I'm afraid to. I mean, think of it. These will determine what college I go to, which will affect what kind of degree I get, which will mean what career I choose, which will determine how much money I make, which will dictate whether I live in a nice house and have a nice family and a nice life!

**Sarah:** *(Pretending to be astounded)* Boy, that is an important envelope!

**Joan:** It's my future. *(Seriously)* It'll mean either I'm something, or I'm nothing.

**Sarah:** You're something, all right, but being your friend I won't say what. Now open the thing!

**Joan:** But what if they say I'm not good enough to go to a good school and get a good job and have a good life?

**Sarah:** Oh, come on. Do you really think your score on this test will determine all those things?

**Joan:** If you want the good life, you've got to live up to a certain standard. *(She holds up the envelope.)*

**Sarah:** *(Skeptically)* OK, if you say so ... *(Impatiently)* Open it!!

**Joan:** Here goes ... *(Hesitating)* Winner or loser? Top or flop? Yes or no? Andy or Barney? Hit or...

**Sarah:** Enough already!! *(She grabs the envelope, quickly rips it open, then takes out and begins reading the enclosed paper.)*

**Joan:** *(Anxiously)* Well? Well? *(Both freeze to end the skit.)*

If you use this skit as a discussion starter, here are possible questions:

■ **Why is it so easy to trust ourselves instead of God?**

■ **How does Romans 4:4-6 apply to the goals we've set for ourselves?**

# ROMANS
# 5:1-5

---

THEME:
Hope

SUMMARY:
At this RETREAT, kids will develop strategies for bringing hope to "hopeless" people.

---

PREPARATION: Advertise this overnight retreat as a "hopeful" event. Send out notices telling kids you "hope" they'll be able to attend. List on your fliers the Scripture passage on which this retreat is based (Romans 5:1-5). You'll need Bibles at the retreat.

As kids arrive, lead a brief worship experience where teenagers name ways they have hope in their lives. For example, kids might say they hope for a peaceful society, for future success, or for better understanding of the Bible. Have kids read aloud Romans 5:1-5 and give thanks for the hope that Christ gives.

Then challenge the group to use this retreat to struggle with this question:

■ **How can we share our hope with people who have little or no hope?**

Form four or five "hope" teams and assign one of the following questions to each team:

■ **How can we offer hope to latch-key children in our community who are lonely?**

■ **How can we offer hope to the poor and the hungry in our community?**

■ **How can we offer hope to peers at school and in our community who are troubled by addiction or living in abusive situations?**

■ **How can we offer hope to the elderly in our community?**

■ **How can we offer hope to kids of all ages who've lost a parent, either through death or divorce?**

(You may want to adapt the situations to fit your own community.)

Have teams spend most of the retreat time developing strategies to give hope to each of these groups of people. Encourage hope teams to develop specific plans for the who, how, when, what, and where of accomplishing their hope-giving tasks.

If possible, have an adult sponsor with a special interest in one of the needy groups guide each team, stimulate ideas, and keep teams focused. You may want to invite representatives of the various needy groups to meet with the teams and answer questions.

Throughout the retreat, have kids create skits, sing songs, and tell stories that help bring the topic of hope to life.

Conclude the retreat by having hope teams present their plans to the larger group. Read aloud Romans 5:1-5 as a closing prayer of hope.

# ROMANS
## 5:6-11

## THEME:

God's friendship

## SUMMARY:
In this SKIT, contestants compete for the title of "Perfect Best Friend."

## THE FRIENDSHIP SHOW

SCENE: A game show setting, similar to *The Dating Game.*

PROPS: You'll need a microphone, three chairs (one for each contestant), and a Bible for the discussion afterward.

CHARACTERS:
**Emcee**
**Self-Centered Sonja**
**Tyler Trueheart**
**Mean-Minded Myrna**

### SCRIPT

**Emcee:** Welcome to *The Friendship Show,* where we present you with three choices for the perfect best friend. Let's give a warm game show welcome to our three contestants for today! First, straight from her room, where she spends most of her time fixing her hair, welcome Self-Centered Sonja.

**Sonja:** I'm so glad you get to meet me!

**Emcee:** Next, meet a person whose favorite hobby is throwing his classmates surprise parties, welcome Tyler Trueheart.

**Tyler:** Thanks, you're really the best bunch of people I've ever met.

**Emcee:** Our final contestant claims her hero is Oscar the Grouch, of *Sesame Street* fame. Please welcome Mean-Minded Myrna.

**Myrna:** Get outta my face, buffalo breath!

**Emcee:** OK, here's the way our game works: I'll ask three questions to which each of you may respond. At the end of this question and answer time, our studio audience will vote on which contestant they'd choose as a friend. Is everybody ready? Here's question #1: What would you say is a fun way to spend time with a friend?

**Sonja:** Well, let me see. There are so many... My friend could give me a new perm or help me reorganize my room or help me get ready for a date.

**Tyler:** First, I'd need to know what this friend really enjoys. Then I'd do what I always do for a new friend—I'd make my friend's favorite food, and hold a party in his or her honor.

**Myrna:** *(To Tyler)* What a waste. I'd think of some way to upset this person, like spreading a rumor about him or her or stealing something from school and blaming it on this so-called friend.

**Emcee:** Thank you, contestants. Now, question #2: It's your best friend's birthday. What present are you going to give?

**Sonja:** A wall-sized poster of...me!

**Tyler:** Well, I'd try to find out what he or she needed most, then see what I could do to give it to my friend.

**Myrna:** I'd send my cousin Guido over to his house to present him with a knuckle sandwich.

**Emcee:** Thanks again, contestants. Now, your final question: What do you consider the most important quality in a friend?

**Sonja:** The ability to know what makes me feel special.

**Tyler:** Love.

**Myrna:** Up-to-date life insurance.

**Emcee:** *(To audience)* You've heard their responses, and now it's time for you to decide. Who would you choose for a friend? Will it be contestant #1, 2, or 3?

Have the audience applaud to select the person they think would best fit the title of "Perfect Best Friend." The contestant who receives the loudest applause wins.

Then, spark discussion about Romans 5:6-11 by following the skit with these discussion questions:

■ **What character in the skit do you tend to act like most?**

■ **How is the way God chose us as friends like or unlike the way we chose friends in this game?**

■ **What can we learn about God from Romans 5:6-11? about ourselves? about choosing friends?**

■ **What's your reaction to the news that Jesus died so you could become friends with God?**

# ROMANS
# 6:8-14

**THEME:**
New life in Christ

**SUMMARY:**
In this OBJECT LESSON, kids will examine items from their past and discuss how Christ brings new life.

PREPARATION: Before the activity, ask group members to bring clothes, toys, books, or other items that they've outgrown to your meeting. Bring a few extra children's things in case some group members forget. You'll also need Bibles.

Begin the meeting by having teenagers create a "display window" (similar to the ones in department stores) using only the items they brought. Afterward, have teenagers gather around the display.

Form groups of no more than four and have kids take turns answering the following questions in their groups. Then have volunteers share their groups' responses with the whole class. Ask:

■ **What do these items in this display remind you of?**

■ **Why do our feelings about certain childhood items change as we grow older?**

■ **What were you interested in as a child that no longer seems important to you?**

Say: **As we grow older, we grow out of some things and grow into others.**

Have one person in each group read Romans 6:8-14 for his or her group. Then ask:

■ **How are the things we've outgrown like or unlike the old ways we're to leave behind as written in this passage?**

■ **How is new life in Christ like the new life that growing up brings?**

■ **In what ways does Jesus give us new life?**

■ **What items from our past do we leave behind when we gain that new life?**

■ **What keeps you from expe-** riencing to the fullest the new life in Jesus that's described in Romans 6:8-14? What can you do about that this week?

Have kids join hands in a circle around the items you displayed. Invite teenagers to participate in a closing prayer by asking them to each think of one part of their old lives to which they've died (such as being greedy or hard-hearted) and one thing they love about their new life in Christ (such as knowing forgiveness or being able to start over).

Open the prayer by saying: **Thank you, God, for new life. Thank you for helping us die to** (have teenagers name parts of the old life). **Thank you for the joys of the new life such as** (have teenagers name what they love about new life in Christ). **Amen.**

# ROMANS
## 7:7

THEME:
Rules

SUMMARY:
In this SKIT, four friends find out what happens when rules are ignored.

## HE WHO LIVES BY THE RULES...

SCENE: Four friends are playing a board game.

PROPS: You'll need a board game

with money, tokens, dice, and a rule book. You'll also need a table, four chairs, and a Bible for the discussion afterward.

CHARACTERS:
Jake
Marie
Albert
Kath

## SCRIPT

*(Jake, Marie, Albert, and Kath are sitting at the table, playing a board game. Marie sits to Jake's left.)*

**Jake:** Awright, my turn. Gimme the dice!

**Marie:** OK, OK, don't get so excited!

**Jake:** *(Chuckling gleefully)* I love this game! *(He rolls.)*

**Albert:** *(Happily)* Six! You got a six! You land on my home space—that'll be 100 bucks, please!

**Jake:** Except, I'm only gonna go four, so I get to land on this "Easy Money" space.

**Kath:** What do you mean you're only gonna go four? *(She looks at the others.)* He can't just go four, can he? *(She grabs the rule book and starts to look through it.)*

**Jake:** Just watch me! *(He picks up an "Easy Money" card.)* "Take $40 from the player on your left."

**Marie:** Don't you even try, Jake! *(He tries, and they fight over the money.)*

**Jake:** Gimme that money!

**Marie:** Forget it! It's my turn, by the way. *(She grabs the dice, rolls, doesn't like the first results,*

*and rolls again.)*

**Albert:** What are *you* doing now? You're allowed to roll only once!

**Marie:** *(Smugly)* Rules are made to be broken.

**Albert:** What? Without the rules, we wouldn't even know how to play the game!

**Marie:** *(Ignoring him)* I'm on your "Reversal of Fortune" space— give me $85!

**Albert:** That's not fair!

**Marie:** Life isn't fair! *(She grabs some money, and Albert pouts.)* Kath, it's your turn!

**Kath:** *(Looking up from the rule book)* OK... *(She rolls and proceeds normally.)* Hmm...the Hotel Sweeney. I'll buy it.

**Jake:** Are you environmentally friendly?

**Kath:** Huh?

**Jake:** I lead a community group that's going to block the sale of the hotel unless you promise to use all-natural products in the care and upkeep of it.

**Kath:** *(She grabs the rule book again.)* Community environmental group? All-natural products? *(She buries her nose in the rule book.)*

**Jake:** Ha, ha! My turn! Where's my piece? *(He looks around. Marie has a smirk on her face)* YOU! *(They both jump up, and he chases her out of the room.)*

**Albert:** Well, as long as they're gone... *(He starts taking their money and putting it with his own.)*

**Kath:** You can't do that!

**Albert:** As I believe someone has already said, "Just watch me." *(He takes all their money and sits back contentedly.)*

**Kath:** *(Frustrated)* None of this is in the rules! I quit! *(She leaves. Albert stuffs his pockets with money and leaves.)*

If you use this skit as a discussion starter, here are possible questions:

■ **How would you feel if there were no rules in life?**

■ **According to Romans 7:7, why are God's laws important for everyday living?**

# ROMANS
# 8:22-25

**THEME:**
The future

**SUMMARY:**
At this RETREAT, kids will explore how they're growing more Christlike as they think about their hope for the future.

PREPARATION: Plan this event as a two-day retreat and don't forget to bring Bibles.

Use Romans 8:22-25 as a guide for this weekend. On the first day of the retreat, focus on the present and where kids are in their spiritual lives. Allow plenty of time for kids to evaluate what they feel most confident about in their faith and what they wish they knew more about.

Then, on the second day, have kids focus on the future and what God might have in store for them spiritually.

Here are some activities to consider for the retreat:

■ Form groups of no more than four and have group members interview each other about what they think God wants them to be like, what pleases God most about who they are now, what they pray God is being patient with them about, and who they hope they'll be someday.

■ Have kids put together a skit titled "Our Youth Group: What We'll Remember." Have kids include (in serious or comical form) events, characteristics, disappointments, and questions they have that record who they are today.

■ Use refrigerator boxes to create a "time tunnel" for kids to crawl through to begin the second half of the retreat. You may want to decorate the tunnel with pictures and souvenirs from past youth group events.

■ Have people who've graduated from your youth program attend the second half of the retreat and discuss the changes they've experienced as they've matured in faith.

■ Have teenagers rewrite Romans 8:22-25 in their own words, then discuss these questions:

■ **Why do you think Paul included these thoughts in his letter to the Romans?**

■ **What makes it hard to wait for God to finish his work on us?**

■ **What can we do to help each other wait patiently and not lose hope?**

■ **If Paul, the apostle were here today, what do you think he'd tell us about this passage of Scripture?**

# ROMANS 8:26-27

**THEME:**
Prayer

**SUMMARY:**
In this CREATIVE PRAYER, kids will discover how the Holy Spirit searches our hearts and helps us pray.

PREPARATION: You'll need Bibles.

Read Romans 8:26-27 aloud. Then have kids share times they've had a difficult time knowing how (or what) to pray.

Say: **This passage helps us see that we can always pray, even when we don't know what words to say.**

Form pairs. Ask the pairs to first tell each other something they're concerned about. Then have partners take turns restating those concerns as prayers. For example, if someone mentions a concern about a non-Christian parent, his or her partner might pray, "Dear God, reach out to Tom's dad and help him to know you."

When partners have finished praying, ask:

■ **How was your partner's prayer like what the Holy Spirit does when we don't know how to pray?**

■ **How is the Holy Spirit's function different?**

■ **What can we do when we're unsure of how to pray for something or someone?**

Say: **Praying for each other is a picture of how the Spirit helps us pray. As your partner prayed, you were praying also.**

Encourage kids to spend at least another five minutes praying for each others' concerns.

# ROMANS 8:28

**THEME:**
Finding good in bad times

**SUMMARY:**
Kids will form rescue teams in this PROJECT to help bring good results from disastrous events.

PREPARATION: You'll need a Bible.

Form "rescue teams" of no more than six. Meet with the rescue teams and read Romans 8:28. Discuss how kids can be a part of fulfilling God's promise in this verse by bringing good to events that seem like disasters. Use the examples that follow to help kids explore ways they can find the good in a bad situation:

■ Your church sponsors an all-church picnic, but only three families attend.

■ Your children's church is out of control. Kids don't seem to be having any fun or learning anything.

■ The church van breaks down just before a senior citizen outing.

■ A family in your church experiences a devastating fire and loses everything.

Have kids think of their own disasters or failures and plan what they could do to bring good out of a bad situation.

Each week, have kids report any "disaster" situations they could step in and help with. Then mobilize your rescue teams and send them out to help in any way possible.

After each rescue operation, have teams meet to discuss how they brought good in bad situations.

Use the theme of Romans 8:28 as the focus for a "finding-the-good-in-things" party. Have kids each bring something they might have otherwise thrown away (such as a pair of old jeans, a cereal box, or an empty candy wrapper) as a ticket to get into the party.

During the party, lead a game where groups compete to see how many uses they can find for the items they've brought. Award used items (such as old tires, broken appliances, or scrap paper) as prizes to the kids who come up with most uses for their items.

End the party by serving "recycled" treats such as cookie crumbs, leftover pizza, and leftover cake frosting on graham crackers.

# ROMANS
## 8:28

---

**THEME:**
Joy

**SUMMARY:**
Kids will celebrate the joy of Romans 8:28 with a PARTY.

---

PREPARATION: You'll need Bibles and a place for the party. You'll also want to collect and set up party decorations and snacks ahead of time.

# ROMANS
## 8:31-39

---

**THEME:**
Impossible things

**SUMMARY:**
Teenagers will play a LEARNING GAME to discover how impossible it is for them to be separated from God's love.

---

PREPARATION: You'll need balloons, markers, and Bibles.

Read aloud Romans 8:31-39. Next, distribute a balloon and a marker to each person. Have kids each inflate their balloons, tie them, and write on them one of the things that won't separate us from God's love, listed in Romans 8:35, 38-39.

Have teenagers form pairs and take turns telling their partners how the things on their balloons might cause them to feel like God is far away. For example, someone might say that going through "troubles" could make it seem like God has forgotten him or her.

When everyone has shared, reread Romans 8:31-39 aloud. Then have kids race to see how quickly they can pop all the balloons without using their hands. After all the balloons are popped, have pairs discuss these questions:

■ **What obstacles seem to get in the way of your relationship with God?**

■ **When do you feel closest to God? Explain.**

■ **How was popping these balloons like what God does to things that could separate us from his love?**

■ **How can Romans 8:31-39 give us hope this week when we feel like God is far away?**

# ROMANS
## 8:31-39

THEME:
    God's inseparable love

SUMMARY:
    In this LEARNING GAME, kids will compare a shadow to the inseparable love God gives us.

PREPARATION: Meet outside near dusk on a sunny day, when kids will have visible shadows. Or set up a large lamp in a corner of your room in such a way as to create shadows. You'll also need Bibles.

Play Shadow Tag with your group. In Shadow Tag, the person who is "It" runs around and tries to tag other people by stepping on or touching their shadows.

After a few rounds, meet in a circle and see who can create the best shadow shape with his or her hands (such as a rabbit, a dog, or a sea monster). Then have kids attempt to make their shadows disappear (without leaving the sunny area).

Afterward, gather everyone in a circle. Have kids take turns reading a verse of Romans 8:31-39 until you've read the entire passage.

For the next series of questions, have kids cross their arms over their chests and take turns sharing responses to each question. When one person shares an answer, allow anyone who thought of the same answer and has nothing more to add to uncross his or her arms. When kids have all uncrossed their arms, ask the next question and repeat the process. Ask:

■ **How is trying to separate yourself from a shadow like or unlike the way Jesus loves us?**

■ **Why is it important for us to know that nothing can separate us from God's love?**

■ **How can you remind yourself of the truth of Romans 8:31-39 when God seems far away?**

Have kids form cross-shaped

shadows by holding their arms parallel to the ground and standing still. As kids are forming these shadows, say: **Like a shadow on a sunny day, Christ's love is always with us.**

Encourage kids to think of Romans 8:31-39 each time they see their shadows during the coming week. Then close with a moment of silent prayer.

# ROMANS
# 10:11-15

### THEME:

Sharing the good news

### SUMMARY:

In this MUSIC IDEA/ADVENTURE, kids will plan ways to share God's good news with others through music.

PREPARATION: You'll need Bibles, songbooks, and someone who can accompany kids on a guitar. Or get a copy of *The Group Songbook* and its accompaniment tapes for kids to use (these are available from Group Publishing). If you use *The Group Songbook* accompaniment tapes, you'll also need a cassette player.

Arrange in advance a place where your group will be singing. Plan for transportation if necessary.

Have kids meet and practice songs that celebrate God's love, such as "Shine on My Life With Your Love," "We Are the Reason," or "Jesus Loves Me." Have kids choose three or four songs they enjoy singing.

Then form pairs and have partners read Romans 10:11-15. In response to the message of this passage, have pairs brainstorm specific ways they can use their music to tell others about Christ. For example, they could put on a sidewalk concert, go "love caroling," or learn how to express their chosen songs through sign language.

Next have pairs join together to form song teams, then send kids out to places they can spread their message through music, such as nursing homes, hospitals, homeless shelters, malls, and city streets.

# ROMANS
# 12

### THEME:
The body of Christ

### SUMMARY:
Teenagers will play a LEARNING GAME to help them understand how members of a body need to work together.

PREPARATION: You'll need to prepare slips of paper that have one of the following parts of the body written on them: right arm, right hand, left arm, left hand, torso, left leg, and right leg. You'll also need a snack reward for everyone and Bibles.

As kids arrive, give them each one of the slips of paper you've prepared. Have kids join with other people who have the same body part. Then move everyone outside to a field or to an empty parking lot.

Tell kids to lie on the ground and work together to form a giant body. (It's OK to reassign some young people if you have too many "hands" or not enough "legs.")

Once the body is made, say: **I'm going to give several simple commands that you must do *as a body*. If you're able to complete all the commands within five minutes, you'll win a snack reward. Here's the list:**

■ **Take five steps.**

■ **Do a somersault.**

■ **Pick up a ball and toss it from one hand to the other.**

■ **Do five jumping jacks.**

■ **Wave your hands while running.**

Time kids to see how long it takes to complete the tasks. Give everyone a snack reward if kids are able to finish in five minutes or less. Then form small groups for discussion and ask:

■ **What was difficult about this activity?**

■ **How did it feel to be a part of the body? Explain.**

■ **How is moving with this body of ours like being a part of the body of Christ?**

Have one person in each small group read aloud Romans 12, and the others summarize the passage in one sentence. Ask:

■ **Why do you think Paul uses the example of a body to describe Christians?**

■ **Why is it important for Christians to work together like a body?**

■ **In what ways is Jesus the head of the church body?**

■ **How would you summarize the picture of Paul's words in verses 10-21, which describe the body of Christ working together?**

■ **What can you do this week to make Paul's word picture in Romans 12 come to life in our church?**

# ROMANS
## 12:1-2

THEME:
God's transforming power

SUMMARY:
In this OBJECT LESSON, teenagers will examine water and a rock to discover the transforming power of God.

PREPARATION: On a table, set out several water-tight containers, such as different-shaped glasses, a bowl, a plastic bag, and a pitcher. You'll also want a lump of clay that can fit in all of these containers. Fill one of the containers with water. Place the clay in a different container. You'll also need newsprint, a marker, and several different versions of the Bible.

Form a circle and ask for volunteers to read aloud Romans 12:1-2 from several different versions. Ask kids to explain what they think the difference is between being "transformed" and being "conformed" (verse 2). Write their responses on newsprint.

Hold up the water-filled container and ask group members to describe the shape of the water. Wait until they say it's the shape of the container. Pour the water into another container and ask them to describe its shape. Again, it's the shape of the container. Repeat this until you've moved the water into several different containers.

Now ask for a revised definition of "conformity"; for example, accepting the mold or taking the shape of a container.

Hold up the container with the clay in it. Ask kids to describe the shape of the clay. Change containers and again ask about the clay's shape. Change one more time and ask kids to describe the clay's shape. Put down the clay and ask kids to volunteer answers to these questions:

■ **In this experiment, what was the difference between the way the clay behaved and the way the water behaved?**

■ **What can we learn from the clay that can help us understand what it means to be "transformed" by God's way of thinking?**

■ **Which are you more like in your life—the water or the clay? Explain.**

■ **In what ways does God transform Christians like a potter transforms clay?**

Say: **As we are transformed by Christ, we stop being like the water and become more like the clay. We stay the same in all kinds of environments in the world but are still able to be molded and transformed by God.**

Have kids think of one area in their lives where they conform to society. Encourage them to commit themselves to letting Christ transform them in that area.

VARIATION: You might also want to add another aspect to the object lesson by having one container that the clay doesn't fit into. Then you could discuss how Christians don't fit into the world system.

# ROMANS
## 12:1-8

THEME:
Giving of ourselves

SUMMARY:
In this AFFIRMATION, kids will determine ways they can serve each other.

PREPARATION: Cut two or three dollar-sized pieces of green paper for each group member. You'll also need an offering plate, pencils, and Bibles.

Give kids each a pencil and two or three dollar-size pieces of paper. Have kids sign their names on their papers and write on each one a service they could do for others in the group during the next week (such as helping with homework, setting up chairs, praying for someone, or helping with chores).

Next, have kids take turns reading a verse of Romans 12:1-8 until the group has read aloud the entire passage. Ask:

■ **How do we serve God when we serve each other?**

■ **Why is it important to serve each other?**

Pass an offering plate around and have kids drop their completed papers into it. Then pass the plate again and have kids each take out one or two papers written by someone else. Have kids find the people who wrote their service and arrange to have them perform that service within the next week. Allow kids to trade papers if they don't need or can't use the service they chose.

Say: **When you perform these acts of service for one another, remember that you're performing them also for Christ.**

Encourage kids to use the ideas they get from this activity to serve one another even after this activity is fulfilled.

# ROMANS
## 12:4-8

THEME:
Working together

SUMMARY:
Kids will work on a PROJECT together and discover how that's like working together as the body of Christ.

PREPARATION: Contact nonprofit businesses in your community to see how your youth group could help them. You'll also need Bibles and snacks.

Arrange for teenagers to do a volunteer project for a nonprofit organization (such as getting a mass mailing ready for the post office, building playground equipment, or organizing a party).

Find an organization that has more than enough work for everyone in your group so that everyone has a role in this endeavor. Some of the best ideas will allow kids to work in an assembly line fashion (for example, folding newsletters or fliers, stuffing them into envelopes, and addressing envelopes).

Take kids to their work site and lead them in doing the job that's been determined. After a long stretch of work, take a snack break and ask:

■ **How does it feel to be working together so closely?**

■ **How does each person's role affect the final product?**

Form discussion groups of no more than three. Have the person wearing the most red in each group read aloud Romans 12:4-8. Ask groups to discuss these questions:

■ **How is the way we're working together today similar to what this passage says about the body of Christ?**

■ **What can we accomplish when we use the gifts we've been given and work together?**

■ **What happens when someone doesn't use his or her gifts?**

■ **What truth from this passage might help us work together more effectively on our project today?**

Pray a prayer similar to this before sending group members to finish their work: **Lord, thank you for showing us the good things that can happen when we all work together. Help us appreciate those we work with and be willing to fulfill our roles effectively, too. In Jesus' name, amen.**

As kids return to work, encourage them to take a minute and thank all the people in their work team by giving them a pat on the back and an encouraging word.

# ROMANS 12:9-21

THEME:
Showing love

SUMMARY:
In this PROJECT/ PARTY, kids will sponsor a festival to show their love and compassion for the community.

PREPARATION: Kids will prepare booths for a variety of activities. You'll need plenty of poster board, markers, and other supplies (determined by what kids choose to do for the festival). You'll also need Bibles.

Have kids volunteer to be on a youth group festival-planning committee. Then hold a planning meeting with those kids to work out how you'll put on the festival.

At the meeting, have kids form pairs and read Romans 12:9-21. Ask pairs to discuss these questions:

■ **In what ways does Romans 12:9-21 encourage Christians to show compassion?**

■ **What implications does this passage have for how we should reach out to our own community with our festival?**

Tell kids that in response to this passage, the theme for the festival will be "compassion." Then have kids brainstorm ways they can show love for their neighbors through a compassion festival. The festival could include booths such as the following:

■ **Service booth**—Kids would take requests from community members for helping out at their homes (raking leaves, shoveling snow, painting trim, and so on). Make sure kids don't commit to more activities than they can truly handle.

■ **Food booth**—Kids would prepare and distribute cookies, punch, and other treats to people who attend the festival.

■ **Music booth**—The musical kids in your group would provide live or recorded music to liven up the festival. Encourage kids to choose uplifting music that speaks of God's love.

■ **Carwash booth (if weather permits)**—Kids would offer free carwashes to people who drive to the festival.

■ **Story booth**—Teenagers who are good with children would read stories to younger children who attend.

■ **Games-for-children booth**—Teenagers can collect several children's games and toys into one booth and invite children to come play while their parents check out the other booths.

■ **Free-stuff booth**—Kids would collect garage sale type items to give away to people who need or want them.

Have kids choose the kinds of activities they feel are most important for this festival. Then help kids plan, publicize, and run this event at your church or at a nearby park.

# ROMANS
# 16:1-16

**THEME:**
Thankfulness

**SUMMARY:**
In this AFFIRMATION, kids will create huge thank-you notes for church members.

PREPARATION: You'll need rolls of adding machine tape, thin-tipped markers, masking tape, and Bibles.

Form groups of no more than four and have a volunteer in each group read aloud Romans 16:1-16. Then have groups discuss these questions:

■ **What's significant about this list of Paul's personal greetings?**

■ **Why do you suppose it's included in the Bible?**

■ **Why is it important to be thankful for people in our lives?**

Give each group a roll of adding machine tape, thin-tipped markers, and masking tape.

Say: **In your group, brainstorm things you're thankful for about the people in this room and in our church. Then work together to write the world's longest thank-you note to each person you think of. Be specific about who you're writing to and why you're thankful. You might want to assign one person in your group to be the scribe who writes your group's thank-yous, or you might want to take turns writing. Ready? Go.**

Encourage groups to fill up one whole side of the adding machine tape with their thanks. Then have kids tape the long strips of paper around the church for other church members to see and appreciate.

VARIATION: An alternative to this idea is to have kids each choose a category of people to write their thanks to, such as missionaries, church staff, community leaders, or family members.

# 1 Corinthians

*"Don't you know that you are God's temple
and that God's Spirit lives in you?"*

*1 Corinthians 3:16*

# 1 CORINTHIANS 1:18-31

THEME:
Wisdom

SUMMARY:
In this ADVENTURE, kids will go on a scavenger hunt for "worthless" items.

PREPARATION: You'll need paper, pencils, Bibles, and as many nickels as you have youth group members.

Form teams of three and give each team three nickels. Then say: **Your challenge is to collect three of the most unimportant items you can find. You'll do this by knocking on doors in the neighborhood surrounding our church.** (If your neighborhood is unsafe, tell teams to bring back to your meeting room the three most unimportant things they can find in your church.)

**When people answer the door, tell them you're from our church and you've been sent on an unusual scavenger hunt. Ask them to give you the most unimportant thing they have in their homes. They can choose anything, even a rubber band or a paper clip. In return, give them one of your nickels. When you've collected three items, return to this room. No matter what, make sure you're back here in 20 minutes. Ready? Go!**

When kids return, give each team a sheet of paper, a Bible, and a pencil. Ask teams to read aloud 1 Corinthians 1:18-31. Then challenge teams to brainstorm reasons their three items *are* important and valuable. Give teams five minutes to brainstorm and tell them the team that lists the most reasons will win a special honor.

Call time after five minutes and ask teams to display their three items and read aloud their important lists. Have the team with the most reasons stand in the middle of the room. On your signal, have the other teams carry out a 10-second "honor explosion" for the winning team members by shining their shoes, rubbing their backs, applauding them, bowing to them, and complimenting them.

Then ask:
■ **How did you feel when I asked you to brainstorm reasons your three items were actually important?**
■ **How is this experience like what Paul writes about in 1 Corinthians 1:18-31?**
■ **What does it mean that God chose the unimportant things of the world to destroy what the world thinks is important?**
■ **Think about your life and the world you live in. What's something that looks foolish to the rest of the world but is actually quite important to God? Explain.**

# 1 CORINTHIANS 2:11-16

**THEME:**
Knowing God

**SUMMARY:**
In this OBJECT LESSON, kids will attempt to read each other's thoughts.

PREPARATION: You'll need paper, pencils, and Bibles.

Form two equal groups and ask kids in each group to line up along opposite walls in your meeting room, facing each other. Say: **Walk straight toward each other until you're standing opposite of one other person. The person you're now facing is your partner for this activity.**

Give each pair a sheet of paper and a pencil and ask them to sit back to back. Tell partners to decide who'll be the mind reader and who'll be the client. Then tell all the clients to pick up the paper and pencil.

Say: **Clients, you have one minute to think of a thought— any thought—then write it on your sheet of paper. When you're finished writing, fold the paper.**

After one minute, say: **Clients and mind readers, turn to face each other. Clients, give your mind reader your folded paper. Mind readers, put the paper to your forehead, concentrate, then tell your client what he or she has written on the paper.**

**When you've guessed, open the paper to see if you were right.**

After all the mind readers have guessed, ask if anyone correctly guessed what was on his or her client's paper. Applaud those who happen to guess correctly. If you have time, have partners switch roles and repeat this activity.

Then gather together and ask:
■ **Is it possible to read someone's mind? Why or why not?**
■ **Mind readers, how did you feel as you tried to figure out what was on the paper?**
■ **Clients, how did you feel when your mind reader guessed what you had written?**

Ask a volunteer to read aloud 1 Corinthians 2:11-16. Then wrap up the activity by asking:
■ **How is the message of this passage like our mind-reading experiment?**
■ **How can we know "the mind of God"?**
■ **What does it mean that we have "the mind of Christ"?**

# 1 CORINTHIANS 3:5

**THEME:**
Trusting God

**SUMMARY:**
In this SKIT, a famous athlete plugs himself on a late-night TV commercial.

## JUST BUY IT

SCENE: A late-night TV commercial.

PROPS: You'll need a Bible for the discussion afterward.

CHARACTERS:
**Marcus Jackson** (an athletic-looking guy)

## SCRIPT
*(Marcus is standing facing the audience, as if he's making a pitch on a TV commercial.)*

**Marcus:** Hi! Do you know me? Unless you've been living in a cave, you do! That's right—I'm Marcus Jackson, world-famous athlete. You know, whether I was scoring the winning touchdown at last year's Super Bowl or shooting a 3-pointer at the buzzer for the Morristown Mosquitoes, I always had my mind on one thing—the thing that kept me going and made everything worthwhile...me! I'm the greatest, and I can trust in me to get me through each day.

And now, you can learn to trust in me by attending one of my Marcus Jackson Self-Enhancement Seminars. When you attend, you'll be treated to a fantastic weekend where you'll learn all about...me!

You'll have your picture taken with a life-size, cardboard cutout of...me! In the evening sessions, Marcusian-trained counselors will assist you in becoming more like...me! That's right, you'll begin to experience the greatness of...me, Marcus Jackson. You'll discover that no hurdle is too high, no defensive line too strong, no fly ball too much in the sun for...me! You, like me, will realize that I can do anything.

And, you'll have a chance to become even more like me by shopping at our special Marcus-Seminar Mart, where you can purchase Marcus Jackson brand cross trainers, Marcus Jackson brand sweat bands, Marcus Jackson brand T-shirts, Marcus Jackson brand tube socks, and Marcus Jackson brand roll-on deodorant directly from...me!

So don't delay—call right now and send a check or charge the low, low price of $395 to any major credit card. You'll be on your way to becoming just like...ME!

If you use this skit as a discussion starter, here are possible questions:

■ **What's the difference between what Paul wrote in 1 Corinthians 3:5 and what Marcus Jackson said in this skit?**

■ **Why are people so consumed with being important?**

■ **What can you do this week to help you imitate Paul's attitude in 1 Corinthians 3:5?**

# 1 CORINTHIANS 3:10-15

## THEME:

Being tested by fire

## SUMMARY:
In this OBJECT LESSON, kids will build an "office building," then determine how the building is like their lives.

PREPARATION: You'll need a match (a long fireplace match is best) and three or four garbage bags. Spread the garbage bags out flat in the middle of the room. You'll also need a Bible and materials with which kids can build, such as sticks, wood blocks, paper, tape, and bricks.

Form five "design teams" (a team can be one person, if necessary).

Say: **Imagine you're all employees at the prestigious architectural firm Buildings 'R' Us. You've just won an important contract to design a four-story office building. The people who've hired you tell you they expect your creation to stand up to rigorous structural tests.**

**Each of you is a member of one of five design teams at Buildings 'R' Us. Four teams will each be responsible for designing one floor of the office building. The fifth team will be responsible for laying the foundation for the building. Both the foundation and the floors should fit on the garbage bags in the middle of the room.**

Tell teams what floor they'll be responsible for and assign one team to lay the foundation. Tell that team they must build their foundation on top of the garbage bags.

Then say: **You each have 10 minutes to build your floor or complete the foundation. Then we'll put all the parts together. You can use anything in this room as building materials or anything on the church grounds. But remember—you only have 10 minutes to gather your materials and build your floor. Ready? Go!**

Have design teams put together the office building and work together until it can stand on its own. Then say: **OK, now let's test this building to see if it's a strong design.**

Light your match. Ask:

■ **Is this building strong enough to make it through a terrible fire? Why or why not?**

■ **If you knew I was going to set fire to your building, how would your team have built its floor or foundation differently?**

Blow out the match, then ask a volunteer to read aloud 1 Corinthians 3:10-15. Then say: **Get together with your design-team members and answer this question: "Knowing that my life is going to be 'tested by fire,' what would I change about the way I'm living my life today?"**

# 1 CORINTHIANS 3:16-17

## THEME:
The body, God's temple

## SUMMARY:
Kids will plan and run a RETREAT based on the theme "Your Body, God's Temple."

PREPARATION: You'll need a Bible.

Help kids plan an overnight retreat with the theme "Your Body, God's Temple." Read aloud 1 Corinthians 3:16-17. Ask each group member to sign up for one of five retreat committees. Then give committees 30 to 45 minutes to brainstorm and plan ideas for their areas of responsibility. Committees include:

**The Holy-Temple Caterers—** This committee is responsible for planning a dinner, a midnight snack, and a breakfast that are completely healthy. The committee members must first determine what food is considered healthy, then decide how to organize the food and how to prepare it for the retreat. This committee must also determine how much to charge each person for the cost of the food.

**The Holy-Temple Athletic Club—** This committee is responsible for planning and organizing four or five fun activities that get people moving. The activities should be active but not so active that nonathletic kids feel left out.

**The Holy-Temple Players—** This committee is responsible for creating and performing a skit that communicates the message of 1 Corinthians 3:16-17.

**The Holy-Temple Entertainers—** This committee is responsible for choosing uplifting music to be played during the evening and for planning two activities that will help people feel closer to God.

They could choose to rent and show uplifting movies such as *Chariots of Fire* or the classic Christian short film *The Music Box.* (Kids can ask your local Christian bookstore about renting these films, or have them call Films, Inc. at 1-800-323-4222, ext. 211 for information on public-performance rights.) Or they might plan a creative worship time that helps group members focus on God's goodness. They could also plan a progressive board game activity; for example, every 15 minutes kids travel to different rooms to play different cooperative board games.

**The Holy-Temple Back Slappers—** This committee is responsible for coming up with at least three affirmation activities designed to build up each person in the group. (You might loan this group a copy of the book *101 Affirmations for Teenagers* to use as a resource. It's available from Group Publishing.)

After committees complete their brainstorming and planning, ask representatives from each committee to meet together and plan a schedule for the retreat and coordinate the details. Pick a date, then have a holy-temple blast!

# 1 CORINTHIANS 4:6-8

**THEME:**
God's good gifts

**SUMMARY:**
Kids will think about their favorite things and thank God in this CREATIVE PRAYER for the many gifts they've received.

PREPARATION: You'll need a Bible, paper, and pencils.

Give kids each a sheet of paper and a pencil. Have kids write at the top of their paper, "A Few of My Favorite Things." Then give kids five minutes to list some of their favorite things. After five minutes, have them gather in a circle with their favorite-things lists in hand.

Have kids look at what they've written, then close their eyes. Say: **Think about the things you've written. How are they like gifts to you? Who gave you these gifts? Now think of one gift in particular. Think of a two-sentence prayer you can offer to God to say "thanks" for this gift. The prayer should go something like "God, (blank) is such a gift to me. I see how good you are when I think about this gift because ... "**

Read aloud 1 Corinthians 4:6-8. Then, starting with the person on your right, go around the circle and have kids each say a prayer.

# 1 CORINTHIANS 6:12-20

**THEME:**
Sexual sin

**SUMMARY:**
In this LEARNING GAME, kids will get tied up with strings and discuss how that's like getting caught up in sexual sin.

PREPARATION: You'll need string and a Bible.

Give kids each a long piece of string (at least 5 feet long). Then have them all tie one end of their strings together with all the other strings—the result should look like a wagon wheel, with the strings as "spokes." Tell kids to hang on tightly to the other end of their strings.

On "go," have kids try to capture as many other players as they can by gently winding them up in their string. (Warn kids to be careful not to wrap string around anyone's throat or cut off anyone's circulation by wrapping string too tightly around arms or legs.) After all kids have come to the end of their strings, call "stop" and have kids sit where they are. Ask:

■ **How does it feel to be wrapped up like you are?**

■ **What would it take to clean up this tangled mess?**

Read aloud 1 Corinthians 6:12-20. Then wrap up the activity by asking:

■ **How would you define "sexual sin"?**

■ **How is this tangled mess like getting caught up in sexual sin?**

■ **Why do you think 1 Corinthians 6:12-20 speaks so strongly against sexual sin?**

■ **What can someone who's already gotten tangled up in sexual sin do to get him- or herself untangled?**

■ **How can you avoid getting tangled up in sexual sin in the future?**

# 1 CORINTHIANS 8:4-13

THEME:
Freedom

SUMMARY:
In this DEVOTION, kids will discover the benefit of giving up a freedom.

PREPARATION: Bring a set of encyclopedia books (from your church library, your home, or borrowed from a church member) to the meeting. Tape a sheet of newsprint to a wall and place a few markers nearby. You'll also need a Bible.

EXPERIENCE
As kids arrive, ask them each to write on the newsprint their name and the one country in the world they'd like to visit.

After everyone has signed the newsprint, ask kids to form groups made up of people who chose the same country (a group can be one person if only one person chose a certain country).

Give groups each the encyclopedia volume that corresponds to the country they chose. Have them find the country in the encyclopedia, then look for the one cultural tradition or habit of that country that seems most unusual (for example, in Papua New Guinea the people drink a homemade, fermented beverage that natives make by chewing a common root, then spitting it into a vat that's left in the sun).

After five or 10 minutes, call time and ask each group to tell about its country's unusual cultural tradition.

RESPONSE
After groups have presented their discoveries, ask:

■ **If you lived in this culture, what freedoms might you have to give up to fit in?**

■ **How would you feel about giving up those freedoms?**

■ **Do you think you could adapt to and live in this culture for the rest of your life? Why or why not?**

Read aloud 1 Corinthians 8:4-13. Then ask:

■ **What are examples of things we could do if we wanted to but that might hurt someone else or cause them to struggle in their relationship with God?**

■ **What's one practical way we can help others grow closer to God by giving up a freedom?**

CLOSING
Have groups each decide on one freedom they can give up for a week and determine how they can serve someone else with the time or money they save by giving up that freedom.

For example, group members might give up television and write letters of encouragement to church staff, missionaries, political leaders, and friends instead. Or they might give up fast food for a week and donate the money they save to the church or a local food-distribution agency.

Next week, ask kids to report on how their "freedom-free" week turned out.

# 1 CORINTHIANS 9:19-23

---

THEME:
Being all things to all people

SUMMARY:
In this ADVENTURE, kids will learn how to reach out to all kinds of people.

---

PREPARATION: You'll need a Bible, paper, a marker, tape, and pencils.

Have kids brainstorm different occupations and life situations (such as social worker, professional athlete, homeless person, accountant, teacher, TV anchorperson, journalist, homemaker, psychologist, construction worker, and so on). As kids shout out their ideas, write them in large print on sheets of paper, then tape them to a wall.

After five minutes, stop the brainstorming and form pairs by matching kids who don't normally spend time with each other.

Say: **You and your partner must quickly decide which of the occupations we've brain-**stormed interests both of you the most. When you decide, run up and grab that occupation off the wall. It's first come, first served—so some other pair might choose your occupation first if you don't agree quickly. If you don't get your first choice, quickly choose another. Ready? Go!

After each pair has an occupation, ask:

■ **Was it hard or easy to agree on an occupation with your partner? Explain.**

■ **What did you learn about your partner as you struggled to decide? Were your differences a help or a hindrance?**

Ask a volunteer to read aloud 1 Corinthians 9:19-23. Then ask:

■ **Paul says he became "all things to all people" so he could "win" them. What does it mean to win someone?**

■ **What's the difference between becoming all things to all people and simply being fake or a hypocrite?**

■ **Why is it important to remember a person's background, such as his or her occupation, when telling that person about your faith?**

Say: **Today we're going to take a risk and make plans for an adventure. Your challenge as partners is to make contact with someone in the occupation you've selected and spend at least two hours with that person in the next two weeks. For example, you might invite that person to lunch or dinner or to a sporting event, ask to tour his or her workplace, arrange an** interview with that person, and so on.

In two weeks, you and your partner should be ready to report about your experience to the group. In addition to telling us about your experience, you should answer the following question: "What would Jesus do to 'win' this person?" Now, get together with your partner and decide on a strategy. I'll be available to help you brainstorm if you need it.

In two weeks, have kids report back to the group about their experience and give their answer to the question.

# 1 CORINTHIANS 9:24-27

**THEME:**
Running to win

**SUMMARY:**
In this LEARNING GAME, kids will participate in a race and discuss what it means to run the race of life.

PREPARATION: You'll need a flag-sized piece of cloth and masking tape. Mark starting and finish lines in your room using the masking tape. You'll also need Bibles.

Form "race-car teams" of five (or "motorcycle teams" of three).

Say: **Each of your teams is now an Indy-style race car** (or a motocross motorcycle). **One of you will be chassis, and the**

others will be the wheels. The wheels must carry the chassis.

When I shout, "Racers, start your engines!" all race cars should line up, side by side. Then when I drop my flag, your race car should race along the outside edge of our meeting room. The first race car to make five laps around the track wins. Ready? Racers, start your engines! Pause, then quickly lower your flag.

When the race is finished, have kids sit together with their teams. Give each team a Bible. Ask a volunteer from each team to read aloud 1 Corinthians 9:24-27, then have teams each discuss the following questions to debrief their experience:

■ What does it mean to "run to win"?

■ Did your team run to win? Why or why not?

■ What does it mean to run to win in life?

■ What's one thing you can do that will help you run to win in your life?

# 1 CORINTHIANS 10:12-13

**THEME:**
Temptation

**SUMMARY:**
In this LEARNING GAME, kids will create spontaneous sculptures to represent temptations and their escape hatches.

PREPARATION: You'll need masking tape and a Bible.

Read aloud 1 Corinthians 10:12-13. Then form groups of three and ask groups to each brainstorm one temptation that everyone must battle. After a minute or two, have groups each plan a "spontaneous sculpture" that tastefully illustrates the common temptation.

Spontaneous sculptures are created using materials found in or around your meeting room—books, chairs, pillows, people, pencils, shoes, and so on. Provide masking tape to groups that need it.

After three minutes, have one group present its sculpture to the rest of the group. Challenge the rest of the groups to guess what temptation the group is illustrating. When someone guesses correctly, that person's group must quickly come up with a spontaneous sculpture to illustrate an "escape hatch" from that temptation. For example, if the temptation is drinking alcohol, the group might create a sculpture showing someone walking away from a party. Have that group form its escape-hatch sculpture in front of the original group.

Have other groups guess what the escape hatch is. When someone guesses correctly, that person's group must come to the front and form its own spontaneous sculpture of a temptation.

Continue until all the groups have formed their sculptures in front of the whole group.

# 1 CORINTHIANS 10:12-13

**THEME:**
Temptation

**SUMMARY:**
In this LEARNING GAME, kids will take risks that illustrate the dangers of giving in to temptation.

PREPARATION: You'll need a large room for this activity—or you may do it outside. You'll also need a Bible.

Use masking tape to mark off a 10×10-foot area. This will be the "bear's cave." Place a knotted rag—the treasure—in the center of the cave. Have a volunteer be the bear who'll guard the treasure. The rest of the kids must try to swipe the treasure without being tagged by the bear. The bear may not pick up the treasure. People tagged inside the cave must freeze where they are. The person who gets the treasure becomes the next bear. If no one gets the treasure within two minutes, the bear wins, and a new bear is picked.

Explain the game. Then play for eight minutes. When time is up, ask:

■ **How did you feel as you played this game? Explain.**

■ **What risks did you take in this game?**

■ **How are those risks like the risks we take when we give in to temptation?**

■ **Did you play this game aggressively or with a wait-and-**

watch attitude?

■ How is the way you played this game like the way you deal with temptations in everyday life?

■ Are temptations dangerous? Why or why not?

Read aloud 1 Corinthians 10:12-13. Ask:

■ What are the dangers associated with temptations you face in real life?

■ What does this passage tell you about how to deal with temptation when it comes?

# 1 CORINTHIANS 10:23-24

## THEME:

Freedom and responsibility

## SUMMARY:
In this SKIT, two guys talk about the importance—and unimportance—of going to church.

## I'M A CHRISTIAN—ISN'T THAT ENOUGH?

SCENE: Two teenagers on their way home from school on a Friday afternoon discuss what to do over the weekend.

PROPS: Have two chairs set up facing the audience to represent the front seat of a car. You'll also need Bibles for the discussion afterward.

CHARACTERS:
Peter
Max

### SCRIPT
*(The scene opens with Peter driving. He sees Max and pulls over.)*

**Peter:** Hey, Max! Need a ride?

**Max:** Sure, thanks. *(He pantomimes opening the door and hops in.)* Boy am I glad you came along. It's a long walk home!

**Peter:** No problem. Where've you been hiding out, anyway? *(Peter continues to drive throughout.)*

**Max:** Oh, you know—going to school, going home, shooting some hoops, watching the tube. Same old stuff.

**Peter:** It just seems like I hardly see you anymore. Especially on Sundays.

**Max:** *(Playing dumb)* On Sundays?

**Peter:** Yeah, on Sundays! We used to have a lot of fun at church, and now I never see you there!

**Max:** Well, it's just that… *(thinking)* I've got other stuff to do now.

**Peter:** Oh. Must be awfully important.

**Max:** It's just… stuff. 'Sides, I was talkin' to my mom, and she said I'm old enough now to choose whether I go to church or not. So…

**Peter:** So, you don't. What do you do, then?

**Max:** You know—stuff! The kind of stuff I don't get a chance to do during the week. This is my street. *(He points right. Peter pantomimes turning the wheel to the right.)*

**Peter:** Such as…

**Max:** Well, shooting baskets, for example. I mean, the courts are almost empty on Sunday mornings. It's great!

**Peter:** *(Not convinced)* Hmm.

**Max:** Or...I also get time on Sunday mornings to catch up on my sleep. I work hard during the week—I've got to get my rest on the weekends.

**Peter:** I guess so. I still wish you'd come around more often. Can't you play basketball some other time?

**Max:** Well...Why don't you join me on Sunday morning for a game! Then we can goof around *together!* You've been to enough Sunday school in your life. I mean, you're a Christian, aren't you? That's all that really matters. Why not have some "fellowship" on the court with me on Sunday?

**Peter:** Nah. I sort of like to go to church on Sundays.

**Max:** Whatever. Here's my house. *(Peter pantomimes stopping the car. Max opens the door, gets out, and leans back in.)* Thanks for the ride! See you around.

**Peter:** OK. I hope so.

Permission to photocopy this skit from *Youth Worker's Encyclopedia: NT* granted for local church use. Copyright © Group Publishing, Inc., Box 481, Loveland, CO 80539.

If you use this skit as a discussion starter, here are possible questions:

■ **Why did God give us so much freedom to make our own choices?**

■ **According to 1 Corinthians 10:23-24, what else do we need to consider?**

■ **What responsibilities go hand in hand with the freedom God has given us?**

# 1 CORINTHIANS 12:4-11

**THEME:**
Spiritual gifts

**SUMMARY:**
In this OBJECT LESSON, kids will paraphrase 1 Corinthians 12:4-11 using items in the room.

PREPARATION: It might be fun to plan this activity for a time when your group is enjoying pizza. You'll also need Bibles, paper, and pencils.

Form pairs and give each pair a Bible, a sheet of paper, and a pencil. Ask a volunteer to read aloud 1 Corinthians 12:4-11 as kids follow along in their Bibles.

Then say: **Today I'm challenging you and your partner to paraphrase this Scripture passage by using an object (or objects) in this room. For example, if you chose pizza as your object, you might write, "There are different kinds of toppings, but they're all on the same pizza. There are different ways to eat pizza, but we all eat it. And we have differences in the brands of pizzas we enjoy, but it's all still pizza..."**

Give kids 10 to 15 minutes to complete their paraphrases. Then have a spokesperson from each pair read aloud their paraphrase.

After all the paraphrases have been read, ask:

■ **Why is it important for us to know that there are many different gifts but they're all from the same Spirit?**

■ **How can we appreciate each other's gifts?**

■ **How can we use our gifts to help others come to know Jesus?**

■ **How will what you've learned from 1 Corinthians 12:4-11 affect what you do this week?**

# 1 CORINTHIANS
## 12:12-27

## THEME:
The body of Christ

## SUMMARY:
This OBJECT LESSON centers on eating things that emphasize unity and diversity in the body of Christ.

PREPARATION: Ask each person to bring one can of soup (no creamed soups), one piece of fruit, and some bread. (Don't explain why you need each item.) You'll need kitchen facilities, a large pot to mix the soup, plates, bowls, glasses, silverware, and napkins. On a large table, place a large bowl, a soup ladle, sharp knives, and a cutting board. Place a chair for each person around the table. You'll also need a Bible.

Gather everyone for a unique, fun experience with food. As kids arrive, have them put the fruit and bread on the table and bring their cans of soup to the kitchen. Gather around the stove, open the cans and prepare the soup putting it all together in one pot. Ask kids to think of ways the youth group is like the soup; for example, "Just as there are many different soups added to one pot, we're each unique individuals who together make up the youth group."

While the soup is heating, sit at the table. Ask the kids to examine their pieces of fruit for a few minutes. Ask kids each how they are like their fruit. Then ask how they are different. Distribute the knives and ask kids to cut up their fruit, remove the seeds, and put the pieces into a large bowl. Read aloud 1 Corinthians 12:12-27, substituting "fruit salad" for "body" and specific fruits for the parts of the body.

Ask for helpers to set the table, then bring out the hot soup. Share the bread and serve the fruit salad. After everyone eats the meal, ask kids to compare their faith to the bread; for example, "My faith is like this bread because it fills me up when I'm spiritually hungry."

After everyone is finished eating, close with prayer. Ask each person to add a word or sentence of thanks for the person on his or her right.

# 1 CORINTHIANS 12:12-27

THEME:
The body of Christ

SUMMARY:
In this LEARNING GAME, kids will discover how we need each other.

PREPARATION: You'll need a Bible and masking tape.

For this activity, take kids into a gym or outside a two-story building. Form teams of three or four and assign each team member one of these four conditions:

■ you have no right leg,
■ you have no left leg,
■ you have no eyes, or
■ you have no hands.

(For three-member teams, assign only three conditions.)

Give each team a piece of masking tape. While acting out their assignments, have teams each race to see which of them can place the piece of masking tape highest on the wall. Encourage kids to be careful, but try not to assist teams any more than necessary.

After the first round, form new teams of kids with the same conditions and have them try it again. For example, combine all kids who have only one leg or combine all kids who have no hands.

After allowing teams several attempts at placing the masking tape higher, congratulate kids for their efforts. Then ask:

■ **How did you feel as your team attempted this activity?**

■ **What did you need to make your job easier?**

■ **Was it easier or harder when your team members all had the same conditions? Explain.**

Read aloud 1 Corinthians 12:12-27. Ask:

■ **How is your team like or unlike being a part of the body of Christ?**

■ **What does this activity tell you about how we should relate to each other in the body of Christ?**

■ **Is it possible to be a healthy Christian apart from Christ's body? Why or why not?**

Say: **We discovered that the missing body parts affected how well each team did its task. The task was easier when all the various body parts worked together. As Christians, we need one another to be what God has called us to be as his church. There's no such thing as a healthy Christian apart from Christ's body.**

# 1 CORINTHIANS 12:12-31

THEME:
Spiritual gifts

SUMMARY:
Kids will create posters of body parts and perform an interactive CREATIVE READING based on the Bible passage.

PREPARATION: You'll need large and small pieces of poster board and markers.

Assign each person one of the following body parts and give him or her a marker and an appropriate-size piece of poster board as indicated in parentheses: a mouth (small), two hands (small), a torso (large), two legs (large), two arms (large), two feet (small), two ears (small), two eyes (small), a nose (small), and a head (large).

**Note:** If you have more than 16 kids in your group, form pairs for each body part or add body parts such as a belly button, knees, hair, and so on. If you have fewer than 16 kids in your group, one person can be both eyes, one can be both ears, and so on.

Tell kids to draw their assigned body parts on their poster board. Then have them gather to form a completed body using their poster-board parts. Kids should stand facing you and position their poster-board body parts to make a standing figure (see illustration).

Have kids sit down, holding their illustrated body parts. Say: **You're going to act out a Scripture passage on how the body of Christ works together. As I read aloud 1 Corinthians 12:12-31, I'll mention various body parts. When you hear your body part, rush forward and position that part on the body.**

Certain body parts aren't mentioned in the passage, so the kids holding those parts should come to the front of the room and position their parts from the start (these include mouth, torso, legs, and arms).

Read aloud 1 Corinthians 12:12-31. As you come to each body part, emphasize it and pause. (Don't forget to emphasize the word "smell" in verse 17.) Kids should run up and position their parts when they hear them emphasized. Afterward, discuss what it means to be part of Christ's body.

# 1 CORINTHIANS 13

## THEME:
Love

## SUMMARY:
In this PROJECT, kids will transform an old boat into a reminder of the greatness of God's love.

PREPARATION: You'll need an old rowboat, white paint (optional), several small cans of black paint, paintbrushes, paint thinner, paint buckets, lots of magazines with photos and illustrations, glue, shellac or clear varnish, and a bottle of sparkling cider. Ask kids to bring old throw pillows from home, or buy inexpensive new pillows. You'll need enough to stuff the boat full of them.

First you'll need to locate an old rowboat. Have kids search classified ads, ask friends and family members, and even call boat shops to find an inexpensive (or free) used rowboat or canoe. Tell kids that the person who locates the boat will win the honor of christening it later on.

Once you have the boat, get kids together to clean it up, both inside and outside. You may also want to paint the outside of the boat with a coat or two of white paint before proceeding.

Tell kids they're going to paint a mural based on 1 Corinthians 13. Form 13 groups and assign each group one of the 13 verses in 1 Corinthians 13. (A group can be one person. Or, if you have fewer than 13 kids in your group, give some kids more than one verse.) Divide the boat's hull into 13 sections, starting at the bow (or front) and circling all the way around the boat and back to the bow on the other side.

The group that's assigned verse 1 should start with the first section at the left front of the hull. Groups must paint the words of their verses at the top of their sections. Then groups may look through the magazines you've provided for pictures to illustrate the message of their verses. As they find pictures, have kids tear them out and glue them onto their sections of the hull. As groups finish their sections, have them paint a coat of shellac or clear varnish over them.

Allow time for the boat to dry, then have kids stuff it with pillows so it's comfortable to sit in. Together, decide where to put your "love boat." Christen it with a bottle of sparkling cider. Then ask:

■ **As you worked on the boat, how did you see others practicing the greatness of love?**

■ **Why is love the greatest of gifts?**

■ **What can you do to exercise your love?**

Your love boat will be a great place to lounge for years to come and a constant reminder of what it means to love.

# 1 CORINTHIANS 15:50-57

---

**THEME:**
Victory over death

**SUMMARY:**
Kids will tour a cemetery, then celebrate God's victory over death with a ADVENTURE/PARTY.

---

PREPARATION: Ask permission from a cemetery's management to lead your group members on a walk through the cemetery at night. Kids will need their Bibles, and you'll need a flashlight. Also, arrange with adult volunteers to have them decorate your meeting room for a "Celebrate New Life!" party while you're away with the group. Have adults use colorful balloons and streamers that say "Congratulations!" Serve pizza (the "food of heaven") and your kids' favorite soft drinks the ("elixir of heaven").

When the preparations are completed, have your volunteers turn off the lights in the room and wait for your return. Encourage them to yell, "Celebrate life!" when kids walk in the door.

Meet kids at a neutral site and take them to a local cemetery. Make sure each of your group members has a Bible for your cemetery walk. Bring a flashlight and ask everyone to be totally silent unless you ask them to speak.

Before you start, have a volunteer read aloud 1 Corinthians 15:50. As you walk around the cemetery, stop the group six times. Each time you stop, have a new volunteer read the next verse in the passage, until you've read through verse 56. Then walk back in silence to your vehicles. On the way back to your meeting room, ask kids to talk about how they felt during the walk.

As you open the door to your darkened youth room, tell kids to find a place to sit silently. Then quickly flip on the lights and join your volunteers in yelling, "Celebrate life!" Have a volunteer read aloud (in a loud voice) 1 Corinthians 15:57. Then celebrate together the eternal life God has promised to those who follow Jesus.

After you've celebrated, ask kids:

■ **What did it feel like to go from a somber experience to a party?**

■ **How is this experience like or unlike God's victory over death?**

# 1 CORINTHIANS 16:13-14

---

**THEME:**
Faith

**SUMMARY:**
In this PROJECT, kids will create and videotape raps based on the Bible passage.

PREPARATION: For this activity, you'll need to bring, borrow, or rent one video camera for every six to eight group members. You'll also need Bibles, paper, pencils, a VCR, and a TV.

Tell kids they're going to star in their own rap videos. Form groups of no more than eight (smaller groups of one or two people are OK) and designate a separate room or area for each. Give each group a video camera, a sheet of paper, a pencil, and a Bible. Before you send groups to their separate rooms, have a volunteer read aloud 1 Corinthians 16:13-14.

Say: **Each group has 20 minutes to create a rap using this Scripture passage as the basis. Study the verses before you write your rap. Then take another 10 minutes to practice performing the rap before you videotape it. Make sure everyone in your group is involved in performing the rap. In 30 minutes, we'll get back together and watch what you've produced. Ready? Go!**

While kids are creating their rap videos, set up a VCR and TV in your meeting room. After 30 minutes, gather kids together and watch the videos. (You could have kids vote on the best video if you want or give a standing ovation to each group.)

Then spend five or 10 minutes exploring the message presented in each video (and in 1 Corinthians 16:13-14).

# 2 CORINTHIANS

*"If anyone belongs to Christ, there is a new creation. The old things have gone; everything is made new!"*

*2 Corinthians 5:17*

# 2 CORINTHIANS 1:3-11

**THEME:**
Comfort in suffering

**SUMMARY:**

In this DEVOTION, kids will explore true stories of suffering and determine how to find comfort in suffering.

PREPARATION: Seek out several adults, leaders, pastors, or teenagers who are known by most of your youth group members. Ask them to each write a one-page personal story about a time they suffered. For example, people might write about the death of a loved one, the divorce of one's parents, a break-up with a boyfriend or girlfriend, being cut from a sports team, rejection by a popular club or group, losing a job, and so on.

Choose three to five stories that best relate to issues your kids are facing and ask the story writers to attend your youth group meeting.

You'll need Bibles, 3×5 cards, and pencils.

EXPERIENCE

Have the people who agreed to share their suffering stories each read (or tell) their story to the group. Ask these volunteers to share the situation as well as their feelings during the situation.

Encourage kids to examine how they feel as they listen to these stories.

RESPONSE

Give a 3×5 card and a pencil to each teenager. On the 3×5 cards, have kids write how they felt as they listened to the stories of suffering. Then form groups of no more than four (include your special guests in the groups) and have kids share their feelings and discuss the following questions for each story:

■ **How would you respond to a close friend if he or she shared a similar experience with you?**

■ **What kinds of things can you say or do to comfort someone experiencing this situation?**

■ **If you've dealt with a similar situation, what comforted you or helped you to feel better?**

Have groups each read 2 Corinthians 1:3-11. Then have them discuss the following questions in their groups:

■ **How did Christ suffer and how does he comfort us in our suffering?**

■ **What can we learn from this passage to help us deal with suffering?**

■ **How can we comfort others in their suffering?**

CLOSING

Ask representatives from each group to share an idea their groups came up with for dealing with suffering. Then have groups form one big circle. Read aloud 2 Corinthians 1:3-4 as a closing reminder of God's comfort in times of trouble.

# 2 CORINTHIANS 3:4-6

THEME:

Power from God

SUMMARY:

In this OBJECT LESSON, teenagers will examine things they're good at and things they're not good at and discover that God's power helps us do great things.

PREPARATION: Divide a large sheet of newsprint into three columns. Title the first two columns "Things I'm Good At" and "Things I'm Not Good At." Leave the third column heading blank.

You'll need markers, bottled soft drinks (but not the kind with the twist-off tops), and bottle openers. You'll also need a Bible.

Have kids write in the appropriate columns on the newsprint things they're good at and things they're not good at. Then form groups of no more than four. Have groups discuss the following questions:

■ How does it feel to have limited abilities?

■ What is one thing you don't do well that you wish you did do well?

Give kids each a bottled soft drink. Have kids attempt to open the bottles without the use of a bottle opener.

Before kids get too frustrated, read aloud 2 Corinthians 3:4-6. Ask:

■ How is trying to open this bottle like trying to do things without God?

■ How does God's power make us able to do great things we couldn't do alone?

Title the third column on the newsprint "With God's Help, I Can..." Then have kids list things God enables them to do through his authority and power (such as praying, studying the Bible, serving others, sharing God's love, and so on). Then give kids bottle openers and let them enjoy the soft drinks and be reminded that God's power makes us able to do great things.

# 2 CORINTHIANS 4

THEME:

God's vessels

SUMMARY:

In this DEVOTION, kids will make foil containers to illustrate our being containers of God's love.

PREPARATION: Gather Bibles and aluminum foil.

EXPERIENCE

Divide 2 Corinthians 4 into three sections (six verses per section). Assign volunteers to read the sections. Ask how our bodies are like "clay jars." Have kids explain how God uses our human weaknesses to fulfill his work.

Next, give kids each a large square of aluminum foil and instruct them to fashion pots or vessels out of the foil. When kids are ready, have each person explain his or her creation.

RESPONSE

Ask kids to think of different things they'd like to put in their vessels and what they think God would like to put in their vessels. Then discuss how Christians are containers for God's love and the message of the gospel.

CLOSING

Close by saying: **Each individual, though important, is only a portion of the bigger picture. We need to join together and work together in Christian groups. We need to love and help each other.**

Have kids work together to fashion their individual foil vessels into one large vessel, then have them discuss how that is like or unlike walking in unity with other Christians.

# 2 CORINTHIANS
## 4:1-2

**THEME:**
Sharing the good news

**SUMMARY:**
In this SKIT, a guy on the street tries to coax passersby to come to his church.

## GET TO YOUR POINT!

SCENE: On a street corner, a teenager is trying to get people to come to youth group.

PROPS: You'll need a Bible for the discussion after the skit.

CHARACTERS:
**Willy**
**Marie**
**Passersby**

SCRIPT

*(Willy is alone on a street corner, calling out to people who are passing by.)*

**Willy:** Hi! How you doin' today? *(He sees someone else.)* Hello, ma'am. My, don't you look like you're enjoying this sunshine today! *(Greeting another person)* Howdy—good to meet you! *(He finally catches someone's attention.)* Hi! Can I tell you something? I belong to an organization that's one of the fastest-growing industries in the nation. For just a few hours each week, your standard of living can be changed forever. All you need to do is attend our Sunday seminars on personal growth and . . . *(Watching as his "customer" walks away)* Miss— can I interest you in an investment opportunity? J. C. Growth Industries has made available a special, one-time offer to new investors. All you have to do is attend one of our Life-Asset Management meetings held every Sunday at . . . *(He watches as another "customer" walks away and sighs. Marie walks in.)*

**Marie:** Hi, Willy! How's it going?
**Willy:** Not so good. I get right into the middle of my spiel, and the

customer walks away.

**Marie:** "Spiel"? "Customer"? Willy, you're not selling mutual funds here. You're trying to get people to attend our church!

**Willy:** Sure, but you've got to have a hook, a drawing card of some sort. *(Marie is skeptical.)* You've got to give people something to show up for!

**Marie:** They *do* have something to show up for! The love of Jesus and friendship with God's people!

**Willy:** And what else? I mean, what will grab them?

**Marie:** You'd be surprised. There are a lot of people out there who don't feel like they experience anyone's love or spend time with anyone who cares about them.

**Willy:** Well, OK. I'll try it, but I just don't know. *(He sees a passerby.)* Excuse me, sir. I just wanted to let you know that we'd be pleased if you could join us at our church for worship. *(He listens as though being talked to.)* No, no gimmick. *(Almost apologetically)* Just the love of Christ and the friendship of God's people. The services are Sunday morning and evening, right down the street at our church. Why, yes. I'll see you there! 'Bye!

**Marie:** See?

**Willy:** And I didn't even have to give anything away! Who would have thunk it?

If you use this skit as a discussion starter, here are possible questions:

■ **Why are we tempted to "sell" Jesus to people? How does that approach compare to the words of 2 Corinthians 4:1-2?**

■ **If you had a chance to tell someone "the plain truth" about Jesus, what would you say?**

# 2 CORINTHIANS 4:5-7

**THEME:**
Being like clay in God's hands

**SUMMARY:**
In this DEVOTION, kids will make clay representations of qualities they want to develop.

PREPARATION: Gather paper, pencils, and a lump of clay or Play-Doh for each person. You'll also need a Bible and a glass or clay dish.

EXPERIENCE

Form a circle and place a glass container or clay dish in the center. Give kids each a sheet of paper, a pencil, and a lump of clay or Play-Doh. Read aloud 2 Corinthians 4:5-7. Ask:

■ **What does the "earthen vessel" or "clay jar" represent?**

■ **What is the treasure?**

Say: **Think of three qualities you'd like to develop in the next year that would reveal God's presence in your life. Write those on your paper.** (Pause.) **Now circle the one quality you'd like to work on in the next month.** (Pause.) **Using your clay, create a** symbol that illustrates the quality you circled. For example, a heart might illustrate love, or open hands might illustrate serving others.

RESPONSE

After kids have been working for a few minutes, have them pause to discuss these questions:

■ **What thoughts go through your mind as you work to create your symbol?**

■ **In what ways are Christians like the clay you're molding?**

■ **How can we make ourselves moldable like clay in the hands of God?**

■ **What can we do this week to let the treasure of God be seen in our lives?**

CLOSING

Give kids a few minutes to complete their symbols. Then ask each person to explain his or her creation to the group and place the symbol in the glass container or clay dish. When kids have all talked about their symbols, hold hands around the glass container and sing a song of surrender to God, such as "Change My Heart, Oh God" or "Lord, Be Glorified." (Both songs are available in *The Group Songbook,* from Group Publishing.)

# 2 CORINTHIANS 4:7-11

## THEME:

God's power

## SUMMARY:

In this CREATIVE READING, kids will read the Bible passage, substituting dictionary definitions for key words to enhance the passage's meaning.

PREPARATION: You'll need paper and a pencil for each person. You'll also need six dictionaries and a Bible.

Give kids each a sheet of paper and a pencil. Have six volunteers each look up one of the following words: defeated, give up, persecuted, leave, hurt, and destroyed.

Have a volunteer read aloud 2 Corinthians 4:7-11, leaving out the above listed words (the words come from The Youth Bible, New Century Version; adjust them as necessary for the translation you use). When the reader comes to one of these words, have the person who looked up that word read aloud the dictionary definition in its place (the definition may need to be modified for clarity).

Then form groups of no more than four and have groups complete the following statement and discuss what the passage means for us today: **Based on 2 Corinthians 4:7-11, we are..., but we are not...**

# 2 CORINTHIANS 5:6-9

## THEME:
Death

## SUMMARY:
In this DEVOTION, kids will visit a mortuary and discuss the temporary nature of life on earth.

PREPARATION: Schedule a visit to a local mortuary or university nursing department. If possible, meet in the embalming room for your lesson. You'll need a Bible.

EXPERIENCE

Go to the mortuary and take a tour. Encourage kids to ask questions during the tour. Then meet in the embalming room or another location for a discussion time.

RESPONSE

Read aloud 2 Corinthians 5:6-9 and then have kids discuss the following questions:

■ **If you've experienced the death of someone close to you, how did you react?**

■ **How do you feel after this tour?**

■ **What affected you most about this tour?**

■ **How do you feel about death?**

■ **What hope does this passage give Christians when they die?**

■ **What does it mean to be present with the Lord?**

■ **How can we please God while we're here on earth?**

CLOSING

Say: **Even though our earthly bodies will someday die, God has promised that those who love him will spend eternity in God's presence.**

Have kids form pairs and pray for their partners, asking God to lead them in following God's ways while on earth and thanking God for the promise of eternal life.

# 2 CORINTHIANS 5:7

## THEME:
Faith

## SUMMARY:
In this ADVENTURE, kids will lead each other blindfolded around playground equipment.

PREPARATION: Find a nearby park or school with playground equipment. Prepare enough blindfolds for each person in your group. You'll also need a Bible, a portable cassette or CD player, and a contemporary Christian music cassette or CD kids will enjoy.

Tell your group members it's time to return to their childhood, then take them to the playground. At the playground, form pairs and have one person be A and the other be B. Have person A blindfold B.

Say: **While the music plays, person A will verbally direct person B around the playground and help him or her enjoy the playground equipment without**

**running into obstacles. You may not lead your partner by touching him or her.**

Play the music for two minutes (or if you don't have music, simply tell kids when to begin and when to end the activity). Then have kids switch roles and repeat the activity. Bring the whole group together and have everyone put on a blindfold. Read aloud 2 Corinthians 5:7. Ask the following questions to wrap up the experience:

■ **How did you feel when you were blindfolded?**

■ **What was it like to be directed by your partner?**

■ **What does it mean to live by what we believe and not by what we can see?**

■ **How is trusting God different from trusting your partner?**

■ **In what areas of life is it easy for you to live by what you believe and not by what you can see?**

■ **In what areas of life is it hard for you to do that?**

# 2 CORINTHIANS
# 5:17

THEME:
New creations

SUMMARY:
In this OBJECT LESSON, kids will refinish a piece of furniture and compare their experience to what it means to be a new creation in Christ.

PREPARATION: You'll need a large piece of furniture that needs to be refinished (such as a coffee table or a dresser). Check garage sales for possible furniture items. Gather sandpaper, stain, rags, brushes, hammers, nails, wood glue, and cleaning supplies. You'll also need a Bible.

Lead the group in refinishing the piece of furniture by sanding it, making minor repairs (such as gluing or nailing broken pieces), filling small holes or scratches, and staining it.

When the work is done, read aloud 2 Corinthians 5:17. Ask:

■ **How is this experience like the meaning of this passage?**

■ **What was the price God paid for you?**

■ **In what ways are we new creations?**

■ **What old things have passed away?**

■ **How is this new piece of furniture like or unlike a new creation in Christ?**

Display your new piece of furniture in your meeting room as a reminder that we're all new creations in Christ. Or have kids donate their symbol of new creation to a needy family.

# 2 CORINTHIANS 8:2-5

## THEME:
Giving

## SUMMARY:
In this SKIT, a girl is interrupted on her day of relaxation by a persistent youth group member looking for help.

## KNOCK OFF THE EXCUSES!

SCENE: Stacy is relaxing in her living room.

PROPS: You'll need a bowl of snack food, a book, a couch or comfortable chair, and a Bible for the discussion afterward.

CHARACTERS:
**Stacy**
**Fred**

### SCRIPT
*(The scene opens with Stacy relaxing on the couch, reading a romance novel or something similar.)*
**Stacy:** Nothing like a day off—nothing to do, nothing to worry about, nothing to take me away from this great book. *(She sighs contentedly and becomes engrossed in the book. A few seconds later, there's a knock at the door.)* Oh! Who on earth could that be! Coming! *(She gets up and pantomimes opening the door.)* Oh, hi.
**Fred:** Hi!
**Stacy:** Can I help you?
**Fred:** I hope so. I'm going through the neighborhood asking people for help.

**Stacy:** *(Doubtfully)* Help?
**Fred:** Yes. We have a lot of families here in town that don't have anywhere to live, so we're trying to help them out. We're collecting funds to ...
**Stacy:** *(Cutting him off)* Oh! Well, I really don't have any extra money—sorry.
**Fred:** That's OK. It isn't just money we're in need of. We're also looking for items that we could fix up and use to furnish some apartments that we're ...
**Stacy:** Well, I'm really sorry, but I just don't have anything that I could donate to help you out. But thanks for stopping by anyway ...
**Fred:** Another form of help we're looking for is people that might be able to spend a day helping fix up the various apartments. You know, swing a hammer, paint, whatever.
**Stacy:** I'm sorry, but I'm just all thumbs when it comes to that kind of stuff. Why don't you check with my neighbors. They just put in a new deck and hot tub. I'm sure they'd be pleased to help! Goodb ...
**Fred:** *(A little bit angry)* You know, you don't have to have any special skills to be of help. We could even use people who could just donate time to help baby-sit or shop for groceries or whatever while the adults try to earn a living. All you have to do is give *time* to play with kids, or clean, or ...
**Stacy:** *Time?!* I'm sorry, but I have less of that than anything else. And right now, I don't have any more time to speak with you! I'm sorry. *(She closes the door, shakes her head, and goes back to*

*the couch, where she resumes eating and reading.)*
**Fred:** *(After a pause, he says to the closed door)* Are you?

If you use this skit as a discussion starter, here are possible questions:

■ **When have you felt like Stacy? like Fred?**

■ **What would 2 Corinthians 8:2-5 have us do?**

■ **How do we know how much of our time or resources to give?**

# 2 CORINTHIANS 9:6-8

**THEME:**
Giving

**SUMMARY:**
Kids will perform a service for the community and explore how they felt doing this PROJECT for free.

PREPARATION: Choose a work project for your group, such as removing graffiti or picking up trash for the city. Contact your local police department or community-service agencies for other ideas about what you can do.

You'll need newsprint, tape, and a marker, Bibles, an instant-print camera, and film.

Before you take kids to the project site, have them brainstorm things they'd be doing if they weren't helping out with the project. List these things on newsprint and have kids assign a dollar amount to each, symbolizing the value they place on these activities. For example, someone who's missing an important baseball game might say the game was worth $15 to him or her.

Attach the newsprint to a wall in your room. Take an instant-print picture of kids before they go to the project site. Tape that picture to the newsprint.

While at the site, take lots of pictures of kids working. Collect these for showing kids after they're done with the work.

When the work is done, return to your meeting room. Pass around the pictures you took. Form groups of no more than four and have them read 2 Corinthians 9:6-8, then discuss the following questions:

■ **How did it feel to do this work for free?**

■ **How do the values you placed on the things you could've been doing compare to the value others received because of your service?**

■ **What's the difference between helping out because we feel we have to and helping out because we want to?**

■ **Is it easier to sacrifice time or money to help someone out? Explain.**

■ **What did you gain from this work-project experience?**

Have kids list the positive things

they learned from this experience on a new sheet of newsprint. Then tape this sheet over the first list and attach the "after" photographs to it.

Close the session by having kids thank God for the gifts they received by helping out others. Then have kids each tell one way they'll give to others in the coming week.

# 2 CORINTHIANS 9:6-8

## THEME:
Giving

## SUMMARY:
At this PARTY, kids will feed each other dinner to explore the idea of giving cheerfully.

PREPARATION: Plan a dinner party with your group at a group member's home. Ask each person to bring one part of the meal (main dish, salad, bread, drinks, side dishes, and desserts). Tell kids they can make the food themselves or have their parents help out. You'll need a Bible.

On the night of the dinner, place the food on a table where kids won't be sitting. On another table, place all the supplies such as plates, silverware, cups, and drinks. After saying a prayer, explain the following rules to be followed during the meal:

■ Rule #1—You can't get any food or drink for yourself.

■ Rule #2—You can't ask for any food or drink for yourself.

■ Rule #3—If you break any of these rules, you must leave the room and can't eat until everyone else is finished.

Keep an eye out for kids who aren't being served and serve them yourself, if necessary.

After dinner, read aloud 2 Corinthians 9:6-8 and discuss the following questions:

■ **What were your thoughts when you heard the rules?**

■ **How did you feel about giving away food you really wanted to eat?**

■ **Did you get everything you wanted to eat or drink? Why or why not?**

■ **How would our world be different if everyone gave as generously and cheerfully as we did tonight?**

# 2 CORINTHIANS 10:3-5

## THEME:
Making our thoughts obey Christ

## SUMMARY:
On this OVERNIGHTER, kids will discover what it means to be a captive and compare that feeling to the Scripture passage's message.

PREPARATION: Plan an overnight retreat based on the theme of captivity. Contact your local police department or county jail to schedule a tour during the retreat.

Plan games and activities that relate to the theme. For example, play any variation of Tag but send kids to a prearranged "jail" when they're tagged. Serve simple foods, such as bread and water, and don't allow kids to have any outside contact after the visit to the jail.

You'll need a Bible, newsprint, and a marker.

Begin the evening by touring the jail. Then return to your retreat site. Ask:

■ **What does it mean to take someone or something captive?**

■ **What is the purpose of taking people captive in jails and detention centers?**

Have someone read aloud 2 Corinthians 10:3-5. Then ask:

■ **What does this passage say about our thoughts?**

■ **How is capturing our thoughts and making them obey Christ like capturing criminals in hope of changing their ways?**

■ **What thoughts do we need to take captive in our lives?**

Play the games you planned and enjoy the time together as "captives." Every hour or so, stop the activities and have kids brainstorm two or three ways they can follow the message of 2 Corinthians 10:3-5. List the ideas on newsprint. Continue adding to the list until the end of the retreat. Then compile the list and make copies for kids to take home with them.

Near the end of the overnight retreat, have kids spend an extended time in prayer, asking God to help them take captive any thought that is contrary to God.

# 2 CORINTHIANS 13:5

**THEME:**
Testing your faith

**SUMMARY:**
In this DEVOTION, kids will take a test and learn that "actions" don't make us Christians.

PREPARATION: You'll need a Bible, photocopies of the "Test of True Faith" handout (p. 244), pencils, a sheet of newsprint, and a marker.

EXPERIENCE
Give kids each a "Test of True Faith" handout and a pencil. Have kids complete the test, answering the questions honestly with a "true" or "false." Tell kids that their tests will be kept private.

After kids have finished, have them score their tests as follows.

Number of answers marked "true":

0 to 1—Ouch.

2 to 4—Oh, ye of little faith.

5 to 7—Lukewarm.

8 to 10—The Pharisees are looking for a few new recruits.

Ask:

■ **How do you feel knowing that no score seems like a good score?**

■ **If you got a similar number of "right" answers on a test at school, what would your grade be?**

■ **How do we "fail" this test of faith in everyday life?**

RESPONSE

Say: **There's one other part to this test. In the space before "Bonus question," write "true" or "false" for this statement: "I have committed my life to Jesus Christ and want to follow him in all I do."**

Read 2 Corinthians 13:5, then say: **If you answered "true" to the bonus question, according to 2 Corinthians 13:5, you pass the test of faith. The first 10 questions, while important parts of the Christian life, do *not* make you a Christian. In fact, someone can practice *all* of these and not be a true Christian at all. The Pharisees practiced nearly all of these exactingly, yet were considered** Christ's enemies. The only question that determines whether or not we're Christians is the bonus question.

Ask:

■ **How does your answer to the bonus question make you feel?**

■ **What implications does this question have for the other 10 questions?**

■ **How can we act on our decision to follow Christ?**

CLOSING

Have kids form groups of no more than four. Ask kids to pray for God to help them act on the faith decisions they've made. Then have groups each form a small group hug.

---

# TEST OF TRUE FAITH

**Answer "true" or "false":**
_____ 1. I study the Bible regularly (at least twice a week).
_____ 2. I attend church regularly.
_____ 3. I am not afraid to pray aloud in front of others.
_____ 4. I listen carefully to sermons in church and try to apply them to my life.
_____ 5. I stand up against sin and ungodliness.
_____ 6. I understand basic theological truths.
_____ 7. I have a hunger for worship and prayer.
_____ 8. I'm involved in youth group activities and leadership.
_____ 9. I tell others about my faith.
_____ 10. I frequently sacrifice things for God (such as time and money).
_____ Score (Total of "true" answers)
_____ Bonus question

---

# GALATIANS

*"But the Spirit produces the fruit of love, joy, peace, patience, kindness, goodness, faithfulness, gentleness, self-control. There is no law that says these things are wrong."*

*Galatians 5:22-23*

# GALATIANS
## 2:16-20

**THEME:**
Faith

**SUMMARY:**
In this CREATIVE READING, kids will choose to open a box that may or may not contain a gift.

PREPARATION: Place a weightless gift (such as a gift certificate to a restaurant) in a medium-sized box and wrap it in colorful paper. You'll also need a Bible and a supply of candy bars.

F orm a circle and give the wrapped gift to a teenager. Tell kids that the box may or may not contain a gift. Read aloud Galatians 2:16-20. Each time kids hear the word "faith" or a name for God, have them pass the gift to the person on their right. Continue until you've read all the verses.

The person who ends up with the gift at the end of the reading may choose to keep it or pass it to the right and take a candy bar instead. Continue passing the gift until someone chooses to keep it instead of receiving a candy bar. Give everyone else a candy bar. Then have the person with the box open it and tell the others what was inside. Have kids wrap up the experience by answering these questions:

■ **How is the belief** (name) **had that there was something in this package like or unlike our faith in God?**

■ **What does the Scripture passage tell us about following the law?**

■ **What does it tell us about living by faith?**

# GALATIANS
## 3:3-4

**THEME:**
Relying on God

**SUMMARY:**
In this SKIT, two football fans watch their team blow a scoring opportunity, then try to figure out why their team is failing.

## WHEN ALL ELSE FAILS

SCENE: Two big football fans are watching a game on TV.

PROPS: You'll need two chairs and a Bible for the discussion afterward.

CHARACTERS:
**Patti**
**Ted**

### SCRIPT
*(Patti is sitting, watching TV. As the skit goes on, she waits longer and longer to respond to Ted's comments.)*
**Patti:** Yes, yes... *(Getting more excited)* Go, go, go... Yes! Yes! NOOO! *(She collapses into a slump in front of the TV, head down.)*
**Ted:** *(Enters and sits down, focusing his attention on the TV.)* Did I miss anything? *(Patti just shakes her head. Ted looks at*

*her.)* Nothing happened? *(Patti shakes her head again.)* I thought I heard something. *(Patti shakes her head again.)* Coulda sworn I heard something.

**Patti:** *(Looking blankly at the TV)* Nope.

**Ted:** *(Finally starting to understand)* Oh, you're kidding—they blew another chance?

**Patti:** Yup.

**Ted:** They didn't make it to the end zone?

**Patti:** Nope.

**Ted:** They didn't even make a field goal?

**Patti:** Nope.

**Ted:** What's going on with these guys? They've had a decent season so far.

**Patti:** Yup.

**Ted:** They've won a bunch of games.

**Patti:** Yup.

**Ted:** They know what to do to succeed.

**Patti:** Yup.

**Ted:** But lately they can't do anything right!

**Patti:** Nope.

**Ted:** I don't know. I mean, it's not as though their coach hasn't worked with them, told them what to do, and showed them the plays!

**Patti:** Yup.

**Ted:** They started the season with such spirit, such drive, such a desire to reach their goals.

**Patti:** Yup.

**Ted:** They could do no wrong. Remember that first game? They were so good, so pumped up, so . . .

**Patti:** Yup.

**Ted:** *(Getting exasperated with Patti)* Is that all you can say? "Yup"? "Nope"? Can't you give me even a single word of encouragement? Some plan of action? Just one word of help for our downtrodden team?

**Patti:** Yup.

**Ted:** Well, then, for gosh sakes, what do you have to say? What can we possibly do?

**Patti:** Pray.

Permission to photocopy this skit from *Youth Worker's Encyclopedia: NT* granted for local church use. Copyright © Group Publishing, Inc., Box 481, Loveland, CO 80539.

If you use this skit as a discussion starter, here are possible questions:

■ **What goals are impossible to reach on our own?**

■ **According to Galatians 3:3-4, what's dangerous about trying to reach our goals without God's guidance and help?**

# GALATIANS
## 4:1-7

**THEME:**
Children of God

**SUMMARY:**
In this MUSIC IDEA, kids will create air-band renditions of familiar hymns or choruses to celebrate being children of God.

PREPARATION: You'll need hymn books and snacks. You may also want portable cassette or CD players and cassettes or CDs of Christian music, though they're not required for the activity.

R ead aloud Galatians 4:1-7. Ask:

■ **What does it mean to be a child of God?**

■ **How can we become children of God?**

■ **How are we God's heirs?**

■ **What are the blessings we receive as children of God?**

■ **How can we celebrate being God's heirs?**

In celebration of being children of God, have an "heir-band" contest. Form groups of no more than four. Have each group choose a favorite hymn or chorus from a church song book. Give groups 10 minutes to practice their songs. Tell groups they can pantomime rock-band, full-orchestra, or country versions of the songs. Ask groups to sing their songs as they pretend to play along. (If your group doesn't enjoy singing, consider providing a variety of contemporary Christian cassettes or CDs and portable players for kids to choose their background music.)

When they've had time to practice, have each group perform its hymn or chorus for the rest of the group.

After a hearty round of applause, declare that we're all winners because we're children of God and heirs to God's kingdom. Celebrate with a snack and close with prayer, thanking God for loving us and for being our heavenly Father.

# GALATIANS 5:13

## THEME:

Freedom

## SUMMARY:
In this SKIT, a guy's quiet evening at home with a friend gets out of hand, leading him into a troubling misunderstanding.

## THE PARTY'S OVER

SCENE: A teenage guy is sitting in a comfortable chair in his home.

PROPS: You'll need a phone, a pizza box, a six-pack of nonalcoholic beer, a Walkman, a can of lemon-lime soda, a rag, and chairs. You'll also need a Bible for the discussion afterward.

CHARACTERS:
**Mom**
**Dad**
**Jay**
**Mel** (guy or girl)
**Rob**

SCRIPT
*(Jay is relaxing in a chair. Mom and Dad are leaving.)*

**Mom:** Now, Jay, here's the number where you can reach us in case of an emergency. We should be back at about two tomorrow afternoon.

**Dad:** We'll probably call and check in on you later. Have a nice evening.

**Mom:** And if you go out, don't track in mud on the carpet. We just had it cleaned.

**Jay:** *(Somewhat bored)* Sure, Mom. I'll probably just stay home tonight and *(yawning)* watch TV or something.

**Dad:** OK.

**Mom:** Bye-bye. *(They leave.)*

**Jay:** *(Waits 'til they're safely out the door, then jumps up.)* Yes! *(Dials phone.)* Hi, Garin? Yeah! They won't be back until tomorrow afternoon. Why don't you bring over those videos you were telling me about? All right. See ya! *(There's a knock at the door. Jay answers it.)* Mel? What are you doing here?

**Mel:** I saw your folks leave with some suitcases, and I figured you'd be in the mood for... *(dramatically)* PIZZA! *(Mel holds a big pizza box up, opens it, balances it, and drops it on the floor—open-side down, of course.)* Oops!

**Jay:** Hey! That carpet was just cleaned!

**Mel:** Don't worry—a little club soda will get that right up!

**Jay:** We don't have any club soda!

**Mel:** Well, what do you have? That's all right—I'll check.
*(Mel exits to the kitchen to look around. There's another knock on the door. Jay goes to answer it. Rob stands in the doorway wearing a Walkman and holding his hands behind his back.)*

**Jay:** Rob? Uh, hi. What...

**Rob:** Garin called me up and told me you were having a party, so here I am! *(He holds up a six-pack of beer he's been hiding behind his back.)*

**Jay:** Oh, great... *(He smacks his forehead. He speaks louder so Mel can hear him.)* I mean, great to have you here. Have a seat. *(Rob sits and cracks open a beer and offers it to Jay.)* No thanks.

**Mel:** *(Entering with can of lemon-lime soda and a rag)* I couldn't find any club soda, but let me try this diet lemon-lime. *(Mel starts to clean the carpet.)*

**Jay:** I wonder where Garin is, anyway? *(Sound effect of phone ringing—could have either Mom or Dad yell out, "Ring ring.")* Maybe that's him calling. *(He goes to answer the phone, waiting for it to ring again.)*

**Mel:** Well, that's not working. Hmm... Hey, Rob! *(Jay picks up phone. Rob is grooving to his headphones.)* Rob! Let me try one of those beers!

**Jay:** Hello? *(Miserably)* Oh hi, Dad.

If you use this skit as a discussion starter, here are possible questions:

■ **What's tempting about freedom?**

■ **According to Galatians 5:13, how did God intend for us to use the freedom he's given us?**

# GALATIANS 5:13-15

**THEME:**
Serving and affirming others

**SUMMARY:**
In this AFFIRMATION, kids will design praise books for each other.

PREPARATION: You'll need a Bible, paper, poster board, markers, pens, and staplers.

Have kids each design a peppy praise book by folding several sheets of paper in half and stapling them inside a piece of poster board that has been cut and folded to make a cover.

Then have kids gather in a circle. Give each person a marker or a pen. Have kids creatively write their names on their covers and illustrate them with symbols representing their interests and hobbies.

Then have a volunteer read Galatians 5:13-15. Ask:
■ **What do these verses tell us about how we should relate to each other?**

Have kids write two or three positive descriptions of themselves in their books. Then have them pass their books to the right and write in other kids' books as many positive descriptions as they can to describe the books' owners. Allow one minute for each person to write in someone's book before passing it to the right. Continue until each book reaches its owner.

Give kids time to read their praise books. Ask:
■ **How does it feel to be lifted up in this way?**
■ **How can we build each other up in everyday situations?**

Reread Galatians 5:13-15 as a final reminder for kids to build one another up in love.

# GALATIANS 5:22-23

**THEME:**
The fruit of the Spirit

**SUMMARY:**
In this LEARNING GAME, kids will work to put puzzles together and discover how they live out the fruit of the Spirit.

PREPARATION: You'll need a 200-piece puzzle for each group of no more than six. Puzzles with illustrations of fruit would be best for this activity. You'll also need Bibles and a supply of fresh fruit.

Form teams of no more than six. Have the youngest person in each team read Galatians 5:22-23 for his or her group.

Then say: **The qualities that make up the fruit of the Spirit are ones that we can practice all the time, in everyday circumstances. Let's play a game right now to see if we can iden-**

tify ways our group members express the fruit of the Spirit in an everyday circumstance.

Give each team a puzzle.

Say: **This is a race to see which team can work together to put its puzzle together first. Signal when your team is finished by standing and yelling, "Fruit of the Spirit!" As you're working on your puzzles, make a mental note of ways that people on your team express the fruit of the Spirit.**

**For example, one person might help calm others down with her patience, while another's joyful attitude might spread enthusiasm through your whole team. Keep a Bible open to Galatians 5:22-23 in case you want to refer to it. Ready? Begin.**

Congratulate the winning team, then give kids each a piece of fruit to enjoy during the discussion time that follows.

Have kids form new groups with people who were on different puzzle teams. Read aloud Galatians 5:22-23 and have groups discuss the following questions. When groups have had time to discuss the questions, have a volunteer from each group share his or her group's ideas with the whole class. Wrap up the activity by asking:

■ **What was the most challenging part of this game for you?**

■ **How did you feel about your team when putting the puzzles together?**

■ **How was the fruit of the Spirit illustrated in your team's attitudes and actions?**

■ **How can you express the fruit of the Spirit in your daily life this week?**

# GALATIANS
## 5:22-23

THEME:
   The fruit of the Spirit

SUMMARY:
   In this DEVOTION, kids will select a piece of fruit that symbolizes one of the qualities listed in Galatians 5:22-23 they see in their lives.

PREPARATION: You'll need a fruit bowl containing grapes, bananas, pears, apples, oranges, and strawberries. You'll also need a Bible and a pitcher of fruit juice.

EXPERIENCE
   Gather kids around the bowl of fruit. Ask a volunteer to read aloud Galatians 5:22-23. Ask teenagers to think about a spiritual quality listed in the passage that they feel is alive and well in their lives right now. As each person decides on a quality, ask him or her to pick from the bowl a piece of fruit that illustrates that quality.

RESPONSE
   When everyone has made a selection, ask kids to show the fruit they chose and explain why they chose it. For example, someone might say, "I picked grapes

because the clusters symbolize how love draws me together with all of you."

CLOSING

After everyone has shared, say: **The fruit of the Spirit isn't just words listed in a book; it's people growing and expressing God's love each day. Let's celebrate that.**

To close, celebrate the gifts God has given by having a love feast. Eat the fruit and serve fruit juice.

# GALATIANS
## 5:22-26

## THEME:

The fruit of the Spirit

## SUMMARY:
Kids will enjoy a PARTY based on the theme of the fruit of the Spirit.

PREPARATION: Publicize this party by delivering "apple invitations" to kids and their families. You can make these invitations by using ribbon or string to tie a strip of paper (listing the party's time and date) to an apple. You'll need "fruity" decorations and refreshments. You'll also need a Bible. If possible, hold the party in a recreation room or large fellowship hall.

As people arrive, have them help decorate the room using posters and pictures of fruit, colorful streamers, and real fruit. Make the decorating activity a time of fun and fellowship. Encourage kids to go wild with the decorations.

Serve refreshments such as fruit salad, fruit punch, and fruit desserts (peach cobbler, apple pie, or strawberry sundaes).

Play games that use fruit. For example, have a pie-eating contest. Or have people run relays using fruit. Think of games you regularly enjoy with your youth group and try to incorporate fruit into them somehow.

During a break in the action, have a volunteer read aloud Galatians 5:22-26. Then have each person choose one of the qualities of the fruit of the Spirit that they most desire to "grow" in their lives.

Next, read aloud Galatians 5:22-26 again and have kids each think of three ways they can live out the fruit of the Spirit in their lives during the coming week. For example, someone might say, "I can help my mom around the house," "I can work on not losing my temper when my brother bugs me," or "I can be patient when things aren't going my way."

Close the party by having kids form groups of no more than four and tell one fruit of the Spirit they see in each other.

# GALATIANS
## 6:9

THEME:
Helping others

SUMMARY:
Kids will perform an exhausting task in this PROJECT and discuss how to keep from getting tired when doing good.

PREPARATION: Set up an experience for kids that will tire them out. This could be anything from painting a house to cleaning out a basement or garage. You'll need a snack for this activity, too.

L ead the kids in the chosen activity. You'll know kids are tiring when they begin to take more breaks and complain about how difficult this activity is.

When kids are tired and need a break, call them together and feed them a snack. Discuss the following questions in groups of no more than four. Ask:

■ **How does it feel to work this hard on a task?**

■ **How is the way we're working on this task like the way we are to work out our faith?**

Have someone read aloud Galatians 6:9. Ask:

■ **What is the harvest we'll receive when we help others?**

■ **How can we re-energize when we're tired of working?**

■ **How is this break like the way we recharge our spiritual batteries at church or when we read the Bible?**

When the discussion time and snacks are finished, dive in with the kids to finish the task. Have different kids read aloud Galatians 6:9 throughout the rest of the working time.

# EPHESIANS

*"I mean that you have been saved by grace through believing. You did not save yourselves; it was a gift from God."*

*Ephesians 2:8*

# EPHESIANS 2:1-9

**THEME:**
Grace

**SUMMARY:**
In this SKIT, a man is shot on the street and lies dying but refuses to accept help from a doctor.

## GUNSHOT

SCENE: A man has been shot and is lying abandoned in a street.

PROPS: You'll need a bandanna and a Bible for the discussion afterward.

CHARACTERS:
**Man**
**Woman**

### SCRIPT

*(A man, shot in the side, speaks as if he's out of breath.)*

**Man:** Help! Please, somebody... Help!

**Woman:** Oh my gosh! What happened to you?

**Man:** Some guy jumped out... stole my wallet... had a gun...

**Woman:** OK, OK. I'm a doctor, just lie quietly. *(She takes a bandanna from her purse.)* I'll try to stop the bleeding, then call for an ambulance.

**Man:** *(Sitting up, struggling to stand)* Got to walk to the hospital...

**Woman:** Walk? You can't walk— you'll bleed to death! Let me...

**Man:** I can do it myself *(He falls.)*

**Woman:** Not for long, you can't! Here, this bandanna will help stop the bleeding.

**Man:** *(Fumbling for bandanna)* Let me do it...

**Woman:** Are you crazy?

**Man:** Got to do it myself...

**Woman:** Look, I'm the doctor here. You just lie still, and I'll try to get this cleaned up.

**Man:** No, go away. I can't pay you... my wallet...

**Woman:** Pay me? Mister, I'm trying to save your life here! You don't have to pay me! Now just lie still and be quiet.

**Man:** Credit card... in my car... let me get it for you...

**Woman:** Please, mister. You're losing a lot of blood. Lie down so I can help you.

**Man:** No. *(Trying to get up)* I'll walk to a phone... call ambulance.

**Woman:** We've got to stop the bleeding first! Then I can go call.

**Man:** Can do it myself. *(He lies very still.)*

**Woman:** No. No you can't—you need me.

**Man:** I'm... tired...

**Woman:** Then stop fighting and let me help you.

**Man:** No... no... no.

*(Characters freeze, then lights go out.)*

If you use this skit as a discussion starter, here are possible questions:

■ **When have you had a hard time asking God for help?**

■ **According to Ephesians**

2:1-9, why is it important for us to understand God's grace?

■ What can we do to help ourselves?

■ How do we receive what God has for us?

# EPHESIANS 2:8-9

---

THEME:

Beginning a relationship with God

SUMMARY:

In this ADVENTURE, kids will survey shoppers about what it takes to get into heaven.

---

PREPARATION: You'll need paper, pencils, and a Bible.

Meet at a shopping center or mall. Form groups of no more than three and give each group paper and a pencil. Have groups each choose a store they'll stand near to get responses for an informal survey on heaven. Be sure kids get permission from the store manager before beginning. If you're unable to get permission for kids to stand near a store, you might want to have them stand in open areas of the mall or shopping center instead.

Have kids survey 10 people leaving the store using a statement similar to this one: We're from (church name), and we're conducting a survey on how to get to heaven. What do you think it takes for someone to get to heaven?

After groups complete their surveys, gather for a devotion time. Have groups share the responses they got from their surveys. Ask:

■ How did it feel to ask strangers about getting to heaven?

■ What did you think about the responses you received?

■ What do you think is the general consensus on how people think they can get to heaven?

In their groups, have kids list significant good things they've done in their lives (such as helping on a missions trip, giving money to the poor, or sharing food with a friend).

After kids have shared their good deeds, ask:

■ How do you feel about your list?

■ According to your list, are you worthy to go to heaven?

Read Ephesians 2:8-9 aloud. Then discuss the following questions. Ask:

■ How do these verses relate to what we discovered in our surveys?

■ What do you think Jesus meant by saying we are "saved by grace"?

■ Why do you think so many people won't accept Christ's free gift?

Say: God knows you can't get to heaven by your good works. He only wants you to accept his free gift of salvation and believe in him.

Pray: Dear God, thank you for your free gift of salvation. Please continue to strengthen our faith. Help us to live a lifestyle that glorifies and honors you. In Jesus' name, amen.

# EPHESIANS
## 3:14-21

**THEME:**
Broken hearts

**SUMMARY:**
Use this SKIT to help kids discover the best way to deal with brokenness in their lives.

## THE BROKEN HEART

SCENE: A dark, empty stage with lights.

PROPS: You'll need a chair, a large heart made of red construction paper, a large heart made of white construction paper, and a Bible.

CHARACTERS:
**Don**
**Villain** (wearing a dark, hooded robe)
**Parent**
**Coach**
**Girlfriend**
**Friend**
**Hero** (wearing a white robe or sheet)
**Reader**

### SCRIPT
*(Lights come up on Don, center stage, with a red heart in his hand.)*
**Don:** I can't believe how hard this week has been. It's only Tuesday, and nothing's going right. I botched my geometry test, and I know I'll end up having to go to summer school. *(Villain enters and stands behind Don with arms crossed.)* If I don't get my grades up, I won't be able to graduate with my friends. I must be stupid. I just can't learn things as fast as other people. I'm not very bright.
*(Villain takes the red heart from Don and tears off a small portion, tosses away the piece, and gives the heart back to Don. Don sits in a chair. Parent enters and paces in front of him.)*
**Parent:** Don, I can't believe the way you've been acting lately. You're acting just like a child. Will you ever grow up? You're the most irresponsible person I know. Why can't you be like your older brother just once?
*(Parent freezes in place. Villain takes Don's heart, tears off another small piece, and returns the heart to Don. Don stands center stage and mimes shooting a basketball. Coach enters.)*
**Coach:** Don, what's your problem? You haven't concentrated on one thing I've said today. And it's not just today. You've been an airhead for two days now. I'm sorry, but I'm going to start Mike in your position for Friday's game.
*(Coach freezes in place. Villain takes the heart, tears another piece off, and returns it to Don. Girlfriend enters and stands center stage with Don. The two stand back to back, miming talking on the phone with each other.)*
**Girlfriend:** Oh...hi, Don. Oh right, we did have a date for

tonight. I guess I forgot to call you. Sorry, but I have to cancel our date. You remember Joey, don't you? From Travis High? Well, he called, and I really want to spend some time with him this weekend. Really, Don, it's nothing personal. I just don't get to see him very often. I'll talk to you next week, OK? 'Bye.

*(Girlfriend freezes in place. Villain takes heart from Don, tears off a piece, and returns the heart to him. Friend and Hero enter and share center stage with Don. Friend is seated in chair, and Don is on his knees. Villain stands next to Don. Hero stands next to Friend.)*

**Don:** *(Loudly)* I can't take this anymore! Everything is all wrong! Nothing ever goes right!

**Friend:** I know how you feel. There are times in my life when nothing seems to go right either. *(Villain snickers.)*

**Don:** Don't give me that. You're always on top of everything. You can't know how I feel.

**Friend:** You're wrong. Bad things happen to me all the time. The only difference between you and me is that I've learned how to face and overcome those problems. *(Villain looks nervous.)*

**Don:** How?

**Friend:** By turning to someone else for strength and comfort in the midst of problems. I can hand my struggles over to him, and he'll make me strong enough to make it through the day. *(Villain wrings his hands nervously, begins to pace.)*

**Don:** But who can do that?

**Friend:** A person named Jesus.

*(Villain cringes at the name.)*

**Don:** He can really do all of that?

**Friend:** He can do much more than just that. But you have to let him do it. It's up to you. What do you say? *(Villain grows fearful.)*

**Don:** I say yes. I want him to do all you've said.

*(Villain pulls at Don's shoulder, grabs the last piece of Don's heart, and tries to tug it away. Don pulls it away from Villain and turns to look into Hero's eyes. Don hands the small piece of heart to Hero. Hero takes the small piece of heart, reaches into his robe, and pulls out a white heart and gives it to Don. Lights fade. Reader reads aloud Ephesians 3:14-21.)*

If you use this skit as a discussion starter, here are possible questions:

■ **When have you felt like Don? What did you do?**

■ **How can Ephesians 3:14-21 encourage you in light of discouraging circumstances?**

■ **What can you do this week to allow Jesus to heal your broken heart?**

# EPHESIANS 4:2-6

THEME:
Unity

SUMMARY:
This OBJECT LESSON will help kids picture and understand the unity described in Ephesians 4:2-6.

PREPARATION: You'll need a Bible.

Ask all group members wearing belts to remove them. Tell the group to fasten the belts together so they form a single belt around the group. This may be a tight squeeze!

Once the belt is fastened around the group (even if it's really tight), have kids freeze in silence and take a mental "picture" of their situation. Then ask:

■ **What did you have to do to make this belt fit?**

■ **How did you feel as you took the mental picture of the group with this weird belt around it?**

Read aloud Ephesians 4:2-6, then ask:

■ **How is this belt like or unlike the unity talked about in this passage?**

■ **This physical belt wrapped around us keeps us restricted, but how does spiritual unity free us in real life?**

■ **What can we do in our group to promote the unity described in Ephesians 4:2-6?**

# EPHESIANS 4:25-5:2

THEME:
Sin

SUMMARY:
In this DEVOTION, kids will compare trash with bad things in their lives.

PREPARATION: You'll need light-colored, plastic garbage bags; a black marker, and Bibles.

EXPERIENCE
Take your kids outside and give them each a plastic garbage bag. Tell group members they've been assigned the duty of trash collection. Explain that, for fun, the trash collection will be a contest. Whoever can retrieve the most trash in 10 minutes wins. Ask kids to make individual piles as they collect the trash. When time is up, announce the winner. Have kids bag the trash, then sit in a circle.

RESPONSE
Have volunteers read aloud portions of Ephesians 4:25-5:2 until the entire passage has been read. Then have kids give you the "thumbs up" sign as you ask the following questions. Give kids a few seconds to think after each question and tell them you'd like to hear lots of interesting responses. When one person shares an answer, allow kids who thought of the same answer and have nothing more to add to lower their thumbs. When kids have all lowered their

thumbs, ask the next question and repeat the process. Ask:

■ **What's your opinion of the trash you gathered?**

■ **How is that like or unlike the way we feel about the "smelly" things in our own lives?**

■ **What are some "trashy" things in our own lives?**

■ **What are some "trashy" things listed in this Scripture that we should throw out of our lives?**

■ **How can we replace those things with the good things listed in this Scripture?**

CLOSING

With a black marker, label each of the garbage bags your teenagers collected with one of these words or phrases from Ephesians 4:25–5:2: lies, sinful anger, stealing, harmful talk, bitterness, angry shouts, and evil. It's OK if a bag has more than one word or phrase on it.

(**Note:** The words and phrases here are adapted from The Youth Bible, New Century Version. Adapt words as needed to fit the Bible translation your group uses.)

Next, take kids and their garbage bags to the garbage-dumping area at your church. One by one, have kids toss the bags into the trash while the group applauds as you symbolically "throw out the garbage" that sometimes fills our lives.

# EPHESIANS 4:29-32

THEME:
Purity

SUMMARY:
In this OBJECT LESSON, kids will compare how an apple cleans a knife to how God cleanses our sins.

PREPARATION: You'll need plastic knives, bread, peanut butter, and apples. You'll also need a Bible.

Form a circle. Give each person a plastic knife, a piece of bread, and peanut butter. Have kids each make a peanut butter sandwich.

When kids are finished, have them look at their peanut butter-covered knives. Say: **These knives represent each of us. The peanut butter represents our sins—those things that separate us from God. Just as the peanut butter sticks to the knives and makes them messy, sin messes up the clean and pure parts of us.**

Give each person an apple. Have kids use their knives to cut the apples in half. The peanut butter will be cleaned from the knives when they cut through the apples.

Say: **These apples represent Christ. Just as the apple cleanses the knife, Christ can cleanse our sins when we ask for forgiveness.**

Ask:

■ **How is this like real life?**

∎ **What sins in your life stick to you like the peanut butter sticks to the knife?**

∎ **How do you feel when sin keeps you from growing closer to Christ?**

Read Ephesians 4:29-32 and ask:

∎ **How do these verses relate to our activity?**

∎ **How does the apple represent Christ in these Scriptures?**

∎ **What areas can you work on to keep your life pure?**

Have kids each tell a person sitting close to them one specific way they'll try to keep their lives pure.

# EPHESIANS
## 4:29-32

**THEME:**
Gossip

**SUMMARY:**
In this SKIT, a girl visits her cousin's school and quickly finds out how ugly gossip can be.

## THE INVITATION

SCENE: High school cafeteria.

PROPS: You'll need trays, paper plates, forks, cups, books or backpacks, a table, chairs, and a Bible for the discussion afterward.

CHARACTERS:
**Teresa**
**Kris**
**Stacey**
**Paula**

SCRIPT
*(Teresa and Kris are sitting in the cafeteria, eating lunch. Stacey enters, talking to Paula.)*

**Stacey:** And this is the ever-dangerous cafeteria. Oh, Teresa, Kris, this is my cousin, Paula Stevenson. She's visiting for a week, and they're letting her go to classes with me today.

**Teresa:** Nice to meet you, Paula. Too bad they had to be serving tuna surprise on the day you're visiting—not a very nice first impression!

**Paula:** *(Laughs)* That's OK. We have tuna surprise back home, too. Actually, everyone's been really nice.

**Stacey:** Oh, I invited Paula to Bible study on Thursday night. I thought she could probably meet a lot of new people there.

**Kris:** Well, she'll meet a lot of people there, all right. People like Jennifer Thomas and Cathy Ivers—they're so stuck up! They only go to Bible study to talk about how many guys they've gone out with!

**Teresa:** Or to show off their new clothes. I'm so sick of them! And they're always flirting with that jerk, Mark Andrews. You know, I heard that he got some girl pregnant over at Washington High.

**Stacey:** Hey, I heard that, too. Only I thought it was at Central... or was it Westview? Anyway, if Jennifer or Cathy ever go out with him, I wouldn't be surprised if it happened again. I heard Cathy went to the mountains with some college guy.

**Kris:** Yeah, but you know, there

*are* some really nice people at Bible study. Like Marissa and Kelly. I mean, they're pretty nice... even if Kelly does have really bad breath. Did you ever notice that? I sat next to her last week, and it was gross. And she totally sings off key, too.

**Paula:** Hmm... that sounds like a really... um... interesting Bible study.

**Teresa:** Yeah, it's a great place to meet people.

If you use this skit as a discussion starter, here are some possible questions:

■ **Why is it so easy to get caught up in gossip?**

■ **According to Ephesians 4:29-32, what are good examples of how we should talk about others?**

# EPHESIANS
# 6:1-3

---

## THEME:
Parents

## SUMMARY:
In this CREATIVE PRAYER, kids will create sentence prayers based on the letters in the phrase "Obey your parents."

---

PREPARATION: On 15 3×5 cards, write out the phrase "Obey your parents," putting one letter on each card.

F orm a circle. Read Ephesians 6:1-3. Discuss the challenges and rewards of obeying your parents. Ask:

■ **Why is it difficult to obey your parents?**

■ **How do you feel when you obey your parents? when you don't?**

■ **According to these verses, how does God want us to act?**

Shuffle the 3×5 cards. Form no more than 15 groups. Have each group choose one 3×5 card. If you have fewer than 15 people in your group, have kids each choose more than one card.

Say: **On your card is a letter. Think of one thing you can do better to show respect for and obedience to your parents. Choose a key word that begins with the letter on your card. Then phrase your idea into a prayer, asking God for help to do the thing you've decided. For example, if your letter is "o," you might say, "Dear God, help me to always be** o**pen with my parents."**

Give kids a few minutes to prepare their prayers. Then gather everyone together. Have kids say what letters they had, then speak their prayers in order of the letters in the phrase "Obey your parents." Close with a group "amen."

# EPHESIANS
## 6:1-4

**THEME:**
Parents

**SUMMARY:**
In this LEARNING GAME, kids will examine how they relate to their parents.

PREPARATION: You'll need a Bible.

Have kids sit in a circle of chairs. Say: **I'm going to read statements that may or may not reflect things that happened with your parents during this past week. If a statement is true for you, move in the direction I indicate. If it's not true for you, stay seated. If someone is in the seat you're supposed to move to, sit on that person's lap.**

Read aloud these "Lap Leap" statements:

- **Move one seat to your right if you said, "I love you" to your parents.**
- **Move two seats to your left if you had an argument with your parents.**
- **Move one seat to your left if you fought with your parents about the bathroom.**
- **Move one seat to your left if you were told to clean your room.**
- **Move three seats to your right if you helped wash dishes.**
- **Move eight seats to your left if you were grounded.**
- **Move one seat to your left if you yelled at your parents.**
- **Move two seats to your right if you talked about school problems with your parents.**
- **Move five seats to your right if you spent time alone with your parents talking.**
- **Move one seat to your right if you helped cook.**

After you've read the last statement, have kids return to their seats. Ask:

- **What did you learn about how you relate to your parents?**
- **Do you think you have a generally good or bad relationship with your parents? Explain.**

Read aloud Ephesians 6:1-4, then ask the following questions to wrap up:

- **Does this passage describe what goes on at your home? Why or why not?**
- **What can you do to make your home life better reflect this passage?**

# EPHESIANS
## 6:10-11

**THEME:**
Armor of God

**SUMMARY:**
In this SKIT, a guy forgets to put on his "spiritual armor," leaving him vulnerable to "attack."

## UNARMED

SCENE: Joe Christian is in his bedroom, wearing shorts and a T-shirt.

PROPS: You'll need a squirt gun (use one and pass it from character to character), books or backpacks, a magazine, and a Bible for the discussion afterward.

CHARACTERS:
**Joe Christian**
**Reader** (offstage)
**Friends 1, 2, and 3**

### SCRIPT

*(Joe wakes up, yawns, stretches, and scratches. Gets up and opens closet door.)*

**Reader:** "Finally, be strong in the Lord and in his great power. Put on the full armor of God so that you can fight against the devil's evil tricks."

**Joe:** Y'know, it's gonna be pretty hot today. I think I'll just wear what I have on. *(He grabs backpack and heads out the door.)*
*(Friend 1 enters, carrying backpack and a squirt gun.)*

**Joe:** *(Stopping Friend 1)* Hey, what're we doing in biology today?

**Friend 1:** Oh, it's really cool. Mr. Evers shows this video on evolution and the big-bang theory. *(He squirts Joe in the face and head with squirt gun.)* Then he talks about how we evolved from squid. *(He squirts Joe's chest.)* Pretty interesting, actually.

**Joe:** Well, I don't believe in evolution, but maybe it'll be a good video.
*(Friend 1 exits, walking past Joe. Joe shivers slightly from his damp T-shirt. Friend 2 enters, carrying a magazine and a squirt gun.)*

**Friend 2:** Joe, you gotta see this picture! *(He shows him the cen-terfold of magazine. Joe takes magazine and Friend 2 squirts him with squirt gun.)* Pretty good, huh?

**Joe:** I don't know... I mean, you really shouldn't read this kind of stuff. *(Friend 2 gives him another squirt.)* But she is something!

**Friend 2:** Yeah, I'll show you the rest later! *(Exits.)*

**Joe:** Brrr—it's getting kind of cold. I thought it was supposed to be hot today!
*(Friend 3 enters, carrying squirt gun.)*

**Friend 3:** Joe, you should hear what your "buddy" Zach is saying about you! *(He squirts Joe.)* Some friend, right? *(He gives another squirt.)* If I were you, I'd be really mad! What a jerk! *(He squirts him again before exiting.)*

**Joe:** *(Shivering)* Why am I so cold?

**Reader:** "Finally, be strong in the Lord and in his great power. Put on the full armor of God so that you can fight against the devil's evil tricks."

If you use this skit as a discussion starter, here are possible questions:

■ **In what situations do you need God's armor?**

■ **Ephesians 6:10-11 says to "put on the full armor of God." How do you do that?**

# EPHESIANS
# 6:10-18

---

### THEME:
Spiritual warfare

### SUMMARY:
In this LEARNING GAME, kids will compare a war game with spiritual war.

---

PREPARATION: Gather enough Laser Tag equipment so each person can have a gun and a sensor unit. You'll also need two "treasures" and a Bible. (If Laser Tag equipment isn't available, substitute water guns for the lasers, and colored construction paper taped to kids' chests and backs for the sensors. Any wet streaks on the construction paper signals a hit.)

Form two teams and establish two home bases at opposite ends of the building—one for each team. Have each team hide a treasure, such as a pillow or a soccer ball. The first team to find the opposite team's treasure and reach home base with it wins. A player is out when he or she receives a deadly sixth hit.

After the game, ask:

■ **What made this exciting for you? Why?**

■ **Is this game like or unlike war? Explain.**

Read aloud Ephesians 6:10-18. Ask:

■ **What does this passage say about war?**

■ **Describe a battle you might fight on an average day. Do you** flee or fight? Explain.

■ **According to Ephesians 6:10-18, how can you win those battles?**

■ **How can other Christians, like our teammates during the game, help during our personal spiritual battles?**

■ **What can you do this week to help you use the battle armor described in Ephesians 6:10-18?**

---

# EPHESIANS
# 6:11-17

---

### THEME:
Armor of God

### SUMMARY:
In this DEVOTION, kids will discover the importance of putting on God's armor to protect themselves from sin.

---

PREPARATION: You'll need balloons, straight pins, duct tape, and a Bible.

EXPERIENCE

Give each teenager a balloon and a straight pin. Have kids blow up their balloons as large as they can. Then have kids cover one half of their balloons in duct tape. Say: **When we're protected with God's armor, sin can't destroy us.**

Have kids stab their straight pins through the duct tape into the balloons. Although the balloons will begin to slowly leak, they will not pop. Move quickly to the next step.

Say: **When we aren't protected with God's armor, sin can damage and sometimes destroy us.**

Have kids stab their straight pins through the untaped side of the balloons. The balloons will pop.

RESPONSE

Ask:

■ **What did you think would happen when the pin entered the taped side of the balloon?**

■ **How did you feel when the pin didn't pop the balloon?**

■ **How did you feel when the pin destroyed the balloon?**

Have a volunteer read aloud Ephesians 6:11-17. Ask:

■ **How is our balloon activity like the message of this passage?**

■ **How can sin damage and destroy us?**

■ **What are ways we can put on God's armor in our daily lives?**

CLOSING

Form groups of no more than three. Have teenagers think of three weaknesses or temptations they're going to guard against in the coming week. Then have each person pray for strength to overcome one of the weaknesses or temptations.

Have kids each tape a small piece of duct tape to their wallets, purses, watches, or other personal items as a reminder to always put on God's armor. Award a prize to the person who can keep the tape on the longest.

# EPHESIANS 6:14-17

THEME:
Armor of God

SUMMARY:

In this LEARNING GAME, kids will put on protective clothing to start a discussion on God's armor.

PREPARATION: Gather two boxes, each containing the following: a belt, a catcher's chest protector, large boots, a garbage-can lid, a football helmet, and a plastic sword (or one made of cardboard). You'll also need a Bible and several pocket-sized Bibles for prizes.

Introduce kids to the armor of God with a relay. Form two teams. For each team, put a box containing the protective clothing on the other side of the room. Begin the game by asking each team to line up single file. Each team member will run across the room to the box and put on the items in the box. Then with sword in hand, the player shouts, "Put on the full armor of God!" He or she then takes off the outfit, runs back to the line, and the relay continues.

Award a pocket-sized Bible to each member of the team that finishes first. Then talk about each of the parts of God's armor as listed in Ephesians 6:14-17.

# Philippians

*"In your lives you must think and act like Christ Jesus."*

*Philippians 2:5*

# PHILIPPIANS
## 1:3-6

**THEME:**
Communicating love

**SUMMARY:**
Kids affirm one another in this AFFIRMATION by writing encouraging notes on "casts"—tube socks pulled over one arm.

PREPARATION: Ask kids to each bring a long, white tube sock to the meeting (collect extras for those who forget to bring one). You'll also need a marker for each person, a cassette or CD player, contemporary Christian cassette tapes or CDs, and a Bible.

Give each person a marker. Ask kids to pull their tube socks over their nonwriting hands all the way up their arms. Each sock will serve as a "cast."

Explain that as the music plays, you want everyone to move around the room and write something positive on other kids' casts. These notes should be brief, focusing on the person's gifts or good character. (Because the markers could bleed through the socks, warn kids wearing long-sleeved shirts to push their sleeves up above the edge of their casts.)

During the activity, play mellow contemporary Christian music such as Steven Curtis Chapman's "I Will Be Here" or Amy Grant's "If These Walls Could Speak." Encourage your group members to be serious throughout. When kids finish, ask:

■ **How did you feel writing something positive about everyone else in the room?**

■ **How did you feel when others were writing something on your own cast?**

■ **Do any of the comments on your cast surprise you? Why or why not?**

■ **What's easier to believe about ourselves: good stuff or bad stuff? Explain.**

Ask a volunteer to read aloud Philippians 1:3-6.

Say: **Sometimes we forget to be thankful for the friends we have. It's good to be remembered by our friends. And when you feel lonely or hurting, just remember this time of affirmation. God has started something good in us, and he'll give us the strength to finish it.**

Ask kids to take their casts home and hang them on a dresser or bedpost as a reminder. They can use the socks to hold special mementos from future youth group meetings.

# PHILIPPIANS
## 2:1-8

**THEME:**
Humility

**SUMMARY:**
In this SKIT, one guy brags about his accomplishments while another focuses on the needs of others.

# BIG MAN ON CAMPUS

SCENE: In a high school cafeteria, two teenagers are eating lunch.

PROPS: You'll need a letter jacket (optional), books, a sports magazine, two chairs, a table, lunch items, and a Bible for the discussion afterward.

CHARACTERS:
**Todd** (wearing a letter jacket, if possible)
**Ryan**
**Shelby**

## SCRIPT

*(Todd and Ryan are sitting at a table eating lunch.)*

**Todd:** So, Ryan, how do you like Central High, so far?

**Ryan:** It's been a good two weeks. I think I'm really going to like it here. Especially if I can get more involved in clubs and stuff.

**Todd:** Yeah, that really helps. I mean, I should know—being student-council president, yearbook editor, and class valedictorian and all.

**Ryan:** Hmm, well, I guess you would know, then. I'm thinking about trying sports, though. Maybe basketball now, then baseball in the spring.

**Todd:** I can tell you all about sports, too. I *am* a four-year letterman ... track, football, basketball, baseball—you name it.

**Ryan:** Pretty impressive.

**Todd:** Well, baseball is my best sport. Last year I was named MVP for our division. It was in all the papers, you know.

**Ryan:** Hmm, guess I missed it. Does Central have a service organization? Like a club that helps out in the neighborhood?

**Todd:** Yeah, but you wouldn't like it. It's full of dorks who don't like the *normal* clubs or aren't good enough for sports.

**Ryan:** Sounds like they need people to help out, though. I'm going to go check the front office for some info. See ya around, Todd.

**Todd:** *(Shaking head)* That guy's not getting off to a good start here.

*(Shelby hurries over, sits down next to Todd, and talks excitedly.)*

**Shelby:** Hey, Todd, I saw you talking to Ryan just now!

**Todd:** Yeah, so?

**Shelby:** Did he say anything about going out for the team this year?

**Todd:** Yeah, he said something about baseball or basketball or something.

**Shelby:** Something? Todd, don't you know who he is?

**Todd:** Ryan? He's just some transfer from Iowa or Ohio or Idaho ...

**Shelby:** Ohio. And he's not just some transfer! He was all-state for three years in basketball and football, division MVP for two years in baseball, and is being recruited by every major college in the United States!

**Todd:** Huh?

**Shelby:** I read about him in this magazine—that's how I found out!

*(Todd looks at magazine and shakes head in disbelief.)*

**Shelby:** So, what did he have to say?

**Todd:** *(Looking in direction where*

*Ryan exited)* Not much. Then again, maybe he said a lot after all.
*(They exit.)*

If you use this skit as a discussion starter, here are possible questions:

■ **After you've bragged about yourself to someone, how do you normally feel? Explain.**

■ **According to Philippians 2:1-8, what does it mean to "give more honor to others than to yourselves"?**

■ **What are specific ways you can follow Jesus' example that's described in verses 6-8 this week?**

# PHILIPPIANS 2:1-11

**THEME:**
Considering others

**SUMMARY:**
Kids get a taste of what it's like to be homeless during this lock-in ADVENTURE that ends with kids actually serving homeless people at a shelter.

PREPARATION: You'll need to recruit adult volunteers to help staff the lock-in. Ask group members to come to the lock-in wearing casual clothes and to bring another change of clothes. Tell them not to bring sleeping bags or blankets so they can get a taste of what it's like to live as a homeless person for a night. Form a lock-in prep team made up of a few kids. Ask prep-team members to coordinate the following tasks:

■ Contact a homeless shelter and offer your group's help in serving a breakfast meal.

■ Gather blindfolds and smelly things and bring them to the lock-in. Ideas for smelly things include sweaty socks, a rotten banana, spoiled milk, and so on.

■ Gather empty but clean soup or vegetable cans (one for each lock-in participant), cans of soup, packages of crackers, and plastic cups.

■ Gather cardboard boxes, old mattresses, scraps of wood, old tires, garbage bags, and other junkyard stuff that can be used as building materials.

■ Record an hour of heavy-traffic noise on a cassette tape and gather a cassette player that can play both sides of a tape continuously.

You'll also need quarters or bubble gum and a Bible.

Plan a lock-in with a homeless theme. Possible activities include:

■ **Unfair Handouts**—Have adult leaders pass out quarters or bubble gum to a few teenagers while the rest watch. Ask: **How does it feel to be a "have" or a "have-not"?**

■ **Guess the Smell**—Blindfold kids to see if they can identify the following items by smell: dirty socks, a rotten banana, spoiled milk, or other smelly things your prep team gathers. Ask: **How would you feel if you were surrounded by these smells all the time?**

■ **Meal**—Serve crackers, cold soup in cleaned-out old cans, and warm water in plastic cups. Ask: **How would it affect you physically, emotionally, and mentally if this were your regular diet?**

■ **Build-a-Bed**—Have kids create their own "sleeping quarters" for the night by using materials found in your "junkyard," located in one corner of your meeting room. Remind them they must sleep in whatever they construct! While they build, ask: **If the shelter you're building were your only home, how would you feel?**

■ **Traffic Noise**—Play the cassette tape of heavy-traffic noise throughout the event. Use an auto-reverse cassette player that can play both sides of the cassette continuously. Ask: **How long would it take you to get used to this noise?**

■ **Patrol Cops**—Have one or two adult leaders roam around the room while kids are sleeping and beat on their "sleeping quarters." They should ask kids to move their belongings and their sleeping quarters to another location in the room.

■ **Breakfast Is Served!**—At about 6:30 the next morning, have kids get up, change their clothes and go serve breakfast at a homeless shelter in your area. Then return to the church. Ask:

■ **How did this lock-in adventure affect you?**

■ **How did it feel to serve breakfast to homeless people?**

■ **What new insights do you have about homeless people?**

Read aloud Philippians 2:1-11. Ask:

■ **How do these verses influence our attitude toward the homeless?**

Say: **If we follow Jesus' example, we'll think of others before ourselves. And we'll treat people the way we want to be treated.**

Close by asking kids to pray for the homeless people they just served.

# PHILIPPIANS 3:12-14

THEME:
Pressing toward the prize

SUMMARY:
Kids go on a RETREAT that's packed with prizes for actions they normally take for granted.

PREPARATION: Publicize the retreat with posters shaped like prize ribbons. Gather food and recreation coupons from local businesses—often provided free to churches! Also, gather as many first-, second-, and third-place ribbons as you can. You'll need a Bible, too.

Plan a retreat based on Philippians 3:12-14. Your plan will be to give away as many prizes and awards as possible during the event. This is not a contest because everyone will win a prize by the end of the weekend. Tell your kids that the retreat will center around winning and that everyone is a winner in God's eyes.

Start as soon as the first person arrives the day of the retreat. Give that person a blue ribbon for being first. Give the next person a red ribbon for being second and the third person a white ribbon for being third.

Next, hand out ribbons to
■ the first three on the bus or van,
■ those who help carry luggage and pack the vehicles, and
■ those who tell good jokes or sing songs while you're on the way.

At the retreat site, give out ribbons to
■ those who are last off the bus or van,
■ those who arrive early for meal times,
■ those who say a blessing over the meal,
■ those who help carry someone's tray or clean up afterward,
■ those who do well in your recreational activities (relays, team sports, or board games),
■ those who arrive early for Bible study sessions, and
■ those who bring their Bibles, take notes, and ask questions during the study.

Start and end your days with prizes for cleanest bunks, brightest smiles, quieting down after lights out, and anything else you can think of! Focus your study sessions on Philippians 3:12-14. Close with a worship service in which

young people lay down their ribbons or prizes before Christ, placing them at the foot of a cross in silent celebration.

# PHILIPPIANS
## 4:1-7

THEME:
Standing firm

SUMMARY:
In this LEARNING GAME, kids will bombard balloon people with "peace thieves."

PREPARATION: Gather paper, pencils, two balloons, a marker, two 3×5 cards, and masking tape. You'll also need Bibles.

Form two teams and give each team several sheets of paper, pencils, and a Bible. Have teams read Philippians 4:1-7. Ask them to look for things in each verse that God says could cause anxiety. For example, verse 2 indicates that disagreement can cause anxiety.

Have teams identify as many "thieves of peace" as they can think of and write them on separate sheets of paper. For example, teams might write, "fighting with friends," "not having enough money," or "flunking a test."

After a few minutes, have teams each read their peace thieves. After each peace thief is read, have team members wad up that sheet of paper and set it aside.

Once all the teams have shared,

have them move the furniture to the edge of the room. While they do this, blow up and tie off two balloons. For each balloon, cut a 2-inch slit in the end of a 3×5 card and slide the tied end of the balloon into the slit. With a marker, draw a face on each balloon. The 3×5 cards will serve as "feet" for the balloons.

Set the prepared balloons in the center of the room. Use masking tape to mark off a 10×10-foot box around the balloons. Have each team bring its pile of peace-thief paper wads and stand on the edge of the box. Say: **God's goal is for us to stand firm in peace, but peace thieves often rob us of God's peace. In this game, your goal is to use your paper peace thieves to keep these balloon "people" from standing firm. The team that moves its balloon farthest away from where it is now wins. You must stand on your line at all times.**

Designate which balloon belongs to which team, then start the game. Afterward, declare the winner. Ask:

■ **How did you feel as you bombarded your balloons?**

■ **How does it feel when you're bombarded by real peace thieves?**

■ **What do you think it means to have real peace?**

Read aloud Philippians 4:6-7. Ask:

■ **What does this Scripture passage say to you?**

■ **What does the passage instruct us to do when we feel anxious?**

■ **How will the message of** Philippians 4:6-7 affect your attitude this week?

# PHILIPPIANS 4:4-9

**THEME:**
Worry

**SUMMARY:**
In this DEVOTION, kids think of things they're anxious about, then learn how useless it is to worry.

PREPARATION: You'll need a roll of masking tape and a Bible.

EXPERIENCE
Ask kids to each find something in your meeting room that represents something they're worried about (for example, a book could represent school). Have kids line up their items in a straight line on the floor from one side of your room to the other (it's OK if there's space between the items). With masking tape, make a #1 on the floor at one end of the line and make a #10 at the other end.

Explain that group members will rate, on a scale of 1 to 10, how worried they are about several issues or problems. One represents little anxiety and 10 represents a great deal of anxiety. Tell kids that after you read an issue, they should each decide how much they worry about that issue and stand somewhere along your "worry-o-meter" line. Sample "worrywarts" include (moving from silly to serious):

■ Will the restaurant serve Pepsi or Coke?

■ Will I have clean socks to wear to school?

■ Will my deodorant give out before I do?

■ Will I find a summer job?

■ Will I get a bad grade in a class at school?

■ Will my family have to move to another city?

■ Will I tell my parents about wrecking the car?

■ Will my boyfriend/girlfriend break up with me?

■ Will my parents get a divorce?

■ Will one of my parents die?

After each question, ask a few young people to tell why they stood where they did along the line. Ask:

■ **Why are some worries more important than others?**

RESPONSE

Ask a volunteer to read aloud Philippians 4:4-9. Ask:

■ **Do you trust Paul's advice about dealing with anxiety? Why or why not?**

■ **How can this Scripture passage help you face problems in your life?**

■ **How should we respond to others who worry about things over which they have no control?**

■ **What should we tell ourselves when we're worried?**

CLOSING

To close, have kids form a circle and join hands. Encourage kids to each ask for God's grace and peace

as they face the worry represented by the object they placed along the line.

# PHILIPPIANS 4:10-13, 19

**THEME:**
Being satisfied

**SUMMARY:**
In this CREATIVE READING, kids perform an updated "reader's theater" version of a Scripture passage on learning to trust God and be satisfied in any situation.

PREPARATION: Make three photocopies of the "Creative Reading for Philippians 4:10-13, 19" handout (p. 278) and put one into each of three different-color folders. Ask three volunteer readers to stand in front of the group with about five feet between them. Give readers each a different-color folder containing their script. The person in the middle is Reader 1—this person should read his or her part slowly and deliberately. The other two are Reader 2 and Reader 3, and they should respond in whatever way their script directs (up, down, happy, or sad).

# CREATIVE READING FOR PHILIPPIANS 4:10-13, 19

**Reader 1:** "I am very happy in the Lord that you have shown your care for me again. You continued to care about me, but there was no way for you to show it. I am not telling you this because I need anything. I have learned to be satisfied with the things I have and with everything that happens."

**Reader 2:** I can face sunshine.

**Reader 3:** Or rain.

**Reader 2:** Ups.

**Reader 3:** Downs.

**Reader 2:** Even life.

**Reader 3:** Or death.

**Reader 1:** "I know how to live when I am poor ... "

**Reader 2:** I'm so hungry. Won't somebody give me something to eat?

**Reader 3:** I'm so cold. Won't somebody give me something to wear?

**Reader 2:** I'm so sick. Won't somebody give me something for the pain?

**Reader 3:** I'm so scared. Won't somebody hold me and tell me it will be all right?

**Reader 1** "and I know how to live when I have plenty."

**Reader 2:** Boy, am I stuffed. I couldn't eat another bite!

**Reader 3:** Look at all my great clothes. I can wear something different every day!

**Reader 2:** Ninety-seven, 98, 99, 100 sit-ups! Am I in great shape or what?

**Reader 3:** Ready to face another day. Ain't gonna let nothing get me down!

**Reader 1:** "I have learned the secret of being happy at any time in everything that happens, when I have enough to eat and when I go hungry, when I have more than I need and when I do not have enough. I can do all things through Christ, because he gives me strength."

**Reader 2:** God, help me to make it through this test. I've studied as much as I could. All I ask is that you help me do my best.

**Reader 3:** One more mile, just one more. Lord, I know I can do it. Carry me if you have to, but let's make this last one the best of all!

**Reader 2:** Jesus, I don't know how much more I can take. My mom and dad seem to be drifting apart, and I'm caught in the middle. Please give me strength to hang in there, to help keep our family together.

**Reader 3:** I keep telling them I don't want to do it, but Lord, it's hard to keep saying no to my friends. I know it's not good for me, and I'll probably wake up in the morning regretting what I did. Please give me the strength to stand up and keep saying no.

**All:** "My God will use his wonderful riches in Christ Jesus to give you everything you need."

# COLOSSIANS

*"Do all these things; but most important, love each other. Love is what holds you all together in perfect unity."*

*Colossians 3:14*

# COLOSSIANS 1:15-20

> ## THEME:
>
> God, the creator
>
> ## SUMMARY:
> In this ADVENTURE, kids participate in a video scavenger hunt that helps them understand God's supremacy.

PREPARATION: Gather four video cameras and four Bibles. You'll also need access to a VCR and a TV. If needed, plan transportation for your group. Bring contemporary Christian music, a cassette or CD player, and popcorn and soft drinks for a snack.

Form four teams (a team can be one person) and give each team a video camera. If you can't locate four cameras, form as many teams as you have cameras.

Give each team a Bible, then have team members read aloud Colossians 1:15-20.

Next, explain that teams will have 45 minutes to complete a video scavenger hunt based on Colossians 1:15-20. Each team should videotape 15 things that reflect their verses (for example, trees, flowers, a courthouse, a police car, a church building, and so on). Teams should be prepared to show their videos to the group and explain why they recorded what they did. Assign an adult volunteer to each team.

After 45 minutes, gather together to view the videos. Ask teams to each explain their shot selections. Ask:

■ **As you brainstormed things to shoot, what thoughts or feelings about God did you have?**

Read aloud Colossians 1:15-20 again. Ask:

■ **Would you say that most people recognize God as creator and master over everything you videotaped? Why or why not?**

■ **What are ways that we can recognize God as creator and master of our world and our lives?**

■ **What's one thing you'll remember about God because of your videotaping experience? Why is that thing important?**

Close in prayer, encouraging kids to thank God for what he's created and to recommit their lives to him. Show the videos again, but this time play Christian music in the background. Serve popcorn and soft drinks to kids.

# COLOSSIANS 2:6-8

> ## THEME:
>
> Staying rooted in Christ
>
> ## SUMMARY:
> In this OBJECT LESSON, kids try to pull an inflatable animal out of a bucket of mud and learn what makes strong roots in their lives.

PREPARATION: You'll need two large buckets, a small inflatable animal (or a small beach ball if you can't find an animal), dry dirt (enough to fill a bucket), and a towel. Inflate the animal or ball prior to the meeting. Fill one bucket with water.

Gather your group members around the buckets. Place the inflated animal inside the empty bucket and pour in the water until the bucket is one-quarter full. The animal should float to the surface. Ask kids to take turns pulling the animal out of the water. (This will be easy.)

Next, pull the animal out of the bucket and pour the water back into the other bucket. Place the animal back inside the empty bucket and surround it with the dirt until the bucket is three-quarters full. Repeat the experiment by asking kids to take turns pulling the animal out of the bucket. It's difficult, but it can be done.

Next, while the animal is still in the dirt-filled bucket, fill the bucket to the top with water. Give it a chance to sink in and form a base of mud at the bottom. Now ask your kids to pull the animal out of the bucket. It's practically impossible! Have a towel handy in case your stronger teenagers pull it out quickly, scattering mud around them. Ask:

■ **Why was it more difficult to pull the animal out of the bucket of mud?**

■ **If you wanted to make sure no one could pull the animal out of the bucket, what would you do?**

Ask a volunteer to read aloud Colossians 2:6-8. Then form pairs and ask partners to discuss these questions:

■ **If you had to choose one of the three things we've used here—water, dirt, or mud—to sink your roots into, which would you say is best?**

■ **How is this like sinking your roots into your relationship with God? Explain.**

■ **What's one thing you can do to make your roots stronger?**

Close by forming a circle around the mud-filled bucket. Ask kids to each come to the bucket, one by one, and dab a little mud onto the back of one hand. As they do, they should silently commit to doing one thing to make their roots in God stronger next week. Ask kids to not wash off their hands until they get home.

# COLOSSIANS
## 2:6-8

THEME:
Faith

SUMMARY:
In this SKIT, one friend leads the other into false teachings.

## BOUND TO KNOW THE TRUTH

SCENE: Two friends run into each other on a Saturday afternoon.

PROPS: You'll need two ropes, a

blindfold, and a Bible for the discussion afterward.

CHARACTERS:
**Kori**
**Chelsea**

SCRIPT
*(Kori and Chelsea walk onstage toward each other.)*
**Kori:** Hey, Chelsea! Good to see you! Haven't seen you at Bible study for a while.
**Chelsea:** Yeah, I know. I've been going somewhere else.
**Kori:** Really? Where?
**Chelsea:** Oh, it's the new Church of American Individualistic Believers.
**Kori:** I've...uh...never heard of that before. Is it a Christian church?
**Chelsea:** Of course. Well, mostly. We accept the teachings of many ancient teachers—not just Jesus.
**Kori:** Really? Like who?
**Chelsea:** *(Taking out a piece of rope while she's talking and beginning to tie Kori's hands behind her back)* Well, like Masamoto Yung, Nampira Abugmbata, and the great guru Vishnishini. We also believe that Shaquille O'Neal is a prophet.
**Kori:** Hmm, that sounds really... uh...interesting.
**Chelsea:** It's wonderful! *(Beginning to tie Kori's feet together)* I mean, I was so sold on that Jesus stuff before, but they really straightened me out.
**Kori:** Sounds like you're really into it.
**Chelsea:** Yeah, everyone there is so accepting of everyone else. We believe that everyone is basically a good person, so there's really no need for Jesus—or even God, for that matter.
**Kori:** *(Pulling a little at the ropes on her hands)* You mean you don't believe in God anymore? Chelsea, I don't know if this is such a great thing.
**Chelsea:** *(Putting a blindfold on Kori)* Oh, come on, Kori. Jesus was just a person like you and me. As long as you're a good person and look out for yourself, who cares what happens when you die?
**Kori:** Hmm. I'm starting to see clearly now. I mean, it all kind of does make sense.
**Chelsea:** It's really great. No rules or restrictions. Just be honest and good and don't worry about tomorrow.
**Kori:** This Church of American Individualistic Believers sounds kind of cool. How'd you get involved?
**Chelsea:** Oh, someone told me. *(Pause.)* Just the way I told you. *(Chelsea leads Kori offstage.)*

If you use this skit as a discussion starter, here are possible questions:
■ **Why are some people swayed by the claims of false religions or false teachings?**
■ **According to Colossians 2:6-8, what are ways we can build our faith strong enough to withstand false teachings?**

# COLOSSIANS
## 3:1-4

### THEME:

Priorities

### SUMMARY:
In this DEVOTION, kids will see how easy it is to place people and things above God.

PREPARATION: Gather newsprint, markers, and masking tape. You'll also need a Bible.

### EXPERIENCE
Form two groups and tell them they each have 20 minutes to create a "human magazine" that specializes in covering things that interest teenagers. Group #1 should think of interests that honor God and are appropriate for all Christians. Group #2 should think of interests that "the world" loves but are inappropriate for Christians. Have groups brainstorm one idea for each person in their group.

Each idea represents an article in the magazine. After groups brainstorm all the ideas they need, have them think of titles for their magazines. Give groups sheets of newsprint, one for each person plus one more, and a marker. On one sheet of newsprint, have them write the magazine's title. Have them write (in smaller printing) their brainstormed ideas on the remaining newsprint sheets, one idea per newsprint sheet.

Then have group #1 line up single file, facing away from the rest of the group. Have an adult volunteer stand in front of the line, facing the rest of the group, and hold the magazine's cover page in front of the line. Have kids hold their newsprint sheets in front of themselves as if they were magazine pages. Then have kids each act out an article as the adult volunteer "turns each page." The leader turns the page by turning kids, one by one, toward the rest of the group. The rest of the kids should try to guess what's being acted out. Repeat this procedure with group #2. Then tape all newsprint articles to a wall.

### RESPONSE
Ask:
■ **What are the differences between things Christians like to do and things non-Christians like to do?**
■ **How do you feel when you see other teenagers doing things you consider wrong?**
■ **How do you think they feel about your favorite interests?**
Read aloud Colossians 3:1-4. Ask:
■ **What does it mean to "think only about the things in heaven"?**
■ **Is it hard or easy for you to focus on the "things above"? Explain.**
■ **What reward will we receive for remaining true to Christ?**

### CLOSING
Seat group members in the shape of a large cross. Ask them to think silently about their favorite interests. Ask them to consider

which interests please God and which may not. After a few minutes, say: **As you sit in silence, ask God what you should do about those interests that aren't pleasing to him.**

Close by singing "Turn Your Eyes Upon Jesus" together.

# COLOSSIANS 3:12-14, 17

## THEME:
Expressing Christ-like qualities

## SUMMARY:
Use this CREATIVE READING to help kids learn how to affirm one another with compassion, kindness, humility, gentleness, patience, and forgiveness.

PREPARATION: Make four photocopies of the "Creative Reading for Colossians 3:12-14, 17" handout (p. 286) for the reading. Ask four volunteer readers to do an echo reading of Colossians 3:12-14, 17. Explain that in an echo reading, readers repeat a word or phrase just after it's been said. Those reading the echoes should use whatever emotion seems appropriate for a particular word or phrase. Readers should be spread out among your group (or the congregation if you do it during your worship service). For a dramatic effect, turn out the lights and have readers use a flashlight to read.

# COLOSSIANS 3:18-21

## THEME:
Family rules of love

## SUMMARY:
In this PROJECT, kids will make "handy cans" to take home that remind family members to love and honor one another.

PREPARATION: Ask kids to each bring one empty soft drink can to your meeting (gather extra cans for those who forget to bring one). You'll need Bibles, paper, pencils, markers, scissors, newsprint, and glue.

At the meeting, have a volunteer read aloud Colossians 3:18-21. Then form discussion groups of three. Ask groups to read Colossians 3:18-21 again, then brainstorm ways these "rules for Christian homes" could apply to their own households. Have groups each appoint a recorder to write each idea on paper. Ideas should start out with "Parents can show love and respect by..." and "Kids can show love and respect by..."

Give groups 10 minutes to brainstorm ideas, then ask them to each appoint a reporter to tell their ideas to the large group. Write a running list of ideas on a sheet of newsprint or a chalkboard.

Then give kids each a sheet of paper, a marker, scissors, and glue. Have kids cut the paper to make labels for their soda cans. Then

# CREATIVE READING FOR COLOSSIANS 3:12-14, 17

**Reader 1:** "God has chosen you and made you his holy people. He loves you. So always do these things: Show mercy to others..."
**Reader 2:** Mercy, mercy, mercy.
**Reader 3:** "be kind..."
**Reader 4:** Kind, kind, kind.
**Reader 2:** "humble..."
**Reader 1:** Humble, humble, humble.
**Reader 3:** "gentle..."
**Reader 4:** Gentle, gentle, gentle.
**Reader 1:** "and patient."
**Reader 3:** Patient, patient, patient.
**Reader 2:** "Get along with each other, and forgive each other."
**Reader 4:** Forgive, forgive, forgive.
**Reader 3:** "If someone does wrong to you..."
**Reader 1:** Lies.
**Reader 2:** Spiteful words.
**Reader 3:** Rejection.
**Reader 4:** "forgive that person..."
**Reader 2:** Forgive, forgive, forgive.
**Reader 3:** "because the Lord forgave you. Do all these things..."
**Reader 1:** Mercy.
**Reader 2:** Kindness.
**Reader 4:** Humility.
**Reader 1:** Gentleness.
**Reader 2:** And patience.
**Reader 3:** "but most important, love each other."
**Reader 4:** Love, love, love.
**All:** "Love is what holds you all together in perfect unity."
**Reader 1:** "Everything you do or say..."
**Reader 2:** At work.
**Reader 3:** At school.
**Reader 4:** At play.
**Reader 1:** "should be done to obey Jesus your Lord."
**Reader 2:** Jesus your Lord.
**Reader 3:** Jesus your Lord.
**Reader 4:** Jesus your Lord.
**All:** "And in all you do, give thanks to God the Father through Jesus."

have them scan your master list of ideas and pick out the 10 best ones—five from each category ("parents" and "kids") to write on their labels. When kids have written their ideas, have them glue their labels to their cans.

Say: **You've just made a "handy can" for your family that you can place on your kitchen table or eating area. Every time someone loves or honors someone in your family by doing something listed on the can (or any other loving act), put a penny in the can. When the can is full, pour out the pennies and use them to buy a treat for the whole family.**

# 1 THESSALONIANS

*"Also, we always thank God because when you heard his message from us, you accepted it as the word of God, not the words of humans. And it really is God's message which works in you who believe."*

*1 Thessalonians 2:13*

# 1 THESSALONIANS 1:2-10

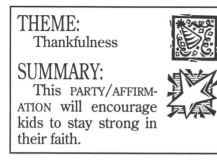

**THEME:**
Thankfulness

**SUMMARY:**
This PARTY/AFFIRM-ATION will encourage kids to stay strong in their faith.

PREPARATION: Prepare a celebration to encourage teenagers and to thank them for all they've done to grow in faith. Gather supplies as needed for the activities you choose. You'll also need a Bible.

Use the following ideas to get your party planning going:

■ **Invitations**—Invite kids to attend this meeting without telling them much about it. Send a simple invitation that reads somewhat like the passage in 1 Thessalonians 1:2-3 and asks kids to attend a meeting to focus on the faith of the youth group.

■ **Decorations**—Decorate the meeting room with lots of memorabilia from previous youth group events. Include pictures of youth group members as well as items representing events and service projects they've done. For example, if kids went on a service project to rebuild homes, include a display of hammers, nails, and paintbrushes near photos of the kids. Also, include lots of colorful streamers.

■ **Fanfare for the faithful Christian**—Keep the youth group room closed until kids arrive. Then, while playing fanfare music (such as the theme from the movie *Rocky* or "Fanfare for the Common Man," by Aaron Copeland), open the doors and announce that the commendation celebration will begin.

■ **Food and entertainment**—Serve your kids' favorite foods, play their favorite music, and lead them in their favorite games. At some point during the party, have kids pause to read 1 Thessalonians 1:2-10.

Say: **The church at Thessalonica was a young church, just as each of you is young. And people were struggling with all kinds of issues that challenged their faith, just as you struggle with issues each day that challenge your faith. This passage is Paul's thanks and encouragement to the church at Thessalonica. And this party is my way of thanking you and encouraging you to continue to be strong and grow in faith.**

Have kids each take a turn standing in the center of the group while others thank that person for specific ways he or she has acted in Christian faith. For example, someone might thank a person for serving at a soup kitchen.

■ **Commendation ceremony**—For each person, prepare badges that have an affirming message on them such as "Up to the Challenge" or "Faithful Follower." Before ending the party, award a badge to each person and say: **We thank God that you continue to hope in our Lord.** Or paraphrase something else from Paul's encouragement in 1 Thessalonians 1:2-10.

# 1 THESSALONIANS 2:13–3:8

> ## THEME:
> Persecution
>
>
>
> ## SUMMARY:
> In this OBJECT LESSON, kids will be "persecuted" for their faith.

PREPARATION: Arrange to have a meeting outside on a nice day. Get the help of three or four sharp-shooting volunteers to position themselves around your meeting area with loaded squirt guns. Tell the volunteers to squirt people whenever they hear them mention faith in Jesus. You'll also need Bibles.

When kids arrive, have them sit in groups of no more than four. Say: **In your groups, tell each other what your faith really means to you. Then tell each other stories about when you shared your faith with someone else. No matter what happens, keep talking about your faith until time is up.**

Encourage kids to keep on talking even though they'll be squirted often by the volunteers. If they complain, encourage groups to keep on talking about their faith and ignore the squirt guns.

After five minutes or so, call the squirters off and ask them to join the groups. Have groups each read 1 Thessalonians 2:13–3:8, then discuss the following questions. Pause after asking each question to allow time for the groups to discuss it. Ask:

■ **How did you feel when you were soaked with water?**

■ **How soon did you realize when you were going to be squirted with the water? Did that change your discussion? Why or why not?**

■ **How is getting soaked by a squirt gun while minding your own business like the persecution the Thessalonian Christians endured?**

■ **How are Christians persecuted today?**

Have groups each come up with one thing they can do to deal with today's persecutions. Have volunteers from each group share their ideas.

Encourage kids not to retaliate against the squirters. Rather, have them pray for the squirters to symbolize the importance of praying for those who persecute us.

# 1 THESSALONIANS 3:12-13

> ## THEME:
> Encouraging bene- dictions
>
>
>
> ## SUMMARY:
> In this AFFIRMATION, kids will encourage each other to keep their faith strong.

PREPARATION: You'll need Bibles.

Form groups of no more than four. Have kids read 1 Thessalonians 3:12-13 in their groups and paraphrase the passage in their own words. Have one person in each group write down the group's paraphrase. When kids are finished, collect each group's paraphrase.

Next, have groups each come up with one way to encourage the members of another group to stay strong in their faith. For example, a group might simply go over and hug another group's members and share encouraging words. Or a group might prepare a song to sing to another group.

While teenagers are preparing their encouragements, send an adult volunteer to photocopy kids' paraphrases. Have the volunteer make enough photocopies for each person to have at least one paraphrased passage. (It's OK if kids have different paraphrases.)

When everyone is ready, have groups take turns acting out their encouragement ideas for each other. Afterward, remind teenagers to continue this kind of encouragement outside of the youth group environment, too.

Give everyone a photocopy of one paraphrase of 1 Thessalonians 3:12-13, then close by having several people read their paraphrases as your benediction.

# 1 THESSALONIANS 4:3-8

**THEME:**
Sexual purity

**SUMMARY:**
In this SKIT, a girl's clean, new T-shirt is ruined by people who smear paint on it as they talk to her about sex.

## KRISTEN'S GIFT

SCENE: Any time, any place.

PROPS: You'll need a beautifully wrapped box containing a plain, white T-shirt; a chair; tempera paint; and a Bible for the discussion afterward.

CHARACTERS:
**Kristen**
**Guys 1, 2, and 3** (all have wet tempera paint on their hands)
**Girls 1, 2, and 3** (all have wet tempera paint on their hands)

### SCRIPT
*(Kristen walks onstage. She sees a present sitting on a chair, then excitedly opens it to find a white T-shirt inside. It's evident that she loves it, and she puts it on immediately.)*

**Guy 1:** *(Walks up, puts arm around Kristen, and smears paint on her shoulder.)* Hey, Kristen, lookin' good, babe! Let's go out again sometime. *(Leering)* I had a great time last night. *(Exits.)*

**Girl 1:** *(Runs on stage, followed by Guy 2.)* Oh my gosh, you've got to hear the joke that Tom just told me... *(She pulls Kristen to her by the front of her shirt, getting paint on it.)*

**Guy 2:** I don't know if Kristen would get it. I mean, it's kind of... *(Kristen acts interested and pulls them to her to hear the joke.) (Guy 2 and Girl 1 whisper the joke to Kristen, putting their hands on the back of her shirt and smearing paint on it. Kristen responds with wide eyes and a disgusted expression. Guy 2 and Girl 1 laugh, then leave.)*

**Girl 2:** *(Walking onstage with Girl 3)* Kristen, I heard that you're going out with Jack. Better be prepared, if you know what I mean. He's got a reputation.

**Girl 3:** But it's OK—as long as you use protection. *(Teasing, she pokes Kristen in the stomach, smearing paint on her. Girls 2 and 3 exit.)*

**Guy 3:** *(Enters and puts arms around Kristen's waist, trying to pull her closer and smearing paint on her.)* Come on, Kristen. You can't make me stop now! *(Kristen pushes him away, and he leaves.)*

*(Kristen looks down at her shirt, now covered with paint. She tries to take it off, but can't. She puts her face in her hands, as if crying, and exits.)*

If you use this skit as a discussion starter, here are possible questions:

■ What did Kristen's T-shirt symbolize?

■ How is this skit like what happens to people's sexual purity in real life?

■ According to 1 Thessalonians 4:3-8, what is God's hope for us?

# 1 THESSALONIANS 4:3-8

**THEME:**
Sexual temptation

**SUMMARY:**
In this LEARNING GAME, kids will examine the temptation of sexual immorality.

PREPARATION: You'll need paper, pencils, and Bibles.

Choose one guy and one girl. Have kids form a tight circle around the girl. If your group is large, form smaller circles of eight to 10 people, each surrounding a female volunteer. Have the male volunteer stand outside the circle and try to break through to tag the female. Allow the male volunteer several tries before having him switch positions with the girl. Once they've switched, have the girl try to tag the guy. Ask:

■ How did it feel to try to tag the volunteers?

■ How did it feel to be in the center of the circle?

■ How might this game illustrate staying free of sexual immorality?

■ **What does the wall of people represent?**

Say: **The wall could represent your strength of will or your decisions to avoid compromising situations. It could represent your friends' help in avoiding temptation.**

Form groups of three. Give each group a Bible, a sheet of paper, and a pencil. Ask groups to read 1 Thessalonians 4:3-8, then rewrite the passage as though they were writing a letter to their school friends.

When groups are finished, have them read their paraphrases aloud. Then ask:

■ **Why should people avoid sexual immorality?**

■ **Why does it matter so much to God?**

■ **If a person has already had sex, what does this passage say to him or her?**

■ **How can we help each other stay sexually pure?**

# 1 THESSALONIANS 4:11-12

THEME:
Peace

SUMMARY:
On this OVERNIGHTER, kids will experience peacefulness.

PREPARATION: Plan an overnight getaway where kids can experience the peacefulness and quiet reflected in this passage. Set up clear expectations before the retreat to help kids know how to get the most from this experience. The object of this retreat is to enjoy a peaceful time, so no radios should be allowed.

Plan ahead so all meals are assigned and ingredients are easy to find. Write instructions for reflection times, silent games, and other activities before you go so you won't have to read them aloud. Gather supplies as needed for the activities you choose. You'll need Bibles.

Encourage kids to start the retreat by silently reading 1 Thessalonians 4:11-12. Then have them go about their responsibilities during the retreat with as little talking as possible. While talking should be kept at a minimum, it's not completely out of the question. But encourage kids to always be respectful of those around them when it is time to be quiet.

Include activities such as the following:

■ prayer times (kids form small groups and share requests for prayer, then pray for an extended time in silent prayer),

■ Scripture-reading times (kids go off on their own to study quietly),

■ discussions on paper (kids communicate solely by writing their dialogue on paper), and

■ worship times (kids quietly hum the tunes to their favorite worship songs).

At the end of the retreat, ask kids questions such as the following:

■ **How did you feel in an environment of peace and quiet?**

■ **How can you live out the message of 1 Thessalonians 4:11-12 at school, home, and church?**

■ **What does the way we live our lives tell non-Christians about us?**

■ **What is the key to living a peaceful life?**

Close the retreat by having kids form a human sculpture representing what it means to live a peaceful life. Let this be their prayer of thanks to God for giving us his peace.

# 1 THESSALONIANS 5:16-18

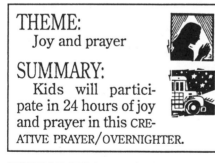

THEME:
Joy and prayer

SUMMARY:
Kids will participate in 24 hours of joy and prayer in this CREATIVE PRAYER/OVERNIGHTER.

PREPARATION: Arrange with your group to have a 24-hour event of continuous joy and prayer at your church. Invite congregation members to participate in this activity. You'll need a Bible.

Set up a location for the prayer to take place. Have kids prepare a banner with the message from 1 Thessalonians 5:16-18 written on it to place at the prayer place. Have adults and teenagers sign up for prayer times in blocks of 15 minutes to cover the entire 24 hours (or a shorter time if necessary). Also, have congregation members submit their prayer requests before the event. Have these available in the prayer room for prayer participants to read and pray about.

Arrange a location in which the joy part of the weekend can take place. Have another 1 Thessalonians 5:16-18 banner placed in this area. Here adults and teenagers can enjoy lots of snacks, fun games, and uplifting activities together. Remind participants that games are to be positive and fun—not competitive or task-oriented.

For example, you might play "no-score" volleyball or softball, low-pressure board games, or community-building games such as the ones found in Denny Rydberg's *Youth Group Trust Builders* (available from Group Publishing). You might want to schedule rowdier games and activities during the daytime and quieter games during the night hours. Again, have people sign up to enjoy the joy activities throughout the entire weekend.

Keep both the prayer room and the joy room open at all times and encourage people to go back and forth between the two rooms during the weekend. In the joy room, begin every hour with one minute of silent prayer. Then continue the activities.

At the end of the 24 hours of continuous joy and prayer, have everyone meet together to give thanks to God for all that happened during the weekend and all that is yet to come.

# 2 THESSALONIANS

*"So, brothers and sisters, stand strong and continue to believe the teachings we gave you in our speaking and in our letter."*

*2 Thessalonians 2:15*

# 2 THESSALONIANS 1:3-4

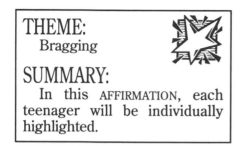

**THEME:**
Bragging

**SUMMARY:**
In this AFFIRMATION, each teenager will be individually highlighted.

PREPARATION: To help kids experience the feelings Paul gave the young Christians at Thessalonica in 2 Thessalonians 1:3-4, secretly arrange to highlight one or more teenagers in your church services until all kids in your group have been highlighted.

Have kids and parents help you collect positive stories and information for each person being highlighted.

During the church service, introduce the bragging time by saying: **Paul modeled encouragement in his introduction to 2 Thessalonians when he wrote, "We must always thank God for you, brothers and sisters... So we brag about you to the other churches of God." In this spirit, we would like to brag about some of the wonderful people in our youth group here at** (name of church).

Tell the congregation about each person being highlighted or have another group member share the bragging rights about members of the group. For added fun, have fanfare music precede the name of the person or people being highlighted at that service.

As a variation on this theme, have teenagers choose people in the congregation to highlight and brag about to the rest of the church. Have kids prepare their speeches and present each person with a memento of the youth group's appreciation for that person (such as a banner or a "key" to the youth room).

# 2 THESSALONIANS 2:1-4

**THEME:**
Jesus' return

**SUMMARY:**
In this SKIT, two friends react to an "expert's" claims that the Second Coming is just days away.

## SIGN OF THE TIMES

SCENE: Outside.

PROPS: You'll need books, newspaper, a grocery bag, chocolate ice cream, chocolate syrup, Twinkies, two chairs (or a bench), and a Bible for the discussion afterward.

CHARACTERS:
**Steve**
**Allison**

### SCRIPT
*(Steve is carrying a stack of books home from the library when Allison runs up to him, screaming frantically. She's holding a folded newspaper and a grocery bag.)*

**Allison:** Steve! Steve! Two more days! We're all going to die! *(The two crash into each other, dropping everything. But Allison continues her frantic raving.)*

**Steve:** What? Allison. Allison! ALLISON! *(Grabbing her)* What are you talking about? Two days 'til what?

**Allison:** 'Til the end! The Second Coming! Armageddon! Whatever you call it, it's all right here in The Daily Dirt *(She points to a newspaper article.)*

**Steve:** *(Reading)* "Today Dr. D. Seever announced that, through careful calculations, he's arrived at a date that he's certain is the prophetic Second Coming of Christ." Allison, you don't honestly believe this guy, do you?

**Allison:** Steve, he's spent his whole life figuring this thing out! How could he be wrong? It totally makes sense! *(While talking, she pulls a container of chocolate ice cream out of the bag and begins to wolf it down.)*

**Steve:** What do you mean it "totally makes sense"? The guy's obviously a few bricks short of a load. *(Short pause.)* What are you doing?

**Allison:** I'm spending my last days eating all the chocolate I want, without worrying about my health, weight, zits... or anything. *(She adds chocolate syrup to the ice cream.)* Anyway, look at the world around us and tell me it doesn't make sense. Wars, famine, gangs, violence, hate—signs of the end times if I've ever seen 'em!

**Steve:** So, you think... uh... Dr. Seever is right about the world ending in two days?

**Allison:** Absolutely.

**Steve:** So you're pigging out on ice cream and chocolate syrup...

**Allison:** And Twinkies *(She pulls out a box, opens them, and eats a Twinkie.)*

**Steve:** And Twinkies. Just because you read about some wacko doctor in the paper who says that Jesus is coming back in two days? Isn't this the same paper that did that story on a wombat born with Elvis' head?

**Allison:** No, don't be stupid. It was a llama! Look, Steve, I've warned you, and if you don't believe me—well, that's your problem. I believe in Dr. Seever. Now, if you don't mind, I'm going to rent all the videos I can carry and spend my last days with my VCR. *(She walks away with grocery bag and leaves newspaper.)*

**Steve:** *(Pauses, then looks at newspaper. Reads, while walking away.)* "Aliens from planet Zortak invade Hollywood and start their own movie studio." Hmm.

If you use this skit as a discussion starter, here are possible questions:

■ **Do you think God wants us to know when the Second Coming will be? Why or why not?**

■ **How can the message of 2 Thessalonians 2:1-4 affect your daily life?**

# 2 THESSALONIANS 2:1-17

THEME:
End-times predictions

SUMMARY:
In this PROJECT, kids will research predictions of the end of the world.

PREPARATION: You'll need Bibles and concordances.

Have kids form research groups of no more than four. Then send groups out to a local library to search out predictions of the end of the world. Small religious groups and cults have for many years predicted that the end was near, so it shouldn't be difficult to find more than a few stories.

After groups have researched the stories, have them compare what they learn to 2 Thessalonians 2:1-17, and to at least four other passages about Christ's return (have groups discover these on their own using concordances).

Encourage kids to do extensive research on this topic. Part of this experience depends on the investment kids make into the research activity.

After groups have completed their research (give them a couple weeks), have them present what they discovered.

Then form small groups and discuss the following questions:

■ **How did you feel as you worked on this project?**

■ **How was your level of dedication to the project like or unlike the dedication of people who believe in the end of the world?**

■ **What surprised you most about this activity?**

■ **How are the surprises you had like or unlike the surprises people have when they think they've discovered when Christ will return?**

Say: **People who predict a specific date for Christ's return put a great deal of devotion into their beliefs. And much of what they believe is based on Scriptures that warn of signs and wonders in the last days. But as the Bible clearly says, we will not know the day and time.**

Close in prayer, asking God to help each person grow in faith and share God's love with others until Christ returns.

# 2 THESSALONIANS 2:15-3:5

THEME:
Peer pressure

SUMMARY:
In this LEARNING GAME, kids will try to influence other kids.

PREPARATION: You'll need a Bible.

Form two teams. Designate one team the "expressions" and the other team the "opposites." Have teams line up facing each other. Tell the expressions to respond to the questions you read with either a goofy grin or a serious frown. Tell the opposites to show the opposite expression of the expressions team. Encourage each team to try to influence the other team's members to change their expressions. Tell team members they must look directly at the team members across from them—they can't look away!

After reading each of the following questions, allow 30 seconds for teams to make their expressions and try to hold them while watching their counterparts. Ask:

■ How do you feel about ice cream on a hot summer day?

■ How do you feel about getting an A on your report card?

■ How would you feel if your best friend moved away?

■ How would you feel if you got terribly sick while on vacation?

■ How would you feel if you won a new CD player?

After all the questions have been read, ask:

■ For those of you on the expressions team, was it hard to decide which expression to make? Why or why not?

■ Was it harder to hold a frown or a smile for 30 seconds?

■ What difference did the expression of the other team make?

■ How did you resist giving in to the pressure to change your expression?

Read aloud 2 Thessalonians 2:15–3:5. Then ask:

■ How is this activity like the message of the Scripture passage?

■ How can we resist negative pressure to change?

■ What help can God give us this week?

# 1 TIMOTHY

*"Do not let anyone treat you as if you are
unimportant because you are young.
Instead, be an example to the believers with
your words, your actions, your love, your
faith, and your pure life."*

*1 Timothy 4:12*

# 1 TIMOTHY
## 1:3-11

> **THEME:**
> False doctrines
>
> **SUMMARY:**
> In this PROJECT, kids will try to "sell" false teachings.

PREPARATION: You'll need art supplies and miscellaneous props. You'll also need a Bible.

Read 1 Timothy 1:3-11 aloud to your teenagers. Then have kids brainstorm a list of today's false teachings (philosophies that go against Christianity). Kids might include things such as "Sex before marriage is OK"; "The more money you have, the more successful you are"; or "You are your own god."

Next, form groups of no more than five and assign each group one of the false teachings. Have each group think of a way to "sell" its false teaching to the rest of the group. Allow 10 minutes for groups to gather props, draw posters, write slogans, and otherwise plan how they'll present their false teachings. Remind kids, if necessary, not to be crude or vulgar in their presentations.

One at a time, have groups attempt to sell their false teachings to the rest of the group. When all groups have completed their sales pitches, have groups discuss the following questions:

■ **How did you feel as you prepared your sales pitch? Explain.**

■ **How easy is it to sell false teachings?**

■ **How is Christian faith watered down by today's false teachings?**

■ **Why do you think Paul started off this letter to Timothy with a warning against false teachings?**

■ **What do you think Paul would say about false teachings if he were to write a letter to our youth group?**

Have kids form a circle and repeat after you as you pray a prayer like this one: **Dear God, help me to know what is true and to avoid the false teachings in our world. In Jesus' name, amen.**

# 1 TIMOTHY
## 1:12-17

> **THEME:**
> Grace
>
> **SUMMARY:**
> Kids will attempt difficult tasks in this LEARNING GAME.

PREPARATION: Gather books, balls, and other props you need for tasks you create. You'll also need a Bible. Before you begin this activity, arrange with volunteers to have a pizza party ready to bring to the meeting on your signal.

When kids arrive, tell them that if they win a game that you teach them, they'll win a prize of a pizza dinner. Explain that the way to win is simply to finish the tasks you give them, but they must be done perfectly and within 10 minutes.

Then begin listing the following tasks (and add your own for fun):

■ Everyone must do 10 jumping jacks while saying the alphabet backward.

■ Kids must form pairs and toss a ball back and forth 10 times in a row without dropping it at a distance of no less than 10 feet.

■ Each person must balance three books on his or her head and walk around the room without dropping the books.

■ Kids must stand on one leg for two minutes without supporting themselves.

■ Kids must form a circle and use their feet to pass around a ball without dropping it once.

Add other nearly impossible tasks to be sure kids can't finish them all within the allotted time.

When kids realize they didn't measure up to your challenge, form a circle and read aloud 1 Timothy 1:12-17. Cue the pizza volunteers to bring on the party. Allow group members to enjoy the food while they discuss how this experience is like the mercy God showed Paul and that God shows us each day.

# 1 TIMOTHY 2:1-8

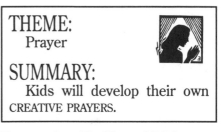

**THEME:**
Prayer

**SUMMARY:**
Kids will develop their own CREATIVE PRAYERS.

Preparation: You'll need Bibles.

Have kids read 1 Timothy 2:1-8. Then form groups of no more than five and have groups each develop a creative way to pray—to express love, praise, thankfulness, and respect to God.

Give kids the freedom to choose any activity they want for their prayers. Remind kids that prayer doesn't have to be expressed in words alone but may be expressed through art, music, motion, actions, and sights—perhaps even smells!

When groups have prepared their prayers, have them follow the advice of 1 Timothy 2:1-8 and offer their prayers to God (without explanation to the other groups). Encourage kids to respect other groups' expressions of prayer and to join with them in a prayerful attitude that fits the style of the prayer being expressed.

This might be a good activity to get kids thinking about how different people pray and the importance of accepting others even though they may express their love for God in different ways.

# 1 TIMOTHY
## 3:1-13

THEME:
Leadership

SUMMARY:
In this PROJECT, kids will interview church leaders.

PREPARATION: You'll need one video camera for every five kids. You'll also need a Bible and a list of past and present church leaders.

Have a volunteer read aloud 1 Timothy 3:1-13 to the whole group. Discuss the qualities in the passage that make a great church leader. Then form groups of no more than five and give each one a video camera. Assign groups the names of people in your congregation who were church leaders in the past or who lead the church today. This could be anyone from a retired pastor to a youth group president.

Send groups out to interview the past and present church leaders. Have kids ask questions such as these:

■ **What role did you play in leading our church?**

■ **How did you get that role?**

■ **What did you do in that role?**

■ **What did you like most about being a leader? least?**

■ **What advice about leadership would you give to new or future leaders in our church?**

■ **Describe why it's important for a leader to fit the qualifications in 1 Timothy 3:1-13**.

Collect the videotapes and, with the help of technically adept members of your youth group or congregation, edit them into one tape chronicling the history of leadership in your church.

Have kids lead an evening service in which they show the videotape to the whole congregation. Enjoy the peek at your church's history while the teenagers practice the leadership qualities they discovered during the videotaping!

# 1 TIMOTHY
## 4:12

THEME:
Being a young
Christian

SUMMARY:
In this CREATIVE READING, teenagers will tell of the importance of youth.

PREPARATION: For each person in your group, make a photocopy of the "Creative Reading for 1 Timothy 4:12" handout (p. 308). Plan a time to present this reading to your church.

At the beginning of the reading, have some teenagers crawl to the front of the church as if they were toddlers while others read the first line for "Teenagers." Have kids follow the rest of the instructions in the reading to help dramatize the value of youth.

# CREATIVE READING FOR 1 TIMOTHY 4:12

**Leader:** "Do not let anyone treat you as if you are unimportant because you are young."

**Teenagers:** *(Crawling up to the front of the church)* When we were toddlers, our parents told us about God. Our Sunday school teachers told us about God. We listened to prayers every night and at every meal. But we were young and didn't know much about God's big world.

**Leader:** "Do not let anyone treat you as if you are unimportant because you are young."

**Teenagers:** *(Standing and pretending to play catch with a playground ball)* As young children, we discovered the great world God created. We marveled at stories of a wall-tumbling trumpet, a sea that opened up, and a flood that covered the whole land. We were fascinated by the stories from the Bible, but we still didn't understand what it meant to be a Christian.

**Leader:** "Do not let anyone treat you as if you are unimportant because you are young."

**Teenagers:** *(Sitting as if in school)* As we grew older, we learned about the world around us. We learned that not everyone is a Christian—not everyone loves God the way we do.

We learned that sometimes bad things happen to good people. And we learned that faith isn't easy, but we still didn't understand God's forgiveness.

**Leader:** "Do not let anyone treat you as if you are unimportant because you are young."

**Teenagers:** *(Standing and speaking to the congregation directly)* Now we are teenagers—young adults, really. We've seen what the world has to offer, and we know that Jesus is the only way. We've experienced the pain of broken relationships and the cleansing of forgiveness. We've seen faith and faithlessness. We've collected years of knowledge about what it means to be a Christian. But we're still learning what it means to grow and mature in faith. We've got a lifetime to learn that and a wealth of resources to learn from.

*(Teenagers go out into the congregation and give hugs and handshakes to congregation members.)*

**Leader:** "Do not let anyone treat you as if you are unimportant because you are young. Instead, be an example to the believers with your words, your actions, your love, your faith, and your pure life."

# 1 TIMOTHY
## 4:12

---

**THEME:**
Mentors

**SUMMARY:**
In this PROJECT, kids will have mentors and be mentors.

---

PREPARATION: Find adults in your church who are willing to mentor teenagers. Secure permission from parents for teenagers to mentor younger children. Develop a list of guidelines for mentors and plan plenty of group activities for the adults, teenagers, and younger children.

Help kids live out the message of 1 Timothy 4:12 by matching up each person in the youth group with an older member of the congregation (to be his or her mentor) and a younger person (to mentor). For safety reasons, be sure to conduct screening interviews of all mentors and ask for references of people you don't know personally.

Plan activities for all three partners to do together to develop strong friendships. Choose mentors carefully to avoid incompatible pairings and meet often with the adults and the teenagers to teach them how to mentor others.

As a model for mentoring, refer to the relationship Paul had with Timothy as outlined in Paul's letters. Teach the adult and teenage mentors how to be active listeners and how to help others discover ways to grow in faith.

As teenagers learn from the more mature adult Christians how to grow, they'll be able to set a good example for the children they mentor—and for their own peers, too.

# 1 TIMOTHY
## 6:6-12

---

**THEME:**
Materialism

**SUMMARY:**
In this ADVENTURE, kids will imagine being wealthy.

---

PREPARATION: Plan transportation to one or more of the following sites: a shopping center, a car dealership, a local bank, a fancy section of town, or a hill or ledge. You'll also need a Bible.

Take kids to one or more of the places in the list above. Point out specific items at each site.

■ At the shopping center, point out an expensive piece of jewelry or a display case filled with jewelry.

■ At the car dealership, point out a fancy car.

■ At the local bank, arrange a tour of the vault. Point out how the vault is structured to protect its contents.

■ In the fancy section of town, point out the biggest house you can find.

■ On the hill or ledge, point out a large section of beautiful land.

At each new place, have kids

form pairs and discuss the following questions for each item:

■ **How valuable do you think this item is?**

■ **What would it be like to own this item?**

■ **How might your life change if you owned this?**

Then return to your youth room and have a volunteer read aloud 1 Timothy 6:6-12. Ask:

■ **How did you feel as you imagined you were wealthy?**

■ **How can we have the same kind of longing for serving God that we have for the things we saw on our field trip?**

■ **What does it mean that "serving God makes us very rich"?**

■ **Why is the love of money dangerous?**

Take kids to a cross in your church and point it out. Ask pairs to discuss the same questions as before, then pray for each other to seek God's riches through serving others.

# 1 TIMOTHY
## 6:7-10

**THEME:**
Materialism

**SUMMARY:**

In this SKIT, two guys toss a football to each other and talk about the money a drug-dealing friend is making.

# FREE AGENT

SCENE: Two friends are tossing a football around in the park.

PROPS: You'll need a football and a Bible for the discussion afterward.

CHARACTERS:
**Mike**
**Rex**

### SCRIPT
*(Two guys continue to toss the football back and forth throughout the dialogue.)*

**Rex:** *(Throwing football to Mike)* He fakes, dodges the outside linebacker, then throws! It's a long bomb to Henderson... *(Mike catches football.)* TOUCHDOWN!! The Oilers win the Super Bowl!

**Mike:** Thanks to Mike "Magic Hands" Henderson, MVP! *(Tosses ball back to Rex.)*

**Rex:** Hey, *(nodding offstage)* isn't that Frank Macelli over there?

**Mike:** Yeah, nice car, huh? You should see the CD player inside!

**Rex:** How do his parents afford that kind of stuff? His dad works with my dad, so I know they don't make that much.

**Mike:** They don't. That's why *he* bought the car.

**Rex:** He bought it! Yeah, right, with all that money he makes bagging groceries!

**Mike:** Catch up, man. He doesn't work at the grocery store anymore! He's self-employed... if you, uh, know what I mean.

**Rex:** Self-employed?

**Mike:** Yeah. He's in sales now.

**Rex:** Sales? Where? What are you *talking* about, Mike?

**Mike:** You really don't know?

**Rex:** Huh-uh.

**Mike:** *(Walking closer to Rex)* Drugs, man. The guy makes big bucks selling.

**Rex:** Get outta here! I grew up with Frank Macelli. He's not like that!

**Mike:** Well, he is now. Told me so himself. He even said he could cut me in on a deal or two to make enough for some new Nikes.

**Rex:** You're not gonna do it, are you?

**Mike:** I dunno. I might. Macelli's doing OK, you know—new clothes, new car, stereos, cash. I could definitely use that kind of stuff.

**Rex:** But it's illegal...and stupid! Cash or not!

**Mike:** It's just a couple of deals, Rex. Nothing serious. *(Tosses football to Rex.)* I gotta go talk to him about it. *(Walks away.)*

**Rex:** Mike! *(Looks at the football, shakes head, and walks the other way.)*

If you use this skit as a discussion starter, here are possible questions:

■ **What evidence of materialism do you see around you?**

■ **How are you tempted by materialism in your daily life?**

■ **According to 1 Timothy 6:7-10, how can materialism lead to destruction?**

# 2 TIMOTHY

*"All Scripture is given by God and is useful
for teaching, for showing people what is
wrong in their lives, for correcting faults,
and for teaching how to live right."*

*2 Timothy 3:16*

# 2 TIMOTHY
## 1:7-14

**THEME:**
Being bold

**SUMMARY:**
In this PROJECT, kids will wear "witnessing" T-shirts.

PREPARATION: Plan to do this project in two sessions. First have kids design the shirts. After the shirts are made, send kids out wearing them. You'll need Bibles.

Have kids read 2 Timothy 1:7-14 and discuss what it means to not be ashamed to tell people about Jesus. Then form three groups. Have the first group develop a slogan that expresses love for Christ in a straightforward way. Have that group also develop a T-shirt design using the slogan and make plans to have the T-shirts made. Have the second group develop a simple and practical way to state what it means to be a Christian. Have the third group prepare a one-page flier inviting others to visit your church and youth group.

Have kids wear the T-shirts to a nearby amusement park or mall—someplace where you'll find lots of teenagers. Then send out groups of two or three to enjoy the day, to seek opportunities to tell others about your church, to give out fliers (if allowed by the location), and to share what it means to be a Christian. Encourage teenagers to be bold about their faith but not obnoxious about forcing it upon others.

Meet at the end of the day to debrief the activities. Read 2 Timothy 1:7 as a closing affirmation that God is always with us when we speak up for what we believe.

# 2 TIMOTHY
## 2:1-7

**THEME:**
Perseverance

**SUMMARY:**
In this SKIT, two girls take a break from running, and one tries to convince the other to keep going.

## SECOND WIND

SCENE: A park or roadside.

PROPS: You could use hand weights, water bottles, sweatbands, and a bottle of Gatorade. You'll need a Bible for the discussion afterward.

CHARACTERS:
**Suzanne**
**Shawna**

### SCRIPT
*(Suzanne and Shawna run into the room, wearing jogging suits and carrying hand weights. Both are out of breath.)*

**Suzanne:** *(Panting)* Five miles! I...give...up! *(Lies down on floor.)* This is impossible!

**Shawna:** *(Pulling Suzanne up)* Sorry, Suzanne. No break yet. First we have to do 50 jumping jacks. Ready—one, two, three ...

*(Suzanne does one halfheartedly, then lies back down. Shawna does a few more before noticing.)* OK, we'll take a short break. Then we'll do the last three miles, 50 push-ups, 100 sit-ups, some wind sprints...

**Suzanne:** Stop! Enough! I give up!

**Shawna:** Then we'll hit the weights.

**Suzanne:** No, Shawna. *You'll* hit the weights. I'm going home. This training thing is too hard. I'm sore, tired, hungry, and missing my MTV.

**Shawna:** *(Pulling Suzanne up)* Come on, Suzanne. We've got to keep training if we're ever going to make it to the Olympics.

**Suzanne:** The Olympics?! I can hardly make it to Circle K! Hey, a Big Gulp sounds really good. *(Starts to walk away.)*

**Shawna:** Get back here. Look, I know it's hard now—dragging yourself out of bed at 5 a.m., drinking raw-egg-and-wheat-germ shakes when your friends get McDonald's, running 'til your body feels like Jell-O... It's hard for me, too!

**Suzanne:** So why do it? Is it really worth it?

**Shawna:** Of course it's worth it. Picture yourself running in the Olympics. *(Suzanne acts out the following in slow motion, maybe humming the* Chariots of Fire *theme song.)* You're passing up other runners left and right. Then it's down to you and one other girl. Suddenly you pour it on, sprinting until you feel the tape against your chest. *(Suzanne falls down in mock exhaustion.)* Now how do you feel?

**Suzanne:** Tired.

**Shawna:** OK, but now you're up on the platform. *(Suzanne stands up, waving to the crowd, hamming it up.)* They put that gold medal around your neck, then play the national anthem. *(Suzanne wipes away tears, waves to crowd.)*

**Suzanne:** Then do I get to be on a Wheaties box?

**Shawna:** Nah, you have to win two medals to do that. *(Jogs away, Suzanne follows.)*

**Suzanne:** Two medals? Who made up that rule? Aw, Shawna, c'mon...

If you use this skit as a discussion starter, here are possible questions:

■ **In your life, when is it hardest to persevere?**

■ **According to 2 Timothy 2:1-7, what does it mean to "compete by the rules"?**

■ **What kind of race is this passage talking about?**

■ **How can we train for this kind of race?**

# 2 TIMOTHY
## 2:1-26

**THEME:**
Being soldiers of Christ

**SUMMARY:**
In this ADVENTURE, teenagers will interview church members.

PREPARATION: You'll need Bibles; transportation for groups; newsprint; a marker; and small, plastic soldiers.

Form four groups (a group can be one person).

Say: **In 2 Timothy, Paul outlines what it means to be a soldier for Christ. Today we'll explore what he meant and search for practical ways to live as soldiers for Christ.**

Assign each group one of the following Scripture passages and themes: 2 Timothy 2:1-2, a soldier of Christ is strong; 2 Timothy 2:5-7, a soldier of Christ follows the rules; 2 Timothy 2:15-16, a soldier of Christ has a sound faith; 2 Timothy 2:24-25, a soldier of Christ must be a servant.

Have each group read its passage and talk about how the passage reflects the assigned theme. Then send groups out to congregation members' homes to ask other church members how to follow the instructions of their assigned passages in practical ways.

Meet with the groups at an appointed time and have volunteers share what they discovered through their reading, discussion, and conversation with congregation members. List the practical advice on newsprint and have kids commit to trying the ideas in the weeks to come.

Before dismissing, give kids each a small, plastic soldier to remind them of the call to be a soldier for Christ.

# 2 TIMOTHY
## 3:1–4:5

**THEME:**
New Age dangers

**SUMMARY:**
In this ADVENTURE, kids will investigate New Age teachings.

PREPARATION: Get parents' permission for kids to go to a New Age store. You'll need Bibles.

With parents' permission, take kids to a New Age store and have them browse through the items. Ask kids to note what is being taught by the various books and trinkets there. Have kids interview the store clerks about the supposed properties of crystals, pyramids, and other items.

If you have time, take kids to a local library to search for more information about New Age philosophies and other false teachings.

Then meet and have volunteers read aloud 2 Timothy 3:1–4:5. Ask:

■ **How did you feel when you were in the New Age store?**

■ How is that feeling like the way Paul might've felt as he was dealing with the false teachings in his time?

■ Based on these verses, what might Paul say about today's New Age teachings?

■ What are the core differences between New Age philosophies and Christian faith?

■ New Agers often claim they're more open to religion than Christians because they're always learning new things that can help them. How is this like or unlike what Paul warns against in verse 7?

■ What other teachings, besides the New Age, is Paul warning Christians about in this passage?

Form pairs and have partners pray for each other to grow in faith and avoid false teachings like New Age philosophies.

# 2 TIMOTHY
## 4:6-8

THEME:
  Faithfulness

SUMMARY:
  In this LEARNING GAME, kids will compete in various races.

PREPARATION: Set up a course for your race. Determine starting and ending points at least 100 yards apart. You'll also need a Bible.

Have kids compete in a fun race in an open field or park. Tell them they must run the race by hopping on one foot the whole time while singing their favorite praise or worship chorus. Remind kids they must be faithful in following the rules and completing the race.

When kids are finished racing, collapse together on the ground and open your Bible. Read aloud 2 Timothy 4:6-8. Ask:

■ How easy was it to be faithful to the rules of our race? Explain.

■ How is that like the way it is or isn't easy to be faithful to God in the race of life?

■ In this passage, Paul reflects on how well he's run the race and been faithful to God. Without answering aloud, how well have you run the race so far?

■ How could you be more diligent in your faith?

Form pairs and have partners pray for each other to "fight the good fight" and "finish the race" in their daily lives of faith.

# TITUS

*"He gave himself for us so he might pay the price to free us from all evil and to make us pure people who belong only to him—people who are always wanting to do good deeds."*

*Titus 2:14*

# TITUS
## 1:5-9

### THEME:
Leadership

### SUMMARY:
In this LEARNING GAME, teen-agers will compare forming shapes of household items to becoming Christlike leaders.

PREPARATION: You'll need several household items with unusual shapes, such as a blender, a toy basketball goal and backboard, or a chair. You'll also need a Bible. (**Note:** This activity works well for teenage leaders or at a youth council meeting.)

Form groups of no less than four but no more than 10 (it's OK if you have only one group). Explain that when you hold up one of the household items and say "go," groups must immediately try to copy the shape of the item you held up in the shortest amount of time. For example, if you hold up a blender, three kids might stand in a circle and lock arms to form the container, while another person might stand to the side and form the handle.

When a group has formed a shape, they should shout out the name of the object to signal they're finished. Have groups form several shapes, and if you have more than one group, check each round to see which had the fastest time.

Afterward, debrief the experience with this discussion. Ask:

■ **What's your reaction to what you just did?**

■ **What was easy or difficult for you about this activity? Explain.**

■ **In what ways is trying to make your group look like a household item like or unlike shaping yourself into a Christlike leader?**

Have the oldest person in each group read aloud Titus 1:5-9 for his or her group. Ask:

■ **How was Paul helping shape Titus into a Christlike leader by putting him in charge of the church in Crete?**

■ **How do you think Titus might've followed Paul's instructions for appointing leaders in the church in Crete?**

■ **Why did Paul consider the qualities listed in Titus 1:5-9 important for a leader?**

■ **What qualities would you add to the list in Titus 1:5-9 for leaders in our youth group?**

■ **What can we do this week to help shape each other into Christlike leaders in our church? our schools? our homes?**

# TITUS
## 2:11-15

### THEME:
Saying no to the world

### SUMMARY:
In this ADVENTURE, kids go on a shopping spree in a mall, looking for things they'd never want to buy.

PREPARATION: You'll need a sheet of paper and a pencil for each person. You'll also need a Bible.

Gather your group at a shopping mall. Hand each person a sheet of paper and a pencil. Explain that you'll all be going on a "non-shopping spree." Instead of looking for things you want to buy, you'll try to spot things you'd never purchase. Ask kids to each list one item per store on their paper. Allow 45 minutes for kids to complete the adventure.

Tell kids to meet in a designated place to compare lists. Ask:

■ **How did you feel looking for something you did not want to buy?**

■ **What about the items you chose was unappealing to you?**

Have a volunteer read aloud Titus 2:11-15. Then ask:

■ **Why was it easy to say no to the things on your list?**

■ **In real life, why is it sometimes hard to say no to the things the world offers us?**

■ **What can help us say no?**

Say: **Each of us has the freedom to say no to things that are bad for us. Sometimes it's hard to exercise that freedom. But we're not in this alone. We have the strength of one another, the strength of God's love, and the help of his Holy Spirit.**

# PHILEMON

*"So, my brother, I ask that you do this for me
in the Lord: Refresh my heart in Christ."*

*Philemon 20*

# PHILEMON
## 8-21

## THEME:
Reconciliation

## SUMMARY:
In this ADVENTURE, kids meet with a pastor, a school counselor, and a marriage counselor to decide what they would do to reconcile broken relationships.

PREPARATION: Set appointments with your senior pastor, a school counselor, and a marriage counselor on the same day. Ask them each to think of a real-life story (not using real names) about a conflict between people in the church (pastor), among students (school counselor), and in a marriage (marriage counselor).

Plan a threefold adventure based on the theme of reconciliation. Meet at the church and prepare the group for its journey by reading aloud Philemon 8-21. Then go to your first appointment.

At each appointment, ask your host to tell about a real-life relational conflict he or she has had to deal with. Then form groups of three and ask each group to discuss how they'd bring about reconciliation in the situation. After five minutes, ask a representative from each group to tell his or her group's answer. Then have the host tell "the rest of the story"—how the situation actually turned out.

After you've gone to each appointment, gather kids back at the church and ask:

■ **How did you feel as you tried to find solutions to the conflicts you heard about?**

■ **Is it always possible to reconcile every conflict between people? Why or why not?**

■ **What keeps people from reconciling?**

■ **In your opinion, what's the key to reconciliation?**

■ **How can Philemon 8-21 help us learn to reconcile?**

Close by holding hands in a circle. Ask kids to each think of someone they need to reconcile with. Then say together: **Lord, teach me how to reconcile with the person who's on my mind right now.**

# HEBREWS

*"God's word is alive and working and is sharper than a double-edged sword. It cuts all the way into us, where the soul and the spirit are joined, to the center of our joints and bones."*

*Hebrews 4:12*

# HEBREWS
## 1:1-4

THEME:
Jesus, the reflection
of God's glory

SUMMARY:
In this OBJECT LESSON, kids
will use shadows to explore how
Jesus "shows exactly what God
is like" (Hebrews 1:3a).

PREPARATION: Darken the room
as much as possible. Hang a large
sheet from the ceiling and place a
bright light behind it. You'll also
need a Bible.

Stand in front of the light but
behind the sheet, projecting a
shadow onto the sheet for kids to
see. Read aloud Hebrews 1:1-4.
Then stay behind the sheet as you
ask the following questions:

∎ **Who do you see when you
look at the sheet?**

∎ **What clues do you have
that I'm the person behind the
sheet?**

∎ **How difficult or easy is it to
see me in my shadow?**

∎ **How am I like my shadow?**

∎ **In what ways does Jesus
reveal more about God than my
shadow reveals about me?**

∎ **In what ways do you see
God in Jesus' personality and
actions?**

∎ **How can we become
"shadows" of God by reflecting
Jesus in our lives this week?**

Close with a prayer, asking God
to help group members become

Jesus' shadows over the next several days.

# HEBREWS
## 3:12-15

THEME:
When it's tough to
love God

SUMMARY:
In this CREATIVE PRAYER, kids
will list times of struggle and
strong faith and pray for each
other.

PREPARATION: You'll need yellow
and white 3×5 cards and pencils.
You'll also need a Bible.

Give kids each a white and a yellow 3×5 card and a pencil.
Read aloud Hebrews 3:12-15. Ask:

∎ **What struggles could turn
someone against God?**

∎ **What is the toughest struggle you've faced?**

∎ **How can we help each
other in our faith struggles?**

Have kids take two minutes to
think about times they struggled
with loving God—times they
fought with fear, disobedience, and
unbelief. Have kids each write on
the white card one of those struggles. For example, someone might
write, "I had a difficult time loving
God when my parents divorced."

Then have kids each list on the
yellow card a past experience of
strong faith—a time they truly felt
God's help or nearness. For exam-

ple, someone might write, "God was near and helped me when I broke up with my girlfriend."

Ask kids to make their statements anonymous and generic, since other kids will be reading them.

Before your group prayer, place the white and yellow cards in separate piles. Then have each teenager take a white card and a yellow card. Have them take turns praying aloud a prayer similar to the following (using the information from their cards): "Lord, in the past you helped my friend by *(summarize the time of strength from the yellow card)*. Now help my friend face *(summarize the struggle on the white card)*."

# HEBREWS 4:1-10

**THEME:**
Rest

**SUMMARY:**
Through this PROJECT, kids will help parents enjoy a day of rest.

PREPARATION: Publicize a "Parent's Day of Rest" in advance so parents can plan accordingly. Gather the necessary supplies for the activities teenagers plan. You'll also need Bibles.

Arrange to have the church facilities available on a specific day for a "Parent's Day of Rest"

sponsored by your youth group. Have church parents drop off young children, and have teenagers prepare games, snacks, and activities for children to enjoy during their stay at the church. If you expect lots of infants, have child-care experts (not parents) on hand to help out.

Teenagers may also choose to spend some of their youth fund on the parents by purchasing magazines, books, or cassettes for parents to enjoy during their time off. Get ideas for these purchases ahead of time and have kids go shopping before the day of rest.

During the child-care experience, have teenagers read and discuss Hebrews 4:1-10.

After the event, have kids debrief the experience by discussing the following questions:

■ **How did you feel offering others a chance to rest?**

■ **When have you felt a need to rest from your own work or activities?**

■ **How is offering someone rest like and unlike what God does by offering us salvation through Christ's sacrifice?**

■ **How would you describe the spiritual rest you enjoy right now?**

# HEBREWS 4:11-13

**THEME:**
God's Word

**SUMMARY:**

In this OBJECT LESSON, kids will compare God's Word to a meat cleaver.

PREPARATION: You'll need a sharp meat cleaver, a cutting board, and beef. Plan this activity to coincide with a youth group barbecue. You'll also need a Bible.

Before starting your barbecue, bring out the meat cleaver. Hold it up and ask:

■ **What are some characteristics of this cleaver?**

Place the beef on your cutting board and begin cutting it with the cleaver. Be dramatic as you slice through the meat. As you're cutting the beef, ask someone to read Hebrews 4:11-13 loudly. Then ask:

■ **How is God's Word like this meat cleaver?**

■ **How does God's Word penetrate into our souls?**

■ **How is the way a butcher trims fat from a steak like the way God's Word can trim sin from our lives?**

Have kids form pairs and tell their partners about one area of disobedience they'd like God to trim out of their lives. Then begin the barbecue. Grill the beef strips for kids to enjoy as a tasty reminder of the power of God's Word.

# HEBREWS 4:14-16

**THEME:**
Temptation

**SUMMARY:**

In this AFFIRMATION, kids will explore temptations they face and be encouraged to overcome them.

PREPARATION: You'll need poster board, markers, magazines, tape, paper, and shoe boxes. You'll also need a Bible.

Have kids use the art supplies to create a "Temptation Alley" in a hallway by making posters listing or picturing temptations teenagers face, such as junk food, money, power, and possessions. **Note:** Caution kids not to be inappropriately graphic in their posters. For example, let teenagers know that nudity and profanity on posters are unacceptable.

Give teenagers each a shoe box and have them turn the shoe boxes into mailboxes by decorating them with paper and markers. Have kids write their names on their mailboxes and place them in Temptation Alley. Have kids spend a couple minutes reading the posters in Temptation Alley, then sit in groups of no more than four to read and discuss Hebrews 4:14-16. Ask:

■ **Why is temptation a problem for Christians?**

■ **What makes it hard to face the temptations in Temptation**

Alley? What can we do about that?

■ How can God help us when we feel tempted?

■ What does it mean that we can "feel very sure that we can come before God's throne where there is grace"?

■ How can the promise of Hebrews 4:16 help us overcome temptation?

■ What can we do this week to help each other overcome temptation by tapping into God's power and grace?

Give group members paper and markers and have them write notes to one another, encouraging one another to be strong in the face of temptation. Kids might write notes such as "Remember—you're not alone when you face temptation" or "Jesus understands your temptations." Have kids deliver one note to each mailbox in Temptation Alley.

To close, have kids silently read their "mail" and pray for God to help them face temptation with confidence.

# HEBREWS
# 5:11–6:3

## THEME:

Christian maturity

## SUMMARY:
In this DEVOTION, kids will be offered both baby food and a real snack as they consider the nature of Christian maturity.

PREPARATION: Gather baby bottles (filled with water) and jars of baby food (consider pureed favorites such as strained carrots, beets, or peas). You'll need a bottle and jar of baby food for each person. Also prepare a real snack consisting of foods your teenagers like. You'll also need a Bible.

## EXPERIENCE
As kids prepare for a snack time, offer them the baby food and bottles of water. Await their reactions, then explain that the baby food is really their snack for today. See if you can get anyone to actually eat some of the food and drink from the bottles.

After a few minutes, get kids' attention.

## RESPONSE
Form groups of no more than four. Have groups place the bottles and baby food in front of themselves and read Hebrews 5:11–6:3. Then have groups discuss the following questions:

■ How did you feel when you saw what your snack would be?

■ How does this compare to the message of this passage?

■ What foods might represent your current level of Christian maturity? Explain.

■ What are ways we can grow so we can enjoy the "food" of mature Christians?

## CLOSING
Have kids pray for their group members to grow in mature Christian faith. Then bring out the other snacks for teenagers to enjoy. As they eat, have kids dis-

cuss practical ways they can mature in faith.

# HEBREWS 8:7-13

## THEME:
The new covenant

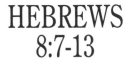

## SUMMARY:
Kids will play a LEARNING GAME using information in old encyclopedias and discuss how God's new covenant supersedes the old covenant.

PREPARATION: You'll need several volumes of an outdated set of encyclopedias. Find volumes that are at least 20 years old if possible (the older the better). Check with congregation members, search garage sales, or contact your local library to find them. Be sure to bring a Bible.

Form teams of no more than four and assign each team a scientific topic to look up. Choose topics that have had lots of advances or that have changed significantly since the encyclopedia was published. Some suggested topics are astronauts, space travel, medicine, solar energy, television, music, and the environment. (Choose the topics in advance to ensure each has at least one bit of outdated information in the entry.)

Have each team read about its topic and create a brief report, using any information that's obso-lete or outdated. Tell teams they can use up to three false facts in an attempt to fool other teams with their reports. For example, a team with the topic "space travel" might say that an aardvark was considered for the first living space traveler, but that a monkey was chosen instead. Teams may add one, two, three, or no false facts to their reports.

Have teams give their reports one at a time. At any time, someone from another team can call out, "False fact!" if they think the information being expressed is false. If they've guessed correctly, that team gets 1 point. If the information was indeed factual, the reporting team gets a point. In addition, each undiscovered false fact at the end of a report earns the reporting team 1 point.

After all the teams have presented, tally the points and determine a winner. Have the winning team read aloud Hebrews 8:7-13. Then discuss the following questions to wrap up:

■ **Why did God make a new covenant with the people?**

■ **How is the old encyclopedia information like the old covenant?**

■ **What is so much better about the new covenant?**

# HEBREWS
## 9:24-28

THEME:
Christ's sacrifice

SUMMARY:
In this OBJECT LESSON, kids will compare fake and real dollar bills and explore how Christ's sacrifice was real.

PREPARATION: You'll need photocopies of dollar bills—color photocopies if possible. Use an enlarging or reducing function on the photocopier to make your bills double- or half-sized (federal law prohibits making actual-sized photocopies). Also, be sure to destroy the bills after this activity to avoid any appearance of counterfeiting. You'll also need a Bible.

Give each person one fake dollar. Have a few real dollar bills available for kids to look at, too. Form groups of no more than four. Have groups brainstorm everything about the fake dollar that's the same as the real dollar.

Call the whole group back together and have representatives from the small groups share what they came up with. Then have kids brainstorm key reasons the fake dollars aren't the same as real dollars. Have kids discuss these reasons and choose the one reason they think is most important.

After kids give that reason, suggest that the most important thing about a real dollar bill is that the government will accept it as legal payment for buying goods. In other words, the most important difference is that a real dollar *works* and a fake dollar doesn't.

Have someone read aloud Hebrews 9:24-28. Then debrief the experience by asking:
■ **Why is it important that Christ's sacrifice was real and accepted?**
■ **How is this difference similar to the difference between fake and real dollars?**
■ **How did Christ's sacrifice succeed in bringing us closer to God?**

# HEBREWS
## 11:1

THEME:
Faith

SUMMARY:
In this DEVOTION, kids will state their beliefs about whether an egg can be broken by squeezing it with one hand, then test their faith with a real egg-crushing test.

PREPARATION: You'll need several fresh eggs and a hammer. You'll also need a Bible.

EXPERIENCE
Say: **Some people claim that it's impossible to crush an egg in your bare hand. What do you think?**
Bring out the eggs and ask for a volunteer who will test this theory. (If no one volunteers, tell kids

you'll be the guinea pig.)

Before you or a volunteer attempts to crush the egg, have kids vote on whether or not the egg will break. Have those who believe the egg will break stand on one side of the room, and those who don't believe the egg will break stand on the other side of the room.

Then set the egg horizontally in the volunteer's palm and have him or her attempt to crush the egg by folding his or her fingers over it and squeezing. It's unlikely that the volunteer will be able to crush the egg. But if he or she does, that's OK. Either option will bring about good discussion.

RESPONSE

Read aloud Hebrews 11:1. Ask:

■ **How is this activity an example of testing our faith?**

■ **What surprised you about this faith test?**

■ **How do you feel about your Christian faith, knowing that you can't test it like you tested this egg?**

■ **What does it mean to live by faith and not by sight?**

CLOSING

Take out the hammer and ask kids if they believe you could break an egg with it. After getting kids' responses, put down the hammer.

Say: **Just as we're sure I can smash an egg with this hammer, we can be sure of God's power to lead us.**

Have kids each take an egg home as a reminder of what it means to have faith in God.

# HEBREWS 11:13, 16a

THEME:
Being citizens of heaven

SUMMARY:
Kids will attend a RETREAT and explore what it means to be an alien in our world but a citizen of heaven.

PREPARATION: Advertise this retreat by sending flying-disc invitations to kids' homes. Write the pertinent retreat information on the discs using permanent markers. Base your retreat on the theme "We're the aliens here!"

Plan to "touch down" at a secret location on the night of the retreat. (You'll want to inform parents of your retreat location but keep it a surprise from kids.) Decorate your church vans, buses, or other vehicles as spacecrafts by placing colorful lights in the windows.

If your kids like costume parties, have them come dressed as aliens. Award prizes for the most outrageous, scariest, and funniest costumes. Prepare alien-looking snacks. Be sure to bring Bibles.

During the retreat, show an alien movie, such as *E.T.— The Extra-Terrestrial,* and discuss the theological themes and implications of the film. For example, with *E.T.* you might discuss the alien's longing to go home and how that relates to the Christian's longing for heaven. Use Hebrews

11:13, 16a as the basis for your discussion.

Serve snacks colored with blue or purple food coloring as your alien treats during the retreat. Play made-up games with strange rules that will make kids feel like aliens.

Throughout the retreat, lead small-group discussions, focusing on the following questions:

■ **What does it mean to be a faithful citizen of heaven while living as an alien on earth?**

■ **How does being a Christian sometimes make you feel like a stranger or an outsider?**

■ **How can we meet the challenge to live our lives as bold examples of Christ?**

# HEBREWS
## 12:1-2

THEME:

Perseverance

SUMMARY:

In this LEARNING GAME, kids will run a race and attempt to overcome hindrances to win.

PREPARATION: You'll need a Bible, several rolls of toilet paper, masking tape, and a prize.

Form two teams. Have teams each choose a "race car"—the person they think would be the fastest and strongest to represent their team in a sprint. Give each team six or seven rolls of toilet paper.

Use masking tape to mark start and finish lines on the floor. If you have a small room, have kids race outside or in a hallway. The longer the race track, the better.

Have the race cars each go to the opposing team to be "prepared" for the race. Have kids wrap all the toilet paper around the opposing team's race car and help him or her over to the starting line. Make sure each team member is involved in wrapping the race cars. If you have a group of more than 10, form more than two teams and have each team wrap another's race car.

When the race cars are ready, start the race. Racers must do all they can to win the race. This will take some perseverance as racers try to get out of their toilet paper entanglements and run.

Award a prize to the winning team, then debrief the activity by reading Hebrews 12:1-2 and discussing the following questions. Ask the race cars:

■ **How did it feel to run a race when you were all tangled up?**

■ **What worked for you as you struggled to get free?**

Ask everyone:

■ **How is this race a good illustration of the Christian race described in Hebrews 12:1-2?**

■ **What kinds of things hold you back in the Christian race?**

■ **How can we persevere in the Christian race?**

# HEBREWS
## 12:1-3

---

**THEME:**
Worldly distractions

**SUMMARY:**
In this SKIT, two guys get ready to go backpacking, but one of them tries to bring too much stuff.

---

## FOR THE LONG HAUL

SCENE: Chris and John are going backpacking in the Grand Canyon for spring break. They're in John's room, the morning of the trip.

PROPS: Gather hiking backpacks, a radio or cassette player, an iron, a box labeled "Beer," a phone, long underwear, pots, pans, heavy things, and a table. You'll need a Bible for the discussion afterward.

CHARACTERS:
**Chris**
**John**
(**Note:** This skit could be performed by two girls instead of guys by simply changing character names and gender references.)

### SCRIPT
*(Chris enters John's room, carrying a full backpack. John is still packing his backpack. Pots, pans, a large radio or cassette player, an iron, and other items are scattered around.)*
**Chris:** All right, the big day is here! We're off to tackle the Grand Canyon! Hurry up and finish packing so we can leave!
**John:** I'm almost done—just a few

more things to fit in. *(Tries to cram the radio into the backpack.)* Having a little trouble with these last few necessities.
**Chris:** John, what are you doing? We're going backpacking—not on a yearlong trek into the jungle! What could you possibly need with all this stuff?
**John:** Well, this *(holding up radio)* is for listening to the ballgame and my new GreenRoadKill Wizards tape. Oh, and I'm trying to win a new car in the Z95 radio contest, too. So I have to be listening all the time. That's also why I'm bringing this *(holds up phone)* so that I can call the radio station to win!
**Chris:** And, uh, this iron? You're taking an iron on a camping trip?
**John:** C'mon, Chris. What if we meet some girls at the Grand Canyon? Can't go looking like some wrinkled-up old hermits.
**Chris:** John, we're not going up there to meet girls! We're tackling the Grand Canyon, from top to bottom, then bottom to top. Remember? This isn't *Love Connection!* If you start messing around up there, we'll never get out by next week!
**John:** Aw, don't worry. We'll be fine! Look, I'm almost done packing. Lemme just figure out a way to fit in this case of beer... *(Brings in a box labeled "Beer.")*
**Chris:** (Slapping his hand to his forehead) Tell me you're joking! You can't take alcohol to the Grand Canyon! Aside from the small fact that it's ILLEGAL, how do you plan to make it in and out in five days if you're drinking?

**John:** Chris, lighten up. It's spring break! OK, looks like I'm ready to go. *(Tries to lift his backpack but can't, hamming it up as he struggles.)*

**Chris:** Oh, we're really going to make tracks this way. John, I'm giving you five minutes to dump all that stuff out; grab your long johns, a map, and your sleeping bag; and meet me in the car. *(Turns and walks out.)*

**John:** Man, I'm glad Chris is heading this thing up. I knew there was something I forgot! *(Grabs long underwear and drags backpack offstage.)*

If you use this skit as a discussion starter, here are possible questions:

■ **Why do you think John was unwilling to let go of all his unnecessary supplies?**

■ **Why are people unwilling to let go of things that interfere with their spiritual growth?**

■ **What keeps you from running the Christian "race," as Hebrews 12:1-3 tells you to do? What helps you?**

# HEBREWS 12:28-29

**THEME:**
Humility

**SUMMARY:**
In this CREATIVE PRAYER/MUSIC IDEA, kids will listen to music about God's holiness as they show reverence with their body positions.

PREPARATION: You'll need a cassette player and cassettes with songs about holiness, or songbooks (such as *The Group Praise & Worship Songbook,* from Group Publishing). You'll also need a Bible.

Tell kids that this is to be a time of prayer and reflection on God's holiness. Give kids the following instructions on how to respond during each song you'll sing or play:

During the first song, have kids bow their heads.

During the second song, have kids kneel and bow their heads.

During the third song, have kids kneel and put their faces to the floor.

Play or sing the songs as kids follow the body position instructions.

After the third song, read aloud Hebrews 12:28-29. Wrap up the experience by asking:

■ **How do you define "worship"?**

■ **How does the posture you**

took reflect respect for God's holiness?

■ How can we see God more clearly when we're humbled?

■ How can we humble ourselves before God each day?

■ How can we show more respect for God in our lives?

# HEBREWS 12:28-29

## THEME:
God's power

## SUMMARY:
In this CREATIVE READING, kids will pose themselves as if near a roaring fire and compare the fire to God's power.

PREPARATION: You'll need a Bible.

Turn out the room lights and have kids close their eyes for this reading. Have teenagers imagine a huge, hot fire burning in one corner of the room. Say: **After I describe the fire in more detail, I'm going to ask you to put yourself into a pose that indicates how you might shield yourself if the fire were real. Stay in that position until I've finished reading the Scripture passage.**
Describe the fire in detail as kids listen with their eyes closed. Say: **The fire has been burning for a few hours now, and it burns brighter than ever be-**

fore. Blue and white sparks fly out in all directions. Glowing ashes float dangerously close to nearby trees. The wind picks up, and the fire begins to roar even higher. Flames now stretch out 10 feet or more. The hungry fire has turned this room into a raging inferno—a furnace looking for more fuel.

Ask kids to pose in response to the description of the fire and listen as you read aloud Hebrews 12:28-29. At the end of the reading, have kids explain their poses. Ask:

■ How is God's power like a raging fire?

■ What causes us to respect the power of fire?

■ What causes us to respect God's power?

■ How can we live to please God?

Close with a prayer of thanks that God uses his awesome power on behalf of God's children.

# HEBREWS 13:9

## THEME:
True religion

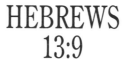

## SUMMARY:
In this LEARNING GAME, kids will create imaginary religions.

PREPARATION: You'll need Bibles.

Form no more than four groups and challenge all but one of the groups to create a wacky religion—an imaginary cult that sounds realistic but preaches at least one "strange teaching" contrary to the Bible.

Have the leftover group's members play the roles of potential religious converts.

Have a representative from each of the wacky-religion groups make a brief presentation to the potential-converts group. Then have the converts each choose which wacky religion they'd like to join. Award a standing ovation to the group that attracts the most converts.

Then have someone read aloud Hebrews 13:9. Ask the wacky-religion groups:

■ **What did you build into your religion to make it appealing to the potential converts?**

■ **How is that like or unlike the way cults attempt to attract teenagers?**

Ask the convert group members:

■ **What attracted you to the religion you chose?**

■ **How is that like or unlike the things that attract people to actual false religions or cults?**

Ask everyone:

■ **What makes these wacky religions contrary to Christian faith?**

■ **What is it about some religions' false teachings that might make them attractive?**

■ **How can we avoid being drawn into groups like these?**

■ **What are the dangers of "strange teachings that lead you into the wrong way"?**

■ **Why do you suppose the writer of Hebrews felt it was important to include the warning of Hebrews 13:9 in this letter?**

■ **What can we do this week to follow the advice of Hebrews 13:9?**

# JAMES

*"But if any of you needs wisdom, you should
ask God for it. He is generous and enjoys
giving to all people, so he will give you
wisdom."*

*James 1:5*

# JAMES
## 1:2-4

**THEME:**
Perseverance

**SUMMARY:**
In this OBJECT LESSON, kids will perform exercises and explore the role of perseverance in faith.

PREPARATION: You'll need a fitness or muscle magazine and a Bible.

Hold up the cover of a fitness or muscle magazine. Say: **Let's see if we can look like this bodybuilder.**

Have everyone perform exercises such as push-ups, sit-ups, and jumping jacks for at least five minutes. Then form groups of no more than four. Have groups discuss the following questions:

■ **How many of you now look like the bodybuilder?**

■ **How long does it take to develop muscles like those on our magazine cover?**

■ **What is the role of perseverance in bodybuilding?**

Ask someone to read aloud James 1:2-4. Ask:

■ **How are difficult situations like exercise?**

■ **In what ways does relying on God build our faith?**

■ **What spiritual muscles grow when we face trials?**

■ **What is the role of perseverance in building your spiritual muscles?**

Say: **We may never physically look like the person on the cover of this magazine, but with perseverance and desire, we can build spiritual muscles that will help us face any difficult situation.**

# JAMES
## 1:5

**THEME:**
Wisdom

**SUMMARY:**
Kids will determine how to pray for wisdom in this CREATIVE PRAYER.

PREPARATION: You'll need Bibles, concordances, paper, pencils, newsprint, and a marker.

Have a volunteer read aloud James 1:5. Ask:

■ **How can we gain God's wisdom?**

Form groups of four. Give each group a Bible, a concordance, paper, and pencils. Have one person be the leader (who encourages group members to participate); another, the recorder (who records on paper the group's responses); another, the reader (who reads the Scripture passages); and another, the reporter (who shares the group's findings with the whole group). If you have groups smaller than four, assign more than one role to each person.

Have kids use their concordances to look up passages about wisdom. Ask kids to discuss what those passages tell us about wisdom. For example, Proverbs 4:5-6 tells us to seek wisdom and understanding because it will protect us.

After 10 minutes, have reporters tell the whole group what they discovered. List the ideas on newsprint.

Have kids form the newsprint ideas into a prayer by adding "Dear God, help us to..." at the beginning and "In Jesus' name, amen" to the end of the list. Then have kids read aloud the prayer, following the advice of James 1:5.

# JAMES
# 1:6-8

THEME:
Doubt

SUMMARY:
Kids will play a LEARNING GAME and discover how doubt is like a wave of the sea.

PREPARATION: Play this learning game at a swimming pool to coincide with a swim party. You'll need a ball that floats and a Bible.

**H**ave kids get into the pool and line up around the perimeter of the pool. Place a plastic ball into the center of the pool. Say: **The object of the game is to get the ball to touch the wall exactly opposite from where you stand. Each person must keep one hand on the pool wall at all times.**

After kids have thrashed and splashed to no avail, have kids form small groups of no more than four. Have someone who's not all wet read aloud James 1:6-8 for the whole group. Then have small groups discuss the following questions to debrief their experience:

■ **How is the game we played like the illustration in this passage?**

■ **Why could the ball never really head purposefully toward a fixed point?**

■ **When have you felt like the ball in our activity?**

■ **How does doubt keep us from reaching our goals?**

■ **How can we focus on growing in faith so we don't bounce between faith and unbelief?**

# JAMES
# 1:12-15

THEME:
Temptation

SUMMARY:
In this SKIT, a girl visiting a blind woman is tempted by a substantial sum of money.

## THE APPLE

SCENE: A blind woman and a young girl are sitting in the woman's home.

PROPS: You'll need two chairs, dark glasses for Mrs. Weathersby, a book, a plastic cup, $50 of play money, and a Bible for the discussion afterward.

CHARACTERS:
**Janine**
**Mrs. Weathersby** (who is blind)

SCRIPT
*(As the scene opens, Janine is in the middle of reading a passage from "Snow White and the Seven Dwarfs," by the Brothers Grimm. Mrs. Weathersby shows her attentiveness by nodding occasionally.)*

**Janine:** "The evil Queen, dressed like a peasant woman, went across the hills to where she knew Snow White was. When she knocked at the door, Snow White called out, 'I dare not let anybody in. The seven dwarfs told me not to.'

'Very well,' answered the Queen, 'I will sell my beautiful apples elsewhere, but, here, take one as a sample.'

'No,' answered Snow White. 'I dare not.'

'But look how beautiful they are!'

"They were indeed beautiful, and Snow White stretched out her hand to take just one, for she could hardly resist."

**Mrs. Weathersby:** And thereby hangs a tale. How I've missed reading since I lost my eyesight! It's been so long since I've heard this story, it's almost like new. Thank you for reading it so far, dear. Could you stop for a moment and get me a glass of water? My throat is quite dry.

**Janine:** Sure, Mrs. Weathersby. Just some water out of the faucet OK?

**Mrs. Weathersby:** That's fine, dear. Let the water run for a few seconds so it gets nice and cold. *(Mrs. Weathersby continues talking while Janine goes to the sink. Janine picks up a plastic cup and turns on the water. While she's waiting, she looks around and notices a stack of money on the counter. She fingers through it without picking it up, looks at Mrs. Weathersby, then back at the money, obviously trying to decide whether or not to steal it.)*

**Mrs. Weathersby:** I've always loved the story of Snow White. It seems to me that it's really a story about all the things we long for in life. With the exception of Snow White, all the characters in the story are searching for something to make their lives complete. The queen will do anything to be the fairest one in all the land. The prince is looking for a beautiful girl to be his wife. And even the dwarfs are miners, looking for riches underneath the earth.

*(Janine looks up just as Mrs. Weathersby makes the next statement)*

**Mrs. Weathersby:** Do you ever think that there's one thing that would make you really happy in life, Janine?

**Janine:** *(Startled out of her internal conflict)* Huh? Uh, no... Well I suppose, money and stuff like that.

**Mrs. Weathersby:** I think the water's cold enough, dear. *(Janine leaves the money alone, fills the plastic cup, turns off the faucet, and comes back over to give it to Mrs. Weathersby.)*

**Janine:** Here you go, Mrs. W. *(Janine gently takes Mrs. Weathersby's hand and places the cup in it.)*

**Mrs. Weathersby:** Thank you, dear. Listen to an old woman when she tells you that "money and stuff" isn't what lasts. Nothing here on earth lasts or will make you truly happy. Snow White thought tasting that delicious apple would make her happy, even for a brief time, and look what happened to her! *(She chuckles.)* Speaking of which, are you going to read me the rest of the story or leave me hanging here in suspense?

**Janine:** Yes, ma'am. *(She picks up the book and continues reading.)* "No sooner had she tasted a morsel of the apple than she fell over dead." *(She looks at the money on the counter, then sighs, knowing she's done the right thing.)*

**Mrs. Weathersby:** Whoops! What did I tell you?

If you use this skit as a discussion starter, here are possible questions:

■ **According to James 1:12-15, what's at the root of the temptations we face?**

■ **What's the best way to resist temptation?**

# JAMES
# 1:16-18

THEME:
Deception

SUMMARY:

In this DEVOTION, kids will make a decision about which beverage to drink and discuss how easy it is to be deceived.

PREPARATION: You'll need two powdered drink mixes (the kind without sugar), water, vinegar, two clear pitchers, sugar, food coloring, and cups. Mix up one of the drink mixes without sugar. Add two or three tablespoons of vinegar to the mixture and stir. Mix the second drink according to the instructions but use food coloring to make the drink a gross color (a dirty brown or gray works best). You'll need equipment for the game you play and a Bible.

EXPERIENCE

Have kids play a rousing game of volleyball, baseball, Freeze Tag, or another energy-burning game. Then invite kids to have a refreshing drink of punch to quench their thirst. Bring out both pitchers and say: **Choose which pitcher you'd like to drink from and form a line behind that pitcher.**

Pour a small amount of punch from the appropriate pitcher into a cup for each person but tell kids not to drink yet. Say: **One of these pitchers of punch contains vinegar. We'll drink all at once and see which of us chose the** poor-tasting punch. And don't worry, if you chose the vinegar punch, you can trade it for the sweet punch after we all drink.

Have everyone take a sip of punch at the same time, then give sweet punch to kids who got the vinegar punch. If no one chose the vinegar-tainted punch, have a volunteer try it and tell the rest of the group how it tasted.

RESPONSE

Have kids form groups of no more than four. Ask:

■ Why did you choose the punch that you did?

■ Were you easily deceived by the look of the punch? Why or why not?

Have someone read aloud James 1:16-18. Then ask:

■ How are people deceived when it comes to faith issues?

■ How can we recognize the good things that come from God?

CLOSING

Have kids form pairs and pour each other a drink of the good-tasting punch. As kids present their partners with the punch, have them say short prayers, asking God to help them avoid being deceived about faith issues.

# JAMES
# 1:17

THEME:
God's goodness

SUMMARY:

In this OBJECT LESSON, kids will share items that represent a favorite hobby, sport, food, or entertainment and discuss how everything good comes from God.

PREPARATION: Let kids know ahead of time that they're to bring an item from home that represents a favorite hobby, sport, food, or entertainment. For example, someone who enjoys listening to music might bring a CD and someone who enjoys sports might bring a basketball.

Form a circle. Have kids describe the items they brought and what they represent. After each person speaks, have the person opposite him or her read aloud James 1:17.

Continue until each person has shared. Then ask:

■ How are these things gifts from God like James describes in James 1:17?

■ What other gifts does God give us?

Have kids each think of one gift they can give back to God and commit to doing that during the coming week.

# JAMES
## 1:19-20

---

**THEME:**
Relating to others

**SUMMARY:**
Kids will explore the message of James 1:19-20 through a variety of RETREAT experiences.

---

PREPARATION: Since this retreat requires kids to speak openly and honestly about difficult subjects, ask kids not to bring guests along. Also, don't use this retreat idea until you're sure your kids feel comfortable sharing with each other.

Plan a "care enough to confront" retreat based on the theme of James 1:19-20. Set ground rules for the retreat so everyone knows the importance of respecting each other's feelings during the time together.

Open the retreat playing get-acquainted games from *Have-A-Blast Games* (from Group Publishing) or another games book. Have kids read James 1:19-20 after the game time to introduce the retreat's theme.

Use the following ideas to focus activities on the retreat's theme:

■ Play Quick to Listen. Form groups of no more than four and have one person in each group tell his or her life story in 60 seconds or less. Then have the other group members each take 20 seconds to retell that person's story to the whole group. Continue until each person has told his or her life story.

■ Explore anger. Have kids form "anger action teams" and have them brainstorm times they've wrongly expressed anger toward another group member, a family member, or a friend at school. Have teams discuss better ways to handle the situations and explore possible actions to take to resolve future situations.

■ Practice forgiveness. Have a "forgiveness free-for-all" during which kids can ask for forgiveness of other group members they've wronged or offer forgiveness to those who've wronged them. Make this a sincere time for kids to rebuild relationships and strengthen friendships.

# JAMES
## 2:1-9

---

**THEME:**
Cliques

**SUMMARY:**
Kids will break down clique barriers in this RETREAT.

---

PREPARATION: Send a cryptic invitation to your kids by writing James 2:1-9 on the invitation and asking kids to attend a retreat based on this passage. Don't say any more about the retreat's theme. You'll need 3x5 cards, pencils, and a Bible.

On the first night of the retreat, give each person a 3x5 card. Have kids privately write on their cards their names and what school cliques they most closely relate to; for example, "jocks" or "rockers."

Collect the cards and create new cliques for the weekend by mixing up people who wrote down different school cliques.

Have these new cliques create things they'll have in common during the retreat, such as always being first for breakfast, choosing the games to play, determining who'll speak first in a discussion, and so on. Allow groups to be creative (but not destructive) with their clique uniqueness. For fun, have cliques each create a new name for themselves based on the things they come up with.

During the first half of the retreat, have cliques practice excluding each other in all the games, meals, and discussion times. Then read aloud James 2:1-9 and have kids discuss the message of this passage and how it relates to cliques. Then, for the last half of the retreat, have cliques practice including each other in all activities. At the end of the retreat, you shouldn't have any cliques left.

# JAMES
## 3:2-12

THEME:
Gossip

SUMMARY:
In this LEARNING GAME, kids will pick up rice with toothpicks.

PREPARATION: Gather uncooked rice, bowls, and toothpicks. You'll also need a Bible. As an added option, you might want to have some upbeat Christian music to play in the background during the game.

Form teams of no more than five (a team should be at least two or three people). Give each team an empty bowl and give each team member two toothpicks. Have teams each choose a referee for the other team.

Have teams each form a circle and have referees station themselves outside the opposing team's circle. Drop a few handfuls of rice on the floor within each team's circle.

On "go," have teams work to pick up the rice from the floor to fill their empty bowls, using only their toothpicks to pick up one grain of rice at a time. (If you brought it, play upbeat Christian music while kids are involved in the game.)

Call time after five minutes. Have the referees each count the grains of rice in the teams' bowls. The team with the most rice in its bowl wins. Next, have kids choose a partner from an opposing team to form pairs for discussion. Ask pairs:

■ **What went through your mind while you picked up the rice one grain at a time?**

■ **How was our picking up rice off the floor like trying to take back the damage done by gossip?**

Have pairs read James 3:2-12. Ask:

■ **In what ways can gossip be**

a damaging force like the things described in this passage?

■ What does James 3:2-12 imply that we should do to stop gossip?

■ How can we judge when our normal conversations turn to gossip?

■ What can we do if we've already been guilty of spreading gossip?

Say: **Like picking up rice one grain at a time or stopping a forest fire once it's started, stopping gossip from spreading is almost impossible. This week, pray each day for God to help you tame your tongue as you work to overcome the temptation of gossip.**

# JAMES
## 3:3-5

THEME:
Taming of the tongue

SUMMARY:
In this SKIT, a host asks three body parts—the Heart, the Brain, and the Tongue—to answer questions about what they'd do in difficult situations.

## WHO'S IN CHARGE?

SCENE: A game show set.

PROPS: You'll need three large name tags with "Heart," "Brain," and "Tongue" printed on them;

pocket breath spray; and a Bible for the discussion afterward.

CHARACTERS:
Host
Heart
Brain
Tongue

SCRIPT
*(Heart, Brain, and Tongue all have their backs to the audience. Host addresses the audience.)*

**Host:** Ladies and gentlemen, you're about to witness the fascinating inner workings of the human body. For our demonstration, we've asked three important parts of the typical teenager to help us out. First, let's have a big round of applause for the Heart! *(Host leads the applause. Heart turns around.)*

**Heart:** *(Heartfelt)* I feel so honored to be part of this exciting demonstration.

**Host:** Thank you, Heart. Second, the Brain! *(Leads applause.)*

**Brain:** *(Turns around, raises an eyebrow with knowing look.)* Of course, it was imperative that I be an integral part of this hypothetical demonstration.

**Host:** Of course. And third, the strongest part of the body, *(Heart and Brain look skeptical)* wielding immense power—the Tongue! *(Leads applause.)*

**Tongue:** *(Turns around, views proceedings with disdain.)* Yeah, yeah, let's get going. I've got a hot date. *(Takes out pocket breath spray and gives himself a shot.)*

**Brain:** You're rather crude, aren't you?

**Tongue:** Get a life, egghead! People may leave you at home when they go out, but I'm always along for the ride! *(Heart is upset. Tongue looks at Heart.)* What are you looking at?

**Heart:** You don't have to be so mean!

**Tongue:** Aw, go soak your aorta!

**Host:** *(Clearly embarrassed)* Uh ... let's get on with the demonstration. I'll present you three with a situation, and you tell me how you'd react. Please feel free to confer with each other. When you arrive at an answer, raise your hand and tell me. Here we go.

You're walking down a hallway at school when you see someone you used to date. You broke up because of an argument about other friends that you didn't like. What do you do? *(Brain and Heart begin to confer.)*

**Brain:** Hmm ... This is interesting—something that we must give much thought to, weigh the possibilities.

**Heart:** I think we should accept the person back into our life. I mean, we really cared for this person at one time, didn't we? *(Tongue raises hand.)*

**Host:** Tongue?

**Tongue:** I go up to this person and say, "I hope you're enjoying all your other jerk friends, you stupid ... "

*(The following three lines are all spoken at the same time:)*

**Host:** *(Interrupting)* Thank you very much, Tongue!

**Brain:** That's highly inappropriate! We would never react that way!

**Heart:** How can you be so insensitive?

**Tongue:** *(With false emotion)* I'm just saying what I feel! I'm just being honest! Please, give me another chance!

**Host:** Very well. Let's try another, shall we?

Your folks let you take the car one night to go out to a movie with some friends. In the parking lot, you're driving a little carelessly and brush up against another car's bumper, putting a long, deep scratch in the side of your folks' car. When you get home, your parents ask if you had a nice time. What do you say?

**Heart:** Now let's take this one slowly. We know they care for us.

**Brain:** But they may get upset, so we need to state our position clearly. *(Tongue raises hand.)*

**Heart and Brain:** *(To Tongue)* NO!

**Host:** Tongue?

**Tongue:** *(Starts to get teary-eyed.)* Um ... Mom, Dad, something happened tonight that I think you ought to know about.

**Heart:** *(Impressed)* I don't believe it—he's going to spill the beans and trust in his parents' forgiveness!

**Brain:** Hmm.

**Tongue:** When I was in the parking lot at the movie theater, something happened to the car. *(Sniffles.)* I was driving real carefully, enjoying a nice, relaxing evening with my friends *(crying)* when suddenly a big, black Buick came racing around the corner and put a huge scratch in the car! *(Pathetically)*

Will you forgive me?

**Brain:** *(Angrily)* That was pathetic!

**Tongue:** Thanks! I thought so, too.

**Heart:** I've never heard such dishonest, manipulative tripe in all my life!

**Tongue:** Aw, cool your ventricles!

**Host:** Unfortunately we're out of time. Tune in next week when our guests will be the Bladder, the Stomach, and the Feet. Thank you!

If you use this skit as a discussion starter, here are possible questions:

■ **Why does your tongue often say things your heart and brain don't agree with?**

■ **According to James 3:3-5, why is the tongue the most powerful organ in our body?**

■ **When has your tongue gotten you into trouble?**

■ **What have you learned about the power of your tongue?**

# JAMES
## 3:3-12

---

**THEME:**
Bragging

**SUMMARY:**
In this ADVENTURE, kids will compare items in nature with the power of the tongue.

---

**PREPARATION:** Use this adventure during a youth group hike or attach it to a retreat based on the power of the tongue. You'll need a Bible.

Take your group to a park or a nearby wooded area. Send kids out in pairs with these instructions: **Find at least three things that are small but have a large impact on the things around them. For example, a seed is small, but it will have a large impact when it grows into a tree.** Let kids know they don't necessarily have to bring the items back. Give pairs 15 minutes to find their three items.

When everyone has returned, have pairs each brag about what they found. Encourage kids to outdo each other in their boasts.

Then have someone read aloud James 3:3-12. Ask:

■ **How are the words we say like or unlike the items we discovered on this adventure?**

■ **How is the way we bragged about our finds like what this passage warns against?**

■ **How can little words of bragging get us into trouble?**

■ **What are other ways that our words get us into trouble?**

■ **Describe a time when someone you know had his or her reputation damaged by a few small words.**

■ **What do the words people use tell about their character?**

■ **How can we use every little word we say to do good things?**

# JAMES
## 4:1-4

---

### THEME:
Materialism

### SUMMARY:
In this DEVOTION, kids will compare building a card tower in a competitive environment to competing for things in real life.

---

PREPARATION: Gather enough 3×5 cards for every group member to have at least five. You'll also need doughnuts (or another treat your group members really like), pencils, and Bibles.

EXPERIENCE

Form teams of no more than four and give each person at least five 3×5 cards.

Show the group a box of doughnuts (or another treat), then say: **The object of this game is to build the highest tower using your 3×5 cards. The team that has the highest tower after three minutes wins this box of doughnuts.**

**There are no other rules. That means things like knocking over another team's tower or building your tower on a table wouldn't be considered cheating. It's every team for itself. Ready? Go.**

Watch as kids compete to build their towers. See if any teams "cheat" by knocking over other teams' towers or by going to great efforts to build their towers on higher objects such as tables or filing cabinets.

After three minutes, call the group back together and award the doughnuts to the winning team.

RESPONSE

Have kids each choose a discussion partner from one of the other teams. Have pairs read James 4:1-4 and discuss these questions:

■ **What's your reaction to your experience during this game?**

■ **Were you tempted to disrupt another team's efforts at building the tower? Why or why not?**

■ **How much influence did knowing what the winners would get have on your actions?**

■ **In what ways did our actions during this game reflect what James talks about in James 4:1-4?**

■ **Why do people fight with each other to get "things"?**

■ **What does James 4:1-4 tell us about God's view of material things?**

■ **What changes would you need to make to reflect the attitude James presents in these verses?**

CLOSING

Give doughnuts to kids who didn't get them earlier. Distribute pencils and make sure everyone has a 3×5 card. Ask kids to write one verse or phrase from James 4:1-4 that's meaningful to them on their 3×5 card. Tell group members to take those cards home as a reminder of what they learned during this devotion.

# JAMES
## 5:16-18

**THEME:**
Prayer

**SUMMARY:**
Group members will create a visible prayer chain in this CREATIVE PRAYER/PROJECT.

PREPARATION: You'll need a Bible, paper clips, 3×5 cards, and pencils.

Gather your group for a discussion of James 5:16-18. Use questions like these to spark exploration of the passage:

■ **Why do you think James encourages us to pray for each other?**

■ **What makes it hard for you to believe prayer will work?**

■ **When have you had a prayer answered in a meaningful way? How did that make you feel? Explain.**

■ **When has it seemed like God didn't answer your prayer? How did that make you feel? Explain.**

■ **How does it make you feel to know that God views your prayers as important as Elijah's?**

Afterward, say: **Let's take God at his word and act on the promises in this Scripture by creating a visible prayer chain.**

Have group members hook paper clips together to create a chain about 20 feet long. Creatively hang the chain on one wall of your youth room. For example, you might hang it in the shape of a P (for prayer), in a circle, or in a stair-step pattern. Make sure kids can reach the chain.

Next, give everyone a 3×5 card and a pencil. Have kids write one or more prayer requests on their cards and hang them on the prayer chain so the requests are visible.

Say: **For the next month, each time you come in this room, pause for a minute or two to read and pray about the requests on this prayer chain. When your request is answered, remove your card and turn it in to me. If you have new requests, write them on new cards and add them to the chain.**

Close your time together with a few moments of silence to pray for the requests on your chain. Then, at the end of the month, bring out the cards kids have turned in to you and show them to the group as an encouragement that God does answer their prayers.

# 1 PETER

*"You have not seen Christ, but still you love him. You cannot see him now, but you believe in him. So you are filled with a joy that cannot be explained, a joy full of glory."*

*1 Peter 1:8*

# 1 PETER
## 1:6-9

---

**THEME:**
Trials

**SUMMARY:**

In this LEARNING GAME, kids will participate in a "bad-hair day" contest and explore what it feels like to suffer through trials.

---

PREPARATION: You'll need hair gel, hair spray, combs, small bottles of shampoo, and hair clips. Also gather straws, plastic forks, yarn, brown paper bags, and a Bible.

Form teams of up to four (at least two people per team). Have kids pick one of their teammates to receive the "bad-hair day" treatment. Give teams each a supply of hair-care products, as well as straws, plastic forks, yarn, and paper bags to use on their volunteers' hair.

Say: **The object of this game is to create the worst possible example of a bad-hair day on your volunteer's hair. Use all the supplies you've been given but be careful not to harm that person's hair.**

Allow five to 10 minutes for teams to create their examples of bad-hair days. Then have kids vote to determine which team created the best example. Award those team members each a small bottle of shampoo as a prize.

Before sending the volunteers away to wash their hair, have someone read aloud 1 Peter 1:6-9. Ask the volunteers:

■ **How did it feel to have your hair "ruined" for everyone to see?**

■ **How is that like the way you feel when you have troubles in everyday life?**

Ask everyone:

■ **How is the way we respond to things like bad-hair days like the way we respond to bigger difficulties in life?**

■ **What does this passage tell us about facing troubles?**

■ **What daily frustrations do you face?**

# 1 PETER
## 2:4-8

---

**THEME:**
Jesus, the corner-stone

**SUMMARY:**
Kids will experience a RETREAT focusing on Jesus' role as the cornerstone of their faith.

---

PREPARATION: To advertise this retreat in a fun way, paint the pertinent information on a large rock and place it in a prominent place in the church. Also, send or deliver to youth group members flat rocks with the information recorded on them (permanent markers write well on smooth rocks). You'll need playing cards, Bibles, sticks and stones, plastic blocks, wooden blocks, paper, tape, and prizes.

Choose a retreat site where you have access to several stone or brick buildings (check out nearby older college campuses or retreat centers). Have kids explore the construction of the different buildings you meet in during the retreat. If possible, have an architect explain the techniques used in constructing the buildings—especially the role of the cornerstone.

Focus the Bible study times on what it means to be built into a spiritual house with Christ as your cornerstone. Use 1 Peter 2:4-8 as the basis for these discussions.

During one meeting, have kids form small groups. Distribute playing cards for groups to build card houses. Discuss how building a card house is like and unlike building a spiritual house.

At other times, have house-building contests using a variety of materials, such as sticks and stones, plastic blocks, wooden blocks, or paper and tape. Award prizes for the most interesting designs. Have kids brainstorm practical ways to build their spiritual houses in the weeks to come.

# 1 PETER
## 2:9-10

THEME:
    Children of God

SUMMARY:
    In this AFFIRMATION, kids will write "royal traits" on each other's paper "robes."

PREPARATION: You'll need person-sized sheets of newsprint, markers, clothes hangers, a stapler, and scissors. You'll also need a Bible.

Read aloud 1 Peter 2:9-10. Say: **Whether we know it or not, we're all children of a king. But we often go through life acting rather "unroyally." And others don't always treat us like royalty.**
    Ask:
    ■ **How can we remind ourselves and others that we're children of God, the King?**

Give kids each a person-sized sheet of newsprint, a marker, a clothes hanger, and scissors. Have kids each lie down on their newsprint with their arms extended out from their sides and their legs parted slightly. Have them use markers to trace each other's shape—from the neck to the shins—to make robes. Have kids write their names on their robes. Then encourage kids to write royal traits on each person's robe. For example, kids might write "Majestic Kindness" or "Prince of Listeners."

When the robes are finished, have kids cut them out, staple them to clothes hangers, and hang them around the room.

# 1 PETER
## 2:11-12

---

THEME:
Sin

SUMMARY:
In this OBJECT LESSON, kids will compare foul-smelling objects to sinful actions.

---

PREPARATION: You'll need blindfolds, a Bible, one item that smells or tastes bad (such as a rotten egg, an old shoe, or an onion), and two items that smell or taste good (such as a bottle of perfume or a candy bar). You'll also need mints for everyone.

Blindfold volunteers for a taste or smell test to determine which item out of three doesn't belong. Give each volunteer a chance to choose the item that's out of place (the foul-smelling or foul-tasting item). Then ask:

■ **How did you determine which item was out of place?**

Have someone read aloud 1 Peter 2:11-12. Ask:

■ **How is the way you determined which item didn't belong like the way we determine what actions aren't appropriate for Christians?**

■ **What kinds of things should we abstain from in our daily lives?**

■ **How can Christians be the sweet-smelling exceptions in foul-smelling situations?**

Distribute mints to everyone and say: **Let this mint remind you this week to concentrate on** sweet-smelling actions instead of letting yourself become involved in foul-smelling ones.

# 1 PETER
## 2:17

---

THEME:
Showing respect

SUMMARY:
Use this SKIT to help kids learn how to understand and respect their parents.

---

## COOL OR CRUEL?

SCENE: Two girls discuss the ways their moms deal with them, each one wanting what the other has.

PROPS: You'll need two phones, two chairs, and a Bible for the discussion afterward.

CHARACTERS:
**Sue**
**Kari**

SCRIPT

*(The girls sit or stand facing the audience about eight feet apart— each talking on a phone.)*

**Sue:** I'm so glad you have time to talk, Kari. My mom's been driving me absolutely nuts!

**Kari:** *(Laughs.)* What's she doing?

**Sue:** Oh, you know—the usual. *(In a nagging voice)* "Sue, your room is a mess! Pick it up or there's no going out later!" "Sue, quit listening to your headphones. Don't you have some homework you should be doing?" Aaah!

**Kari:** Yeah, it can be pretty bad sometimes. My mom's a pain, too!

**Sue:** No way! You're mom is so cool—she lets you do anything. You can come and go as you please, with no questions.

**Kari:** *(Not too thrilled)* Yeah.

**Sue:** She never cuts down your friends or cares what kind of guys you date.

**Kari:** Yeah.

**Sue:** You're free to ditch if you want, and you say she never looks at your report card or asks you how school is going or anything!

**Kari:** Yeah.

**Sue:** She lets you make your own decisions and doesn't bother you with her opinions. You're free to do as you wish. Face it— your mom's the greatest!

**Kari:** *(Not convinced)* I guess so. *(Hears something in another room.)* What's that, Mom? You're going out? *(Pauses.)* When will you be coming home? *(Pauses.)* Oh, well, I'll see you when I see you, I guess. 'Bye.

**Sue:** What was that?

**Kari:** Oh, my mom's got a new boyfriend. They're going out and won't be back 'til late, I guess.

**Sue:** Cool! You get the whole house to yourself! *(Kari looks forlornly around.)* Your mom is so COOL!

**Kari:** Yeah, well... *(Sadly)* I guess I'd like it if my mom were a little less cool and a little more...

**Sue:** Hang on. *(She holds the phone down and listens to someone in another room.)*

**Kari:** ...a mom.

**Sue:** *(To her mom)* What, Mom? I know, I know! Don't nag me! Sheesh—I talk on the phone for a couple of minutes, and you'd think the world is coming to an end! *(Into phone)* I gotta go— the incredible human nagging machine is on the warpath. Have fun tonight. I wish I had *our* house all to myself—how cool! 'Bye! *(She hangs up.)*

**Kari:** *(She hangs up.)* Yeah, cool... and lonely.

If you use this skit as a discussion starter, here are possible questions:

■ **Which character could you relate to most?**

■ **What does 1 Peter 2:17 say about how we should treat family members?**

■ **Why is it sometimes difficult to respect your parents?**

■ **What's one way you can show them respect every day?**

# 1 PETER 3:9-14

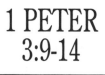

**THEME:**
Retaliation

**SUMMARY:**
Kids will play a LEARNING GAME and learn what it's like to show love to people who've hurt them.

PREPARATION: You'll need to meet in an auditorium or outside for this game. Also, you'll need a Bible and a supply of playground balls.

Form two teams (team A and team B) and play Dodge Ball for a few rounds. Then stop the game and have each team huddle for a pep talk at opposite ends of the playing field. Secretly tell team A they need to be as aggressive as possible during the next game. Suggest that they even bend the rules a bit to win. Then secretly tell team B to be overly polite when playing the next game. Tell members of team B to intentionally miss the other team members and, whenever hit by a ball, to go over to the person who hit them and apologize.

Begin playing. Team A's competitive spirit will quickly dwindle, but play until everyone from team B is hit.

Call the teams together and have everyone sit in a circle. Ask members of team A:

■ **How did you feel when the other team reacted as they did?**

■ **What happened to your competitive spirit in this game?**

Have someone read aloud 1 Peter 3:9-14. Have teenagers tell about situations where they've been verbally attacked and wished they could retaliate with their own harsh words. Ask:

■ **How is the game of Dodge Ball like real life?**

■ **What does this game teach us about situations when we're attacked?**

■ **What does 1 Peter 3:9-14 tell us about retaliation?**

■ **How should we "repay" those who wrong us?**

Have kids close with a group hug.

# 1 PETER 3:14-16

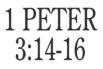

THEME:
Sharing Christ

SUMMARY:
Use this LEARNING GAME to start a discussion about presenting the gospel effectively to others.

PREPARATION: You'll need a Bible.

Have kids mix up their shoes in a pile at one end of the room. Form pairs to create teams of two at the opposite end of the room. The first person on each team is the "detective." The second person on each team describes his or her shoes to the detective, who runs to find them in the shoe pile and bring them back.

If the detective brings back the wrong shoes, he or she gathers more clues and searches again. If the detective brings back the right shoes, the owner puts them on and becomes the detective. Repeat the process until one team finds all its shoes. Declare the winning team.

After the game, ask:

■ **What was difficult about this game?**

■ **Were you surprised at how easy or how difficult it was to**

describe your shoes to someone who didn't know what they
looked like? Why or why not?

Read aloud 1 Peter 3:14-16. Ask:

■ **How is describing your
shoes to a friend similar to presenting the gospel to your
friends?**

■ **What might happen if we
don't present the gospel clearly?**

■ **How can we become more
effective at sharing Christ with
others this week?**

# 1 PETER
## 4:10-11

| THEME:  Serving others  SUMMARY:  In this DEVOTION, kids will receive gifts they can use to serve someone else. |
|---|

PREPARATION: Collect enough
items for each group member to
have one "helping" gift. Helping
gifts should be simple things that
can be used to help another person,
such as combs, hand lotion, breath
mints, or soft drinks. Gifts can be
wrapped or put in a paper sack.
You'll also need a Bible.

EXPERIENCE

Form two groups. Give each
person in one group a helping gift.
Have these kids open their gifts
and find a partner from the other
group (someone who doesn't have
a gift). Have gift holders serve

their partners using the gifts. For
example, a gift holder might serve
someone by brushing his or her
hair, feeding him or her a breath
mint, or helping him or her drink
the soft drink. Kids who are being
served may not use their hands in
any way.

Repeat the activity by giving
helping gifts to the people who
didn't have them the first time.

RESPONSE

After everyone has finished,
read aloud 1 Peter 4:10-11. Ask:

■ **How did it feel to receive a
gift?**

■ **How did it feel to help
another person?**

■ **How did it feel to be served?**

■ **How is using these gifts
you were given like the way
we're supposed to use the gifts
and abilities God's given us?**

Say: **God has given us many
wonderful gifts and wants us to
use these gifts to serve others.**

CLOSING

Ask:

■ **What gifts and talents have
you been given?**

■ **How can you use those to
serve others?**

Form groups of no more than
four and have kids discuss the individual gifts and talents of each
member. Challenge each person to
choose one way to serve others
with their gifts and talents in the
coming week. When you meet
again, have kids tell what they did
and how they felt using God-given
gifts to serve others.

# 2 PETER

*"But God is being patient with you. He does not want anyone to be lost, but he wants all people to change their hearts and lives."*

*2 Peter 3:9b*

# 2 PETER
## 1:5-7

THEME:
Building on a
strong foundation

SUMMARY:
In this OBJECT LESSON, kids
will build a platform to stand on
and compare it to the qualities in
2 Peter 1:5-7.

PREPARATION: Gather bricks,
newsprint, tape, paper, pencils,
Bibles, and markers.

Form groups of seven or more,
and give each group seven
bricks, paper, pencils, a Bible, and
a marker. If you have fewer than
seven people, simply form one
large group.

On each brick, have kids write
one of the qualities listed in 2 Peter
1:5-7. Tell kids they're going to use
the bricks to create a platform for
the group to stand on, but they
must examine each of the qualities
in order to do it.

Say: **Before you can set out a
"quality" brick for your platform, you must discuss and
write responses to each of these
questions:**

■ **How would you define this
quality?**

■ **Why is this quality important to Christian living?**

■ **What would happen if this
quality were or weren't a part of
your everyday life?**

Write the questions on newsprint and tape it to the wall. Then
say: **When you've answered the
questions for each quality, you
must bring the responses to me
so I can check them. Only then
can you move on to the next
quality. And there is one other
catch: You have only five minutes to complete this task. Go!**

When time is up, some groups
will have fewer than seven bricks in
their platform. That's OK. After you
call time, read aloud 2 Peter 1:5-7.
Tell groups they must all stand on
their platforms for 30 seconds—no
feet may be touching the floor.

After 30 seconds, wrap up the
activity by asking:

■ **What was hard about having
the group stand on the platform?**

■ **Did having fewer bricks
make standing harder or easier? Explain.**

■ **How is standing on these
bricks like building your life on
the qualities they represent from
the passage?**

■ **What happens in real life
when one or more of these qualities is missing from your life?**

■ **How can we work on
adding these qualities, as the
Scripture instructs us?**

# 2 PETER
## 1:5-15

THEME:
Faith

SUMMARY:
At this ice-cream PARTY, kids
will create sundaes and determine what traits they most want
to add to their faith.

PREPARATION: You'll need ice cream, seven ice-cream toppings (such as hot fudge, peanuts, caramel, strawberries, marshmallow sauce, chocolate sprinkles, and whipped cream), bowls, spoons, napkins, paper bags, paper, and markers. You'll also need a Bible.

Write the seven traits listed in 2 Peter 1:5-7 each on a separate sheet of paper. The traits are: goodness, knowledge, self-control, patience, service for God, kindness, and love. On a table, place one trait in front of each ice-cream topping. Then cover the toppings with paper bags or boxes so kids can only see the trait labels.

Invite the youth group to an ice-cream party based on 2 Peter 1:5-15. When kids arrive, have each person get a bowl and a spoon. Serve the ice cream but tell kids not to eat it yet.

Form a circle and have a volunteer read aloud 2 Peter 1:5-15. Ask:
■ **What would a sundae be like without any toppings?**
■ **How is the added flavor that toppings bring to a sundae like the added richness that the traits listed in verses 5-7 bring to our faith lives?**

Have kids choose one to three traits (from those listed on the labels) that they'd like to add to their faith. Then have kids remove the paper bags and place those toppings on their ice cream to create faith sundaes. If kids don't like the toppings they end up with, have them trade sundaes with each other until they're happy.

# 2 PETER
## 2:20-22

**THEME:**
Sin

**SUMMARY:**
In this OBJECT LESSON, kids will taste orange juice after brushing their teeth and compare the bad taste to sin.

PREPARATION: You'll need cups of orange juice, toothbrushes, and toothpaste. You'll also need a Bible.

Have kids sit at a table and give them each some orange juice but ask them not to drink it yet. Ask:
■ **What is the popular world attitude about issues such as drinking, wealth, premarital sex, popularity, success, and other similar issues?**
■ **How do people approach these issues in pursuit of acceptance and happiness?**
After your discussion, have teenagers drink some of their orange juice. Ask:
■ **How did it taste?**
■ **How is the way the orange juice tasted like the way sin might taste to people?**
Next, have everyone brush their teeth using a mint-flavored toothpaste. Say: **Imagine that this brushing represents the cleansing that Christ gives us when we become Christians.**
Ask: **How does your mouth feel? taste?**
Read aloud 2 Peter 2:20-22. Then

have kids drink the rest of the orange juice. Wrap up the experience by asking:

■ **How is the way the orange juice tastes after cleansing your teeth like the way sin "tastes" after Christ has cleansed us?**

■ **Why is it important not to return to sinful ways once we've become Christians?**

■ **How can Jesus help you avoid being trapped by sin's unpleasantness this week?**

# 2 PETER
## 3:8-9

**THEME:**
Time

**SUMMARY:**
In this SKIT, a student sitting through a boring lecture can't believe how slowly the time goes.

## IT'S ABOUT TIME

SCENE: Scott is sitting in an extremely boring class while the clock ticks slowly on.

PROPS: You'll need a chair, a desk, a wristwatch, and a Bible for the discussion afterward.

CHARACTERS:
**Teacher**
**Scott**

### SCRIPT
*(Scott sits with chin in palms, eyes glazed, pretending to listen to Teacher. Teacher is babbling on.)*

**Teacher:** Blah blah blah blah *blah* blah blah. Babble babble babble babble. Blah blah blah blah... *(Keeps moving lips as though she's still talking.)*

**Scott:** *(Talking to himself)* Oh, man... This class is the *pits*. Listen to the teacher babble on!

**Teacher:** Babble *babble* babble...

**Scott:** Oh, well. She's been going for quite a while now. It should be about time for the bell to ring. *(He looks at his watch.)* What? *(Taps watch with finger, looks at it closely, holds it up to his ear, and looks dismayed. Meanwhile, Teacher quietly says, "Blah, blah, blah..." the background.)* I can't believe it. There's still half an hour to go! The teacher's been talking forever! Maybe my watch is broken. Would it be too obvious if I turned around and looked at the clock? *(He stretches, turns, and looks back. A look of disappointment crosses his face. He turns back around.)* Rats!

**Teacher:** Babble babble babble...

**Scott:** Why is it always this way? I can be playing sports, playing a great game, and there's never enough time on the clock to do what I want to do. But put me in a situation like this, and the time just crawls by.

**Teacher:** Blah, blah, blah, blah, blah, blah, blah, blah...

**Scott:** I mean, who cares about any of this junk anyway? *(Looks at watch again, puts head in hands.)* How is it possible that five minutes could feel like 30? It's like I'm trapped in some weird, science fiction time warp or something. *(Dramatically)* Next thing you know I'll be on the cover of some supermarket tabloid. *(Scanning a headline in the air with his fingers)* "Teenager Trapped in High School Classroom for Years." "Boring Lecture Creates Rift in Time: Entire Class in Suspended Animation." *(Laughing)* It sounds like an old *Twilight Zone* episode: *(in a deep voice)* "Submitted for your approval. One teenager named Scott. All was normal that school day until his third-period teacher began to talk and talk, and..."

**Teacher:** Don't you think so, Scott?

**Scott:** *(Startled)* Huh? I mean, yes, ma'am. I would say so. I mean... What was the question?

**Teacher:** I said, don't you think you'd best be leaving, considering class is over and everyone else is gone?

**Scott:** Uh, yeah, sure...Thanks! *(He leaves, looking bewildered.)*

**Teacher:** *(Humming* Twilight Zone *theme)* Doo *doo* doo doo, doo *doo* doo doo.

If you use this skit as a discussion starter, here are possible questions:

■ **According to 2 Peter 3:8-9, why does God sometimes seem to move slowly?**

■ **When has God seemed to have moved slowly in your life?**

■ **In retrospect, do you see a reason why God moved slowly?**

# 2 PETER 3:10-14

## THEME:
Heaven

## SUMMARY:
In this PROJECT, kids will create globes representing the old earth and the new earth after Christ's return.

PREPARATION: You'll need a supply of magazines, two large beach balls, and glue. You'll also need a Bible.

Have someone read aloud 2 Peter 3:10-14. Form two groups and give each group a beach ball. Have one group glue magazine pictures to its beach ball to create a representation of the "old earth" (the world we live in today). Have the other group glue magazine pictures to its beach ball to create a representation of the "new earth" (heaven) as described in the Scripture passage.

When the two globes are finished, have kids describe why they chose the pictures they did to illustrate their globes. Next have someone read 2 Peter 3:10-14 again, then deflate the old-earth ball to illustrate the message of the passage. Place the new-world ball in your youth room as a constant reminder of the promise of a new world upon Christ's return.

# 1 JOHN

*"But if we confess our sins, he will forgive our sins, because we can trust God to do what is right."*

*1 John 1:9a*

# 1 JOHN
## 1:1-4

**THEME:**
A tangible God

**SUMMARY:**
In this CREATIVE READING, kids will look up and read aloud hymns describing God in tangible terms.

PREPARATION: You'll need hymn books and chorus books, Bibles, newsprint, and markers. (*The Group Songbook,* from Group Publishing, is a great resource for familiar and new youth group choruses and songs.)

Form groups of no more than four and give each group a hymn book. Have groups look up songs that describe God using human characteristics. For example, songs that describe God as "looking upon us" or "hearing our cries" depict the human senses of sight and hearing. Have groups each come up with at least three phrases like these and write them together on a large sheet of newsprint.

Then have kids read in unison 1 John 1:1-4, followed by sequentially reading the phrases listed on the newsprint.

After the reading, ask:
■ **Why is seeing God in tangible ways important to people?**
■ **Was it important to the Apostle John?**
■ **How can we experience God in tangible ways?**

To close, have teenagers select a song and sing it as praise to God.

# 1 JOHN
## 1:8-9

**THEME:**
Forgiveness

**SUMMARY:**
Demonstrate God's forgiveness through the cleansing blood of Jesus with this vivid OBJECT LESSON.

PREPARATION: You'll need four pint-sized jars. Fill three with water and one with unscented bleach. Put blue food coloring in the first jar of water, green in the second, and red in the third. Find a white, pure-cotton cloth and tongs. You'll also need a Bible. Be sure to practice this demonstration beforehand.

Display the four jars. Dip one portion of the cloth into the blue liquid to demonstrate sins in our lives that only God knows about. Dip another portion of the cloth into the green liquid to demonstrate sins known both by God and other people. Then dip another area of the cloth into the red liquid to demonstrate sins of omission, such as when we fail to help others.

Hold the stained cloth for everyone to see. Ask:
■ **What happens when we say, "Jesus, forgive me. Take my sins away, wash me white as**

snow, and help me start fresh again, living in you"?

Have a volunteer read aloud 1 John 1:8-9. When the volunteer is finished, swish the cloth in the bleach to demonstrate the cleansing. Close with prayer, thanking God for using his power to wash us clean from the stain of sin.

# 1 JOHN
## 1:8–2:2

**THEME:**
Sin

**SUMMARY:**
In this OBJECT LESSON, kids will confess sins and experience how God forgives our sins.

PREPARATION: You'll need a cardboard crown about three or four inches wide, nails, small slips of paper, and pencils. You'll also need a Bible. This activity is best used while sitting around a campfire or a wood-burning fireplace.

Form a circle and give each person a nail. Say: **I'm going to pass around a cardboard crown, representing Jesus. As you're handed the crown, tell the whole group one sinful thing people do that hurts God. Then puncture the crown from the inside out with your nail and pass the crown to your left. Leave the nails in the crown.**

Encourage kids to be serious and reflective during this activity. When the crown is filled with nails,

collect it and read aloud 1 John 1:8–2:2. Ask:

■ **What does it mean to confess our sins?**

■ **Why is it important to acknowledge when we've done something wrong?**

Give each person a small slip of paper and a pencil. Have kids write a key word that represents a sin they've recently committed and want to confess to God. Pass the nail-covered crown around and have kids attach their slips of paper to it by piercing it with one of the nails.

Collect the crown and close with prayer, asking for forgiveness for the sins represented on the slips of paper. Place the crown in the bonfire or fireplace and have kids silently watch as Jesus takes the punishment for their sins. Afterward, ask:

■ **How does it feel to know that Jesus was the sacrifice for our sins?**

■ **How does it feel to confess our sins?**

■ **How does God make us pure when we confess our sins?**

# 1 JOHN
## 2:9-11

**THEME:**
Living in the light

**SUMMARY:**
In this PROJECT, teenagers will go into the community and replace burned-out light bulbs as a symbol of the light that comes from being a Christian.

PREPARATION: You'll need a large supply of different sizes of light bulbs. Collect these ahead of time from church members who are willing to donate them. Or use youth group funds to purchase light bulbs. You'll also need a flashlight and a Bible.

Meet with kids at the church in a dark room. Using a flashlight, read aloud 1 John 2:9-11. Then ask:

■ **How can we show that we're living in the light?**

■ **What are practical ways to show love to those around us?**

Form "light teams" of no more than four and give kids each a supply of light bulbs. Then send kids out into the community to visit homes and offer to replace burned-out light bulbs for people who need or want them. Tell kids they can actually replace bulbs if offered the opportunity by the resident, but they can also simply give them away.

Encourage kids to leave a handwritten copy of 1 John 2:9-11 at each home as a way of explaining their task. You may also want to have kids leave information about your church.

# 1 JOHN
## 3:1-2

---

**THEME:**
Children of God

**SUMMARY:**
In this CREATIVE READING, kids will describe their family members and be thankful to be called children of God.

---

PREPARATION: Invite kids to bring family photos for this activity. Have kids see how far back they can collect the photos of grandparents, great-grandparents, and so on. You'll also need paper, pencil, and Bibles.

Display the family photos on a table. Have kids spend a few minutes looking at the photos. Next, have kids write the names of as many of their parents, grandparents, and great-grandparents as they can think of within a two-minute time limit. Then form a semicircle around the table. Ask:

■ **What thoughts go through your mind as you look at these pictures and names?**

■ **In what ways are we like the people represented in these pictures and lists of names?**

Say: **As children of our parents, grandparents, great-grandparents, and so on, we reflect the history of our families. But 1 John 3:1-2 tells us that we're also children of God. As we look at these pictures and these names, let's take a moment to reflect on how we're children of**

**God with this creative reading.**

Have kids complete the following reading by filling in the names of their parents, grandparents, and great-grandparents in the appropriate places.

Say: **These family pictures and names remind us of those who've gone before us: our parents** (have kids take turns telling their parents' names), **our grandparents** (have kids tell their grandparents' names), **our great-grandparents** (have kids tell their great-grandparents' names), **and many others** (have kids tell any other names they found that go farther back than great-grandparents).

**While we know that no earthly parents are perfect, we understand the importance of families and of parents' caring for their children.**

**But even more than this, we now say** (have kids read aloud 1 John 3:1-2 ).

**May God grant us the grace to accurately reflect what it means to be a child of God. And may we continually look forward to the day when Christ returns because then we'll truly become like God's Son, Jesus. Amen.**

Close the reading by having volunteers say prayers of thanks for being called God's children.

# 1 JOHN
# 3:16-18

**THEME:**
Loving through actions

**SUMMARY:**
In this PROJECT, kids will give to help others.

PREPARATION: You'll need drivers to help transport kids around the community. Also, collect information from local social-service agencies about needy families in your community. You'll need a Bible.

Have kids go through their rooms at home to find clothing they can give to needy families. Encourage kids to be unselfish in their choices of what they'll give up.

Then have kids go around to church members' homes and collect adult and children's clothing, as well as blankets and food donations.

When you've collected a large supply of items, have kids break into teams and take clothing to the homes you've determined have the greatest need. Encourage kids to stay and talk with the families about what it means to be a Christian.

When kids arrive back at church, read aloud 1 John 3:16-18. Ask:

■ **How have we lived out this passage today?**

■ **How can we live out the**

message of this passage every day?

# 1 JOHN
# 4:20-21

## THEME:
Loving others

## SUMMARY:
In this SKIT, a teenager eating lunch misses the point of what it means to share Christ's love.

## THAT'S WHAT IT'S ALL ABOUT

SCENE: A high school cafeteria.

PROPS: You'll need a table, chairs, a sandwich, chips, and a Bible.

CHARACTERS:
**Alexis**
**Bob**
**Terry**

### SCRIPT

*(Alexis is sitting in the cafeteria nibbling on a sandwich and reading her Bible. Bob walks in, sits down across from her, and begins eating chips—loudly but not purposely so.)*

**Alexis:** *(Looking at Bob, more than a bit annoyed)* Excuse me, but could you eat more quietly? I'm trying to read God's Word.

**Bob:** *(With a mouthful of chips)* Thorry. I didn't realithe I wath dithturbing you.

**Alexis:** Well, you are—and quit spraying those chips all over! Go back to the band room!

**Bob:** *(With an unbelieving look)* Hey! What have I ever done to you?

**Alexis:** Just leave me alone with the Lord, OK?

**Bob:** *(Sarcastically)* OK, Moses! *(He walks away.)*

**Terry:** *(Walking over to Alexis)* You were a little hard on him, weren't you?

**Alexis:** Hard on him? I was trying to study God's Word, and he comes over chomping on his chips and interrupts me. I hate the smell of chips on someone's breath!

**Terry:** Come on, the guy was just trying to be friendly.

**Alexis:** I have enough friends, thank you. God, save me from too many friends!

**Terry:** God save you, all right, but not from that.

**Alexis:** *(Irritated)* What's that supposed to mean?

**Terry:** It means that if you don't have enough heart for someone like Bob, how can you possibly have enough for God? *(Terry and Alexis freeze.)*

If you use this skit as a discussion starter, here are possible questions:

■ **What's the main reason people hate others?**

■ **According to 1 John 4:20-21, why is it impossible for us to love God if we can't love the people around us?**

# 2 JOHN

*"And now, dear lady, this is not a new command but is the same command we have had from the beginning. I ask you that we all love each other."*

*2 John 5*

# 2 JOHN
## 4-6

### THEME:

Loving one another

### SUMMARY:
In this LEARNING GAME, kids toss a ball around a circle and discover that it's sometimes difficult to say what we love about others.

PREPARATION: You'll need a tennis ball, newsprint, and a marker. You'll also need a Bible.

Ask your group to sit in a circle. Explain that you're going to toss a tennis ball to someone across the circle. The receiver is to pick out another person across the circle and toss the ball to him or her. Continue tossing until everyone has had a chance to catch and toss the ball.

Repeat the pattern, catching and tossing to the same people as before. But this time, ask kids to each say one thing they really "love" (basketball, skateboarding, french fries, movies, and so on) before they toss the ball to someone else.

On the third round, repeat the catch-and-toss pattern, this time asking kids to each say one thing they really love about the person they're tossing the ball to (this will probably be much harder than the previous round).

After the game, read aloud 2 John 4-6. Ask:

■ **How did you feel when** someone told you something he or she loved about you?

■ **Why is it easier to talk about things we love than about what we love in others?**

■ **What's one thing we can do in our group to show we love each other?**

Write kids' answers to the last question on newsprint. Then vote on the best idea and do it at each meeting.

# 2 JOHN
## 7-11

### THEME:

False teachings

### SUMMARY:
In this LEARNING GAME, kids try to guess the one person in the group who's lying.

PREPARATION: You'll need a stack of 3×5 cards, one for each person. You'll also need a Bible.

Shuffle a stack of 3×5 cards, one of which is marked with a smiley face. This card is considered the "joker" for the activity. Be sure to shuffle the stack face down so no one can spot the joker card.

As you pass out the cards, tell kids that one of them will get the smiley-face joker. They should not let anyone else see their card. The object of the game is to see how long the joker can keep everyone else from finding out who he or she is.

Each person will get to ask one question of anyone else in the room. No obvious questions such as "Are you the joker?" or "Is your name Steve?" are allowed. The joker must always answer any question with a lie, and everyone else must always tell the truth.

Only "yes" or "no" questions such as "Have you always lived in this town?" "Are you in any of my classes at school?" or "Do you like pizza?" are allowed. Kids must try to guess who the joker is. But here's the catch: The only time kids can guess the joker's identity is just *before* they ask a question. So everyone should listen carefully to what others are saying.

When someone knows, he or she should say, "I know who the joker is" and make a guess before he or she asks a question. If the guess is right, have the group surprise the joker with a pile-on hug. Change the surprise with each round you play (a group back-scratch or lifting the person overhead, for example).

Play a few rounds, then ask a volunteer to read aloud 2 John 7-11. Wrap up the game with these discussion questions:

■ **How is this game like trying to spot false teachers?**

■ **How do you know when a teaching is false?**

■ **What can you do to keep from getting caught off guard by false teachers?**

# 3 JOHN

*"My dear friend, do not follow what is bad;*
*follow what is good."*

*3 John 11a*

# 3 JOHN
## 9-12

### THEME:
Lies

### SUMMARY:
In this DEVOTION, blindfolded kids roam around the room, hearing whispered comments that are both negative and positive.

PREPARATION: You'll need a blindfold for each person. You'll also need a Bible.

EXPERIENCE

Blindfold all group members. Then choose two teenagers to help you and remove their blindfolds. One will act as "Dio," and the other will act as "Dem." Their task is to move around the room, whispering in the ears of other group members. Dio should whisper lies and gossip, such as "You're about to step in a hole" and "Did you hear about so-and-so? It's really juicy! I'll tell you about it later!" Dio should whisper in the left ear of everyone in the room.

Meanwhile, Dem should whisper only positive things, such as "Hang in there!" and "You're the greatest thing that ever happened to this youth group!" Dem should whisper in the right ear of every-one in the room.

Tell the rest of the blindfolded kids they should carefully roam around the room whispering, "Is anyone out there? Does anyone care?" Have them try it a few times to make sure they understand. Tell them that others will be whispering words in their ears. Remind them to keep moving.

Play the game a few minutes or at least until Dio and Dem have whispered to everyone in the room.

RESPONSE

Ask your kids to remove their blindfolds and sit on the floor. Ask:

■ **How did you feel walking blindly around the room?**

■ **How did the negative comments you heard make you feel? What about the positive comments?**

■ **Were you tempted to want more of the juicy gossip? Why or why not?**

CLOSING

Ask a volunteer to read aloud 3 John 9-12. Then wrap up the activity by asking these questions:

■ **What's the major difference between Diotrephes and Demetrius?**

■ **Which one are you more like?**

■ **How can you become more like Demetrius this week?**

# JUDE

*"God is strong and can help you not to fall. He can bring you before his glory without any wrong in you and can give you great joy."*

*Jude 24*

# JUDE
# 3

THEME:
Taking a stand

SUMMARY:
In this SKIT, a guy's family is concerned about a fight he got into, until they realize what he was standing up for.

## LEAVE IT TO WEASEL

SCENE: A typical, middle-class home.

PROPS: You'll need "black eye" makeup, a chair, a newspaper, and a Bible for the discussion afterward.

CHARACTERS:
**Announcer**
**Jane** (Weasel's mom)
**Gord** (Weasel's dad)
**Weasel**
**Ollie** (Weasel's older brother)

SCRIPT
*(The cast is lined up facing the audience.)*
**Announcer:** *(Pretentiously)* And now it's time for "Leave It to Weasel," featuring (insert the actual names of your group members) _____, _____, _____, and _____, as the Weasel!
*(Announcer, Jane, Ollie, and Weasel all exit. Gord takes a seat and begins to read the paper. Jane enters, concerned.)*
**Jane:** Gord, I'm worried about the Weasel.
**Gord:** Hmm? What's that, Jane?

**Jane:** Well, it's awfully late, and he's not home from school yet. And Ollie said he heard Weasel got into trouble at school today.
**Gord:** Probably just the typical mischief a boy Weasel's age seems to get into. I'm sure it's nothing serious. He probably stopped to play with some friends on the way home.
*(Weasel enters and hurries across behind them looking down with a hand covering one eye.)*
**Weasel:** Hi, Mom. Hi, Dad. Well, I better get upstairs and do my homework! *(He starts to leave.)*
**Gord:** Just one minute, young man. You've got some explaining to do to your mother.
**Jane:** Weasel, where have you been? What's wrong with your eye? *(Weasel takes his hand down. He has a black eye.)* Oh, Weasel!
**Gord:** *(Impressed at first)* Wow, what a shiner! I mean, son, you know how your mother and I feel about fighting. You go right to your room.
**Weasel:** But Dad, I . . .
**Gord:** No "but Dads," young man. Get to your room!
**Weasel:** *(Trudging off)* Yes, sir.
**Jane:** Gord, don't you think you were a little hard on the Weasel?
**Gord:** Now, Jane, you know we need to be strict . . .
**Ollie:** *(Entering)* Hi, Mom, Dad. *(Tattling)* Dad, Weasel got into a fight today.
**Gord:** We know, Ollie. What was it about?
**Ollie:** Um, I think it had something to do with cheating.
**Jane:** *(Horrified)* Our Weasel cheating?

**Ollie:** No, Mom—someone wanted to cheat off of him, but he wouldn't let 'em. It was Freddie Rascal's little brother. I guess the Weasel really told him off—said cheating wasn't the way he was raised and that no one who was any good did it. That's what started the fight.

**Gord:** WEASEL!

*(Weasel enters as Jane exits.)*

**Weasel:** *(Fearfully)* Yes, sir?

**Gord:** Ollie told me about your fight. At least you were standing up for what you believed.

**Weasel:** Yes, sir.

**Gord:** You know, when I was a boy...

**Jane:** *(Stepping in briefly)* Boys, wash up. Dinner's ready!

**Weasel and Ollie:** Thanks, Mom!

*(Everyone goes happily off.)*

Permission to photocopy this skit from *Youth Worker's Encyclopedia: NT* granted for local church use. Copyright © Group Publishing, Inc., Box 481, Loveland, CO 80539.

If you use this skit as a discussion starter, here are possible questions:

■ **According to Jude 3, what does it mean to "fight hard for the faith"?**

■ **What's one way you can fight for what's right in your daily life?**

# JUDE
## 3-7

**THEME:**
Heroes

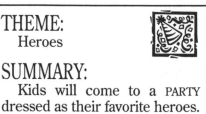

**SUMMARY:**
Kids will come to a PARTY dressed as their favorite heroes.

PREPARATION: When advertising this party, let kids know they're to come as their favorite childhood heroes. Encourage kids to dress up in fun or outrageous costumes that represent these heroes. You'll need hero sandwiches, cassette tapes of songs with hero themes, a cassette player, and a Bible.

During the party, have a humorous lip-sync contest. Use songs with a hero theme such as "Hero," by David Crosby, or "Wind Beneath My Wings," by Bette Midler. Have guys lip-sync the girls' voices and vice versa.

Play a few other games, then serve hero sandwiches as refreshments.

After refreshment time, form a circle. Have kids look closely at each person in the group. Then have teenagers turn and face outside the circle and change one thing about their costumes (unbuttoning one button, removing a watch, turning a collar inside out). Then have kids turn around and see if they can spot all the changes in others' costumes.

Form groups of no more than four and ask:

■ **How easy was it to spot the**

changes in our costumes?

■ **How is this like or unlike how easy it is to spot negative traits in heroes?**

Have someone read aloud Jude 3-7. Ask:

■ **What warnings does this passage give us that could apply to heroes?**

■ **Why do so many real-life heroes fail?**

■ **What are the dangers of looking for role models in our heroes today?**

■ **Who are some appropriate heroes for us to admire?**

# JUDE
## 17-21

**THEME:**
Perseverance

**SUMMARY:**
In this LEARNING GAME, kids will attempt to finish a series of crazy games.

PREPARATION: Plan to have this event in a fellowship hall, gymnasium, or outdoors (during good weather). You'll need a few 3×5 cards, a Bible, and chairs.

Lead your kids in the following silly exercises to test their endurance. Have kids perform each activity for at least 15 seconds. Follow each activity immediately with the next one from the list. If your kids seem like they can keep going after you've used up the

activities, repeat those you liked best (or make up your own).

■ Have kids hop on one foot while turning clockwise.

■ Have kids flap their arms like a chicken while squatting up and down.

■ Without using chairs, have kids "sit" as if they were in invisible chairs by bending their knees and pressing their backs against the wall for 60 seconds.

■ Have kids balance hymns book on their heads and walk as quickly as they can around the room while clapping their hands. If someone's hymn book falls, he or she must start over.

■ Have kids run around a chair backwards, clapping their hands and barking like a dog.

■ Have kids sing "Row, Row, Row Your Boat" three times while balancing on one leg.

After the activities, have kids collapse in a circle for a brief discussion. Ask:

■ **What was it like to keep up with all these activities?**

■ **What role did endurance or perseverance play in this game?**

■ **How could you build better endurance for a game like this?**

Read aloud Jude 17-21. Ask:

■ **How is the game we played like the ups and downs we face in everyday life?**

■ **Why is it important to persevere in our faith the way Jude describes?**

■ **What are ways we can build our spiritual endurance this week?**

# JUDE
# 24-25

**THEME:**
Leaning on God

**SUMMARY:**
In this OBJECT LESSON, kids will attempt to fall to the ground without crashing.

PREPARATION: You'll need a Bible and enough pillows for everyone to have one.

Have everyone stand an arm's length apart, with a pillow behind each person. Tell kids to place their feet together and their hands at their sides.

Say: **The object of this activity is to sit gently on the ground without crashing. You may not move your feet or use your hands. Ready? Go.**

Most group members will probably fall on the way to the floor or at least have a little "thud" at the end.

After everyone is seated on his or her pillow, congratulate kids for their efforts, then form pairs and repeat the activity. This time, have partners stand back to back as they attempt to sit down. For most, having a partner will make sitting down much easier.

After pairs have attempted this activity, repeat it one more time. This time, have partners sit back to back and lock arms as they attempt to sit.

Next, form a circle. Ask:

■ **Why was it difficult to sit without falling the first time?**

■ **How did you improve during the second and third attempts?**

Have someone read aloud Jude 24-25. Then finish the activity and debriefing by asking:

■ **What are ways we fall in everyday life?**

■ **How is the way your partner kept you from falling like or unlike the way God can keep us from falling?**

■ **How can we lean on God when we feel like we're about to fall in life?**

# REVELATION

*"Here I am! I stand at the door and knock. If you hear my voice and open the door, I will come in and eat with you, and you will eat with me."*

*Revelation 3:20*

# REVELATION
# 3:15-16

**THEME:**
Lukewarm faith

**SUMMARY:**
In this DEVOTION, kids will answer questions and discuss how important it is to be on fire for God.

PREPARATION: Hang three signs on the wall at one end of your meeting room: "Hot (Yes)," "Warm (Maybe)," and "Cold (No)." Spread the signs evenly apart, with "Warm" in the middle.

EXPERIENCE
Explain that you're going to ask the group a few questions. After hearing each question, teenagers are to sit or stand beneath the sign that best describes their answer to that particular question. Have kids explain why they responded the way they did. Then move on to the next question. Ask:
■ Is it OK to play basketball with friends instead of attending church?
■ Is it OK to attend parties where you know alcohol will be served?
■ Is it OK to work every day of the week?
■ Is it OK to disobey your parents?
■ Is it ever OK to kill someone?
■ Is it right to have sex before marriage?
■ Is stealing OK?
■ Is it right to hide the truth or to lie?

RESPONSE
After discussing the questions, read Revelation 3:15-16. Ask:
■ Why is it easy to choose the middle ground with difficult questions?
■ In light of this passage, how should we respond to questions that affect our faith lifestyle?
■ What does it mean to be "hot" or "cold" for God?
■ Why does God hate lukewarm Christians?
■ How do we hurt others when we're indifferent?

CLOSING
Close with a time of commitment, encouraging teenagers to "turn up the heat" in their faith during the week.

# REVELATION
# 3:15-16

**THEME:**
Lukewarm faith

**SUMMARY:**
In this OBJECT LESSON, kids will compare lukewarm soft drinks to people with lukewarm faith.

PREPARATION: Gather two cups per person, ice, and room-temperature soft drinks. You'll also need blindfolds and a Bible.

For each person, fill one cup with the room-temperature soft drink and another cup with ice and soft drink. Blindfold kids and have them each take a taste from both cups to see which they prefer. Afterward, ask:

■ **Which soft drink did you like? Why?**

■ **What's wrong with the lukewarm soft drink?**

Have a volunteer read aloud Revelation 3:15-16. Ask:

■ **How is a lukewarm soft drink like a person with lukewarm faith?**

■ **Why does God prefer someone totally turned off to him rather than someone who is lukewarm to him?**

■ **How would you describe a lukewarm Christian?**

Finish by saying: **Cold people understand that they're far from God, so they're more apt to come to God wholeheartedly. Lukewarm people think they're OK because "at least they're doing something good." Think about your actions. Do they show that you're lukewarm, cold, or on fire for God?**

# REVELATION 3:19-20

THEME:
Beginning a relationship with God

## SUMMARY:
In this DEVOTION, kids will see how easy it is to become deaf to God's voice.

PREPARATION: For each teenager, you'll need two pieces of play money and a pencil. You'll also need two real dollar bills and a Bible.

EXPERIENCE

Give each person two pieces of play money and a pencil. On one side of the play money, have kids write three to five things they enjoy (music, movies, being with a girlfriend, skateboarding, and so on).

When kids are finished writing, say: **Cover your ears with the play money, blocking out as much sound as possible. On the signal, start singing: "Row, Row, Row Your Boat" as loudly as you can. Ready? Go!**

As kids are singing, face away from the kids and quietly say: **I'll trade two real dollar bills for any two fake ones. All you have to do is come up and get them.** No one should be able to understand you, but if someone does, go ahead and trade with him or her. After a couple of minutes, get kids' attention and have them stop singing.

## RESPONSE

Explain the deal you were willing to give while kids were singing. Then ask:

■ **Could anyone hear what I was saying? Why or why not?**

■ **How did you feel when you found out I was willing to trade real money for fake?**

Have someone read Revelation 3:19-20. Ask:

■ **What kinds of things block us from hearing God's invitation?**

■ **What can we do to unblock our ears and hear God?**

Form a circle and have kids set their fake money on the floor. Start knocking softly on the door (or floor) and read Revelation 3:19-20 again. Say: **Before we can grow in faith, we must hear God's knock.**

## CLOSING

Have kids look at things they wrote on their play money. Have kid pray silently that the items listed on their money won't cause them to become deaf to God's voice.

# REVELATION
# 3:20

**THEME:**
Responding to Christ's call

**SUMMARY:**
In this SKIT, a teenager is so overwhelmed by all the influences in his life that he can't hear Jesus knocking on the door.

# SOMEONE'S KNOCKING

SCENE: A bare room with a chair in the middle.

PROPS: You'll need a piece of paper, a chair, a cassette player, and a rowdy-sounding heavy-metal cassette. You'll also need a Bible for the discussion afterward.

CHARACTERS:
**Chris**
**Mom**
**TV Announcer**
**Jean**

### SCRIPT

*(Chris sits center stage in a chair and looks woefully at a piece of paper. The other characters stand behind Chris with their heads bowed, only coming to life when it's their turn to speak.)*

**Chris:** Oh, man... Look at these midterm reports! Mom's gonna hit the roof!

**Mom:** *(Wagging her finger at Chris)* What is the meaning of this? I'll tell you what—if these grades don't come up by end of semester, there'll be no more going out, and no more TV! It'll be study, study, study! You better believe it! *(She bows her head when done.)*

**Chris:** *(Frustrated, doesn't know what to do)* I've gotta get my mind off of this. Maybe there's something good on the tube. *(Chris reaches forward and pretends to turn on the TV.)*

**TV Announcer:** *(Smiling absurdly the whole time)* And now it's time for "Those Crazy Kids!"—the wacky new show about the chaos that's caused when a couple of professional carpet installers inherit a working goat farm! Today's episode: "That Spot's Never Going to Come Out!" *(Bows head.)*

**Mom:** *(Interrupting)* No more TV! Study, study, study! *(Bows head.)*

**Chris:** *(Puts hands over ears.)* I should call Jean. She always seems to have it together.

**Jean:** Yeah, you should call me. We should get together. You need to relax, and I've got just the thing to help you. And it comes in your choice of colors—red or black label! *(Bows head.)*

**TV Announcer:** *(Making goat sounds)* Baa, baa, baa... *(Talking like a husband)* Honey, open the gate please! *(Bows head.)*

**Mom:** Get those grades up or you're grounded! Do you hear me? Grounded! *(Bows head.)*

**Jean:** Come on—just take a shot. It'll do you good! Relax you! *(Bows head.)*

**Chris:** *(Shakes head as if to clear it.)* If I can just make it through to summer. Then the guys and I can practice and maybe get good enough to play a few gigs. Anything to relieve some of this stress! *(Turns on the tape player with the volume fairly loud.)*

*(At this point, all of the other characters look up and read the lines below simultaneously, repeating desired portions for effect. As the lines are spoken, a knocking begins offstage, growing louder until the lines are finished, then knocking clearly three more times.)*

**Mom:** Stop banging away on those drums! I didn't pay for three years of music lessons for you to play that kind of junk! I don't know how you have time to practice when you should be studying! Remember—those grades had better come up, or you'll be spending your summer at school!

**TV Announcer:** *(As a husband)* Honey, did you feed the herd? *(As a wife)* No, dear. I thought you did! *(As a husband)* Well, if you didn't feed them, and I didn't feed them, then what are they eating? *(As goats)* Baa, baa, baa! *(As a wife)* Oh, no! It's that roll of shag we were going to install tomorrow afternoon! *(As a husband)* Aargh!

**Jean:** Just a little alcohol won't hurt you. I drink it all the time, and it's never hurt me! If that doesn't do much for you, I've also got some other stuff I've been saving for a special occasion. Everybody's got to have something to help them relax— some things just work a little better and faster than others, that's all.

*(Chris clamps his hands over his ears during the above. When they are finished, a knock is heard.)*

**Chris:** *(Goes to an imaginary door and opens it.)* Oh, good. You're here. I was hoping it was you.

If you use this skit as a discussion starter, here are possible questions:

■ **Why is it sometimes hard to hear God "knocking on our door"?**

■ **According to Revelation 3:20, what will Jesus do if we open the door? What does that mean?**

# REVELATION 4:1-11

**THEME:**
Heaven

**SUMMARY:**
In this PROJECT, kids will create a model of the throne in heaven to illustrate Revelation 4:1-11.

PREPARATION: You'll need modeling clay, "trick" candles (the kind that aren't easily blown out), matches, and other easily obtainable craft supplies. You'll also need a Bible.

Form groups of no more than five and have groups sit around tables. Place modeling clay (and other craft supplies) on each table. Explain to teenagers that they are going to construct a throne scene to illustrate Revelation 4:1-11.

Read the passage carefully beforehand, highlighting items that are to be constructed. Then assign different sections of the Scripture to each group. Have those groups create the items referred to in that passage.

Some of the items groups might create include: a throne, someone seated on the throne, a rainbow, 24 small thrones, people seated on the smaller thrones, white robes, crowns of gold, lightning, seven lamps, a sea of glass, four creatures (a lion, a calf, a man, and a flying eagle).

Encourage groups to be as creative as possible in building their assigned figures. After 20 to 30 minutes, have groups assemble the finished throne scene and place it on one of the tables. Then ask:

■ **How did working on this project help you understand the Scripture passage?**

■ **How would you compare your finished throne scene to what's waiting for us in heaven?**

■ **What would you like to know about heaven?**

■ **What do you know about heaven that you'd like to tell someone else?**

■ **How do you feel knowing you'll never fully understand what heaven will be like until you get there? Explain.**

Place the seven trick candles around the scene. If kids created the seven lamps, place the candles in these and light them. Have someone turn out the lights as you read Revelation 4:1-11 by candlelight to close. If it's appropriate, display the model in your church foyer for a month or so as a tool to help church members think about the heaven that awaits them.

# REVELATION 5:11-13

**THEME:**
Worship

**SUMMARY:**
In this MUSIC IDEA, kids write new words to familiar songs to express the message of Revelation 5:11-13.

PREPARATION: You'll need Bibles, hymn and chorus books, paper, and pencils.

Form groups of no more than three. Make sure each group has a Bible, paper, pencils, and access to hymn and chorus books. Have someone read aloud Revelation 5:11-13.

Say: **Each group is going to write new words to a familiar tune, using this Scripture passage as a guide. Use the hymn and chorus books to find a song everyone will know.**

Examples of some popular songs that most people know are "I Love You, Lord," "Awesome God," "Open Our Eyes," "Joy to the World," "Silent Night," and "O Come, All Ye Faithful." Tell kids they may also choose familiar children's songs, such as "Three Blind Mice," "Hickory, Dickory, Dock," and so on.

Have groups base their new worship songs on the message of Revelation 5:11-13, focusing on verse 12. After about 15 minutes, ask groups to share their new "hit songs" by singing them. Have other kids sing along if groups are uncomfortable singing alone. Ask:

■ **How can we make our lives a "worship song" for God this week?**

Encourage kids to follow through on their ideas.

Close by having kids sing "Glory and Praise to Our God" (in *The Group Songbook,* from Group Publishing) or another familiar worship song.

# REVELATION 12:1-9

**THEME:**
Spiritual warfare

**SUMMARY:**
Kids will participate in a RETREAT based on a "boot camp" theme as they explore the meaning of Revelation 12:1-9.

PREPARATION: When you advertise this event, let kids know they'll be coming to train for the spiritual battles that lie ahead in their lives. Gather supplies as needed for the activities you choose. You'll also need Bibles.

Hold a retreat to help teenagers explore Revelation 12:1-9 and the idea of spiritual warfare. Try any or all of the following activities during the retreat:

● **Let the Banner Wave—** Have teenagers create a banner or flag based on Revelation 12:9. Display the banner in your meeting room.

● **War Zones**—Focus at least one group discussion on Revelation 12:1-9. Have kids discuss the following questions:

■ **What battles do you face at school? home? church? among friends?**

■ **What can we learn from the battle described in Revelation 12:1-9 to help us in our own spiritual battles?**

■ **What is the message of Revelation 12:1-9?**

● **Misdirection Trap**—Choose three volunteers. Blindfold one and have the other two serve as "voices" who will verbally lead this person through a human maze. Then have the rest of the group form a human maze by positioning themselves around the room. Have the voices direct the blindfolded teenager from one side of the room to the other without hitting any other person. Before beginning, secretly tell one of the voices to misdirect the blindfolded person. Repeat this activity with different volunteers. Then discuss who the different voices in this game represent in real life.

Play plenty of competitive games (such as Capture the Flag or sports competitions) and have kids explore how the games are like or unlike the real battles they face in life.

Close the retreat by having kids devise a "battle plan" consisting of a specific list of things they'll do in the coming weeks to grow closer to God and prepare their hearts for difficult times.

# REVELATION 15:1-4

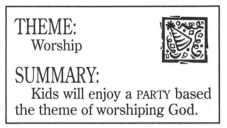

**THEME:**
Worship

**SUMMARY:**
Kids will enjoy a PARTY based the theme of worshiping God.

PREPARATION: Send invitations to this party on pure white paper and encourage kids to attend wearing white clothes. Gather supplies as needed for the activities you choose. You'll need Bibles.

Use the following ideas to enliven a party based on Revelation 15:1-4. At the beginning of the party, have someone read aloud the passage.

Play games such as the ones that follow to help bring the Scripture passage to life in fun ways:

● **What Is It?**—Play recorded excerpts of several instruments (such as a trumpet, drums, a saxophone, and a flute). Hold a contest to see who can identify all of the instruments. Award a plastic harmonica to the winner.

● **Musical Split**—Form groups of three to five by giving each person a slip of paper on which you've written the name of a Christmas song (such as "Away in a Manger," "Jingle Bells," "The First Noel," or "Joy to the World"). You'll need three to five slips for each song title. On "go," have kids read their slips and form groups by singing their songs loudly and finding others with the same song. Then have these groups discuss Revelation 15:3. Ask:

■ **What song might you sing in the presence of God?**

■ **Why is music so often used to worship God?**

■ **How can we worship God more fully today?**

● **Pure Worship**—Form groups of no more than five. Have groups each come up with one way to worship God in a pure and holy way. For example, a group might choose to sing a hymn a cappella while kneeling. Then have small groups take turns leading the rest of the group in a worship experience. Remind kids to make this a sincere time of worship, like that described in the Scripture passage.

# REVELATION 20:11-15

**THEME:**
God's judgment

**SUMMARY:**
Kids will act out a SKIT illustrating God's judgment of sinners.

## MALL JUDGMENT

SCENE: Two girls, one a Christian and one a non-Christian, are shopping in a local mall.

PROPS: You'll need an oversize jacket (for Mannequin #1), a wild-colored jacket (for Mannequin #2), chocolate chip cookies (for the Cookie-Store Clerk to hold), and a white robe (for the Angel to wear). You'll also need a Bible for the discussion afterward.

CHARACTERS:
**Non-Christian** (girl)
**Christian** (girl)
**Mannequin #1**
**Mannequin #2**
**Cookie-Store Clerk**
**Angel**
**God** (an offstage voice)

SCRIPT

*(Have the Mannequins and the Cookie-Store Clerk stand in a line, facing the audience. The Mannequins must stand still during the whole skit. The skit begins with the Christian and Non-Christian looking at the Mannequins and discussing the clothes.)*

**Christian:** What about that jacket? *(Pointing to Mannequin #1)* I think Ben would love that jacket.

**Non-Christian:** *(Looking at the jacket)* I don't know. I mean, it does look nice, and I do want to get Ben something to wear this year... but... I just can't make up my mind. Everything is so expensive.

**Christian:** *(Moves over to Mannequin #2.)* What about this one? I know it's a little wild, but Ben does like to make a statement, y'know. And *(looking at price tag)* it's a great price, too! What do you think?

**Non-Christian:** *(Looking closely at Mannequin #2's jacket)* It is kinda different, isn't it? *(Pauses.)* Y'know, I think I like it, but I'm just not sure I'm ready to make up my mind.

*(They continue to look at the jack-*

*ets.)*

**Christian:** Have you thought any more about what we talked about last Wednesday?

**Non-Christian:** You mean about Jesus and all that?

**Christian:** *(Smiling)* Yeah, Jesus and all that.

**Non-Christian:** Yeah, I've thought about it. But I'm just not sure this Christianity thing is for me. I mean, it fits you well, but I'm just not sure...

**Christian:** If you still have some questions, I'd love to...

**Non-Christian:** *(Interrupting)* It's not that, it's just that I'm not sure I want to make any commitments right now. I've got plenty of time to think about those things. And besides, I'm hungry.

*(Both walk over to the Cookie-Store Clerk and buy chocolate chip cookies.)*

**Christian:** I don't mean to beat you over the head with this issue, but you never know when your time is going to come.

**Non-Christian:** My "time"?

**Christian:** You know—when you'll die.

**Non-Christian:** *(Surprised)* Don't get so morbid on me. I'm just not sure if Christianity is my kind of thing.

*(Non-Christian bites into her cookie, begins to choke, then falls to the floor dead. Rest of the cast turns and faces away from the audience. The Angel enters from stage right and goes over to the Non-Christian. The Angel helps her up and walks her to center stage, facing the audience.)*

**Angel:** *(Looking skyward)* Here's

another one. She was a good-natured girl who went to church once in a while with one of your most faithful servants.

**God:** *(Offstage)* Well, young lady, did you choose to follow me?

**Non-Christian:** Well... Thought I'd have more time... I just couldn't make up my mind...

**God:** I'm sorry, but I can.

*(Everyone freezes.)*

If you use this skit as a discussion starter, here are possible questions:

■ **What thoughts come to your mind after watching this skit?**

■ **Read Revelation 20:11-15. What do you think God's final judgment will be like?**

■ **How does a person get his or her name "written in the book of life"? How do you know whether or not it's too late for you?**

# REVELATION 22:12-17

## THEME:
God's reward

## SUMMARY:
In this LEARNING GAME, kids will run an easy or difficult relay race and explore how the path of faith is a difficult one.

PREPARATION: Set up half of your meeting room as a "straight-shot" race track from one end to the other, with no obstacles along the way. Set up the other half as an obstacle course, placing chairs, tables, and other items in the race path. Make sure each race path is wide enough to accommodate two runners at a time. You'll need snack rewards and a Bible.

Form teams of no more than four. Explain that each team will run a relay race to the other side of the room, using either the straight-shot track or the obstacle course. Tell kids that only one member from each team may run a course at a time, although both runners may run the same course at the same time, if they choose. Explain that you'll be outside the room and unable to see who runs which course.

Leave the room and have kids run the relay. Ask kids to use the "honor system" to determine the winner (the team that gets all its members across the room in the quickest time).

When the races are finished, come back into the room. Have kids each tell which track they ran. Have those who ran the straight track sit on your left, and those who ran the obstacle course sit on your right. Give those on your right a reward, such as a piece of bubble gum, candy, or a soft drink.

Read Revelation 22:12-17. Then wrap up the experience by asking:

■ **How is the way I gave rewards like or unlike the way God rewards people?**

■ **How are your choices in this race like or unlike the faith choices you make as you follow Christ?**

■ **Why is Christianity a difficult path to run?**

■ **How does Jesus invite you to "come" and follow his path to God's eternal reward?**

■ **How can we better prepare for the obstacles in our path?**

# REVELATION 22:20-21

## THEME:
Jesus' return

## SUMMARY:
For this CREATIVE READING/CREATIVE PRAYER, kids will create an impromptu poem, asking Jesus to come soon.

PREPARATION: You'll need paper and pencils. You'll also need a Bible.

Have someone read aloud Revelation 22:20-21. Then form groups of no more than three and distribute paper and pencils to each group.

Next, give groups two minutes to discuss this question:

■ **Why would it be good for Jesus to return today?** (Tell kids their answers can be based on either personal reasons or more global reasons.)

After two minutes, tell groups to use their answers to the question to create a two- to four-line poem about why it would be good for Jesus to return today. For example, kids might write:

"If Jesus Christ returned today,
he'd wipe out sin and hate,
and stay
forever bringing love our way."

When groups are ready, have kids all kneel together in a circle. Say: **Let's take turns reading our group poems as a prayer to God. After each group is finished with its poem, let's all repeat in unison, "Amen. Come, Lord Jesus."**

Have groups read aloud their poems one at a time. Close the prayer with the final repetition of "Amen. Come, Lord Jesus."

# NEW TESTAMENT SCRIPTURE INDEX

Matthew 1:1-17 (p. 9)
Matthew 1:18-23 (p. 10)
Matthew 2:1-12 (p. 10)
Matthew 2:1-18 (p. 12)
Matthew 3:1-12 (p. 13)
Matthew 4:1-11 (p. 14)
Matthew 4:17-22 (p. 15)
Matthew 5:1-12 (p. 16)
Matthew 5:3-12 (p. 17)
Matthew 5:4 (p. 17)
Matthew 5:9-12, 21-22, 38-48 (p. 18)
Matthew 5:13 (p. 19)
Matthew 5:14-16 (p. 20)
Matthew 5:27-28 (p. 21)
Matthew 5:38-42 (p. 22)
Matthew 6:19-21 (p. 23)
Matthew 6:25-34 (p. 24)
Matthew 6:28-34 (p. 25)
Matthew 7:13-14 (p. 26)
Matthew 7:24-29 (p. 27)
Matthew 8:18-20 (p. 28)
Matthew 9:9-13 (p. 29)
Matthew 10:39 (p. 30)
Matthew 11:28-30 (p. 31)
Matthew 13:1-23 (p. 31)
Matthew 14:22-33 (p. 32, 33)
Matthew 15:1-20 (p. 34)
Matthew 16:24-26 (p. 35)
Matthew 17:1-13 (p. 35)
Matthew 18:1-5 (p. 36)
Matthew 18:15-17 (p. 37)
Matthew 18:19-20 (p. 37)
Matthew 18:21-35 (p. 38)
Matthew 19:16-30 (p. 39)
Matthew 20:25-28 (p. 39)
Matthew 21:1-11 (p. 40)
Matthew 22:34-40 (p. 42)
Matthew 24 (p. 42)
Matthew 24:36-44 (p. 43)
Matthew 25:14-30 (p. 44, 45)
Matthew 25:31-46 (p. 46, 47)
Matthew 26:17-30 (p. 48)
Matthew 26:17-46 (p. 49)
Matthew 26:47–28:15 (p. 49)
Matthew 27:32–28:7 (p. 52)
Matthew 27:62–28:15 (p. 53)
Matthew 28:1-7 (p. 55)
Matthew 28:18-20 (p. 59)

Mark 1:9-11 (p. 63)

Mark 1:9-13 (p. 63)
Mark 2:1-12 (p. 64)
Mark 2:13-17 (p. 65)
Mark 2:15-17 (p. 66)
Mark 3:31-35 (p. 67)
Mark 4:1-9, 13-20 (p. 67, 68)
Mark 6:1-6 (p. 69)
Mark 6:7-13 (p. 69)
Mark 6:30-44 (p. 72)
Mark 6:32-34 (p. 74)
Mark 6:32-44 (p. 74)
Mark 6:45-51 (p. 75)
Mark 7:1-13 (p. 76)
Mark 7:14-23 (p. 78)
Mark 8:27-30 (p. 78)
Mark 9:1-8 (p. 79)
Mark 9:33-37 (p. 80)
Mark 10:17-27 (p. 80)
Mark 10:17-31 (p. 82)
Mark 12:41-44 (p. 83)
Mark 14:32-40 (p. 84)
Mark 15:15-32 (p. 84)
Mark 15:21 (p. 86)
Mark 16:1-8 (p. 87)

Luke 1:26–2:20 (p. 91)
Luke 2:7 (p. 92)
Luke 2:21-40 (p. 92)
Luke 4:1-13 (p. 93)
Luke 4:31-35 (p. 94)
Luke 6:17-49 (p. 94)
Luke 6:27-31 (p. 95)
Luke 6:43-45 (p. 96)
Luke 6:46-49 (p. 97, 98)
Luke 8:16-18 (p. 98)
Luke 8:22-25 (p. 99)
Luke 8:26-39 (p. 100)
Luke 9:46-48 (p. 101)
Luke 9:57-62 (p. 102)
Luke 10:30-37 (p. 102, 103)
Luke 11:33-36 (p. 104)
Luke 11:37-41 (p. 104)
Luke 12:13-21 (p. 105)
Luke 12:35-40 (p. 108)
Luke 13:18-30 (p. 109)
Luke 14:15-24 (p. 110)
Luke 15:1-10 (p. 111)
Luke 15:11-32 (p. 112, 113)
Luke 16:1-12 (p. 116)
Luke 17:11-19 (p. 116, 117)

Luke 18:9-14 (p. 117)
Luke 19:1-10 (p. 118)
Luke 21:1-4 (p. 119)
Luke 21:5-38 (p. 120)
Luke 22:39-46 (p. 121)
Luke 24:13-35 (p. 122, 123)

John 1:1-5, 14 (p. 127)
John 1:35-51 (p. 127)
John 3:1-10 (p. 128)
John 3:16 (p. 129)
John 3:16-18 (p. 130)
John 4:1-26 (p. 131)
John 4:4-26 (p. 132)
John 6:1-13 (p. 133)
John 7:25-32, 45-49 (p. 134)
John 8:1-11 (p. 134, 135)
John 8:12 (p. 137)
John 8:31-36 (p. 137)
John 9:1-34 (p. 138)
John 10:10 (p. 139)
John 11:1-43 (p. 140)
John 11:1-44 (p. 140)
John 12:1-11 (p. 141)
John 12:12-19 (p. 142)
John 12:20-26 (p. 143)
John 13:1-17 (p. 143, 144, 145)
John 13:31-35 (p. 146)
John 14:1-4 (p. 146)
John 14:6 (p. 147, 148)
John 14:7-14 (p. 149)
John 14:15-24 (p. 150)
John 14:26-27 (p. 151)
John 15:1-4 (p. 151)
John 15:5-11 (p. 152)
John 15:10-11; 16:24 (p. 153)
John 15:12-16 (p. 154)
John 15:12-17 (p. 155)
John 15:13 (p. 156)
John 16:32-33 (p. 157)
John 17:20-23 (p. 158)
John 18:15-18, 25-27 (p. 158)
John 19:1–20:18 (p. 158)
John 20:11-18 (p. 161)
John 20:24-29 (p. 162)
John 21:15-17 (p. 163)

Acts 1:7-14 (p. 167)
Acts 2:5-13 (p. 167)
Acts 3:1-10 (p. 168)
Acts 3:17-26 (p. 169)
Acts 4:1-21 (p. 170)

Acts 4:32-35 (p. 171)
Acts 4:32-37; 9:23-27; 11:22-30 (p. 172)
Acts 5:1-11 (p. 172)
Acts 6:8-15; 7:51–8:1 (p. 173)
Acts 7:51-60 (p. 174)
Acts 7:54–8:1 (p. 175)
Acts 8:1-8 (p. 176)
Acts 10:9-16, 34-36 (p. 177)
Acts 13:46-52 (p. 178)
Acts 15:1-2, 22-31 (p. 179)
Acts 16:16-35 (p. 180)
Acts 17:16-34 (p. 181)
Acts 18:24-26 (p. 182)
Acts 19:11-20 (p. 183)
Acts 20:17-24 (p. 184)
Acts 21:39–22:16 (p. 185)
Acts 24:5-16 (p. 186)
Acts 26:8 (p. 187)

Romans 1:16-17 (p. 191)
Romans 2:1-3 (p. 192)
Romans 3:21-28 (p. 193)
Romans 3:23-24; 6:23 (p. 194)
Romans 4:4-6 (p. 195)
Romans 5:1-5 (p. 196)
Romans 5:6-11 (p. 197)
Romans 6:8-14 (p. 198)
Romans 7:7 (p. 199)
Romans 8:22-25 (p. 201)
Romans 8:26-27 (p. 202)
Romans 8:28 (p. 202, 203)
Romans 8:31-39 (p. 203, 204)
Romans 10:11-15 (p. 205)
Romans 12 (p. 205)
Romans 12:1-2 (p. 206)
Romans 12:1-8 (p. 207)
Romans 12:4-8 (p. 208)
Romans 12:9-21 (p. 209)
Romans 16:1-16 (p. 210)

1 Corinthians 1:18-31 (p. 213)
1 Corinthians 2:11-16 (p. 214)
1 Corinthians 3:5 (p. 214)
1 Corinthians 3:10-15 (p. 216)
1 Corinthians 3:16-17 (p. 217)
1 Corinthians 4:6-8 (p. 218)
1 Corinthians 6:12-20 (p. 218)
1 Corinthians 8:4-13 (p. 219)
1 Corinthians 9:19-23 (p. 220)
1 Corinthians 9:24-27 (p. 221)
1 Corinthians 10:12-13 (p. 221, 222)
1 Corinthians 10:23-24 (p. 223)

1 Corinthians 12:4-11 (p. 224)
1 Corinthians 12:12-27 (p. 225, 226)
1 Corinthians 12:12-31 (p. 226)
1 Corinthians 13 (p. 228)
1 Corinthians 15:50-57 (p. 229)
1 Corinthians 16:13-14 (p. 229)

2 Corinthians 1:3-11 (p. 233)
2 Corinthians 3:4-6 (p. 234)
2 Corinthians 4 (p. 234)
2 Corinthians 4:1-2 (p. 235)
2 Corinthians 4:5-7 (p. 236)
2 Corinthians 4:7-11 (p. 237)
2 Corinthians 5:6-9 (p. 238)
2 Corinthians 5:7 (p. 238)
2 Corinthians 5:17 (p. 239)
2 Corinthians 8:2-5 (p. 240)
2 Corinthians 9:6-8 (p. 241, 242)
2 Corinthians 10:3-5 (p. 242)
2 Corinthians 13:5 (p. 243)

Galatians 2:16-20 (p. 247)
Galatians 3:3-4 (p. 247)
Galatians 4:1-7 (p. 248)
Galatians 5:13 (p. 249)
Galatians 5:13-15 (p. 251)
Galatians 5:22-23 (p. 251, 252)
Galatians 5:22-26 (p. 253)
Galatians 6:9 (p. 254)

Ephesians 2:1-9 (p. 257)
Ephesians 2:8-9 (p. 258)
Ephesians 3:14-21 (p. 259)
Ephesians 4:2-6 (p. 261)
Ephesians 4:25–5:2 (p. 261)
Ephesians 4:29-32 (p. 262, 263)
Ephesians 6:1-3 (p. 264)
Ephesians 6:1-4 (p. 265)
Ephesians 6:10-11 (p. 265)
Ephesians 6:10-18 (p. 267)
Ephesians 6:11-17 (p. 267)
Ephesians 6:14-17 (p. 268)

Philippians 1:3-6 (p. 271)
Philippians 2:1-8 (p. 271)
Philippians 2:1-11 (p. 273)
Philippians 3:12-14 (p. 274)
Philippians 4:1-7 (p. 275)
Philippians 4:4-9 (p. 276)
Philippians 4:10-13, 19 (p. 277)

Colossians 1:15-20 (p. 281)
Colossians 2:6-8 (p. 281, 282)

Colossians 3:1-4 (p. 284)
Colossians 3:12-14, 17 (p. 285)
Colossians 3:18-21 (p. 285)

1 Thessalonians 1:2-10 (p. 291)
1 Thessalonians 2:13–3:8 (p. 292)
1 Thessalonians 3:12-13 (p. 292)
1 Thessalonians 4:3-8 (p. 293, 294)
1 Thessalonians 4:11-12 (p. 295)
1 Thessalonians 5:16-18 (p. 296)

2 Thessalonians 1:3-4 (p. 299)
2 Thessalonians 2:1-4 (p. 299)
2 Thessalonians 2:1-17 (p. 301)
2 Thessalonians 2:15–3:5 (p. 301)

1 Timothy 1:3-11 (p. 305)
1 Timothy 1:12-17 (p. 305)
1 Timothy 2:1-8 (p. 306)
1 Timothy 3:1-13 (p. 307)
1 Timothy 4:12 (p. 307, 309)
1 Timothy 6:6-12 (p. 309)
1 Timothy 6:7-10 (p. 310)

2 Timothy 1:7-14 (p. 315)
2 Timothy 2:1-7 (p. 315)
2 Timothy 2:1-26 (p. 317)
2 Timothy 3:1–4:5 (p. 317)
2 Timothy 4:6-8 (p. 318)

Titus 1:5-9 (p. 321)
Titus 2:11-15 (p. 321)

Philemon 8-21 (p. 325)

Hebrews 1:1-4 (p. 329)
Hebrews 3:12-15 (p. 329)
Hebrews 4:1-10 (p. 330)
Hebrews 4:11-13 (p. 331)
Hebrews 4:14-16 (p. 331)
Hebrews 5:11–6:3 (p. 332)
Hebrews 8:7-13 (p. 333)
Hebrews 9:24-28 (p. 334)
Hebrews 11:1 (p. 334)
Hebrews 11:13, 16a (p. 335)
Hebrews 12:1-2 (p. 336)
Hebrews 12:1-3 (p. 337)
Hebrews 12:28-29 (p. 338, 339)
Hebrews 13:9 (p. 339)

James 1:2-4 (p. 343)
James 1:5 (p. 343)
James 1:6-8 (p. 344)

James 1:12-15 (p. 344)
James 1:16-18 (p. 346)
James 1:17 (p. 347)
James 1:19-20 (p. 348)
James 2:1-9 (p. 348)
James 3:2-12 (p. 349)
James 3:3-5 (p. 350)
James 3:3-12 (p. 352)
James 4:1-4 (p. 353)
James 5:16-18 (p. 354)

1 Peter 1:6-9 (p. 357)
1 Peter 2:4-8 (p. 357)
1 Peter 2:9-10 (p. 358)
1 Peter 2:11-12 (p. 359)
1 Peter 2:17 (p. 359)
1 Peter 3:9-14 (p. 360)
1 Peter 3:14-16 (p. 361)
1 Peter 4:10-11 (p. 362)

2 Peter 1:5-7 (p. 365)
2 Peter 1:5-15 (p. 365)
2 Peter 2:20-22 (p. 366)
2 Peter 3:8-9 (p. 367)
2 Peter 3:10-14 (p. 368)

1 John 1:1-4 (p. 371)

1 John 1:8-9 (p. 371)
1 John 1:8–2:2 (p. 372)
1 John 2:9-11 (p. 372)
1 John 3:1-2 (p. 373)
1 John 3:16-18 (p. 374)
1 John 4:20-21 (p. 375)

2 John 4-6 (p. 379)
2 John 7-11 (p. 379)

3 John 9-12 (p. 383)

Jude 3 (p. 387)
Jude 3-7 (p. 388)
Jude 17-21 (p. 389)
Jude 24-25 (p. 390)

Revelation 3:15-16 (p. 393)
Revelation 3:19-20 (p. 394)
Revelation 3:20 (p. 395)
Revelation 4:1-11 (p. 397)
Revelation 5:11-13 (p. 398)
Revelation 12:1-9 (p. 398)
Revelation 15:1-4 (p. 399)
Revelation 20:11-15 (p. 400)
Revelation 22:12-17 (p. 402)
Revelation 22:20-21 (p. 402)

# NEW TESTAMENT THEME INDEX

## A

accepting others—Mark 2:13-17 (p. 65); John 4:4-26 (p. 132)
ambition—Acts 19:11-20 (p. 183)
appreciating others—Luke 17:11-19 (p. 117)
armor of God—Ephesians 6:10-11 (p. 265); Ephesians 6:11-17 (p. 267); Ephesians 6:14-17 (p. 268)

## B

Beatitudes—Matthew 5:3-12 (p. 17)
beginning a relationship with God— Ephesians 2:8-9 (p. 258); Revelation 3:19-20 (p. 394)
being all things to all people— 1 Corinthians 9:19-23 (p. 220)
being beautiful inside—Luke 11:37-41 (p. 104)
being bold—2 Timothy 1:7-14 (p. 315)
being citizens of heaven—Hebrews 11:13, 16a (p. 335)
being the greatest—Mark 9:33-37 (p. 80)

being important—John 9:1-34 (p. 138)
being like a child—Matthew 18:1-5 (p. 36); Luke 9:46-48 (p. 101)
being like clay in God's hands— 2 Corinthians 4:5-7 (p. 236)
being "salty" Christians—Matthew 5:13 (p. 19)
being satisfied—Philippians 4:10-13, 19 (p. 277)
being soldiers of Christ— 2 Timothy 2:1-26 (p. 317)
being tested by fire— 1 Corinthians 3:10-15 (p. 216)
being a young Christian— 1 Timothy 4:12 (p. 307)
body of Christ—Romans 12 (p. 205); 1 Corinthians 12:12-27 (p. 225, 226)
body, God's temple— 1 Corinthians 3:16-17 (p. 217)
bragging—Luke 18:9-14 (p. 117); 2 Thessalonians 1:3-4 (p. 299); James 3:3-12 (p. 352)

broken hearts—Ephesians 3:14-21
(p. 259)
building on a strong foundation—
Matthew 7:24-29 (p. 27); Luke 6:46-
49 (p. 96); 2 Peter 1:5-7 (p. 365)

## C

celebration—Luke 24:13-35 (p. 122)
children of God—Galatians 4:1-7
(p. 248); 1 Peter 2:9-10 (p. 358);
1 John 3:1-2 (p. 373)
Christian maturity—Hebrews 5:11–6:3
(p. 332)
Christ's sacrifice—Hebrews
9:24-28 (p. 334)
cliques—James 2:1-9 (p. 348)
comfort in suffering—
2 Corinthians 1:3-11 (p. 233)
commitment—Matthew 10:39 (p. 30)
communicating love—Philippians
1:3-6 (p. 271)
confrontation—Matthew 18:15-17
(p. 37)
consequences—Acts 5:1-11 (p. 172)
considering others—Philippians
2:1-11 (p. 273)
cost of following Jesus—Matthew 16:24-
26 (p. 35)

## D

death—John 11:1-44 (p. 140);
2 Corinthians 5:6-9 (p. 238)
deception—James 1:16-18 (p. 346)
describing Jesus—Mark 8:27-30
(p. 78)
doubt—Matthew 14:22-33 (p. 32); John
20:24-29 (p. 162); James 1:6-8 (p. 344)

## E

Easter—Matthew 26:47–28:15
(p. 49); Matthew 28:1-7 (p. 55);
John 19:1–20:18 (p. 158);
John 20:11-18 (p. 161)
encouraging benedictions—
1 Thessalonians 3:12-13 (p. 292)
encouraging each other—Acts 4:32-37;
9:23-27; 11:22-30 (p. 172)
end times—Matthew 24 (p. 42)
end times predictions—
2 Thessalonians 2:1-17 (p. 301)
excuses—Luke 14:15-24 (p. 110)
expressing Christlike qualities—
Colossians 3:12-14, 17 (p. 285)
expressing Jesus to others—Mark 6:7-
13 (p. 69)

## F

faith—1 Corinthians 16:13-14 (p. 229);
2 Corinthians 5:7 (p. 238); Galatians
2:16-20 (p. 247); Colossians 2:6-8
(p. 282); Hebrews 11:1 (p. 334);
2 Peter 1:5-15 (p. 365)
faith and actions—Acts 4:1-21 (p. 170)
faith stories—Acts 21:39–22:16
(p. 185)
faithfulness—Luke 16:1-12 (p. 116);
2 Timothy 4:6-8 (p. 318)
false accusations—Acts 24:5-16
(p. 186)
false doctrines—1 Timothy 1:3-11
(p. 305)
false teachings—2 John 7-11 (p. 379)
family histories—Matthew 1:1-17
(p. 9)
family rules of love—Colossians 3:18-21
(p. 285)
fathers—John 14:7-14 (p. 149)
favoritism and cultural differences—
Acts 10:9-16, 34-36 (p. 177)
fear—Luke 8:26-39 (p. 100)
feeding the 5,000—John 6:1-13
(p. 133)
feeding God's sheep—John 21:15-17
(p. 163)
finding good in bad times—Romans
8:28 (p. 202)
focusing on God—Mark 14:32-40
(p. 84)
following Jesus—Matthew 28:18-20
(p. 59); Luke 9:57-62 (p. 102); Acts
3:17-26 (p. 169)
forgiveness—Matthew 18:21-35
(p. 38); John 8:1-11 (p. 135);
1 John 1:8-9 (p. 371)
freedom—1 Corinthians 8:4-13
(p. 219); Galatians 5:13 (p. 249)
freedom and responsibility—
1 Corinthians 10:23-24 (p. 223)
friends—John 15:12-16 (p. 154)
friendship—Mark 2:1-12 (p. 64); John
11:1-43 (p. 140)
friendship with God—Luke
24:13-35 (p. 123)
fruit of the Spirit—Galatians
5:22-23 (p. 251, 252); Galatians
5:22-26 (p. 253)
future—Romans 8:22-25 (p. 201)

# G

gifts and talents—Matthew 25:14-30 (p. 45); Mark 6:32-44 (p. 74); Luke 8:16-18 (p. 98)

giving—Luke 21:1-4 (p. 119); John 12:1-11 (p. 141); 2 Corinthians 8:2-5 (p. 240); 2 Corinthians 9:6-8 (p. 241, 242)

giving Jesus our burdens—Matthew 11:28-30 (p. 31)

giving of ourselves—Romans 12:1-8 (p. 207)

giving thanks—Luke 17:11-19 (p. 116); John 10:10 (p. 139)

God, the creator—Colossians 1:15-20 (p. 281)

God's comfort—Matthew 5:4 (p. 17)

God's control—Acts 16:16-35 (p. 180)

God's family—Mark 3:31-35 (p. 67)

God's friendship—Romans 5:6-11 (p. 197)

God's gift of Jesus—John 3:16 (p. 129)

God's good gifts—1 Corinthians 4:6-8 (p. 218)

God's goodness—James 1:17 (p. 347)

God's grace—Romans 3:21-28 (p. 193); Romans 4:4-6 (p. 195)

God's house—John 14:1-4 (p. 146)

God's inseparable love—Romans 8:31-39 (p. 204)

God's judgment—Revelation 20:11-15 (p. 400)

God's love—John 3:16-18 (p. 130)

God's peace—John 16:32-33 (p. 157)

God's perspective—John 8:1-11 (p. 134)

God's power—Acts 26:8 (p. 187); 2 Corinthians 4:7-11 (p. 237); Hebrews 12:28-29 (p. 339)

God's provision—Mark 6:30-44 (p. 72)

God's reward—Revelation 22:12-17 (p. 402)

God's transforming power—Romans 12:1-2 (p. 206)

God's vessels—2 Corinthians 4 (p. 234)

God's Word—Hebrews 4:11-13 (p. 331)

good from bad—Matthew 27:32–28:7 (p. 52)

good Samaritan—Luke 10:30-37 (p. 102, 103)

gossip—Ephesians 4:29-32 (p. 263); James 3:2-12 (p. 349)

grace—Ephesians 2:1-9 (p. 257); 1 Timothy 1:12-17 (p. 305)

greed—Luke 12:13-21 (p. 105)

# H

hard-to-love people—Matthew 25:31-46 (p. 47)

heaven—2 Peter 3:10-14 (p. 368); Revelation 4:1-11 (p. 397)

helping others—Mark 6:32-34 (p. 74); Galatians 6:9 (p. 254)

heroes—John 12:12-19 (p. 142); Jude 3-7 (p. 388)

Holy Spirit, the—John 14:26-27 (p. 151); Acts 2:5-13 (p. 167)

home—Matthew 8:18-20 (p. 28)

hope—Romans 5:1-5 (p. 196)

humility—Philippians 2:1-8 (p. 271); Hebrews 12:28-29 (p. 338)

hypocrisy—Matthew 15:1-20 (p. 34)

# I

impossible things—Romans 8:31-39 (p. 203)

including or excluding others—Mark 2:15-17 (p. 66)

# J

Jesus' birth—Luke 1:26–2:20 (p. 91)

Jesus' birth and life—Matthew 2:1-12 (p. 10)

Jesus calms life's storms—Mark 6:45-51 (p. 75); Luke 8:22-25 (p. 99)

Jesus came for sinners—Matthew 9:9-13 (p. 29)

Jesus can heal us—Acts 3:1-10 (p. 168)

Jesus changes our lives—Matthew 17:1-13 (p. 35)

Jesus, the cornerstone—1 Peter 2:4-8 (p. 357)

Jesus' death—Mark 16:1-8 (p. 87); John 12:20-26 (p. 143)

Jesus is the way to God—John 14:6 (p. 147); John 14:15-24 (p. 150)

Jesus, our King—Matthew 21:1-11 (p. 40)

Jesus knows and loves us—John 4:1-26 (p. 131)

Jesus, the light—John 8:12 (p. 137)

Jesus, our power source—John 1:35-51 (p. 127)

Jesus, the reflection of God's glory—Hebrews 1:1-4 (p. 329)

Jesus' rejection—Mark 6:1-6 (p. 69)

Jesus, our rock—Luke 6:46-49 (p. 97)

Jesus' resurrection—Matthew
27:62–28:15 (p. 53)
Jesus' return—Matthew 24:36-44
(p. 43); Luke 12:35-40 (p. 108); Acts
1:7-14 (p. 167); 2 Thessalonians 2:1-4
(p. 299); Revelation 22:20-21 (p. 402)
Jesus' suffering—Mark 15:15-32
(p. 84)
Jesus, the vine—John 15:1-4
(p. 151); John 15:5-11 (p. 152)
Jesus, the Word—John 1:1-5, 14
(p. 127)
John the Baptist—Matthew 3:1-12
(p. 13)
joy—John 15:10-11; 16:24 (p. 153);
Romans 8:28 (p. 203)
joy and prayer—1 Thessalonians 5:16-
18 (p. 296)
judging others—Romans 2:1-3 (p. 192)

### K
kingdom of God, the—Luke
13:18-30 (p. 109)
knowing God—1 Corinthians
2:11-16 (p. 214)
knowing Jesus—Luke 4:31-35
(p. 94)

### L
lamp of the body—Luke 11:33-36
(p. 104)
leadership—1 Timothy 3:1-13
(p. 307); Titus 1:5-9 (p. 321)
leaning on God—Jude 24-25 (p. 390)
learning about our faith—Acts
18:24-26 (p. 182)
lies—3 John 9-12 (p. 383)
living in the light—1 John 2:9-11
(p. 372)
love—John 13:31-35 (p. 146);
1 Corinthians 13 (p. 228);
loving God—Matthew 22:34-40
(p. 42)
loving one another—2 John 4-6
(p. 379)
loving others—1 John 4:20-21 (p. 375)
loving through actions—1 John 3:16-18
(p. 374)
loving your enemies—Luke 6:27-31
(p. 95)
lukewarm faith—Revelation
3:15-16 (p. 393)
lust—Matthew 5:27-28 (p. 21)

### M
making our thoughts obey Christ—
2 Corinthians 10:3-5 (p. 242)
materialism—Luke 12:13-21
(p. 105); 1 Timothy 6:6-12
(p. 309); 1 Timothy 6:7-10
(p. 310); James 4:1-4 (p. 353)
mentors—1 Timothy 4:12 (p. 309)
mercy—Matthew 25:31-46 (p. 46)
money—Matthew 19:16-30 (p. 39)

### N
narrow way—Matthew 7:13-14
(p. 26)
New Age dangers—2 Timothy 3:1–4:5
(p. 317)
new birth—John 3:1-10 (p. 128)
new covenant—Hebrews 8:7-13
(p. 333)
new creations—2 Corinthians 5:17
(p. 239)
new life in Christ—Romans 6:8-14
(p. 198)
night of Christ's arrest—Matthew
26:17-46 (p. 49)
no room at the inn—Luke 2:7 (p. 92)

### O
obeying Jesus—Luke 6:46-49 (p. 98)
opposition to the faith—Acts 8:1-8
(p. 176)
overcoming doubt and fear—Matthew
14:22-33 (p. 33)

### P
parable of the seeds—Matthew 13:1-23
(p. 31)
parents—Luke 2:21-40 (p. 92);
Ephesians 6:1-3 (p. 264); Ephesians
6:1-4 (p. 265)
Passover—Matthew 26:17-30 (p. 48)
peace—1 Thessalonians 4:11-12
(p. 295)
peer pressure—John 18:15-18,
25-27 (p. 158); 2 Thessalonians
2:15–3:5 (p. 301)
persecution—Acts 7:54–8:1 (p. 175);
1 Thessalonians 2:13–3:8 (p. 292)
perseverance—2 Timothy 2:1-7
(p. 315); Hebrews 12:1-2 (p. 336);
James 1:2-4 (p. 343); Jude 17-21
(p. 389)
possessions—Matthew 6:19-21
(p. 23); Mark 10:17-27 (p. 80)

power from God—2 Corinthians 3:4-6
(p. 234)
power of good news—Romans 1:16-17
(p. 191)
prayer—Matthew 18:19-20 (p. 37);
Mark 9:1-8 (p. 79); Luke 22:39-46
(p. 121); Romans 8:26-27 (p. 202);
1 Timothy 2:1-8 (p. 306); James 5:16-
18 (p. 354)
pressing toward the prize—Philippians
3:12-14 (p. 274)
pride—Matthew 2:1-18 (p. 12)
priorities—Colossians 3:1-4 (p. 284)
prodigal son—Luke 15:11-32 (p. 112,
113)
producing good fruit—Luke
6:43-45 (p. 96)
promised savior—Matthew 1:18-23
(p. 10)
purity—Ephesians 4:29-32 (p. 262)
putting God first—Acts 17:16-34
(p. 181)

Q

questions about our faith—John 7:25-
32, 45-49 (p. 134)

R

reaching out to non-Christians—Luke
15:1-10 (p. 111)
reactions to the gospel—Acts 20:17-24
(p. 184)
reconciliation—Philemon 8-21
(p. 325)
relating to others—James 1:19-20
(p. 348)
relying on God—Galatians 3:3-4
(p. 247)
rescued from sin—Romans
3:23-24; 6:23 (p. 194)
responding to Christ's call—Revelation
3:20 (p. 395)
responses to evangelism—Acts 13:46-52
(p. 178)
rest—Hebrews 4:1-10 (p. 330)
retaliation—1 Peter 3:9-14 (p. 360)
revenge—Matthew 5:9-12, 21-22, 38-48
(p. 18)
riches—Mark 10:17-31 (p. 82)
rules—Romans 7:7 (p. 199)
running to win—1 Corinthians 9:24-27
(p. 221)

S

sacrifice—John 15:13 (p. 156)
sacrificial love—John 15:12-17 (p. 155)

saying no to the world—Titus 2:11-15
(p. 321)
seeds and soil—Mark 4:1-9, 13-20
(p. 68)
Sermon on the Mount—Luke 6:17-49
(p. 94)
servanthood—John 13:1-17 (p. 145)
service—Matthew 20:25-28 (p. 39);
John 13:1-17 (p. 143, 144)
serving and affirming others—Galatians
5:13-15 (p. 251)
serving Jesus—Mark 15:21 (p. 86)
serving others—1 Peter 4:10-11 (p. 362)
sexual purity—1 Thessalonians 4:3-8
(p. 293)
sexual sin—1 Corinthians 6:12-20
(p. 218)
sexual temptation—
1 Thessalonians 4:3-8 (p. 294)
sharing—Acts 4:32-35 (p. 171)
sharing Christ—1 Peter 3:14-16 (p. 361)
sharing the good news—Romans 10:11-
15 (p. 205); 2 Corinthians 4:1-2
(p. 235)
shining God's light—Matthew 5:14-16
(p. 20)
showing love—Romans 12:9-21 (p. 209)
showing respect—1 Peter 2:17 (p. 359)
signs of the end times—Luke 21:5-38
(p. 120)
sin—Mark 7:14-23 (p. 78); Ephesians
4:25–5:2 (p. 261); 1 Peter 2:11-12
(p. 359); 2 Peter 2:20-22 (p. 366);
1 John 1:8–2:2 (p. 372)
spiritual gifts—1 Corinthians 12:4-11
(p. 224); 1 Corinthians 12:12-31
(p. 226)
spiritual growth—Mark 4:1-9, 13-20
(p. 67)
spiritual warfare—Ephesians 6:10-18
(p. 267); Revelation 12:1-9 (p. 398)
standing firm—Philippians 4:1-7
(p. 275)
staying rooted in Christ—Colossians
2:6-8 (p. 281)
Stephen's stoning—Acts 6:8-15;
7:51–8:1 (p. 173)

T

taking a stand—Acts 7:51-60 (p. 174);
Jude 3 (p. 387)
taming of the tongue—James 3:3-5
(p. 350)
tangible God—1 John 1:1-4 (p. 371)

telling others about Jesus—Matthew
   4:17-22 (p. 15)
temptation—Matthew 4:1-11 (p. 14);
   Mark 1:9-13 (p. 63); Luke 4:1-13
   (p. 93); 1 Corinthians 10:12-13
   (p. 221, 222); Hebrews 4:14-16
   (p. 331); James 1:12-15 (p. 344)
testing your faith—2 Corinthians 13:5
   (p. 243)
thankfulness—Romans 16:1-16
   (p. 210); 1 Thessalonians 1:2-10
   (p. 291)
time—2 Peter 3:8-9 (p. 367)
tradition—Mark 7:1-13 (p. 76)
trials—1 Peter 1:6-9 (p. 357)
Trinity—Mark 1:9-11 (p. 63)
true religion—Hebrews 13:9 (p. 339)
trusting God—1 Corinthians 3:5
   (p. 214)
truth—Luke 19:1-10 (p. 118); John 14:6
   (p. 148)
truth and freedom—John 8:31-36
   (p. 137)

## U

unity—John 17:20-23 (p. 158); Acts 15:1-
   2, 22-31 (p. 179); Ephesians 4:2-6
   (p. 261)

using God's resources—Matthew 25:14-
   30 (p. 44)

## V

value—Mark 12:41-44 (p. 83)
values—Matthew 5:1-12 (p. 16)
victory over death—1 Corinthians
   15:50-57 (p. 229)
violence—Matthew 5:38-42 (p. 22)

## W

walking the narrow road—Matthew
   7:13-14 (p. 26)
when it's tough to love God—Hebrews
   3:12-15 (p. 329)
wisdom—1 Corinthians 1:18-31
   (p. 213); James 1:5 (p. 343)
working together—Romans 12:4-8
   (p. 208)
worldly distractions—Hebrews 12:1-3
   (p. 337)
worry—Matthew 6:25-34 (p. 24);
   Matthew 6:28-34 (p. 25); Philippians
   4:4-9 (p. 276)
worship—Revelation 5:11-13 (p. 398);
   Revelation 15:1-4 (p. 399)

# NEW TESTAMENT TEACHING-STYLE INDEX

## ADVENTURES

Matthew 2:1-12 (p. 10)
Matthew 5:3-12 (p. 17)
Matthew 6:28-34 (p. 25)
Matthew 7:24-29 (p. 27)
Matthew 11:28-30 (p. 31)
Matthew 26:17-46 (p. 49)
Mark 1:9-13 (p. 63)
Mark 2:13-17 (p. 65)
Mark 6:7-13 (p. 69)
Luke 6:46-49 (p. 97)
Luke 8:26-39 (p. 100)
Luke 24:13-35 (p. 123)
John 11:1-44 (p. 140)
John 14:1-4 (p. 146)
John 14:6 (p. 147)
Acts 1:7-14 (p. 167)
Acts 3:17-26 (p. 169)
Acts 7:54–8:1 (p. 175)
Acts 15:1-2, 22-31 (p. 179)

Romans 10:11-15 (p. 205)
1 Corinthians 1:18-31 (p. 213)
1 Corinthians 9:19-23 (p. 220)
1 Corinthians 15:50-57 (p. 229)
2 Corinthians 5:7 (p. 238)
Ephesians 2:8-9 (p. 258)
Philippians 2:1-11 (p. 273)
Colossians 1:15-20 (p. 281)
1 Timothy 6:6-12 (p. 309)
2 Timothy 2:1-26 (p. 317)
2 Timothy 3:1–4:5 (p. 317)
Titus 2:11-15 (p. 321)
Philemon 8-21 (p. 325)
James 3:3-12 (p. 352)

## AFFIRMATIONS

Matthew 5:14-16 (p. 20)
Matthew 6:19-21 (p. 23)
Matthew 25:14-30 (p. 45)
Mark 12:41-44 (p. 83)

Luke 6:46-49 (p. 98)
Luke 11:33-36 (p. 104)
Luke 17:11-19 (p. 117)
John 3:16 (p. 129)
John 8:1-11 (p. 134)
John 12:12-19 (p. 142)
John 15:12-16 (p. 154)
John 21:15-17 (p. 163)
Acts 19:11-20 (p. 183)
Romans 12:1-8 (p. 207)
Romans 16:1-16 (p. 210)
Galatians 5:13-15 (p. 251)
Philippians 1:3-6 (p. 271)
1 Thessalonians 1:2-10 (p. 291)
1 Thessalonians 3:12-13 (p. 292)
2 Thessalonians 1:3-4 (p. 299)
Hebrews 4:14-16 (p. 331)
1 Peter 2:9-10 (p. 358)

## CREATIVE PRAYERS

Matthew 18:19-20 (p. 37)
Matthew 25:31-46 (p. 46)
Mark 9:1-8 (p. 79)
Luke 21:5-38 (p. 120)
Luke 22:39-46 (p. 121)
John 10:10 (p. 139)
John 14:26-27 (p. 151)
Acts 7:54–8:1 (p. 175)
Romans 8:26-27 (p. 202)
1 Corinthians 4:6-8 (p. 218)
Ephesians 6:1-3 (p. 264)
1 Thessalonians 5:16-18 (p. 296)
1 Timothy 2:1-8 (p. 306)
Hebrews 3:12-15 (p. 329)
Hebrews 12:28-29 (p. 338)
James 1:5 (p. 343)
James 5:16-18 (p. 354)
Revelation 22:20-21 (p. 402)

## CREATIVE READINGS

Matthew 1:18-23 (p. 10)
Matthew 14:22-33 (p. 32)
Matthew 21:1-11 (p. 40)
Mark 6:1-6 (p. 69)
Mark 6:45-51 (p. 75)
Mark 9:33-37 (p. 80)
Mark 15:21 (p. 86)
Luke 1:26–2:20 (p. 91)
Luke 6:17-49 (p. 94)

Luke 10:30-37 (p. 103)
Luke 12:13-21 (p. 105)
Luke 15:11-32 (p. 112)
John 15:5-11 (p. 152)
John 17:20-23 (p. 158)
John 18:15-18, 25-27 (p. 158)
Acts 26:8 (p. 187)
1 Corinthians 12:12-31 (p. 226)
2 Corinthians 4:7-11 (p. 237)
Galatians 2:16-20 (p. 247)
Philippians 4:10-13, 19 (p. 277)
Colossians 3:12-14, 17 (p. 285)
1 Timothy 4:12 (p. 307)
Hebrews 12:28-29 (p. 339)
1 John 1:1-4 (p. 371)
1 John 3:1-2 (p. 373)
Revelation 22:20-21 (p. 402)

## DEVOTIONS

Matthew 5:1-12 (p. 16)
Matthew 8:18-20 (p. 28)
Matthew 10:39 (p. 30)
Matthew 16:24-26 (p. 35)
Matthew 19:16-30 (p. 39)
Matthew 25:31-46 (p. 47)
Matthew 28:18-20 (p. 59)
Mark 2:1-12 (p. 64)
Mark 2:15-17 (p. 66)
Mark 4:1-9, 13-20 (p. 68)
Mark 7:14-23 (p. 78)
Mark 15:15-32 (p. 84)
Luke 10:30-37 (p. 102)
Luke 12:13-21 (p. 105)
Luke 12:35-40 (p. 108)
Luke 21:1-4 (p. 119)
John 4:4-26 (p. 132)
John 8:12 (p. 137)
John 14:6 (p. 148)
John 15:13 (p. 156)
John 16:32-33 (p. 157)
Acts 2:5-13 (p. 167)
Acts 4:1-21 (p. 170)
Acts 13:46-52 (p. 178)
Acts 20:17-24 (p. 184)
Acts 24:5-16 (p. 186)
Romans 1:16-17 (p. 191)
Romans 3:23-24; 6:23 (p. 194)
1 Corinthians 8:4-13 (p. 219)
2 Corinthians 1:3-11 (p. 233)
2 Corinthians 4 (p. 234)
2 Corinthians 4:5-7 (p. 236)
2 Corinthians 5:6-9 (p. 238)

2 Corinthians 13:5 (p. 243)
Galatians 5:22-23 (p. 252)
Ephesians 4:25–5:2 (p. 261)
Ephesians 6:11-17 (p. 267)
Philippians 4:4-9 (p. 276)
Colossians 3:1-4 (p. 284)
Hebrews 5:11–6:3 (p. 332)
Hebrews 11:1 (p. 334)
James 1:16-18 (p. 346)
James 4:1-4 (p. 353)
1 Peter 4:10-11 (p. 362)
3 John 9-12 (p. 383)
Revelation 3:15-16 (p. 393)
Revelation 3:19-20 (p. 394)

## LEARNING GAMES

Matthew 2:1-18 (p. 12)
Matthew 4:1-11 (p. 14)
Matthew 5:9-12, 21-22, 38-48 (p. 18)
Matthew 5:38-42 (p. 22)
Matthew 7:13-14 (p. 26)
Matthew 18:15-17 (p. 37)
Matthew 18:21-35 (p. 38)
Matthew 22:34-40 (p. 42)
Mark 6:32-34 (p. 74)
Mark 8:27-30 (p. 78)
Mark 10:17-27 (p. 80)
Luke 2:7 (p. 92)
Luke 6:27-31 (p. 95)
Luke 8:16-18 (p. 98)
Luke 9:57-62 (p. 102)
Luke 16:1-12 (p. 116)
Luke 19:1-10 (p. 118)
John 1:1-5, 14 (p. 127)
John 3:1-10 (p. 128)
John 4:1-26 (p. 131)
John 7:25-32, 45-49 (p. 134)
John 8:31-36 (p. 137)
John 9:1-34 (p. 138)
John 11:1-43 (p. 140)
John 14:15-24 (p. 150)
Acts 3:1-10 (p. 168)
Acts 4:32-37; 9:23-27; 11:22-30
    (p. 172)
Acts 6:8-15; 7:5–8:1 (p. 173)
Acts 8:1-8 (p. 176)
Acts 21:39–22:16 (p. 185)
Romans 3:21-28 (p. 193)
Romans 8:31-39 (p. 203, 204)
Romans 12 (p. 205)

1 Corinthians 6:12-20 (p. 218)
1 Corinthians 9:24-27 (p. 221)
1 Corinthians 10:12-13 (p. 221, 222)
1 Corinthians 12:12-27 (p. 226)
Galatians 5:22-23 (p. 251)
Ephesians 6:1-4 (p. 265)
Ephesians 6:10-18 (p. 267)
Ephesians 6:14-17 (p. 268)
Philippians 4:1-7 (p. 275)
1 Thessalonians 4:3-8 (p. 294)
2 Thessalonians 2:15–3:5 (p. 301)
1 Timothy 1:12-17 (p. 305)
2 Timothy 4:6-8 (p. 318)
Titus 1:5-9 (p. 321)
Hebrews 8:7-13 (p. 333)
Hebrews 12:1-2 (p. 336)
Hebrews 13:9 (p. 339)
James 1:6-8 (p. 344)
James 3:2-12 (p. 349)
1 Peter 1:6-9 (p. 357)
1 Peter 3:9-14 (p. 360)
1 Peter 3:14-16 (p. 361)
2 John 4-6 (p. 379)
2 John 7-11 (p. 379)
Jude 17-21 (p. 389)
Revelation 22:12-17 (p. 402)

## MUSIC IDEAS

Matthew 25:31-46 (p. 46)
Luke 24:13-35 (p. 122)
John 15:12-16 (p. 154)
Romans 10:11-15 (p. 205)
Galatians 4:1-7 (p. 248)
Hebrews 12:28-29 (p. 338)
Revelation 5:11-13 (p. 398)

## OBJECT LESSONS

Matthew 4:17-22 (p. 15)
Matthew 5:14-16 (p. 20)
Matthew 15:1-20 (p. 34)
Matthew 17:1-13 (p. 35)
Matthew 24 (p. 42)
Matthew 27:32–28:7 (p. 52)
Mark 1:9-11 (p. 63)
Mark 4:1-9, 13-20 (p. 67)
Luke 4:1-13 (p. 93)
Luke 6:43-45 (p. 96)
Luke 6:46-49 (p. 96)

Luke 11:37-41 (p. 104)
John 1:35-51 (p. 127)
John 3:16-18 (p. 130)
John 12:20-26 (p. 143)
John 15:1-4 (p. 151)
John 20:24-29 (p. 162)
Acts 5:1-11 (p. 172)
Acts 17:16-34 (p. 181)
Romans 6:8-14 (p. 198)
Romans 12:1-2 (p. 206)
1 Corinthians 2:11-16 (p. 214)
1 Corinthians 3:10-15 (p. 216)
1 Corinthians 12:4-11 (p. 224)
1 Corinthians 12:12-27 (p. 225)
2 Corinthians 3:4-6 (p. 234)
2 Corinthians 5:17 (p. 239)
Ephesians 4:2-6 (p. 261)
Ephesians 4:29-32 (p. 262)
Colossians 2:6-8 (p. 281)
1 Thessalonians 2:13–3:8 (p. 292)
Hebrews 1:1-4 (p. 329)
Hebrews 4:11-13 (p. 331)
Hebrews 9:24-28 (p. 334)
James 1:2-4 (p. 343)
James 1:17 (p. 347)
1 Peter 2:11-12 (p. 359)
2 Peter 1:5-7 (p. 365)
2 Peter 2:20-22 (p. 366)
1 John 1:8-9 (p. 371)
1 John 1:8–2:2 (p. 372)
Jude 24-25 (p. 390)
Revelation 3:15-16 (p. 393)

## OVERNIGHTERS/ RETREATS

Matthew 18:1-5 (p. 36)
Matthew 24:36-44 (p. 43)
Mark 7:1-13 (p. 76)
Luke 8:22-25 (p. 99)
John 14:7-14 (p. 149)
John 19:1–20:18 (p. 158)
Romans 5:1-5 (p. 196)
Romans 8:22-25 (p. 201)
1 Corinthians 3:16-17 (p. 217)
2 Corinthians 10:3-5 (p. 242)
Philippians 3:12-14 (p. 274)
1 Thessalonians 4:11-12 (p. 295)
1 Thessalonians 5:16-18 (p. 296)
Hebrews 11:13, 16a (p. 335)
James 1:19-20 (p. 348)
James 2:1-9 (p. 348)

1 Peter 2:4-8 (p. 357)
Revelation 12:1-9 (p. 398)

## PARTIES

Matthew 3:1-12 (p. 13)
Matthew 5:4 (p. 17)
Matthew 7:13-14 (p. 26)
Mark 3:31-35 (p. 67)
Luke 2:21-40 (p. 92)
Luke 15:1-10 (p. 111)
Luke 17:11-19 (p. 116)
Luke 24:13-35 (p. 122)
John 13:1-17 (p. 143)
Acts 10:9-16, 34-36 (p. 177)
Romans 8:28 (p. 203)
Romans 12:9-21 (p. 209)
1 Corinthians 15:50-57 (p. 229)
2 Corinthians 9:6-8 (p. 242)
Galatians 5:22-26 (p. 253)
1 Thessalonians 1:2-10 (p. 291)
2 Peter 1:5-15 (p. 365)
Jude 3-7 (p. 388)
Revelation 15:1-4 (p. 399)

## PROJECTS

Matthew 1:1-17 (p. 9)
Matthew 5:13 (p. 19)
Matthew 13:1-23 (p. 31)
Matthew 20:25-28 (p. 39)
Matthew 25:14-30 (p. 44)
Matthew 26:17-30 (p. 48)
Mark 6:32-44 (p. 74)
Mark 14:32-40 (p. 84)
Mark 16:1-8 (p. 87)
Luke 4:31-35 (p. 94)
Luke 9:46-48 (p. 101)
Luke 14:15-24 (p. 110)
Luke 22:39-46 (p. 121)
John 6:1-13 (p. 133)
John 12:1-11 (p. 141)
John 13:1-17 (p. 145)
John 13:31-35 (p. 146)
John 15:10-11; 16:24 (p. 153)
John 15:12-17 (p. 155)
John 20:11-18 (p. 161)
Acts 4:32-35 (p. 171)
Acts 18:24-26 (p. 182)
Romans 8:28 (p. 202)
Romans 12:4-8 (p. 208)
Romans 12:9-21 (p. 209)
1 Corinthians 13 (p. 228)

1 Corinthians 16:13-14 (p. 229)
2 Corinthians 9:6-8 (p. 241)
Galatians 6:9 (p. 254)
Colossians 3:18-21 (p. 285)
2 Thessalonians 2:1-17 (p. 301)
1 Timothy 1:3-11 (p. 305)
1 Timothy 3:1-13 (p. 307)
1 Timothy 4:12 (p. 309)
2 Timothy 1:7-14 (p. 315)
Hebrews 4:1-10 (p. 330)
James 5:16-18 (p. 354)
2 Peter 3:10-14 (p. 368)
1 John 2:9-11 (p. 372)
1 John 3:16-18 (p. 374)
Revelation 4:1-11 (p. 397)

## SKITS

Matthew 5:27-28 (p. 21)
Matthew 6:25-34 (p. 24)
Matthew 9:9-13 (p. 29)
Matthew 14:22-33 (p. 33)
Matthew 26:47–28:15 (p. 49)
Matthew 27:62–28:15 (p. 53)
Matthew 28:1-7 (p. 55)
Mark 6:30-44 (p. 72)
Mark 10:17-31 (p. 82)
Luke 13:18-30 (p. 109)
Luke 15:11-32 (p. 113)
Luke 18:9-14 (p. 117)
John 8:1-11 (p. 135)
John 13:1-17 (p. 144)

Acts 7:51-60 (p. 174)
Acts 16:16-35 (p. 180)
Romans 2:1-3 (p. 192)
Romans 4:4-6 (p. 195)
Romans 5:6-11 (p. 197)
Romans 7:7 (p. 199)
1 Corinthians 3:5 (p. 214)
1 Corinthians 10:23-24 (p. 223)
2 Corinthians 4:1-2 (p. 235)
2 Corinthians 8:2-5 (p. 240)
Galatians 3:3-4 (p. 247)
Galatians 5:13 (p. 249)
Ephesians 2:1-9 (p. 257)
Ephesians 3:14-21 (p. 259)
Ephesians 4:29-32 (p. 263)
Ephesians 6:10-11 (p. 265)
Philippians 2:1-8 (p. 271)
Colossians 2:6-8 (p. 282)
1 Thessalonians 4:3-8 (p. 293)
2 Thessalonians 2:1-4 (p. 299)
1 Timothy 6:7-10 (p. 310)
2 Timothy 2:1-7 (p. 315)
Hebrews 12:1-3 (p. 337)
James 1:12-15 (p. 344)
James 3:3-5 (p. 350)
1 Peter 2:17 (p. 359)
2 Peter 3:8-9 (p. 367)
1 John 4:20-21 (p. 375)
Jude 3 (p. 387)
Revelation 3:20 (p. 395)
Revelation 20:11-15 (p. 400)